R. R. BOWKER: MILITANT LIBERAL

R. R. BOWKER

MILITANT LIBERAL

BY

E. McCLUNG FLEMING

UNIVERSITY OF OKLAHOMA PRESS

NORMAN

Library of Congress Card Catalog Number 52–11604

Copyright 1952 by the University of Oklahoma Press
Publishing Division of the University
Composed and printed at Norman, Oklahoma, U. S. A.
by the University of Oklahoma Press
First edition

TO MY FATHER

Daniel Johnson Fleming

ANOTHER YANKEE PURITAN

AUTHOR, REFORMER, CITIZEN OF THE WORLD

AND MILITANT LIBERAL

≈

Preface

RICHARD ROGERS BOWKER planned to write a volume of memoirs similar to his intimate friend Everett P. Wheeler's *Sixty Years Of American Life*—a topical recollection of public events with a minimum of personal material. From time to time after 1920 he dictated short paragraph summaries of his activities in various fields, and also the first draft of three chapters dealing with his family and early boyhood. After Bowker's death in 1933 it was hoped that these fragments might be edited into some suitable memorial. Mr. Trumbull White was engaged to undertake the task, but illness prevented him from doing more than sorting some of the papers. In 1936, Professor Allan Nevins of Columbia University was invited to complete what Mr. White had begun, but found it impossible to accept.

Meanwhile, the enormous quantity of material bearing on his many activities which Bowker had carefully collected and preserved during a long lifetime was gradually sorted and classified. Portions were given to the Library of Congress, to the Stockbridge (Massachusetts) Library, and to the Brooklyn Public Library. The larger part was given to the New York Public Library, where it filled 158 manuscript containers of letters, unpublished manuscripts, and papers; 47 containers of diaries and journals; 17 containers of letter-books; and 8 chests of scrapbooks, clippings, pamphlets, and miscellaneous printed ephemera. This now constitutes one of the largest collections of papers belonging to one individual in the library's Manuscript Division.

It was an interest in the Mugwumps and a desire to investigate the circle of Independents which played such a conscientious but largely ineffectual role in American political life during the last quarter of the nineteenth century which led to my first knowledge of Bowker and, through Professor Nevins, of the Bowker papers. After an examination of these materials, a proposal for a biography was presented to and accepted by the executors of the Bowker estate. By 1943 a first draft was completed. My subsequent service in the Army of the United States and exacting administrative duties in a small college delayed the final preparation of my manuscript for publication.

From the beginning I have received the cordial help of many of Bowker's friends and associates, and to all of them I express my gratitude. I wish to mention in particular the following persons, who have generously lent material, supplied data, or made suggestions on manuscript: For Bowker's personal and early life: the late Carolyn T. Bowker, Mrs. Edwin P. Farnham, and Mr. W. N. Seaver; for his relations with the College of the City of New York, Professor Donald A. Roberts; for his relations with the *Publishers' Weekly,* Mr. Armond Frasca; for the Stockbridge chapter, Mr. Bernhard Hoffman; for library relations: Dr. Harry M. Lydenberg, and especially Miss Helen E. Haines, who has given generously of her time to discuss problems, read large parts of the manuscript, and make many valuable suggestions.

Professor Allan Nevins has borne the brunt of counseling each step of the work with his usual good sense, wide sympathies, and helpful encouragement. Staff members of the Manuscript Division, Newspaper Division, and Picture Collection of The New York Public Library, and James T. White and Company have given especially friendly co-operation. The directors of the R. R. Bowker Company, the Brooklyn Institute of Arts and Sciences, the Brooklyn Public Library, the Stockbridge Library Association and the Laurel Hill Association of Stockbridge, Massachusetts, have given valuable aid. The author's wife has supplied the kind of secretarial and editorial assistance in season and out of season that surely only love could ask or give. Finally, Miss Rose Weinberg, out of devoted loyalty to the memory of R. R. Bowker, whom she admired as an employer and a friend, has given unsparingly of her time and energy to help locate materials, check bibliography and manuscript, arrange interviews, and secure illustrations. Her assistance has been a good fortune as rare as it is undeserved. To each of these I want to express my very sincere appreciation.

E. McClung Fleming

Parkville, Missouri
June 15, 1952

Contents

ॐ

Illustrations

Introduction

In 1930 it was my happy privilege to make repeated calls on Richard Rogers Bowker, then well past eighty years of age and totally blind, but mentally alert and full of fascinating memories of the past. His attention had been attracted by volumes I had written on Grover Cleveland and the history of the New York *Evening Post,* and he told me much of importance on topics connected with both themes. Having been literary editor of the New York *Evening Mail* not long after the Civil War, he recalled William Cullen Bryant when that venerable poet was dividing his time between translations of Homer and the conduct of the *Post.* He had had an intimate personal acquaintance with Bryant's distinguished editorial successors, Carl Schurz, Edwin Lawrence Godkin, and Horace White. He remembered many striking details of Godkin's battles against Tammany in the days of Boss Richard Croker and Mayor "Hughie" Grant, a struggle in which Bowker himself had struck shrewd blows. He recalled many details, too, of the dramatic contests over the tariff and free silver—of the defeat of the reformers in the McKinley Tariff and their short-lived victory with the Wilson Tariff of 1894, of the critical battle against Bryan's sixteen-to-one doctrine, and of the subsequent alliance of most American liberals with Bryan on the issue of anti-imperialism.

Mr. Bowker took credit to himself, and rightly, for a great part in that Mugwump movement which alone made possible the momentous victory of Grover Cleveland over James G. Blaine in 1884. He still spoke of the movement with something like passion—the passion of a great reform cause, enlisting many of the best spirits of the nation: George William Curtis, Charles Francis Adams, Jr., Henry Ward Beecher, and Carl Schurz; the best educators from Charles W. Eliot down; and the best writers. Mr. Bowker had initiated in 1879 the "Young Scratchers" revolt against the dictatorial course of Roscoe Conkling in forcing on the Republican party of New York, merely to serve Conkling's national ambitions, a highly improper nomination for governor. Out of that revolt grew the far broader Mugwump uprising. Mr. Bowker had helped Cleveland gather in 1884 the crucial margin of votes needed to carry New York and the nation; he had strengthened Cleveland's arm by sponsoring the first civil service reform law in New York and by supporting the resistance to spoilsmen throughout the national government; and he had been one of Cleveland's trusted advisers at various moments. No history of liberalism and reform in America during the period from the Civil War to 1900 can be complete if it omits a due account of Bowker's incessant political activities.

All these activities, however, were but a small part of his public services. Of still greater importance were his many-sided accomplishments in the interest of librarians, publishers, and writers—that is, of all literary work in the United States. Not himself an author of original talent (though he published essays and poetry of value, and useful volumes on various phases of economic and political reform), he was one of the truest friends that American writers had in the long period 1875–1925. He did more than anyone else, as London representative of Harper Brothers in the early 1880's, to give *Harper's Magazine* a conspicuous place in British reading, and thus make Britons better acquainted with American literature. Already he had been one of the founders of the American Library Association, and as editor of the *Library Journal* he did as much as anyone to place library work on the high professional footing it attained before 1900. It was as a just tribute to his labors that he was chosen the first president of the New York State Library Association; it was evidence of his indefatigable interest that, becoming trustee of the Brooklyn Public Library in the 1880's, he held that post until his death in 1933. He and George Haven Putnam were long the two most conspicuous figures in championing the movement for an international copyright agreement, laboring decade after decade until they finally gained a large measure of success.

Publishers in particular owe a great debt to Mr. Bowker. In publishing even more than in most other business callings it is important constantly to remind firms and men that their undertakings are affected with a public interest, that success in purely commercial terms is really failure, and that larger considerations must be kept in view. Mr. Bowker, acquiring control of the *Publishers' Weekly* at the close of the 1870's and becoming active editor a few years later, strove to defend every right of publishers and to promote business enterprise in the marketing of books. But he never forgot that publishing is a department of public education and enlightenment and a mainstay of literature; and he made his magazine an invaluable agency of general culture. His humane spirit and sense of civic responsibility were infused into its pages, and he handed on to his successors in that powerful journal a torch that they have kept alight.

No one who knew Mr. Bowker could doubt that his was one of the finest spirits of his time. He has paid a certain penalty for the many-sided range of his labors; had he been less versatile, had his ardor for efficiency, liberalism, and reform been confined to fewer channels, he might have made a deeper if narrower impression. But the United States needed and will always need men of his wide reach of public interests and unquenchable zeal in lending a hand to diverse useful endeavors. E. McClung Fleming has given his career the careful study which it deserved. He has captured, by skillful use of Mr. Bowker's papers, the flavor of his idealism and energy; he has vividly portrayed the contests in which he engaged. We have in this book much more than the portrait of an arresting personality and the record of a noble career; we have a vigorous study of some of the principal strands of American liberalism in a period which needed all the liberalism that it could find.

ALLAN NEVINS

R. R. BOWKER: MILITANT LIBERAL

I

A Salem and New York Boyhood

THROUGHOUT HIS LIFE, Richard Rogers Bowker was proud of his Salem background. Both grandfathers were substantial Salem merchants, both parents were born and reared in Salem, and the nine years of his own Salem boyhood left him with memories which a subsequent residence of seventy-six years in New York City never dimmed. Bowker cherished his early link with New England. Perhaps it was not an accident that his personality combined the traits of the Puritan and the Yankee.

Young Rogers was fortunate in his grandparents.[1] Grandfather Joel Bowker was a successful and respected Salem merchant whose large, hospitable home was the center of the family's activities. When Rogers knew him, he was a formidable old patriarch in his mid-seventies; a tall, spare man so scrupulously exact and exacting that, according to Salem tradition, he would walk a mile to collect a cent owed him, and two miles to pay a cent he owed. Born in Scituate, Massachusetts, Joel had first worked as a farmer's assistant, next as a blacksmith, then as a ship-smith's apprentice. At the age of eighteen he set out with one suit of clothes and ten dollars in his pocket to make his fortune in Salem, then at the height of its foreign trade and promising a large field for youthful energies. He immediately got a job in the grocery store of Billy Gray, Salem's largest shipowner, and before long was permitted to send "ventures" in his employer's fleet as a reward for faithfulness. Soon going into business for himself, Joel became a merchant and part owner of several sailing vessels. The Bowker store was located alongside Bowker's Wharf near the South Salem bridge, and was rebuilt after the "Great

[1] This chapter is based on R. R. Bowker's typescript MS, "As to Forebears and Salem Town"; Mrs. Edwin P. Farnham's typescript MSS, "My Old Home" and "Memories of the Garden of My Childhood."

3

Salem Fire" of 1844 as a substantial brick warehouse at 8 and 10 Fish Street, where it still stands. Some of Joel's later investments include the purchase of forest lands in Michigan.

Joel married three times. By the first wife he had a son and two daughters. The second died childless. By the third he had three sons and two daughters.[2] The second and third wives were sisters and came from an Ipswich family of Rogers, whose ancestors included the Reverend John Rogers, burned at the stake in 1555 as the first Protestant martyr under Mary Tudor;[3] the Reverend Doctor John Rogers, fifth president of Harvard; and Captain Daniel Rogers of Revolutionary fame. Richard Rogers Bowker was always proud to have been named after his grandmother's distinguished family.

Early in his business career, Joel leased the big, three-story, red brick home at 9 Crombie Street, and in 1814 purchased it. With the earnest approval of his wife, he paid taxes on pews in two churches in Salem, though he took his family regularly to only one, the Old Salem Tabernacle. His chief recreations were the newspaper, which he read daily from end to end, his greenhouse, and his gardens. The greenhouse made him a notable grape grower and in it he cultivated the Hamburg grape from which he made his own wine. The garden was an excellent example of his thrift and enterprise, for here he grew at least thirty-eight different varieties of flowers and fifteen different kinds of berry bushes and fruit trees. One of these was the Bowker Seedling, so named by the Horticultural Society for a peach tree raised and exhibited by Joel and grafted on trees all over the country.

Rogers was equally fortunate in the grandparents on his mother's side. Grandfather Richard Savory, born in Portsmouth, New Hampshire, of Huguenot ancestry, had come as a young man to Salem and prospered as a successful cooper. Operating three factories and acquiring considerable estate,[4] he purchased a handsome home on Derby Street, from whose lofty cupola one might watch the ships enter and

2 Joel Bowker was born on July 4, 1775, the sixth son of Benjamin Bowker. His first wife was Eunice Pearson, daughter of Eliphalet Pearson of Newbury, possibly later the president of Andover Theological Seminary and of Phillips Academy. Joel's children by his first wife were Eunice, who married Rev. George Torrey and went to Michigan; Joel, Jr.; and Nancy, who married George Curtis of Hanover. His children by his third wife were Daniel, father of Richard Rogers Bowker; Lucretia, who married Brackett H. Clark; George; Charles; and Susan, who married Samuel Pearce Richardson.

3 George Wilson Hoke, *George Halford Clark*, 3–4. R. R. Bowker was convinced that this John Rogers died without issue and that he could not therefore have been descended from him. (R. R. Bowker, MS Memoir.)

4 A. W. Savory, *Genealogical and Biographical Record of the Savory Families* (Boston, 1893). Richard Savory married Betsy Lewis on September 11, 1803, and died February 12, 1841. His wife was born in 1786 and died on September 2, 1861.

clear Salem harbor, and here Rogers' mother Theresa Maria was born in 1826. Grandfather Richard was a liberal spirit, being one of the founders of the Universalist Church in Salem, to which he went every Sunday with his wife on his arm and his large family of six boys and five girls in attendant procession. Rogers was too young to know him personally, but he was glad to bear his name, and he loved to visit the Derby Street home and listen to his Savory uncles tell of their exciting adventures at sea. Two of his mother's brothers were sea captains.[5] There was Captain Hardy Millet, who made long voyages to the ends of the earth, particularly to the "Indies" and to China. There was Uncle George, who had founded in New York the notable firm of George Savory and Company, with a branch house in Buenos Aires; and Uncle William, who was following up Commodore Perry's bold action off Yokohama with early voyages to Japan[6] and who was later to establish a steamer service to the Río de la Plata.

Fortunate in the security of his grandparents on Crombie and Derby streets, Rogers seemed to be fortunate in his parents as well. His father, Daniel,[7] was Grandfather Joel's oldest son by his third wife. Simple in tastes and no scholar, he showed early signs of ambition and independence. As soon as he became of age, he left the strict Calvinist orthodoxy of the Old Salem Tabernacle in which he had been brought up, and attended St. Peter's Episcopal Church. Though of a deeply religious temperament and well versed in the Bible, he had no liking for creeds and ceremonies and did not have his children baptized. When he early became a Republican, it was in spite of severe criticism from his fellow Whigs.

Daniel first entered into business association with Joel, but soon attracted the attention of Stephen C. Phillips, a prominent Salem merchant, and at the latter's invitation became the junior partner of the firm of Phillips, Goodhue, and Bowker. This firm did business at Phillips' Wharf at the end of Derby Street and was very successful. It exported Wenham Lake ice to London, possibly for the first time;[8] it supplied the coal to the Lawrence and Lowell mills over the Salem and Lowell Railroad, in which it was interested, and it imported tea. It also had an interest in Lowell Island outside Salem Harbor, on which

5 The Salem Marine Society possesses an album of Society members which contains portraits of five of these uncles. In the East India Museum is the portrait of the sixth.

6 In 1864, William Thomas Savory rescued the young Japanese student Neesima, who later became a pioneer in modern Japanese development. (A. S. Hardy, *Life and Letters of Joseph Hardy Neesima*, 1, 2.)

7 Born February 24, 1820. Obituary in *Publishers' Weekly*, November 9, 1895, p. 805.

8 R. R. Bowker to Edwin Bulkley, May 24, 1904.

there was a summer hotel, and in the steamboat which plied between the Salem wharf and the island. Daniel did much of the custom house business of the firm and, over in the old brick office not far from Phillips' Wharf, came to know Nathaniel Hawthorne, whom he described as "rather silent and uncompanionable."

In 1846, Daniel began courting the spirited young Theresa Maria Savory, who had finished her education at the Charleston Female Seminary, then the most noted educational establishment for Boston and Salem young ladies. When his firm launched a new schooner that year, Daniel caused it to be christened the *Maria Theresa* after his fiancée; and she, not to be outdone by this romantic gesture, made for it, with her own hands, a full set of colors. The young man then sailed away to Brazil as "supercargo" on the new ship, of which he later became the owner.[9] On his return, the handsome couple were married and moved into the new house which Daniel had built for his bride on St. Peter's Street. At this time it was considered a marvel of modernity, for, in addition to velvet carpets, it contained a bathroom and gas lighting which Grandmother Savory was sure would sooner or later blow her beloved daughter to bits. Two children were born to the young Bowkers, Richard Rogers on September 4, 1848, and four years later, Carolyn.

It was a happy childhood for Rogers. The St. Peter's Street home with its shed and garden were full of possibilities for fun. On sunny days Rogers could ride the Shetland pony given him on his fourth birthday and play with his big, black, Newfoundland dog, Rover, that for many years could carry him almost as well as the pony could. Another favorite playground was Grandfather Joel's home, with its spacious barn, greenhouse, and garden. So was the attic of Grandmother Savory's house, which was a wonderland of curious bric-a-brac brought by his seafaring uncles from the ends of the earth, though not quite as impressive as the East India Museum on Essex Street with its strange figures in Oriental garb, its ship models, and its carved ivory. There were Sunday walks to the North Bridge, the "Great Pastures" beyond Essex Street, and Gallows Hill on which the witches were martyred; and there were steamboat excursions to Lowell Island.

The seasons moved pleasantly by. In the mellow September afternoons came the peach-eating orgies, when the children would stop at Crombie Street after school to pick up the ripe fruit and splatter themselves with its juice, pausing long enough to carry baskets of peaches to ministers, doctors, and friends in the neighborhood. Thanksgiving was a high feast day, with Grandfather Joel's children and grand-

[9] C. S. Osgood and H. M. Batchelder, *Sketch of Salem* (Essex Institute, Salem, 1879), 177.

children assembling from far and near around the well-provided table in the lovely McIntyre dining room in the Crombie Street home. For seventy-five years not a Thanksgiving was to go by without at least three Bowkers present at that table to help welcome the turkey on an elaborate menu that remained an unvarying family ritual through three generations. Winters were often severe, and sometimes Essex Street was heaped so high with snow on either side that arches had to be cut through to permit pedestrians to cross. With the Fourth of July came green peas and strawberries and a marvelous program of burlesque and serious orations, of comic and solemn processions. For schooling, Rogers was going to Marm Percy's, on Essex Street, where his mother had gone before him, and where several ancient ladies presided over a simple program of studies pursued by both boys and girls.

It was a friendly, promising, broad-horizoned world on which young nine-year-old Rogers would look out when he climbed to the roof of Grandfather Joel's house. Behind, in Essex Street, was Marm Percy's school; farther along was the Bowker Block where Uncle George and Uncle Charles were carrying on Joel's business together as the Bowker Brothers,[10] and behind that was Rogers' own home. To the south, past the new railroad station and near the South Salem bridge, he could see the Bowker warehouse and the Bowker's Wharf, where his father's handsome schooner, the *Maria Theresa,* was moored. Around to the east, but out of sight, was the great Derby Wharf where Elias Derby had startled the town by launching the giant *Grand Turk* sideways, the custom house where Hawthorne had just written the *Scarlet Letter,* and a little way farther on the House of Seven Gables which he was to immortalize. In the other direction was Chestnut Street, perhaps the most civilized street in America, whose beautiful, dignified homes were a tribute to the architectural genius of Samuel McIntyre. These structures expressed the serenity and solidity of purpose which belonged to the Salem of the Crowninshields and Nathaniel Bowditch, the man who had made American ships the fastest that sailed the seas. Out beyond all these familiar sights was the great blue ocean over whose expanse Rogers' father and his grandfather and his numerous uncles had sailed and fished and traded as far as Patagonia and Cathay.

At nine years of age, Rogers was indeed a fortunate young fellow. With respected grandparents, a prosperous father, and a comfortable home, the present was secure and the future seemed bright. Suddenly, however, came the Panic of 1857 and with it a radical change in the family fortunes.

10 At 227 and 229 Derby Street. Cf. Bowker Brothers' advertisement in *Salem Directory,* 1857, p. 55.

The business depression of 1857 was to have far-reaching effects on Rogers' family. In that year the senior partner of Phillips, Goodhue, and Bowker was killed in a steamboat explosion on the St. Lawrence. With his death and because of the hard times succeeding the Panic of 1857, the firm was dissolved. Daniel Bowker now decided to move his small family from Salem to New York and there begin a new business career. He invested in a barrel-making factory utilizing a new, patented, stave-making machine, located on the southwest corner of Sixth Avenue and Forty-seventh Street. Things went fairly well for a while, but in the spring of 1861 Daniel Bowker experienced a series of business disasters that put the household in straitened circumstances.

The barrel factory had occupied a frame building which was properly insured against fire, but which was blown down in a great storm as an almost total loss. This disaster was doubled when the working exhibit of the stave-making machinery which Daniel installed in New York's Crystal Palace was destroyed in the fire which gutted that supposedly fireproof edifice, ruining exhibits and exhibitors. A final calamity occurred when the mill, which Daniel and his brother-in-law Brackett H. Clark had installed in Virginia to turn out the rough staves for use in the New York factory, was fired by a hostile community that suspected the two hated Northerners of designs upon the slaves. Brackett Clark rallied from the disaster, set up a much-improved stave-making factory in Rochester and later became associated with George Eastman in organizing the Eastman Kodak Company.[11] Daniel Bowker, however, never again succeeded in establishing himself in business or in recovering his business confidence.

The decline in the family fortunes was reflected in the successive moves of the family residence uptown. During the first three years, the family lived at the St. James, a family hotel at the southeast corner of Fourth Avenue at Fourteenth Street, fronting on Union Square; in 1860, it moved to a boardinghouse at 5 West Twenty-fourth Street, across the way from the new Fifth Avenue Hotel; in 1861, to a brownstone boardinghouse at 72 West Forty-seventh Street, close to the northern limit of the city; and then to Jamaica. It was a trying progression. In Union Square young Rogers raced with ribboned "hoople-sticks" and played "old mother tippy-toe" with such socially privileged children as the young Roosevelts, Croppers, Weeks, and Postleys. Uncle George Savory, whose New York firm was prospering, played Santa Claus, frequently inviting the family to dinner at his residence in the fashionable Metropolitan Hotel on the corner of Prince Street, to the theater, and for week-end visits at his country home on Staten Island.

11 George H. Clark to the author, February 15, 1943.

When in 1860 the young Prince of Wales visited New York incognito as Baron Renfrew, a member of the New York University faculty known to the family arranged that Rogers' little sister be delegated to present the Prince with a huge bouquet. Meanwhile, both Rogers and Carolyn attended the dancing salon of General Ferrero on Fourteenth Street, which rivaled Dodsworth's fashionable dancing academy on Fifth Avenue. But on Forty-seventh Street, the meals became more meager; the sight of the squatters' shanties and the numberless goats just to the north on Sixth Avenue depressed Rogers' mother; and the cattle which were driven down Fifth Avenue to be slaughtered in the Bull's Head region on the East Side frightened sister Carolyn and her little friends.

Perhaps the most important result of the collapse of the family fortunes was the change it necessitated in Rogers' plans for college. It had always been assumed that he would go to Harvard, where two centuries before a Rogers ancestor had been president. Now this was absolutely out of the question, and the Bowkers felt fortunate in being able to steer their son toward New York's Free Academy. True, Uncle George's two sons, although they could easily have afforded it, scorned the thought of going to college and did not see why Rogers must do so. But Rogers' mother absolutely insisted on it. Since the prerequisite for admission to the Free Academy was a year's attendance at a public school, Rogers in 1862 entered Ward School No. 48 on Twenty-eighth Street, just west of Sixth Avenue. Mrs. Bowker was almost in tears that her son should be obliged to seek an education in public school, a course of action which impressed her as being not commendably democratic, but just plain plebeian.

Rarely has a life more strikingly illustrated the old adage, "As the twig is bent, so the tree inclines." By the time he was twelve, young Bowker had clearly developed many of the interests and habits which were to mark him for the rest of his life: travel, sightseeing, the theater, journalism, politics, voluminous letter writing and record-keeping, and business management.

Rogers could never get enough of travel. He made regular visits to his cousins in Salem, often by the big Sound boats which plied between New York and Fall River; he looked forward to hot-weather sojourns at Portchester, week-end visits to Uncle George's summer home at Blanquard's on Staten Island, summer vacations with his Aunt Nancy Curtis at Hanover Four Corners. He reveled in an opportunity to visit his Uncle Brackett Clark's new barrel factory in Rochester, thrilling at the view of the Upper Falls of the Genesee and sending back to his sister rhapsodic birch-bark letters about Niagara Falls. He found excitement as well as profit in an ambitious stamp collection which

9

necessitated poring over the maps in his atlas. Meanwhile, around New York, young Bowker exhibited the insatiable curiosity of the born sightseer. At the age of eleven he was recording in a journal his trips to see "the golden images taken from the ancient graves at Chiraque," the American Institute Fair at the Palace Gardens, the exhibition of "The mammoth balloon 'City of New York,' and the aerial ship 'Leontine,' " some gorillas on view at 635 Broadway. And, as in Salem, he never missed a parade. "I did not go to school today," he cheerfully noted in his journal, "as it was the day of the firemen's parade." "It is St. Patrick's Day," he noted when he was twelve, "and the Irish have a procession, but it was not good for much, as they were nearly all Free-Masons."

Similarly, he seemed fascinated by the theater, the newspapers, and politics. He loved the spectacles offered at Niblo's Garden behind the Metropolitan Hotel, from the dizzy acrobatic performances of the Revels and Dan Rice's circus to the productions by the Barney Williams troupe of "O'Flanigan and the Faies," and "In and Out of Place." He devoured the fare at the Winter Garden, from "Dot and Smike" to the appearance of General Tom Thumb. Newspapers had a strange attraction for young Bowker. To his Aunt Lizzie he wrote on February 19, 1859:

> The great topic with the New York papers about this time is the Grand Complimentary Ball at Washington to Lord and Lady Napier, the British Minister. I send you the *New York Herald* of Feb. 18th, which gives some account of it, and Monday I will send you that of the 19th which gives the particulars in full. Also the *Ledger* for today. I suppose you have heard of Robert Bonner, the Editor and Publisher.

Into his journal were copied, verbatim, long paragraphs taken from various newspapers on a bewildering range of current events in this country, Europe, and Asia. An early interest in politics was exhibited during the first contest for the presidency of the Mercantile Library, an election which, to many New Yorkers, was more exciting than that of president, governor, or mayor. Rogers kept careful note of the rival organizations represented, discussed breathlessly the rumors that votes had been bought on both sides, studied the long queue of voters which formed in the street, and exulted with the rest of the family when the son of the Bowker's boardinghouse-keeper, Charles, was elected and found himself in the newspaper headlines.

In addition to these abiding interests, Bowker early showed habits and qualities which were to mark him throughout his life. Even at the age of nine he was a prodigious letter writer, maintaining a lively correspondence with Salem relatives and with his parents during their trips away from New York, which was striking for its evidences of alert observation and mature responsibility. At the same time he was engaged in the meticulous preservation of all personal papers and records. Copies of all his outgoing and incoming letters were kept in a formidable, green paper-covered copybook. As an eleven-year-old, he carefully filed his compositions, copybooks, class exercises, and scrapbooks of poems clipped from the press. A "Stamp Account" and "Ledger" were filled with meticulous entries of purchases and sales. Under the influence of a school teacher he started a journal which he kept faithfully for more than a year. In it he recorded systematically what he had learned in history and mythology, the books he was reading, passages memorized, the minister's Sunday texts, and his outings with his cousin George.

Most striking of all, however, was his knack for sober business management when still in knee pants. During his father's frequent absences from town, he acted as volunteer superintendent of the manufacturing establishment. The reports of affairs at the factory written by the child of eleven are clear and concise. The following is typical.

New York, March 19, 1859

Dear Father,

Today I went down to Briggs and after waiting awhile for him, I got the money. I then went up to the mill and gave James $30, after which I went down to Mr. Stanton and got a receipt for $20, which sum I paid his son. James gave Alex Burns $10 out of the $30. James said that the painter came soon after I left and he has now the first coat on both jointers. James is now busy putting in the floor, which they tore away, and having the barrels of heads filled up. Did you wish more than one coat of paint on the jointers? If you did, please write to me and let me know . . . .

Yours truly
RICHARD R. BOWKER

Rogers early developed a profitable stamp-collecting program. From a merchant in Salem who traded with South America he procured "big Brazils" which he sold at handsome prices to the stamp dealers on Nassau Street. Apparently on his own initiative he thought up the scheme of buying small pieces of English and French gold and sending these to postmasters in the colonies with a request for an equivalent value in unused stamps, which he then sold locally at a handsome profit. He became American correspondent of the Liverpool firm which preceded the Scott Company, and of Erich Ritzau in Copenhagen, and maintained accounts with correspondents in Germany, Newfoundland, New Brunswick, and Nova Scotia. Part of the profits from this small business were regularly deposited in a savings account on which Rogers earned carefully noted interest.[12]

There is no doubt that the family situation increased the premature sense of duty of this serious young man who was old beyond his fourteen years. Rogers worried about his father, realized clearly that he must prepare himself to support the entire family, and drew away from his carefree cousin Georgie who had more spending money. It was fortunate for young Bowker that, during the days of relative family security, he had developed habits of self-reliance, industry, and order, for he was now in need of them. Someone had to take the family situation seriously. Far from being able to expect his parents to look after him, Rogers was finding it necessary to look after his parents. Probably, however, this only reinforced an innate earnestness. When some adolescents in the neighborhood threatened to overturn the ash barrels on the street, Rogers' sense of social responsibility was so outraged that he had a fight with them on the issue. Justifiably or not, Uncle George and even Carolyn's young friends came to think of him as a bit of a prig.

Meanwhile, young Bowker's formal schooling, both religious and secular, was conscientious. Every Sunday he went without fail to Sunday School at the church of St. Bartholomew at Lafayette Place and Fourth Street, then joined his parents in the family pew for the morning and evening service led by Dr. Cook. On weekdays he went, first, to the co-educational "dame-school" of Miss Day and her sister Mrs. Leonard on Eighteenth Street just west of Fourth Avenue. From school notes that survive, it would seem that in his twelfth year he was reading *Nicholas Nickleby,* the *Merchant of Venice, Hamlet,* and fragments of Leigh Hunt, and that he "had a very pleasant time reading Burns' works." Ward School No. 48, which he next attended, had several excellent teachers, and Rogers, of course, did well. In a class of thirty-four he stood first in ten subjects with an average of 97. Consistently, month after month, he received an official certificate "for regular and punctual attendance, correct deportment and diligent attention to study." In June, 1863, he was duly pronounced eligible to become a member of the Introductory class of the Free Academy.

[12] R. R. B., "Plain Talks on Economics," *The Million,* No. 1 (September 20, 1884).

II

The Free Academy and the City College

THERE IS a special fitness in the fact that young Bowker received his education at the College of the City of New York.[1] The man and the institution were born in the same year and became embodiments of the same democratic faith. From this faith, the city had caught a vision of how a commonwealth might be enriched by extending the benefits of learning to all its sons. The vision became a college. The college so inspired the young man that he served the college and the city as student and citizen-alumnus through seventy years, incarnating the democratic faith in a multitude of good works whose effects were not confined to his city or his country.

The foundation of New York City's grammar school system had been laid in 1804 by the organization of the Public School Society. No action, however, was taken to extend the range of free instruction until Townsend Harris, later to be the first American ambassador to Japan, became president of the Board of Education. Under his vigorous leadership, the board in 1847 proposed that the city should establish a free college or academy which would be " in no way inferior to any of our Colleges in the character, amount, or value of the information given to the pupils." "If the wealthy part of the community," the board argued, "seek instruction to enlarge the minds of their children, why should not an opportunity be given to the sons of toil to give the *same*

[1] This chapter, where other sources are not indicated, is based on the following four articles written by R. R. Bowker in the *City College Alumnus* of 1926 under the general title "College Days and College Ways": I. "The Early Faculty" (March); II. "The Old Building and Early Curriculum" (June); III. "Student Activities in the '60's" (September); IV. *"Obit Academia, Crescit Collegium"* (December); and his address, *"Ave Atque Salve,"* delivered before the alumni dinner on November 24, 1928, printed in the *City College Alumnus* of November, 1928.

advantages to their children?" Legal authorization for the new venture was given in 1847, the new building was erected during 1848, and on January 15, 1849, the first municipal institution of free higher education in the world opened its doors to 143 picked students. During Bowker's junior year the institution had nearly 250 students in its collegiate classes and was assured an annual income of $125,000 from the city.[2]

Bowker entered the Introductory class of the Free Academy in the fall of 1863. It then occupied a large, five-storied, red brick building plastered with brown stucco, located on the southeast corner of Lexington Avenue and Twenty-third Street. The design was English Collegiate Gothic, with impressive buttresses and tall turrets at each corner. No less impressive was the institution's president, Horace Webster, a graduate of West Point and for eight years a professor there. Both the Academy's architecture and the Academy's president embodied the founders' hope that the institution would be a "Civic West Point" which would do for the citizens of the city what the Military Academy did for the soldiers of the nation. Before long young Bowker came to think of Webster as having a stronger passion for petty discipline than for true scholarship, and he hated Webster for this. Webster, for his part, soon came to think of Bowker as an insubordinate rebel and made him suffer for it. But there were other men on the faculty whom Bowker found both talented and inspiring and well able to give him a solid grounding in several important fields.

The Free Academy had established one of the pioneering professorships in English language and literature, and the post was most ably filled by the Reverend J. G. Barton. This tall, serious man, with the face of an owl and a capacity for withering satire, was a great teacher and commanded absolute respect from his students. Bowker eagerly responded to Barton's leadership, and the thorough training in literature and composition which he received from this master became the foundation of his professional career in journalism, book reviewing, and editorial management.

No less important for his future was the solid grounding received in the natural sciences. It was a department in which the Academy was particularly strong. Oliver W. Gibbs, the famous chemist, had just completed his four-year professorship when Bowker entered. Gibbs' place was filled by Robert Ogden Doremus, also a prominent chemist and inventor, who had been the first private pupil and for seven years the assistant of the great natural scientist, John W. Draper. Descendant

2 M. E. Cosenza, *The Establishment of the College of the City of New York,* 12–33; City College memorial requesting a local chapter of Phi Beta Kappa, July, 1867.

of a well-known New York family and fond of entertaining in his private home at Fourth Avenue and Eighteenth Street, Doremus was a showman of handsome appearance and elegant manner who enjoyed doing things on a large scale, giving brilliant lectures and impressing his students with his fertile imagination. He was probably the most brilliant experimentalist in the country,[3] and his expert investigations in toxicology not only had a great influence on medical jurisprudence, but necessitated his testimony at murder trials, an activity which won him an enormous reputation with the students. His success as a teacher within the college was matched by the civic role he played without. A fine musician himself, he was host to many of the musical celebrities who came to the United States, including Adelina Patti, Christine Nilsson, and Ole Bull, and served as president of the Philharmonic Society at a difficult period of its history.[4]

In addition to Doremus, the science department included John C. Draper, son of the famous John W. Draper and brother of the brilliant astronomer Henry Draper, both of whom were teaching at the University of the City of New York (New York University). Bowker studied natural history under Draper and chemistry and physics under Doremus at a time when the Academy's well-designed and equipped laboratories were among the first in any American college. From these teachers he acquired a profound respect for science which accompanied a conviction that there was no conflict between it and liberal religion. Both men remained for many years his warm personal friends.

Another member of the faculty who exerted a strong and beneficial influence on young Bowker was Adolph Werner, professor of German. There was a quality of real greatness about him which few of his students missed. Bowker said of him that he "was a great teacher because he was a great man, most beloved of all our instructors, popular in the best and highest sense with every class and every man coming under his influence." Werner had a genius for friendship and could remember the names of his students fifty years after they had passed through his classroom. For two-score years Bowker prized his association with this fine teacher-companion whom he called the "Golden Hearted."

In addition to his courses in English, natural science, and German, Bowker did a great deal of work in the exceptionally strong department of mathematics. He also took courses in art, history, political economy, logic, moral and mental philosophy, Greek and Latin, and a flourish of international and constitutional law. It was not an easy

[3] E. P. Wheeler, "Chapters from the Life of a Lawyer," *City College Quarterly*, March, 1917. pp. 16–17.

[4] "Robert Ogden Doremus" in *Dictionary of American Biography*.

program. Bowker thought that "the work was hard, the examinations tough, and the marking rigid."[5] He did, nevertheless, earn a high record of proficiency in his studies. As a result of his increasing extracurricular activities, Bowker's averages dropped from 99.3 at the end of the first term to 98 for the second year, and 89.45 for his senior year. He graduated fifth in his class.

There is good evidence that Bowker was not a mere bookworm, but had an independent and inquiring mind. It was typical of him that, on one occasion when his own reason balked, he challenged the statement of his mathematics textbook that the circumference of a circle was made up of an infinite number of straight lines. It was also typical that, on the same occasion, he admired his professor for being sufficiently free from rote methods of instruction to give up most of the class hour to a clarification of the disputed point, and that he had only disgust for his classmates who effusively thanked him after class for saving them a recitation. When a student once undertook to prompt him during a Latin recitation, Bowker rebuked him fiercely in open resentment. It was probably because he was genuinely interested in political economy that Bowker insisted on discussing the material which Professor G. W. Huntsman presented in class. Huntsman, however, utterly lacked the ability to maintain classroom discipline and apparently was rattled by this bold demand for extemporaneous explanations. He reported Bowker to President Webster for "repeated disorder and disobedience," complaining that "he continues to talk and to ask questions—frivolous questions—after I have told him not to do so."

An educational influence second only to that of the curriculum and the men who taught it was Bowker's membership in the fraternity of Alpha Delta Phi which brought him into close association with a fine group of undergraduates and alumni. Of his undergraduate fraternity brothers, Bowker came to have most in common with Edward Morse Shepard (class of 1869), who was recognized as one of the best college writers, speakers, and debaters, a man who quickly became a leader of his class, as he was later to become a leader in his city and state. Bowker found another especially congenial spirit in Graham McAdam (class of 1870), who like himself was preparing for journalism and was interested in liberal reform movements.[6] Of the alumni

---

[5] R. R. B., "Edward Morse Shepard," *City College Quarterly*, December, 1911.

[6] Other fraternity brothers with whom Bowker was intimate were: William Murray and Ernst Eurich of the class of 1867; Albert Delafield, Robert Bach McMaster, Miner Knowlton, and Henry Chapman of his own class; George A. Baker, Frank L. Wing, E. T. Hiscox, and Neilson Olcott of the 1869 delegation. His closest friend in his freshman year was Gilbert Holmes Crawford, later class valedictorian. The two were said to be as hard to separate as the Siamese twins.

Richard Rogers Bowker about 1890

Two Civic Interests: *(Top)* The Great Tower of the City College; *(Bottom)* Brooklyn Academy of Music Building

brothers, Bowker came into association with such liberal leaders as Everett P. Wheeler and Russell Sturgis (1856) and General Henry E. Tremaine (1860), all of whom represented a high ideal of public service. In 1865 he accompanied the Manhattan chapter delegation to the national convention at Brown University in Providence, and in 1868 attended and reported for the *Evening Mail* the proceedings of the national convention held in New York City at which George William Curtis, John Jay, and J. H. Choate were present. Bowker gave lifelong devotion to his fraternity associations, and through them received not only the satisfaction of lasting friendships, but also the stimulus of capable minds.

Other formative impressions were received at the theater and concert hall. Bowker witnessed many performances from the topmost gallery of the old Academy of Music at Irving Place. One of these was the American debut of the charming Swedish singer, Christine Nilsson, whose carriage Bowker and his friends afterwards drew to the residence of Professor Doremus, where they serenaded her. Bowker long remembered a reading given by Dickens at Steinway Hall on his second visit to this country in 1867; the time when he and his friends were paid a small sum to act as extras in "The Flying Scud" at Wallack's Theatre; and the several farces put on by his fraternity at its chapter house.

From instructors, books, and associates, from the theater, concert hall, and lecture platform, Bowker acquired important ideas and ideals. He was deeply impressed by the instruction in moral and intellectual philosophy. This was grounded on the assumption that there were eternal realities which could be known by the spiritual sense as surely as the truths of physical science. He gave complete inward assent to the further propositions that the moral structure of the universe was certain and ascertainable, and that it was as important to understand and obey these moral principles as to understand and obey the laws of physical nature.[7] Through lectures, reading, and conversation, he seized and pondered the epochal doctrines of evolution and social progress then being championed by Darwin, Huxley, Spencer, and Fiske. Through Wheeler, Sturgis, Shepard's guardian Abram S. Hewitt, and George William Curtis he sensed the importance of civic responsibility and of political liberalism.

Three surviving college compositions indicate how well Bowker had hammered these various ideas into a philosophy of his own. The chief themes emphasized by the youth, moreover, were to remain the lifelong convictions of the man: the social importance of culture, the

[7] Wheeler, "Chapters from the Life of a Lawyer," *City College Quarterly*, March, 1917, pp. 16–17.

emancipating role of invention, the divine governance of the world, and the Christian philosophy of history which understood the extension of liberty to be the goal of modern progress. The first composition, entitled "The Use of Culture," is a vigorous defense of free higher education against those who cried down college culture as effeminate or a superfluous luxury. "Culture directs thought," Bowker wrote, "and thought directs life. True action implies thought and is not possible without it,—thought and action include all labor, and life is only labor." "There is an unfortunate but prevalent suspicion that energy and culture are incongruous" he pointed out, "that America to preserve the one must reject the other. . . . While we labor to found firmly a new nation, let us not vaingloriously ignore all times but our own, all people but ourselves. Culture vivifies and does not weaken."

The second composition, Bowker's Junior Exhibition oration entitled "The Inspiration of Invention," analyzed the important contribution made by technology to social progress, but warned against a humanistic pride which forgot that the compass, steam engine, camera, and telegraph were "only instruments in the hands of God."

The third piece, entitled "The Goal of Modern Progress," won Bowker a gold medal in the annual prize poem contest in the spring of his junior year. It was a fervid expression of Christian liberalism's philosophy of history. In the garden of the Lord, so the poem goes, there blooms the tree of liberty whose leaves are green for the healing of the nations. Christ first taught men to cultivate this tree. From time to time shoots are transplanted to new lands. Man's duty is to care for these outgrowths, train them, and carry seedlings to new fields until the tree of liberty blooms over all the world, for nothing can prevent the fulfillment of this great movement through the ages. The American Civil War was an important step, but the work must go on: it was the special task of Bowker's generation to promote the idea of the self-determination of all people and the establishment of free trade.

While he was appropriating these solid Victorian ideas, young Bowker showed definite qualities of leadership. During his freshman year, he was appointed class marshal for the Free Academy procession that followed Lincoln's funeral cortege through the city.[8] In his sophomore year, the state legislature passed an act transforming the Free Academy into the College of the City of New York, and Bowker organized an ambitious celebration for the occasion, complete with a torchlight procession, a band, and rites performed by Orator, Prophet,

8 Bowker long kept, and finally donated to the College, one of the small silk flags and the baton of gilt and black paper wound around a hoople stick which he carried in the procession.

and Poet. He himself, as sponsor, christened the infant college on the stroke of midnight by breaking (on the third attempt) a bottle of lager beer upon the building while the assembled multitude roared out the specially written Christening Song.[9] It was in his junior year, however, that Bowker really showed his mettle. He launched his college's first campus newspaper, initiated the first attempt at student self-government in his or any American college, edited and published a collection of college songs, secured a charter for the City College chapter of Phi Beta Kappa, and meanwhile served as vice-president of the Clionian Society, chairman of his class cane committee, and president of the Junior class.

His journalistic accomplishment was notable. On November 21, 1866, there appeared the first number of the *Collegian*, the student newspaper of which Bowker was founder, editor, manager, publisher, and proprietor. College journalism was then in its infancy; only three campus papers (as distinct from college magazines) pre-dated Bowker's: the Harvard *Advocate*, the Yale *Courant*, and a third at either Hamilton, Williams, or Brown. The *Collegian* consisted of eight pages published on alternate Wednesday mornings and was advertised as "For sale by all City Booksellers and Newsdealers." It featured local news, correspondence from other colleges, essays, poems, editorial promotion of various student activities such as a committee to select the college color (incidentally urging the color "lavender" which was officially selected and is still used), and a student council.

President Webster thought the *Collegian* improper and insubordinate, and it was not a financial success. On both counts Bowker had to assume full and sole responsibility. Of advertisements it had practically none, and the price of ten cents, later raised to fifteen, proved more than student budgets could then afford, even though the paper always seemed popular. At the end of the first five numbers, paid up subscriptions totaled $454, unpaid $20, but the balance in the treasury was only $55. The eighth number was the last. This paper, which was not revived until 1875, and then for only four numbers, was probably never surpassed by students at the college.[10] It provided Bowker excellent training in journalism, for he did not only the reporting, but the leader writing also, and was on hand at the printing office for the proofreading, make-up, and other practical details.[11] It also brought him contacts

---

[9] See Robert Abbe in Philip J. Mosenthal and Charles F. Horne (eds.), *The City College—Memories of Sixty Years*, 239–43. On the morning of May 1, the *Tribune's* column of Deaths and Births contained solemn reference to the demise of the Academy and the blessed arrival of the College.

[10] See Gamma chapter of Phi Beta Kappa Minutes of June 19, 1933.

[11] Charles Wingate, *Views and Interviews on Journalism*, 184.

with professional journalists. During his senior year he secured from Charles Sweetser of the *Evening Mail* several reporting assignments on that paper.

Another service which Bowker did his college this year was to chair a committee of five which edited and published a handsomely bound volume of the *Songs of the College of the City of New York.*[12] According to the preface the work was issued

> to promote cordiality and good feeling, and to lend to college life a charm which only music can. Turning into a proper channel that overflow of spirits which else too often breaks its proper bounds, song is at the same time one of the most pleasant, most refreshing, and least injurious of College amusements.

The sixty selections were taken from the songs of Amherst, Bowdoin, Dartmouth, Harvard, Kenyon, Williams, and Yale, and included a good many original City College songs. Bowker also served as one of the contributing editors of the *Carmina Collegensia* brought out in 1868 by Henry Randall Waite, which was perhaps the most complete collection of the kind then or since attempted.

A third enterprise which Bowker initiated, and which was first proposed in one of his *Collegian* editorials, was a student council. It was probably the first endeavor at student self-government in any American college. Bowker's purpose was to promote an *esprit de corps* in the student body which would relieve the faculty from exercising petty discipline and the student body from suffering "nursery" supervision. Bowker was chosen chairman of a committee to draft the council's first constitution. This document named the new body, somewhat pompously, the Academic Senate and provided that the Senate should consist of five elected delegates from each class. In the fall of 1867, Bowker was elected a representative from the Junior class and temporary president.

The Academic Senate was short-lived. Its most popular achievement was an indignant refutation of the charge that a City College student had thrown a cabbage at a Columbia dandy making a formal oration in the annual Junior Exhibition. Almost from its inauguration it encountered faculty opposition. President Webster had absolutely no use for such an organ of student self-government and poured his wrath on it. It soon expired. Nevertheless, Bowker always thought it the germ of a good idea, had the satisfaction of knowing it provided a precedent for later action, and watched with interest the gradual establishment of student councils in almost all American colleges.

12 New York, Walter Gibson, 59 Liberty Street, 1866.

The Free Academy and the City College

In addition to his leadership of the Academic Senate, Bowker secured valuable experience in public speaking and parliamentary procedure through the college literary societies. There were two of these in friendly rivalry at the college, the Clionian and the Phrenocosmian. The meetings consisted chiefly of essays and debates and were held in the lecture room of the old Clinton Hall in Astor Place. Bowker took a prominent part in the Clionian Society, being elected vice-president in his junior year and president in his senior year. In the spring of 1866 he had the happy inspiration of inaugurating a yearly joint debate. Assuming the name X. L. C. Orr in order to give his proposal added prestige, he wrote to both societies and President Webster offering a "handsomely bound" copy of *Chambers' Cyclopedia of English Literature* and a large edition of *Cushing's Parliamentary Rules* to the best speakers in an extemporaneous debating contest. The proposal was an instantaneous success. So much so, that to conceal its adolescent origins, Bowker induced his father to represent himself to the president as the sponsor, and in the end President Kelly of the Board of Education was moved to institute a permanent medal for such an annual contest. Bowker later stated that electioneering experience in his fraternity and parliamentary practice in the literary societies provided useful training for practical politics.

While the *Collegian* was still appearing and the Academic Senate was still in session, Bowker did his college a fourth signal service by securing the charter for a local chapter of Phi Beta Kappa. This scholars' fraternity had been organized by states, and in 1866 there were seventeen chapters. Alpha and Beta chapters in New York had been organized at Union College in 1817 and at New York University in 1858 respectively, and to the latter President Webster and nine Free Academy professors had been elected in 1859. It occurred to Bowker that it would be a feather in the college cap to establish its own chapter, especially since Columbia had none. It further occurred to him that it would be a splendid thing if the City College chapter might make New York City the scene of an annual Phi Beta Kappa oration similar to the one justly famous at Harvard. Consequently he initiated correspondence with the appropriate officials and sponsored a memorial from the eight honor men of the Junior and Sophomore classes requesting a charter. This was granted on December 18, 1867, the eighteenth of the fraternity.[13] Shortly afterwards, some Columbia students requested Bowker's assistance in securing a chapter for their college. Bowker felt he could

[13] R. R. B. to J. S. Battell, January 12, June 29, 1904; to L. S. Burchard, December 14, 1925; A. Dickson, *History of the Gamma Chapter of New York Phi Beta Kappa, 1867–1931*, 3–5.

not "decently refuse co-operation," and the result of his friendly guidance was that in 1869 Columbia became the Delta of New York and the twenty-first chapter of the fraternity.

Ironically, when it came time to elect students from Bowker's class to the organization, President Webster blackballed Bowker because of his "insubordinate" activities in founding the *Collegian,* the student Senate, and the Phi Beta Kappa chapter.[14] The faculty protested, but to no avail. The injustice rankled. As soon as Webster retired in 1870, Bowker was voted in, but he declined the tardy honor. Not until 1904, and then only through the intervention of his close friend, Professor Werner, did he finally accept election.

Bowker had made good use of his opportunities at college. He had conscientiously studied composition and had been so successful in his campus newspaper that he had a position waiting for him on a metropolitan journal at graduation. He had acquired such a thorough grounding in physics that he was able, years later, to master the technical intricacies of the new electrical industry and help to develop it as manager of the largest electric-lighting company in the world. He had discovered an enthusiasm for political science and political economy, had tried his hand at campus politics with some success, and had gained considerable confidence in his own managerial ability. He had acquired a personal philosophy which indicated where his duty lay and a personal faith which mobilized his will to do his duty. He had acquired a fine company of loyal friends who respected him for what he was and what he had done. City College was to Bowker truly an *Alma Mater.*

Bowker discharged his debt to the college with lifelong loyalty. Through sixty-five years he remained an active, interested alumnus willing to serve on committees, raise money, rally fraternity brothers and classmates to reunions, counsel with faculty and presidents, write articles and memorials. Sixty years after graduation a fellow alumnus paid him warm tribute.

It was you, I am sure, who lit in the heart of Shepard the flame that never died, who cheered Crawford, and inspired Miller. You made them dream your dreams. I see in the undergraduate *you* the *fons et origo* of all that has lifted the student spirit of sixty classes from the routine atmosphere of a municipal academy to peerage with the famous colleges of the land, that brought college conscious-

14 R. R. B. to M. R. Cohen, May 12, 1927; Dickson, *History of the Gamma Chapter of the New York Phi Beta Kappa*, 6.

ness, college pride, and college emulation into those narrow rooms and on that merely theoretical "campus."[15]

Commencement was held at the old Academy of Music, and Bowker reported it in full for an evening newspaper.[16] In spite of his many extracurricular activities he was the fifth of the eight honor men in his class entitled to deliver "orations" on the commencement stage. The following morning he was at his new desk in the office of the *Evening Mail.*

[15] Lewis Sayre Burchard to R. R. B., September 4, 1928; see also Minutes of Gamma Chapter, Phi Beta Kappa, June 19, 1933.

[16] New York *Evening Mail,* July 2, 1868; hereafter referred to as *Evening Mail.*

III

Journalism
1868–1875

BOWKER BEGAN his career in journalism and never lost a close touch with the profession. From 1868 to 1874 he was first city editor and then literary editor of the New York *Evening Mail*. From 1875 to 1878 he wrote a weekly column of book news for the New York *Tribune*. Meanwhile he wrote articles and editorials for the Cincinnati *Commercial*, the New York *Press*, the *Jeweler's Circular*, the Boston *Globe*, and the London *Athenaeum*. From 1880 to 1882 he was editor of the European edition of *Harper's Magazine*, and in 1896 he was invited to become the manager of the New York *Times*. He edited one free-trade monthly in 1876 and another in 1888; in 1896 he edited the campaign handbook of the national Democratic party. For over half a century he was editor of both the *Library Journal* and the *Publishers' Weekly*. He was an inveterate writer of letters and articles for newspapers and periodicals and placed his journalistic experience and skill at the service of the friends, institutions, and causes dear to him, composing manifestoes, platforms, and creeds for various liberal movements and memorials for a host of departed friends. Bowker's career is an interesting example of how useful a journalistic training can be.

Law, business, and journalism had all appealed to young Bowker as a future calling. The legal interests of his close friends Wheeler, Delafield, and Shepard inclined him to join them, but his successful experience with the *Collegian* had led to contacts which finally decided him in favor of the newspaper world. By graduation he was invited to consider two offers: the post of city editor at fifteen dollars a week on the *Evening Mail* and a reporter's post at slightly higher pay on the *Commercial Advertiser*. Bowker accepted the former, and the morning after receiving his diploma reported for work at 11 Frankfort Street.

24

The young City College graduate entered New York City journalism at a time when many of the great metropolitan papers were in existence and their founders still active. The *Herald,* started in 1835 by James Gordon Bennett, was still the unprincipled, colorful paper which its editor kept it. Horace Greeley was very much the master of the *Tribune,* which he had launched in 1841. The New York *Times* was laying its long-maintained reputation under Henry J. Raymond, who, with his associate George Jones, had founded the paper in 1851. Charles A. Dana was just taking over the *Sun,* then thirty-five years old. William Cullen Bryant was sole editor of the *Evening Post.*

The paper which Bowker elected to join was not yet a year old. It had been launched as the *Evening Gazette* in 1866 by Charles H. Sweetser and S. J. Ahern in the loft building at 11 Frankfort Street. The next year Sweetser sold out the *Gazette* to Ahern and launched the *Evening Mail,* taking his old staff with him into another part of the same building in the expectation that the *Gazette* would thus become worthless. Ahern attempted to carry on as publisher and proprietor, but was soon obliged to abandon the paper.[1]

The *Mail's* staff was a small but energetic one. Bowker's new employer was himself a young man and not too stable. Sweetser had graduated from Amherst only six years previously. He was an inventive and brilliant journalist, starting six papers in four years, each with novel ideas;[2] but he was always in financial hot water and even imposed on the gullibility of his Amherst professors for credit. The four young men whom he gathered together to run the *Evening Mail* had, however, considerable ability. J. B. F. Walker was the very capable general editor; Bronson Howard, later well known in American drama, handled editorials and dramatic criticism; D. O'C. Towneley, a witty and brilliant Irishman, served as art critic; Bowker was city editor; society news was supplied by a colorful Mrs. Francis Jerry Fairfield, alias "Sophie Sparkle," remembered by Bowker for the scandalous amount of makeup she used and for her atrocious handwriting. The establishment did not take up much room: presses were located in the basement, composing rooms at the front, and editorial offices at the back of an upper floor.

Judging from his contributions to the paper during the first summer, Bowker worked hard and successfully. In addition to editing the regular city news, he wrote a surprising number of brisk, colorful feature articles. There were stories on everything under the sun from soda-

1 *Jersey City Herald,* July 29, 1871; R. R. B., MS Memoir; R. R. B. to Billings, June 10, 1901; to S. W. Dean, December 29, 1926.
2 Wingate, *Views and Interviews on Journalism,* 190.

water manufacturing, campaign badges, and paper collars to an old Irish woman selling apples on a street corner. There was also an ambitious and technical set of articles dealing with photography, lithography, and printing, including six accurate, authoritative studies of newspaper publishing, type, machinery, presses, and pressroom. One is impressed, on reading these pieces, by the excellent quality of Bowker's journalistic work. There is clearly evident, moreover, much that distinguished him in later life: a relish for accurate, full data; facility in digesting detailed technical material with precision and order; ease in obtaining an authoritative grasp of a subject; a cool, conscientious, orderly mind; and a style that was always simple, crisp, consistently free of padding, and illumined by touches of light humor.

Within six months of his arrival on the paper, Bowker was plunged into the first of the many journalistic crises he was to know. Sweetser's inventive temperament brought bankruptcy, and by Christmas, 1868, he was obliged to sell the controlling interest in the paper to James S. Johnston. It was Sweetser's confident hope that he could ruin the *Evening Mail* by a second audacious walkout with his entire staff, and then start afresh with a new evening paper. Bowker, however, was not the man for this kind of game, and Johnston had far more vigor than Ahern. He had served for ten years as business manager of the *Evening Post* and while there had formed a high regard for Major Jonas M. Bundy, for three years the *Post's* literary, dramatic, and musical critic. He now induced Bundy to become editor-in-chief of the *Evening Mail*. For a month Bundy and Bowker kept the paper going alone; for another three months they had only Towneley's help. To make matters worse, Johnston died and was succeeded by his less able brother. It was an up-hill fight and a small staff, but it was enough to break Sweetser and establish the paper.[3]

Major Bundy was steadier and more capable than Sweetser. Only thirty-three years old, he nevertheless had considerable experience behind him as a reporter on the daily *Evening Wisconsin,* editor-in-chief of the *Wisconsin Daily Sentinel,* and since 1866 the literary, musical, and dramatic critic of the *Evening Post.* He had also studied law at Beloit, served as judge in a Colorado mining district, and seen Civil War action as one of General Pope's staff officers. Cool-headed, agreeably-mannered, and possessing the cultivated courtesy of a gentleman, Bundy had the good sense to give a good measure of freedom to his

[3] R. R. B. to C. F. Wingate; Wingate, *Views and Interviews on Journalism,* 190; *Jersey City Herald,* July 29, 1871. James S. Johnston was succeeded by his brother Robert, a banker and treasurer of the American Press Association. Sweetser, after spending a few years trying to launch *The City,* a magazine about New York, died in 1871 at the age of thirty.

subordinates. He also had great energy and initiative and often galvanized the office staff into united action to achieve notable "beats," such as on the occasions of Henry J. Raymond's death, the defeat of the French Army at Sedan, and the Orange riots.[4] The editorial rooms were continued at 11 Frankfort Street and a public office opened at 34 Park Row.

By 1870 Bundy was ready to expand his staff and the paper.[5] The number of editors was increased from three to six, capable correspondents were secured in Washington, London, Paris, Berlin, Vienna, and Rome. In 1872, the *Mail* was encouraged to launch a weekly edition, renamed in 1873 the New York *Weekly Mail*. It appeared on Wednesdays and included the best features in all the departments of the daily editions. These policies were so successful in increasing the circulation and value of the property that Cyrus W. Field purchased one-third of the stock for $50,000. The *Mail* had taken the lead among New York's two-cent afternoon papers.

The paper, under Bundy's new regime, became the very model of a wholesome, liberal, crusading journal. The *American Newspaper Reporter* described it as "such a paper as a tired merchant or banker would like to read on the cars, on his way up town, and then hand to his wife or daughters for their edification, without fear of taint or contamination." It ruled out all notices of engagements to marry as objectionable pruriency; it indulged in no malicious attacks on individuals. It described itself as "a thoroughly Independent Organ of the honest men of both political parties who hate official corruption . . . ." Good causes were vigorously supported: Cuban freedom, free trade, civil service reform, temperance, higher education, the reduction of unnecessary federal legislation. Unchristian forces were unhesitatingly attacked: land and railroad monopolies, corporations, Tammany Hall, "atheistic European Socialism, Communism, and Positivism." Bowker considered Bundy's editorials to be "the most vital and telling in current journalism."

As part of this new staff shake-up, and at his own request, Bowker became the literary editor. As usual, however, he was able to make himself useful in other capacities. He also served as an unofficial assistant editor and did much of the work of managing editor. Such was the confidence that he enjoyed, indeed, that on more than one occasion, in Bundy's absence, he acted as editor-in-chief.[6] His passion for efficiency around the office sometimes resulted in ruffled feelings. One of his

[4] R. R. B., MS Memoir; *Jersey City Herald,* July 29, 1871.
[5] *Evening Mail* Weekly Edition, January 1, 1872.
[6] R. R. B. to Parke Godwin, October 26, 1874.

schemes was a procedure for timing and disciplining the office boys. Robert Johnston, the publisher, chided Bowker for his impatience at delays. "The trouble all appears to be that you are in too great a hurry to get things at a moment's warning," he complained. "I think you won't find this office behind in anything,—but don't carry all the time the idea you appear to have formed years ago—that nobody outside of the editorial rooms knows anything." Yet Johnston approved of many of Bowker's schemes and in general appreciated his enterprise. "I am conscious of your ability, faithfulness, and conscientiousness in the discharge of your important duties," he wrote, "and the zeal and enthusiasm with which you have worked up your department."[7]

From the moment Bowker had entered the newspaper field he had set out to master it. The articles for the *Mail* describing the various aspects of newspaper publishing could only have been written on the basis of intensive observation of several different printing rooms. Writing articles and editorials for seven different newspapers and weeklies widened his experience and contacts. His essay "The Small-Talk of Journalism" in the *Aldine Press*[8] proves that he was carefully studying the special features of all the leading New York and Boston papers. He was also keeping notes for a history of journalism and starting a collection of important editions. In the summer of 1872 he planned an ambitious article on the future of journalism which would discuss both American and European trends, and some of this material was worked into two long essays for the *Mail*.[9] C. F. Wingate's *Views and Interviews in Journalism* in 1875 contains an interview with Bowker which further indicates his wide-ranging interest in the problems of the profession.

Early in his journalistic career, Bowker decided that it was not economical "for a fifty-dollar man to do any part of the work a twenty-dollar man could do as well," and so hired a series of capable young college graduates as personal assistants who would also thus have the benefit of an apprenticeship in journalism. Graham McAdam, a fellow City College alumnus, was the first to accept the post of assistant. This arrangement freed Bowker for more and more outside work. Already in the fall of 1868, he had supplied the Cincinnati *Commercial* with a series of letters on current New York doings and sayings.[10] The following year he prepared editorials for both the New York *Press* and the *Jeweler's Circular*, doing much of the work in the early morning at home, before he left for his own office. A few years later he sought to

7 R. Johnston to R. R. B., December 18, 1871; November 13, December 14, 1872.
8 August, 1870. See the *Mail's* editorial on this subject, August 6, 1869, probably by R. R. B.
9 "Journalism," I, II, *Evening Mail* Weekly Edition, February 5, 12, 1873.
10 Cincinnati *Commercial*, October 30, November 14, 1868.

become an occasional correspondent of the London *Athenaeum* when it was arranging for a New York column. On the *Mail,* Bowker contributed a great deal of occasional brevier writing in such columns of small talk as "Spinnings," "Short Paragraphs," "All Sorts," "Personal Gossip," "Freshest Gleanings," "College Chat," and "Journalistic."[11] But the most important professional work he did at this time, from the standpoint of its effect on his future career, was the half-time assistance he gave to Frederick Leypoldt in managing and writing editorials for his weekly book-trade journal, the *Publishers' Weekly.*

With his appointment in 1870 to the literary department of the *Evening Mail* Bowker's general journalistic interests became focused somewhat of necessity on one particular field: the writing, publishing, selling, and reviewing of books and magazines. From 1870 to 1872 his regular contributions were made under the heading "Literary Notes." When the *Weekly Mail* edition was created, he set up a new feature called "Our Book Table," and supplemented it with such additional weekly features as "The Literary Outlook" and "The Magazine Outlook." Bowker's natural ambition and thoroughness were immediately evident. "It is our intention," he announced in 1870, "that . . . the *Evening Mail* shall be second to no daily journal in the country in the freshness and scope of its literary matter." He pledged that his reviews would be "unusually prompt and . . . liberal," "thorough, well-informed, fair, fearless, and useful." His purpose, he said, was to be "an enterprising chronicler . . . and a useful guide to those desiring to keep up with the current literature of the language as expressing the movement of the world's thought and life."

Book reviewing was a serious responsibility to Bowker, and he frequently discussed it with his close friends George Haven Putnam and Richard Watson Gilder, then junior editor of *Scribner's Monthly.* To him the *Nation* was as guilty of one extreme in being too negatively critical as George Ripley's literary columns in the *Tribune* were guilty of the other extreme in being too appreciative. Ripley was an unusually well-informed man in his field and had become a kind of "one-man power" in the American literary world. Bowker, however, was one of those who felt that he lacked "virile positiveness" and failed to exert the constructive influence on letters that the critics of Poe's day had. It was the reviewer's practical responsibility, according to Bowker, to help mold a creative tradition of writing by seeing justice done to promising young writers, by encouraging discrimination in both readers and publishers, and by "the heartiest appreciation of good and the most fearless and unsparing rebuke of bad books." In discharging this re-

11 R. R. B., "Small Talk of Journalism," *Aldine Press,* New York, August, 1870.

sponsibility, Bowker did not hesitate to assume the roles of teacher, preacher, and legislator.

Bowker's patient efforts to do justice to young writers earned him the heartfelt appreciation of many struggling for recognition.[12] There were the young novelist E. P. Roe, and George W. Cable, who long remembered Bowker's encouraging review of his early work and prophecy of his future success. He gave friendly encouragement to Mrs. Adeleine D. Train Whitney when other critics were denouncing her as a sentimentalist. He followed with interest the career of Mrs. Frances Hodgson Burnett, took pains over the verse of Laura C. Redden, and joined E. C. Stedman in helping C. F. Woolson. He won many friends by responding conscientiously to scores of little, time-consuming requests for favorable notices of this and that, for the promotion of this and that, for information, for talks before literary societies, for employment, for literary markets in behalf of friends and strangers.

It seemed to Bowker a great age in which to be reviewing books. The years 1868–70, he asserted, would "hereafter be distinguished in the history of literature as almost a golden era. For many decades no period has been so wonderfully prolific in great books from great authors." Writing early in 1872, he listed some of the forces giving vitality to American literature, such as the stimulus of war, the healthy revolt against "the scum of society, the shams and shoddyites" rising to the surface after Appomattox, the stirring development of the West, the security and "highly developed culture" of a large part of the people. He attributed the excellent quality of the American translations of European classics issued by James R. Osgood and Company to "our catholic, all-absorbing position among the nations." As for New York, Bowker frequently said that it was rapidly recovering the prestige and leadership enjoyed in the time of Irving and since yielded to Boston. "We may at this day safely assert," he wrote in 1874, "that New York is fast becoming the metropolis of literature as well as of trade: its literary circles are many, wide, cultured, and aesthetic, authors are gravitating hither from West and East, its criticism is becoming distinctively appreciative without fulsomeness and receptive of all schools alike."[13]

Bowker's judgments were generally sound, occasionally capricious. He was skeptical of Joaquin Miller's permanent worth, held that John Hay's *Pike County Ballads* would give him "average rank among minor poets," and was enthusiastic about *A Chance Acquaintance* by W. D. Howells. Bowker wrote of Mark Twain's *Gilded Age* that "it was the most trenchant satire on American life and morals since *Martin Chuz-*

12 See correspondence with individuals mentioned in R. R. B. Papers.
13 *Christian Leader*, February 14, 1874.

zlewit." He said of Whitman's writing that "behind his silly affected-ness and dry cataloguing there is a fresh, broad, wholesome American-ism"; but he couldn't resist the temptation to burlesque Whitman in a piece entitled "Yawp Hitman Again," printed in the *Mail* and reprinted in the Hartford *Courant*.[14] Bowker's greatest praise, however, was re-served for Mrs. A. D. T. Whitney's *Real Folks,* which he described as "that book of the year in fiction which will live, as for all time, and ultimately be considered greatest." Bowker tried to encourage regional studies and novels "sticking to the soil." He attacked the "child of na-ture" school which "exercises no self-restraint, but throws everything hot from the brain and crude to an alarming degree straight into the hopper of the printing press."[15] Where morality was concerned, he gave no quarter to the "art for art's sake school," ripping into Edgar Faw-cett's *Purple and Fine Linen* and Wilkie Collins' *The New Magdalen.*

European writers were given attention in Bowker's columns. He was critical of Ruskin, charging that "his sublime faith in things abso-lute gives way to a painful distrust of the world as it is." He had un-restrained praise for Turgenev's *Nest of Nobles,* pronouncing it "a *very* great novel." George Eliot he considered as "easily first among living writers, challenging place among the greatest of all time," but criticized her *Daniel Deronda* in a long and painstaking review[16] as lacking in continuity, marred by unfamiliar words, and representing a lapse by the writer in both literary and artistic taste. Bowker ap-plauded, however, the moral affirmation of man's freedom in this work and wrote that, in this respect and in comparison with *Adam Bede* and *Middlemarch,* "it was as though George Eliot had got out into the free air and found hope in life after all."

Bowker's book reviewing was not confined to the *Mail.* Several of his essays appeared in the *Cosmopolitan,* the *International Review,* and the *Christian Leader.*[17] Bowker's most ambitious and wholesale review, "Literature in America in 1871," was written at Frederick Leypoldt's request for the third edition of his *Annual American Catalogue.* This was a thoroughly workmanlike affair, confidently noting and comment-ing upon 240 books grouped under fifteen heads.

Bowker's professional work of reviewing, indeed, in no way in-hibited him from trying his own hand at essays and verse. Between 1870 and 1879 he had forty-three contributions published in thirteen mag-

14 September 14, 1871.

15 *Christian Leader,* February 14, 1874.

16 *International Review,* January, 1877, pp. 68–76; H. B. Barnes to R. R. B., February 2, 1877.

17 *Christian Leader,* June 28, July 26, August 30, 1873; February 14, 1874.

azines, with at least as many refused.[18] Of the published total, twenty-seven were verse, and represent a wide range of experimentation in meters and forms. In subject matter several were about children and for children, a few described natural scenes, most were of a religious and moral nature. Two of these were translations from the German: Bayard Taylor's *"Jubel Lied Eines Amerikaners,"* which first appeared in the *Mail* but attracted so much attention that it was soon reprinted in the *Cosmopolitan;* and Salis' "Evening Sadness," printed in *Old and New.* One, "Toll Then No More," was deemed by William Cullen Bryant to merit inclusion in his *Library of Poetry and Song.* Another, "My Lady's Voice," was contributed to Thomas Niles' *Masque of Poets* in his No Name Series. A much finer piece was Bowker's sonnet on Thomas a Kempis, first published in *Scribner's* and later included in Stedman's *American Anthology.*

Thomas a Kempis: De Imitatione

Turn with me from the city's clamorous street,
Where throng and push passions and lusts and hate,
And enter, through this age-browned, ivied gate,
For many summers' birds a sure retreat,
The place of perfect peace. And here, most meet
For meditation, where no idle prate
Of the world's ways may come, rest thee and wait.
'Tis very quiet. Thus doth still Heaven entreat.

With rev'rent feet, his face so worn, so fair,
Walks one who bears the cross, who waits the crown.
Tumult is past. In those calm eyes I see
The image of the Master, Christ, alone.
And from those patient lips I hear one prayer:
"Dear Lord, dear Lord, that I may be like Thee!"

Writing verse became a relaxation and recreation for Bowker, and hardly a year went by without new compositions, often done when traveling. For each one printed there were scores which remained in Bowker's notebooks. Although constant application brought real improvement, so that some of his later pieces have genuine literary merit, Bowker never referred to himself other than as a "poetaster" or "magazine poet." At its best, Bowker's verse during these years exhibited the virtues of pith, compactness, and pleasing rhythm, but the form was

18 See bibliography.

often ragged. R. W. Gilder was accurate in describing Bowker's pieces as "bright and thoughtful," but W. D. Howells was more discerning when he rejected two of Bowker's poems for the *Atlantic* with the comment that there were "true poetic thoughts and feeling . . . but there is too great ambition and unsimplicity in their conception and expression." Bowker almost always had important things to say, but neither the time nor the art to express them in true poetic form. He acknowledged as much himself, and once noted that he had been "diverted from climbing further up Parnassus by more pressing occupations." The prose which Bowker contributed to the periodical press during these years was far better than the verse. In these articles he exhibited his real gift for concise and telling statement. The subjects represent a wide range of interests in social problems, science, religion, health, and camping. Much of his best writing was done in editorials for the *Publishers' Weekly*.

In addition to the association with newspaper men and publishers, Bowker's literary work brought him into close touch with magazine editors. He was particularly familiar with the staff of *Scribner's Monthly;* he knew well R. W. Gilder and J. G. Holland, and became somewhat acquainted with the Scribners themselves. Mary Mapes Dodge made *St. Nicholas* magazine a neighborly enterprise for him. He frequently visited in the home of Henry Alden, editor of *Harper's Magazine*. Washington Gladden and Joshua Leavitt of the *Independent* were both well known to him as fellow free traders. He was being drawn into acquaintance with G. W. Curtis of *Harper's Weekly* through common college fraternity ties and common interests in free trade, civil service, and Independent Republicanism. In Boston he could count on the friendly hospitality of Edward E. Hale of *Old and New* and the cordial interest of William Dean Howells of the *Atlantic*.

Bowker formed a warm literary friendship with E. C. Stedman which lasted for more than a quarter of a century.[19] When Bowker came to know him, Stedman was still in his thirties, but he had made such a reputation for himself that Bowker's generation thought of him as a "venerated if not venerable person." It was Bowker's work on the *Mail* which prompted Stedman's offer of friendship in the fall of 1873 and a note referring to Bowker as "a fellow craftsman." The two men discussed the best advice to give young writers whom they both wished to encourage, the best way to summarize English reviews in the Ameri-

[19] See the correspondence between the two men in the R. R. B. Papers, some of it quoted in Laura Stedman and G. M. Gould, *Life and Letters of Edmund Clarence Stedman*.

can press, and articles for Bowker to write with materials which Stedman would help to provide. Bowker was extended a standing invitation to drop in at the poet's home for dinner, and Stedman expressed his appreciation of Bowker's friendship in many letters.

There were other warm literary friendships. Bowker's association with Richard Watson Gilder, then assistant junior editor of *Scribner's Monthly* lasted well on into life. Gilder and Bowker spent many Sunday afternoons together discussing common interests, and Bowker became Gilder's confidant in his successful courtship of Helena de Kay, granddaughter of Joseph Rodman Drake, New York's first poet. Edward Eggleston became a friend of the entire Bowker family. "I have long wanted to be acquainted with you on general principles," he wrote Bowker in 1874, and there followed many mutual visits. When Moses Coit Tyler left the editorial rooms of the *Christian Union* for Ann Arbor, he sent a most affectionate farewell.

There was lively and unconventional correspondence with many literary figures too far away for close acquaintance. Thomas Bailey Aldrich frequently betrayed his lighthearted irreverence, Frank R. Stockton and Bret Harte discussed Bowker's reviews, Harvard's Charles Eliot Norton exchanged tirades on current American sculpture. Closer by, Bowker had running exchanges with Richard Henry Stoddard, J. G. Holland, and others.

As journalist, critic, and literateur, a handsome young man who could assist in making a reputation and in selling literary merchandise, Bowker found himself *persona grata* in several New York literary circles. Stedman on several occasions invited Bowker to attend the meetings of the Century Club, that distinguished group of luminaries in letters and the arts who gathered in the dignified mansion at 109 East Fifteenth Street under the presidency of William Cullen Bryant. Finally convinced that the young man had won his spurs, Stedman extended the offer of formal nomination for membership, but Bowker felt it best to decline.[20] One of the choicest New York literary salons of the seventies was held by the Gilders in their charming home, "The Studio," on East Fifteenth Street, and in this early-day Bohemia, Bowker was always welcome. For many years he was also a frequenter of the notable Saturday evening "open house" held by Miss Mary L. Booth, editor of *Harper's Bazaar*, and her friend Mrs. Wright; of the somewhat less popular receptions given by Mrs. Oliver B. Bunce, wife of the editor of *Appleton's Journal;* and of the New Year's Day receptions of Mary Mapes Dodge. Professor

[20] R. R. B., MS Memoir; R. R. B. to Miss Laura Stedman, April 23, 1901; to S. E. Mezes, May 26, 1926; to Stedman, June 28, 1900. Other offers of election came later, when a multiplicity of club relations made it undesirable for Bowker to join.

and Mrs. John C. Draper of the City College gave him a standing invitation to their Friday evening musical soirees as well as invitations to Sunday dinners, concerts, and receptions at the Century.

With these pleasant associations in New York, it is not surprising that a trip to Boston in the spring of 1872 proved to be rich in literary introductions. "I have seen *her*,—Mrs. A. D. T. Whitney," he wrote his sister in the midst of a whirl:

> Called Saturday evening and saw her daughter also. . . . Am to meet Miss Alcott tomorrow or next day, and Scudder gives me a tea Tuesday.[21] Monday I am to take tea with Mr. E. E. Hale, up Roxbury way. . . . Had a delightful chat with Prof. Childs, at Cambridge. . . . Monday at three Emerson gives a conversation on Literature, to which I mean to go. Spent 10–12 last evening at Haskell's room here chatting, he is editor of the *Transcript*. . . . *Glorious* sermon and service at Mr. Hale's church, and dinner at Thomas Bailey Aldrich's . . . lovely house and family—and I had a *most* lovely time. Aldrich's twins are rightly famous in literary circles—about Gerty's age, and so I had my usual romp in double quantity. . . . Tonight go to hear Phillips Brooks and afterward the finish of an oratorio. Haven't got half round yet and have already made lots of new friends. Am having a glorious time.

Between 1872 and 1874 Bowker had established something of a reputation for himself in New York literary circles. There is every indication that his reviews were widely read and respected and that he was considered one of the city's qualified, accepted, and promising young journalists. As early as 1871, one press notice asserted that he was "fairly entitled to some of the credit for [the *Mail's*] success as a newspaper"; another spoke of him as "well known as a brilliant and conscientious journalist of the metropolis." The Jersey City *Herald* said of his literary department that "none is more discriminating or exhaustive in its reviews of current publications." Mary Dodge declared that he had "a genius for catching at all the salient points of current literature, and making them more pointed."[22] The *American Stationer* thought highly of Bowker's talents:

> Mr. Bowker possesses special qualifications for a successful journalistic career. He is versatile, has quick perceptions, a 'nose for

21 W. D. Howells wrote R. R. B. regretting that he could not attend.
22 Utica *Daily Observer*, May 25, 1876; New York *Evening Post*, September 21, 1879; *Jersey City Herald*, July 29, 1871; M. M. Dodge to R. R. B., July 24, 1872; June 20, July 23, 1873.

news,' . . . great energy, a love for hard work, courtesy in dealing with visitors, independence, and unusual executive capacity. As a literary critic he has shown both fairness and candor, while he has sympathy for the shortcomings of authors.[23]

E. C. Stedman wrote Bowker a handsome recognition of his services to the literary community in New York:

I have been in the habit of observing your method as a reviewer and the conscientious care which you bestow upon the best current literature. You have really given the *Mail* a decided position among evening papers, as the journal of authors and the book-world,—such as the *Post* had in its early days. I consider your department as most important to literature, and especially to New York authors,—who for so many years have scarcely received *at home* the fostering recognition which Boston so lavishly bestows upon her own clansmen. We few who have stuck to our posts here, against many discouragements, are at last beginning to see hope and to find our reward in the cordial discriminative interest of reviewers like yourself. For all this I beg to tender you my sincerest thanks.[24]

Just as a career in journalism and literary criticism was thus fairly launched, financial mismanagement of the *Mail* forced Bowker to abandon this career and undertake a second one in the book trade. The *Mail* had never paid him a decent salary. As early as 1871 he had pointed out this fact, and it had been admitted by the publisher to be true but beyond immediate remedy.[25] Early in 1874 Bowker entered into an agreement with Johnston whereby he was to get a stated percentage of the paper's profits. But Bowker was never able to collect a cent on this agreement.[26] This interest in the *Mail's* earnings, however, enabled Bowker to learn certain details about Johnston's business management which utterly dismayed him. Johnston, he concluded, was recklessly using the *Mail* to feather his own nest. Bowker rebelled, threatened to demand an investigation and an accounting, and was only prevented from this by a direct appeal to his personal loyalty by Major Bundy, who assured him that a public disclosure might break up the enterprise. Bundy then told Bowker that he had arranged with friends to buy out Johnston and that if Bowker would quietly resign,

23 "A Journalistic Change," *American Stationer*, April 8, 1875.
24 E. C. Stedman to R. R. B., November 30, 1873.
25 R. Johnston to R. R. B., December 18, 1871.
26 R. R. B. to R. Johnston, January 11, 13, 1876.

it would not be long before he could return to the *Mail* and help Bundy run it.

This placed the young literary editor in a cruel dilemma. He had worked hard and long to build up his department and was devoted to it. He was, moreover, acutely dependent on his editor's salary, for his father was still without employment, heavy family responsibilities had descended upon his own shoulders, and he had no other material resources. Nevertheless, he decided to act on Bundy's advice and, consequently, in the fall of 1874, began looking for another job.

Other literary jobs proved hard to get. The departments of the *Evening Post* and the *Tribune* were filled, and his vigorous attempts to enter them, even with the backing of Stedman, came to nothing.[27] Whitelaw Reid even turned down Bowker's column of "Literary Notes" for the *Tribune,* although Bowker undertook to guarantee "the freshest and most full department of this sort in the country." The Chicago *Tribune* was similarly approached, but proved equally cold. Christmas came and went, and no new employment had been found. Except for the part-time relation with the *Mail* and with the *Publishers' Weekly,* Bowker found himself a journalist without a job, and it was slight comfort to reflect that this had come about through no fault of his own except an overready loyalty to Bundy, his editorial chief. It was an ordeal Bowker never forgot. Happily this uncertainty was short-lived, for, at the end of December, Whitelaw Reid offered Bowker a weekly assignment on the *Tribune,* and soon thereafter he entered into permanent relations with the *Publishers' Weekly.* Meantime, throughout the first eight months of 1875, he wrote weekly editorials for the *Jeweler's Circular.*

Bowker did not easily give up the hope of continuing his career as a literary editor of a metropolitan newspaper. In the fall of 1876 he once again, but unsuccessfully, sought a place in the literary department of the *Evening Post.* He tried to arrange a talk with Bundy concerning a renewal of relations with the *Mail,* but, much to Bowker's irritation, this proved fruitless.[28] As late as 1878 he still hoped to return to newspaper work as either editor or manager of a New York evening paper committed to liberal reform. As a matter of fact, however, Bowker's career as a newspaperman came to an end in 1875. He now left the world of the fourth estate and entered the world of books.

27 R. R. B. to Parke Godwin, October 26, 1874; to Whitelaw Reid, October 26, 1874; E. C. Stedman to R. R. B., October 28, 1874; Whitelaw Reid to R. R. B., October 30, 1874.

28 R. R. B. to R. Johnston, January 11, 1876; to W. H. White, October 3, 1878.

IV

The Publishers' Weekly
1872–1880

T HE CAUSE of the book runs like a golden thread through all the varied interests and activities of Bowker's long life. As for the writing of books, he came to know intimately many of the most prominent American and British authors and described in frequent magazine articles their working habits, their homes, and their special fields of interest. He became, himself, an author of several books and many pamphlets, was an early member of the Authors Club, and later served on its executive council. He was a leader in the fight to protect the rights of authors through an adequate law of international copyright, serving as chairman of the American Copyright League's executive committee, later as its vice-president and acting president, becoming a member of the Authors' League of America, and writing several books on this subject.

As for the publishing and marketing of books, there were probably several times in Bowker's life when no one had a more comprehensive perspective on the entire book trade of this country. With the exception of a few years, he was editor and owner of the most important American book-trade journal, the *Publishers' Weekly,* from its inception in 1872 to his death in 1933. He assisted in the organization of the first American Book Trade Association and was later an honorary member of the American Booksellers' Association. For two years he was the London representative of one of the most important American publishing houses. At his death the National Association of Book Publishers referred to him as "the Dean of American Publishers." As for the reviewing of books, Bowker earned his bread by this craft for five years as literary editor of the *Evening Mail.*

In addition to familiarity with the writing, publishing, selling, and reviewing of books, Bowker came into a unique position with relation to the American bibliographical profession, starting as the assistant of its great pioneer Frederick Leypoldt in his herculean efforts to launch the *American Catalogue,* and after Leypoldt's death continuing not only this vast enterprise, but the several other bibliographical devices which made the office of the *Publishers' Weekly* the bibliographical center for the country. Finally, Bowker was a pioneer in building up the library profession of the United States, being one of the three men who founded the American Library Association, serving on its council and being elected one of its honorary presidents; a trustee of the Brooklyn Public Library, president for twenty-four years of the Stockbridge (Mass.) Library Association, a founder and the first president of the New York Library Club, a fellow of the American Library Institute and of the Library Association of the United Kingdom. He was also one of the three founders of the *Library Journal* and was its owner and editor for more than fifty years. At his death in 1933 it was said of Bowker that his life was "perhaps more closely interwoven with books than anyone else's now living."[1]

Not one of these relations with the world of books brought Bowker fame or fortune. Indeed, except for the *Publishers' Weekly,* which earned its owner a small interest on his investment, they each incurred an almost continuous deficit. Moreover, this work was costly in its enormous toll of daily physical energy and put such a strain on eyesight that Bowker actually went blind through his devotion to it. Bowker, however, would have been the first to emphasize the enormous rewards of his long-continued association with the world of books in rich, personal friendships, in the adventurous pioneering of new policies, in battles fought and won, in the enormous satisfaction—especially gratifying to a crusading liberal—of knowing that books were a supreme agency in the liberation of man's spirit and that he was playing a determining role in the perfection of this agency.

Bowker's informal introduction to the book trade came when he was appointed literary editor of the *Mail* in 1870. Publishers well realized the value of a good notice to their trade sales and sought to keep on friendly terms with the young reviewer. On his side, Bowker became increasingly interested in the book world. Two articles in the *Cosmopolitan* entitled "Bibliomania—A Noble and Useful Insanity"[2] indicate that, even by the end of 1870, he had determined to familiarize himself thoroughly with the book trade in general and such special

---

[1] Editorial in *American Book Collector,* December, 1933, p. 305.
[2] The second article is dated January 28, 1871.

aspects as rare editions, private libraries, bookstores, book collectors, and booksellers. On one occasion he wrote a description of the Christmas preparations and Christmas offerings of thirty leading New York bookstores.[3] From time to time he published in the *Mail* accounts of book-trade problems and the treatment of authors. When one publisher had the brass to bring out part of a story by Bret Harte and then commission another man to finish it, Bowker sprang to the injured writer's defense in a scorching editorial entitled "A Literary Outrage."[4]

Bowker's more formal introduction to the book trade came in 1872 when he associated himself with Frederick Leypoldt, who had just founded the *Weekly Trade Circular*. His first service for Leypoldt was the review of American literature in 1871, which ran serially in the *Circular* and then became an integral part of Leypoldt's *Annual American Catalogue*.[5] He joined the staff of Leypoldt's book-trade journal on January 1, 1873, at the very moment it adopted the name by which it was henceforth to be known, The *Publishers' Weekly*. He began as a part-time assistant editor while continuing with the *Mail,* an arrangement which lasted until the winter of 1875 when Bowker severed his last connections with the *Mail* and became a full-time editor of the *Weekly*. The association proved to be a lifelong one. With the exception of the years 1880–82 when he was out of the country, Bowker continued to edit the *Publishers' Weekly* until his death in 1933, and from 1878 on he owned it.

Bowker's employer was a remarkable man. Leypoldt was colorful, warmhearted, a man of "small stature but of large presence," who combined masculine intellect with feminine charm. Bowker referred to "the quickness and alertness of his manner which suggested French blood" and his "French stateliness and grace."[6] Leypoldt's wife referred to "his fire and poetry and romance and his intense longing for, and dependence on, expressed sympathy."[7] Leypoldt combined the intellectual vigor of a scholar with the meticulous precision of a scientist and the imagination of an artist. But in all business matters he was utterly naïve. Original, inventive, with an enormous capacity for hard work, he remained a dreamer and was thrown into fits of black depression by business losses. His complete lack of practical judgment, indeed, on several occasions led to his being victimized and swindled and finally reduced to bankruptcy.

3 "Santa Claus Library," *Evening Mail*, December 24, 1873.
4 *Evening Mail*, December 31, 1873.
5 R. R. B., "Literature in America in 1871," *Publishers' and Stationers' Weekly Trade Circular*, January 18, February 8, 22, 1872.
6 R. R. B., "Frederick Leypoldt," *Publishers' Weekly*, April 5, 1884.
7 Mrs. A. Leypoldt to R. R. B., March 31, 1885.

THE

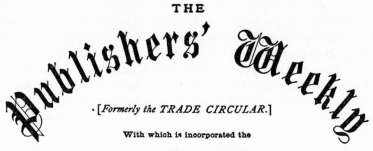

Publishers' Weekly

· [*Formerly the TRADE CIRCULAR.*]

With which is incorporated the

American Literary Gazette and Publishers' Circular,

Established in the year 1852.

OFFICIAL ORGAN OF THE PUBLISHERS' BOARD OF TRADE.

F. LEYPOLDT, EDITOR AND PUBLISHER, 712 BROADWAY, NEW YORK.

VOL. III. No. 1.   NEW YORK, Thursday, January 2, 1873.   WHOLE No. 51.

Leypoldt's career had been devoted entirely to the book trade. Arriving penniless in the United States from Germany at the age of nineteen, he had at first been employed as a clerk by F. W. Christern, then the leading foreign bookseller in the United States. After a return trip to Germany at Christern's suggestion to study book-trade methods there, Leypoldt opened his own foreign-language bookstore in Philadelphia and made a reputation for himself as a dealer and publisher of translations. Moving to New York, he opened a branch publishing house specializing in language-study texts, and in 1865 entered into a publishing partnership with young Henry Holt. By 1871 however, it became clear to Leypoldt that his heart was not in publishing, but in book-trade bibliography. He therefore sold his publishing interest to Holt and settled down to the field of his real lifework.

Leypoldt's decision brought about an almost perfect union of experience and need. To his assumption of leadership in the American field he brought an extraordinary knowledge of the home and foreign book trade in all the relations of retailing, publishing, and importing; newsroom, circulation, and library. In addition to this, he had a singular devotion to bookdealing itself as a trade and the determination to help promote that trade into what he always deemed it to be—a profession.

At this time the book trade in America was growing rapidly and gave promise of a bright future, but the organization of the trade and its necessary tools had received very little attention. Back in 1863 Leypoldt had written an article expressing surprise that practical-minded America could be so slow in establishing those indispensable aids, a well-supported central trade organ and good catalogues.[8] Since nothing was done during the next ten years to fill this need, Leypoldt decided to fill it himself. Between 1868 and 1872 he conceived and initiated the main features of the great system of trade services for which he became justly honored.[9] These were essentially three in number: a means of communication between book publishers and book buyers; a means of communication between book publishers and booksellers; and a systematic, authoritative, book-trade bibliography.

The first service gradually evolved into the *Literary News,* an eight-page monthly review of current literature which attained a circulation, for some issues, of over 100,000 copies and continued publication until 1904. The second service took the form of a weekly trade paper which,

[8] *The American Publishers' Circular and Literary Gazette,* February 2, 1863.

[9] Useful summaries of Leypoldt's trade services can be found in R. R. B., "Frederick Leypoldt," *Publishers' Weekly,* April 5, 1884; the seventy-fifth anniversary number of the *Publishers' Weekly,* January 18, 1947, Section One; J. W. Beswick, *The Work of Frederick Leypoldt, Bibliographer and Publisher.*

after several metamorphoses, became the *Publishers' Weekly*. The third service, most nettlesome of all, was to include weekly, monthly, annual, and specially classified finding lists of books published, as well as an annual compilation of publishers' catalogues. The weekly and monthly lists were issued in the *Weekly*. The annual lists evolved into the *American Catalogue,* and the publishers' catalogues into the *Publishers' Trade List Annual.* The specially classified lists included the *Stationers' Hand Book,* the *Index Medicus,* and half a dozen reading guides and library aids.

Leypoldt knew exactly what he wanted to do, and he had made an excellent start by 1872, but he needed help. More specifically, he needed a steady managerial hand and a sound business judgment to guarantee the continuation of the services he had launched. He also needed some general editorial assistance, for he was not yet entirely at home in the English language. It was to provide this "personal assistance" that Leypoldt called upon Bowker and that Bowker entered the office which was to remain until this day a nerve center of the book trade in the United States.[10]

Bowker and Leypoldt immediately formed a close working partnership and a warm personal friendship. In the working team, Leypoldt from the beginning centered his attention on the bibliographical enterprises, Bowker on the editorial and business aspect of the *Weekly*. In this relation, the former exhibited his original, creative genius; the latter, his organizing ability, sound practical judgment, and steady nerve. The personal friendship of the two men rested on many common traits: moral earnestness, idealism, probity, capacity for hard work, dislike for publicity, and trust in their fellow men. Both, moreover, were ardently patriotic, had a keen sympathy for political reform movements, and believed in international copyright.

The *Publishers' Weekly* office, located at 712 Broadway, just south of Astor Place, was not only functionally but geographically at the center of the American book-trade world. A few doors south were Henry Holt and Scribner's, across the street was E. P. Dutton; a few doors north were Dodd, Mead and Company and A. D. F. Randolph, and in near-by Astor Place were Hurd and Houghton, John Wiley and Sons, and the site of the Leavitt Trade Sales. In the Bible House was the religious bookshop of Thomas Whitaker, while Macmillan's American agent was near by on Fifth Avenue. Farther away were the Harper House on Franklin Square, D. Appleton & Co. on lower Broadway, and G. P. Putnam's Sons at Fifth Avenue and Twenty-third Street. Such leaders as public-spirited William H. Appleton and the four

10 F. Leypoldt to R. R. B., July 16, 1872.

enormously capable Harper brothers helped New York City to set the pace. Boston was second to New York as a publishing center, and Philadelphia third, with Cincinnati and Chicago the only other centers of note. Bowker estimated that in 1871 American book production was worth $40,000,000; and that in 1877 there were 800 publishers, 4,476 books copyrighted, and 10,000 retail bookstores.[11] The book trade was still in the horse and buggy era, with no telephones or typewriters,[12] but it was growing.

Bowker and Leypoldt found the years 1872 to 1875 a hard, uphill fight. Although the *Weekly* had become the official organ of the Publishers' Board of Trade and the American Book Trade Union, the cooperation of publishers was hard to secure, business was generally depressed, and none of the office ventures earned a decent living. A turning point, however, came in 1875. The two men boasted that the *Weekly* had become "the most complete book trade paper published anywhere," not being surpassed even by the daily German trade organ. What's more, they announced that its subscribers represented nine-tenths of the country's retail book trade and that it had at last begun to make a "reasonable living profit."[13] Leypoldt cheerfully acknowledged Bowker's part in assuring this success, declaring that he had been "friend, counsellor, and executive, standing by him faithfully from the early struggles to the successful period of the journal." Meanwhile, since 1873, the office had been located in the old Potter Building at 37 Park Row to be nearer to the printers Waldron and Payne and to the newly established post office.

The office staff was growing. The first important addition after Bowker was Miss Marian M. Monachesi, a young lady of Italian parentage and strong book interests, who had been in charge of Leypoldt's circulating library in Philadelphia. In 1873 she joined the *Weekly* office force to help with the accounts and to write notices of books. Her brother, Nicolo di Rienzi Monachesi, acted as advertising solicitor for a short period, being followed in 1874 by William A. Stewart, a tall, red-haired young Scotsman who had entered the office as a bookkeeper. In 1877 the staff was strengthened by Adolf Growoll, who began by helping Leypoldt in the preparation of the *Educational Catalogue,* but who soon became Bowker's "efficient and most valued chief assistant." Growoll was a studious young man of American birth and German parentage, two years Bowker's junior, who had started as a printer with Waldron and Payne. The two men were fellow liberals with many in-

11 R. R. B., "Books and the Book Trade in America," *Catalogue of the Collective Exhibit of the American Book Trade* (Paris Exposition) (Cambridge, 1878), *vi.*

12 F. A. Stokes, *A Publisher's Random Notes, 1885–1935,* 12–13.

13 "The New Year," *Publishers' Weekly,* January 1, 1876.

terests in common and soon became fast friends. Mrs. Leypoldt, the spirited wife of the bibliographer, devoted herself to serving her husband's many personal needs, but steadily increased her contribution to the work of the office and after 1880 must be counted a regular and very capable member of the staff.[14] Two temporary assistants were good-natured Richard Brinckerhoff, manager of the *Literary News,* and Bowker's fraternity brother, L. E. Jones, chief compiler of the *American Catalogue.* The men and women whom Leypoldt gathered around him proved to be a congenial and devoted group of fellow craftsmen. Bowker maintained an unbroken association with the office for sixty-one years, W. A. Stewart for forty-five years, Miss Monachesi for thirty-six, Growoll for thirty-two, and Mrs. Leypoldt for thirty-one.

Bowker contributed his share to the spirit of the group. Steaming in from the *Evening Mail* around the corner in Frankfort Street and dashing off to political meetings or free-trade conclaves, he supplied a certain drive to the office. "The quietude and tranquillity that settled down on us upon your departure," wrote a member of the staff when Bowker left on his vacation, "has not yet been broken and we are as hopelessly dull as you could desire." At the first Christmas of his absence in London the staff chided him for missing the holiday with them. "If I were you," one of them wrote, "I would reproach myself for taking the heart out of the blessed season for so many people. But you *would* go away . . . and now see what you've been and gone and done! You Truant, taking the edge off so many jokes, and the spirit out of so much mirth."[15]

Bowker's primary and increasing responsibility was for the *Publishers' Weekly.* He began by editing the general book news for which his literary department on the *Mail* had become such an authoritative source. He also handled business relations with the publishing houses[16] and gradually took the initiative in planning as well as writing the editorials along the lines projected by Leypoldt. It was evident that Leypoldt intended the *Weekly* to become the focus of the entire book trade, expressing not only the interests of publishers, but of booksellers, librarians, literary editors, and all agents of book dissemination. He wished it to help the trade to make more money, but also to serve as a clearinghouse for opinions and discussions which might lead to better

[14] Mrs. Augusta Leypoldt was one of six remarkable daughters of Rudolph Garrigue, a German immigrant who had become president of the Germania Insurance Company and who was a brother-in-law of F. W. Christern. One of her sisters married Professor Lewis C. Mott. Another, Charlotte, in 1878 married Professor Thomas Masaryk, later the first president of Czechoslovakia.

[15] Cf. G. H. Putnam to R. R. B., November 29, 1873.

[16] *Weekly Trade Circular,* January 18, 1872.

understanding, the reform of abuses, and the cultivation of "such high standards and friendly relations, and the supply of such educational and professional tools, throughout the American book trade, as should give it rank where it properly belonged, second only to the learned professions."[17] These informational and educational objectives were accomplished through regular departments which presented lists of publishers' announcements, literary and trade news, obituaries, notes on foreign developments, official notices of book-trade organizations, and careful editorial discussion of all trade topics.

Shortly after he had taken over the editorial reins, Bowker listed his own platform:

> Cheap books, provided they are honest books, well made, and fairly paying the man who sells them; . . . that the interests of the trade and the interests of the public are identical in the long run; . . . that one publisher has [not] the right to take the fruits of another's labor by "jumping claims" even if that publisher is not protected by law; . . . the full remuneration of authors, foreign and American; . . . international copyright; . . . that the makers of books should [not] be used by the makers of type to keep the materials of book-making at a higher tariff than books themselves; . . . that the most liberal administration of the postal department best pays.[18]

Editorial adherence to this platform was a discouraging, uphill affair, and Bowker had few illusions about his success. "The part of the trade most directly concerned," he confessed in 1880, "does not care much for these discussions, and they have not been of much effect." There were some, however, who felt otherwise.[19] When an illness forced Bowker to leave the office for several weeks, Putnam expressed the loss to the trade. "We have missed you in more ways than one," he wrote Bowker. "The bookmen seem to have lost their voice, and the best expression of themselves, when your pen is no longer scratching in their behalf."

In addition to his editorial work on the *Weekly*, Bowker frequently took a hand with the bibliographical work of the office. This meant, first of all, supervising the preparation of the "Weekly Record" of books published, that "bookseller's alphabet and protoplasm of American trade bibliography."[20] In this task he secured the adoption of the new bib-

17 "The New Year," *Publishers' Weekly*. January 1, 1876.

18 *Publishers' Weekly*, June 26, 1880, pp. 655–56.

19 G. H. Putnam to R. R. B., January 16, 1877; Cf. testimonials printed in *Publishers' Weekly*, July 3, 1880.

20 Madeleine B. Stern, "The First Half-Century of *Publishers' Weekly*," *Publishers' Weekly*, January 18, 1947, Section One, p. 288.

liographical rules formulated by the young American Library Association which he had helped to found, and substituted concise bibliographical notes, joined to the title, for the indefinite puffs which had formerly been given. It also meant working from time to time, as everyone in the office sooner or later did, on the *American Catalogue*. This brought Bowker right into the midst of one of the most intense bibliographical enterprises of the day.

Bibliography was Leypoldt's great passion and his real life mission. It was a curious one. Bowker described bibliography as "a science in its principles and an art in its varied applications having singular fascination for many minds." To the average man, however, nothing could seem more deadly dull or forbidding: being an obscure calling, it would guarantee no fame; being a restricted and costly one, it would certainly earn few profits and quite likely incur large deficits. To the average man, indeed, bibliography was to be shunned like the plague.[21] And yet this exacting profession has attracted many notable figures, and of these Leypoldt is perhaps the outstanding American example. He was, indeed, one of the few great original geniuses in American bibliography.

The *American Catalogue* was a systematic record of American publications, starting with all American books in print on July 1, 1876, and then presenting an annual finding list of books in print and for sale, arranged alphabetically according to author, title, and subject. It was the most important, the most ambitious, and the most exacting of all Leypoldt's bibliographical enterprises. He described the project in the *Weekly* issue of September 13, 1873, and in December announced his determination to commence the work as soon as six hundred subscriptions of twenty-five dollars each were secured. The business depression delayed commencement of the work until 1875, and then every available office worker and every ounce of energy were commandeered to complete the mammoth task. The work was carried on day and night, in the office and in Leypoldt's home. The latter became, as his loyal wife put it, "a second workshop" where "many good housewives looked in amazement at tables strewed with papers and the makings of catalogues, . . . while I made paste for the work and dinners for the helpers."[22] Delays, however, seemed unavoidable. The Centennial year passed, and the next year, and not until the fall of 1878 was the first part of the first volume ready for issue.

21 See "The Bibliographical Urge," *A Quarter Century of Cumulative Bibliography* (New York, 1923), 37; W. T. S. Stallybrass, Preface in W. S. Sonnenschein, *The Best Books, xiii–xvi*.

22 Augusta Leypoldt, "Some Memories," *Publishers' Weekly*, December 25, 1909, p. 1943.

The entire first volume of author and title entries was not published until 1880, and the second volume, of subject entries, not until 1881. The work, when finally published, consisted of 1,500 large quarto double-column pages, including over 125,000 entries representing 70,000 titles and more than 900 publishers. It incurred a deficit of $300 on a total expenditure of $27,622, which included no compensation at all for the enormous labor which Leypoldt put into it.[23]

There were three major problems of the trade to which Bowker particularly addressed himself: book distribution, postal reform, and international copyright. The system of book distribution was ruining the small book dealers, a group with a cultural role which Bowker thought to be important:

Books may be taxed by weight, but the scales can never test their power. The Bookdealers are themselves claiming rank next to the church and the schoolhouse. To put the right book into the hands of the right man is to do much in education. And the next best thing to being a genius oneself is to strike the spark that shall kindle genius in another.[24]

What made book distribution ruinous was the trade sale and the discount system. The trade sale was the means of getting new books from the publishers to jobbers and retailers, but for all its pleasant camaraderie and humor it was a primitive system, unfortunate in its results, and one of the sorest grievances of the trade. The discount system was vitiated both by the fictitious nature of most discounts and the practice of some publishers of extending the same discounts to private consumers as to local booksellers, thus threatening the existence of the latter.

With Leypoldt's encouragement, Bowker took up the cudgels. On the one hand he denounced current malpractices,[25] on the other he did everything he could to encourage the organization of a booksellers' association to supplement the work of the Publishers' Board of Trade. The first step was to set up the Booksellers' Protective Union in 1873 and then enlarge it into the American Book Trade Association the following year. Bowker attended the meetings at Cincinnati and Put-in-Bay, Ohio, in 1874; and at Niagara and New York City in 1875. He

23 "Literary Note," printed circular advertisement for the *American Catalogue, 1878*. R. R. B., "Books and the Book Trade in America," *Catalogue of the . . . American Book Trader,* usefully summarized in Beswick, *The Work of Frederick Leypoldt,* 46–50.
24 New York *Tribune,* July 24, 1875; hereafter cited as *Tribune.*
25 R. R. B., "Cutting Under," *Evening Mail,* February 26, 1873.

put pressure on the large publishers to subscribe one hundred dollars apiece to promote the association's membership. He made many friends, kept in close touch with the president of the association, was appointed secretary of the committee on assemblies, wrote full reports for the *Weekly* and the *Tribune*,[26] and impressed everyone by his energetic co-operation. He was gratified when the association voted to abolish the trade sale in favor of a legitimate semiannual book fair, to be called the Booksellers' Exchange and Clearing House, and chronicled its initial success.[27] In an address to the New England Book Trade Association, he joined A. D. F. Randolph, F. H. Dodd, and W. H. Appleton in persuading the Boston men to adopt a uniform 20 per cent discount rule, also soon adopted by Philadelphia.[28] In spite of all his hopes and his efforts, however, the movement died. The Centennial meeting of the association made no recommendations on retail prices, failed to support the 20 per cent rule, and refused to reduce nominal prices to real prices.[29] The Autumn Book Fair of 1876 proved to be the last, and with the return to the old trade sale, the association was through. Nothing was to mitigate the return to the old ways of book distribution until 1890.[30]

The second problem on which Bowker worked was postal reform. Postal laws were a basic element in the book trade's existence, and postal reform had figured prominently in the *Weekly's* news and editorial columns from it first issue. Bowker took utmost pains to see that every suggestion, bill, committee, amendment, and vote was fully reported and discussed. In October, 1878, he was appointed, with H. O. Houghton and J. W. Harper, Jr., to the Committee on Resolutions of the New York Postal Conference. This conference had been called with the sanction of the Post Office Department to bring it and the public into more direct relations and to increase support for the generally favored postal bill then pending before Congress. The boards of trade of various cities and the publishers' committees of Boston, New York, Philadelphia, and Chicago, in all about two hundred, took part. The report of Bowker's committee was hotly debated. At the adjournment of the general conference, Bowker was appointed to its continuing work-

26 *Publishers' Weekly*, November 1, 1873; *ibid.*, February 22, 1874, pp. 78–84; Aston to R. R. B., August 29, 1874; articles appearing July 22, 23, 1874.

27 R. R. B., "Frederick Leypoldt," *Publishers' Weekly*, April 5, 1884; Hellmut Lehmann-Haupt, *The Book in America*, 204; R. R. B., *Tribune*, July 8, 20, 24, 1875.

28 *Publishers' Weekly*, November 21, 28; *ibid.*, December 19, 1874.

29 "American Book Trade Association Convention," *Publishers' Weekly*, July 22, 1876; R. R. B., "Frederick Leypoldt," *Publishers' Weekly*, April 5, 1884, p. 39.

30 "What Has Become of the Book-Trade Association?" *Publishers' Weekly*, February 10, 1877; "ABTA," *Publishers' Weekly*, April 14, 1877; Lehmann-Haupt, *op. cit.*, 205.

ing committee. The bill was finally passed in the spring of 1879, and its code became the fundamental law for the post office, one of the most important sections providing bulk rates for periodicals at two cents a pound. This was the first important legislation in which Bowker had had a hand, and he found the experience most congenial.[31]

A much more complicated and controversial problem was that of international copyright. Bowker dealt almost weekly with its many developments, and by thorough attention to the subject became a recognized authority. Since the problem was essentially one of protecting literary property, it involved the interests of author, publisher, and reading public. In both England and America these three parties were all affected, though in varying degrees, by the absence of international copyright.

American publishers could and did reprint any work of any English author without compensating him, an obvious injustice. An American publisher, however, was himself likely to suffer if he made a token royalty payment to the English author and spent any money in advertising his own edition, for he was quite likely to see a cheap competing edition appear overnight and threaten to ruin him. The American author also suffered. He had to compete with English books that could be published in the United States without royalty payments, and he therefore never received adequate royalties from his American publisher. Furthermore, when an English publisher could pirate an original American edition, he gladly did so.

It has been suggested that this situation not only prevented writing from becoming a profession in this country until after the first international copyright law of 1891, but may even have contributed to the low standards of American writing.[32] The American public suffered from both the discouragement to American writing and the miserably-prepared pirate editions resulting from the cutthroat competition.[33] Finally, this literary piracy definitely strained international cultural relations. And yet, in spite of the support of presidents, clergy, and professional associations, favorable legislation was delayed for a discouraging length of time because of ignorance, inertia, and isolationism combined with the early opposition of the Philadelphia publishers and the house of Harper.

Frederick Leypoldt was a steadfast advocate of the cause, and from the first issues of the *Weekly,* he and Bowker filled its pages with the

31 In various issues of the *Publishers' Weekly,* September 14, 1878, to March 8, 1879.

32 Lehmann-Haupt, *The Book in America,* 167.

33 Stokes, *A Publisher's Random Notes,* 24; Lehmann-Haupt, *The Book in America,* 161–68.

views of authors and publishers on the subject.[34] To Bowker it was a simple problem in social morality, and he entered the lists with the fervor of a crusader, finding the enemies of this cause and the enemies of liberalism to be the same: nationalism and the protective tariff. "International copyright is bound to come, sooner or later," he cried, "as the wider and wiser policy of giving each man his rights the world over sweeps away the narrow restrictions which stunt national as well as human growth by opposing the interests of the man of one nation to those of the man of another nation."[35] He did not confine his support of the movement to the pages of the *Weekly,* but fervently preached the gospel in the *Mail,* the *Tribune,* and the London *Athenaeum.*[36]

In 1878 some real hope of progress arose. In November, Harper and Brothers proposed to the Secretary of State a draft treaty which modified the unpopular Clarendon proposal of 1870.[37] In December, Bowker prepared and circulated a questionnaire intended to stimulate public opinion and focus the view of American authors and publishers on some practicable plan. Replies received from forty-one American authors and seventeen American publishers and printed in the *Weekly*[38] showed a shocking lack of interest and information, but a general agreement on the need for action. In addition to the questionnaires, Bowker kept the *Weekly* vibrant with editorials, articles, and correspondence on the copyright question, and the pressure for a treaty continued.

Two further instances of Bowker's vigorous efforts to promote a community of interest in the highly individualistic book trade deserve to be mentioned. In 1876 the *Weekly* gave hearty support to the joint book-trade exhibit sponsored by the American Book Trade Association at the Philadelphia Centennial,[39] and it deserves a good deal of the credit for the splendid results achieved. Ninety-six individual exhibi-

[34] See Thorvald Solberg, "Index to Copyright Articles, *Publishers' Weekly,* 1872–1882," *Publishers' Weekly,* June 16, 1883, pp. 708–12.

[35] "International Copyright," London *Athenaeum,* June 15, 1878, pp. 764–65.

[36] R. R. B., "Copywrong," *Evening Mail* Weekly Edition, February 26, 1873; "The Nation's Library," *Evening Mail* Weekly Edition, February 17, 1874. "Charles Reade's Letter on Copyright," *Tribune,* July 24, 1875. "The British Copyright Report," *Tribune,* June 1, 1878. W. D. Howells to R. R. B., August 22, 1878. "International Copyright," London *Athenaeum,* June 15, 1878, pp. 764–65.

[37] Harper and Brothers to Secretary Evarts, November 25, 1878, in R. R. B., *Copyright, Its Law and Its Literature,* 30–31.

[38] *Publishers' Weekly,* February 15, May 3, December 27, 1879, January 31, 1889; the original signed replies now form part of the Bowker Collection in the Library of Congress.

[39] See especially such editorials as "Books at the Centennial," *Publishers' Weekly,* April 15; "The Opening of the Exhibition," *ibid.,* May 13; "The Centennial Exhibition," *ibid.,* May 20, 1876.

tions were finally presented, including several notable ones from Europe. Bowker gave an ambitious boost to the entire book trade through a special Centennial Exhibition Number of the *Weekly* which he undertook singlehanded and which was completely successful. The following year he worked just as hard to secure wide participation by American publishers in the American book-trade exhibit at the Paris World's Fair.[40] A master stroke was the preparation of a neat, ninety-page octavo *Catalogue of the Collective Exhibit of the American Book Trade,* and for this Bowker wrote three admirable introductory articles printed in both English and French on "Books and the Book Trade in America," "Trade Bibliography," and "The Library System."

Bowker found a number of opportunities to utilize his growing familiarity with the book-trade field in addition to his "Literary Notes" in the *Mail* and his work on the *Publishers' Weekly*. During 1873, 1874, and 1875 he contributed occasional news letters at two pounds apiece to the London *Publishers' Circular*. Throughout much of 1874 and 1875 he wrote fortnightly and then monthly columns of book news at ten dollars apiece for the Boston *Daily Globe*.[41] On January 15, 1875, he transferred his "Literary Notes" from the *Evening Mail* to the *Tribune*. Early in 1878, with the death of Bayard Taylor, Bowker asked Reid for fuller employment in the *Tribune's* literary department, but Reid replied that the staff was already too large. Three months later he terminated Bowker's relations altogether, apparently, because of Bowker's refusal to participate in Reid's vendetta against Appleton's for giving him inadequate entry in their *Cyclopedia of American Biography*.[42] When Fletcher Harper died on May 29, 1877, Bowker wrote a first-rate, eleven-page memorial for the *Publishers' Trade List Annual*.[43] When the Stationers' Board of Trade held its annual dinner in 1878, Bowker was one of the guest speakers along with Whitelaw Reid, A. D. F. Randolph, and H. W. Curtiss.[44]

In the late fall of 1878, there developed a second crisis in Bowker's affairs. Leypoldt was brought face to face with bankruptcy. It had become abundantly evident, as the *Publishers' Weekly* office grew into a center of more and more enterprises, that Leypoldt had far more enthusiasm and good will for book-trade ventures than business ability to

40 "The Paris Exposition," *Publishers' Weekly,* October 27, 1877; "Publishers' Co-operation in America," *Publishers' Weekly,* May 18, 1878.
41 G. H. Putnam to R. R. B., March 11, September 31, 1873; letters from E. M. Bacon to R. R. B., February 19, 1874, through September 25, 1875.
42 R. R. B. to W. Reid, March 5, 1878; W. Reid to R. R. B., March 8, 1878; W. Reid to R. R. B., June 10, September 26, 1878; R. R. B., MS Memoir.
43 R. R. B., "The Harper Brothers," *Publishers' Trade List Annual, 1877, v–xvi.*
44 *Geyer's Stationer,* November 21, 1878.

make them pay. He already had sunk something like five thousand dollars apiece in the *Library Journal,* the *Index Medicus,* and the *American Catalogue,* and this when he had no cash in hand as capital.[45] When Nicolo Monachesi left the office, he owed Leypoldt several thousand dollars which the latter did not know enough to miss. "I don't blame Nicolo for all that," Mrs. Leypoldt later told Bowker. "I blame a business when it is possible to steal two or three thousands without the *head knowing* it!" More than once it happened that three o'clock arrived with notes due for which there was no money in the bank—a situation that invariably precipitated the kindly bibliographer into a state of extreme nervous agitation. The *Journal* was running a deficit. The *Weekly,* for lack of capital, was prevented from adopting important new features which Bowker felt were necessary to its usefulness. The *American Catalogue* developed such heavy expenses that it looked as though the whole enterprise would have to be abandoned before the first volume was published. Leypoldt was clearly at the end of his resources. How successive business "deals" struck the spirited and practical-minded woman who was his wife is indicated in a letter which she wrote Bowker two years later.

> I never believed in the *Library Journal,* because I knew it would not pay. . . . I disapproved of the *management* of the *American Catalogue;* I *denounced* the borrowing of money on *false pretenses,* for any fool could see that the *Catalogue* would take much longer to bring out than was stated to the Publishers that gave the money. The *Index Medicus* I thought was a Literary Medical Paper and I had been told Mr. Leypoldt had been guaranteed against loss, so I said nothing until I saw the first number, and when I found it was merely an *index,* consequently only of use to writing doctors, I opposed that and have quarrelled that it should be given up for many months. "Shopping Guides," and "Coney Island Guides," etc. etc. I have always fought tooth and nail. . . . I have committed the unpardonable fault to say that I think the accounts of all Mr. L's various enterprises should be kept distinctly separate and let those that cannot pay for themselves fall through and stop. . . . I believe in the *Publishers' Weekly.* I always said *you* would make it pay.

> Mr. L. never speaks to me about business now and only frets and stews and worries in a general way, whenever he is upset. I have all the bother of it without the satisfaction of really *knowing* what all this fuss is about. . . . I think if Mr. L. were making $30,000

45 R. R. B. to Herbert Putnam, July 3, 1916.

a year, he would be using $30,000. I think him a splendid worker, industrious and fair, but I do not think he understands business at all, and he never will. . . . If Mr. L. were to die today, where would his children be after all his work and worry?[46]

Leypoldt's extremity was also Bowker's extremity. The latter's connection with the *Tribune* had just been terminated by Whitelaw Reid, and an attempt to form a new connection with the *Evening Mail* came to nothing. He therefore worked out a plan to save both Leypoldt and himself. Two immediate measures were clearly called for: to separate the bibliographical from the journalistic activities of the office so as to gain from separate management and yet not lose the benefits of close collaboration; and to save the *American Catalogue* by immediately raising several thousand dollars in cash as fresh capital. These objectives would be secured if the *Weekly* could be sold to a friendly party who would edit and manage it in co-operation with Leypoldt's bibliographical program. Bowker was obviously the man, and Leypoldt cordially admitted this to be so.

Sometime in December, 1878, Bowker purchased the *Publishers' Weekly* for $5,000 in cash.[47] Having no intention at this time of becoming permanently tied up to the journal, but seeing it as a sound investment, he carefully specified in the terms of agreement that Leypoldt should have the right to repurchase the property on the same terms plus any increment in value. As a result of this transaction, Bowker became, in January, 1879, full owner and manager of the *Weekly*, with Leypoldt cited as the bibliographical editor. In a joint statement the two men specified that absolutely no difference of opinion was signified by the change and that the new arrangement provided a reunion of interests "so that the ultimate aim of both parties may be fulfilled in the final establishment of a fully systematized central office, covering every desirable field of American bibliography."[48] Leypoldt retained sole control of the *American Catalogue*, the *Trade List Annual, Literary News, Monthly Book List,* and *Index Medicus.* The office was now moved for a second time, and made its third home at 13-15 Park Row.

Bowker's plan was to manage the *Weekly* on half his time and supplement its $3,000 net per year with enough outside literary work to bring his income to $5,000. In May, 1880, however, Harper and Brothers invited Bowker to enter their employ as London representative of the firm, and Bowker's acceptance necessitated a drastic revision

46 Mrs. Leypoldt to R. R. B., September 18, 1880.
47 R. R. B. to C. Cutter, January 3, 1879; to Daniel Bowker, August 22, 1881; to Nelson Spencer, March 12, 1906.
48 *Publishers' Weekly,* January 25, 1879.

of his understanding with Leypoldt. He realized that one course would be to sell the *Publishers' Weekly* to the American News Company, but he felt that this firm monopolized "sufficient power already without controlling all the trade organs,"[49] and that such an arrangement would not be fair to Leypoldt's interests. Furthermore, he did not care to burn his bridges behind him until it should become clear whether his Harper association would be permanent or not. Consequently he entered into a fresh agreement with Leypoldt whereby the latter technically leased back the *Weekly*, but with the expectation of his early repurchase of it. Meanwhile it was agreed that after the deduction of a stated yearly sum to cover Bowker's investment, all profits were to accrue to Leypoldt.[50] When Bowker wrote his parting editorial in the *Weekly's* issue of June 26, 1880, he did not expect to return to that journal, and said so.

At a farewell dinner given by the *Weekly* office at the Manhattan Beach Hotel, several testimonials indicated the extent of Bowker's achievement. It was probably either Putnam or Randolph who said:

> I speak for the others as well as for myself, in saying that neither in Europe nor at home have the various problems and questions affecting the publishing and bookselling trade ever received anything like the conscientious accuracy of presentment, or the intelligent and scholarly breadth of treatment, that have been given them in the columns of the *Publishers' Weekly*.[51]

Leypoldt's own acknowledgment of his debt to Bowker was a handsome and a sincere one:

> The trade, not less than the *Weekly* suffers an irreparable loss by the departure of Mr. Bowker. . . . Without his assistance, all the work that after many years has at last found its recognition and support by the best of the trade, could not have been accomplished. No one has studied the interests of the book trade more thoroughly and defended them more ably and conscientiously.[52]

[49] R. R. B. to J. W. Harper, May 8, 1880.
[50] "Notice," by R. R. B., *Publishers' Weekly*, June 26, 1880, p. 651.
[51] Quoted by Leypoldt in his editorial of July 3, 1880, p. 11.
[52] *Ibid.*

V

The Library Journal and the A.L.A.
1876–1880

THE YEAR 1876 was a dramatic one for the American people. On the one hand it was a year of shocking political corruption, of a disputed national election that for a time threatened civil war, and of continuing depression. Yet on the other hand the centennial celebration of the birth of the United States was an occasion for fitting pride in many solid achievements and confidence in the country's future. At the striking World Exposition in Philadelphia there was substantial evidence of the promise of American life. The uncritical exuberance of the late sixties had gone, and Americans everywhere were making a sober self-examination.[1] The war issues were finally dead. New interests, new issues, new leaders held the nation's attention. Bowker entered fully into the experience of the Centennial year, writing vigorously of its meaning for Americans and feeling the inspiration of it in his own life.

Of all the meetings which Bowker attended during the busy Centennial year, none proved of more lasting significance for his own career than those which led to the inauguration of the *Library Journal* and the American Library Association. The community of interest among librarians had been rapidly expanding with the continued growth of public and private libraries in number, size, and complexity of administration. In 1853, eighty distinguished librarians convening in New York City had laid a most auspicious foundation for a national library movement.[2] The group was never again called together, but the library movement continued to grow. By 1876 there were in the United States

[1] Allan Nevins, *The Emergence of Modern America*, 311–13.
[2] R. R. B., "Seed Time and Harvest," *Library Journal*, October 15, 1926.

3,647 libraries of 300 or more books, totaling 12,276,964 volumes.[3] Most public libraries were still operated on the subscription basis. Bound catalogues were just beginning to be replaced by catalogue cards, which were still handwritten and of many different sizes. There was no accepted scheme of classification, no free access to the shelves, no school libraries, no children's departments.

As a young idealist committed to the great liberal crusade, Bowker found that his interest was easily aroused in this great educational agency for the advancement of democracy. The excellent news story on the Library of Congress which he wrote for the *Evening Mail* in 1874 indicates an early enthusiasm.[4] It was through Leypoldt, however, that Bowker really entered into partnership with the library movement.

As journalism had led Bowker to the book trade, so the book trade now led him to the library movement. It was natural that Leypoldt, through his book-trade interests, should be drawn into contact with the library field and quickly realize its growing importance as a means of book distribution. As early as October, 1872, he had issued a special "Library Number" of the *Weekly*. When Melvil Dewey, a young college librarian at Amherst College suggested the inclusion of library notes in the *Weekly*, Leypoldt was quick to act, and the issue of January 10, 1874, inaugurated the "Library Corner."

> Under this head [either Bowker or Leypoldt explained] we propose . . . to gather together such matter as may be of interest to the managers of, and those interested in, libraries, in the way of practical suggestions, descriptions of new improvements in arrangements or methods of work, summaries of library reports . . . notes and queries regarding library economy, etc. The libraries of the country have at present no special organ of communication, and as they need the same information as the book sellers . . . and are . . . subscribers to the *Weekly*, it seems eminently proper that their interest should be especially consulted in this publication.

Between January 10, 1874, and January 30, 1875, the "Library Corner" appeared twelve times, but then disappeared for nine months. On November 6, 1875, it reappeared as "Library and Bibliographical Notes," continuing intermittently to September 16, 1876. Interest and materials soon suggested the desirability of launching a separate library periodical, and Leypoldt occasionally discussed such a project with Bowker.

In April of the Centennial year the *Publishers' Weekly* summarized a suggestion made to the London Academy that there be an interna-

---

3 United States Bureau of Education *Report on Libraries,* 1876.
4 R. R. B., "The Nation's Library," *Evening Mail,* February 17, 1874.

tional congress of librarians to discuss common problems of the profession. It then added editorially, "In these days of International Congresses, it is strange that no attempt should have been made to convene a Congress of librarians."[5] This announcement, and the impression that some sort of library journal might be started in New York, was of enormous interest to the enterprising young Melvil Dewey. For several years Dewey had been thinking over a plan for a national association of librarians, a library journal, a library bureau, and eventually a library school. Without knowledge of the *Publishers' Weekly's* interest in the subject, he had secured the interest of several editors and publishers in a library journal to be organized in Boston.[6] On noting that a similar move was likely in New York, Dewey decided to make a trip to that city for a conference with Leypoldt and Bowker.[7]

The three men met early in May in the offices of the *Publishers' Weekly*. The conclusions they reached proved momentous for the library field: that the library could not rise to its full opportunity without a library profession, that a library profession could not develop without a journal and a national association, and that therefore these two should be organized immediately.[8] The superior advantages enjoyed by the *Weekly* in its relations with the book trade and in its unsurpassed bibliographical facilities convinced Dewey that the new journal should be issued from Leypoldt's office.[9] The three pioneers succeeded in their double undertaking. The *Library Journal* appeared in September, and the American Library Association was organized in October. Leypoldt contributed experience, leadership and financial capital. Dewey supplied what Bowker paid tribute to as "indomitable courage, energy, and persistence."[10] Bowker brought a steady executive hand, cool decision, and sound practical judgment.

The proposed plan of library organization came partly from the old 1853 conference of American librarians and partly from the success of the recently formed American Book Trade Association in which Bowker had been interested. Bowker drafted a circular letter and a telegram which was signed by all three men and sent to a score of prominent librarians urging them to issue a call for an organizing conference. The responses were almost entirely favorable, and John Eaton, commissioner

[5] *Publishers' Weekly*, April 22, 1876.

[6] R. R. B., "The Library and Library Organization: Postscript," *Library Journal*, February, 1896, p. 52; Grosvenor Dawe, *Melvil Dewey*, 96.

[7] M. Dewey, "What the A. L. A. Was Intended To Be and To Do," Wisconsin *Library Bulletin*, February, 1917.

[8] A. Esdaile, *Library Journal*, December 1, 1933, p. 1011.

[9] Dewey, "What the A. L. A. Was Intended To Be and To Do," Wisconsin *Library Bulletin*, February, 1917, p. 43.

[10] R. R. B. to G. H. Putnam. July 3, 1916.

THE

AMERICAN
Library Journal

[MONTHLY]

ASSOCIATE EDITORS:

JUSTIN WINSOR, *Boston Public Library;* J. L. WHITNEY, *Boston Public Library;* FRED. B. PERKINS,
Boston Public Library; CHAS. A. CUTTER, *Boston Athenæum;* EZRA ABBOT, *Harvard University;*
JOHN FISKE, *Harvard University Library;* REUBEN A. GUILD, *Brown University Library;*
J. CARSON BREVOORT, *Astor Library;* H. A. HOMES, *New York State Library;*
S. B. NOYES, *Brooklyn Mercantile Library;* FRED. VINTON, *Princeton College Library;*
L. P. SMITH, *Philadelphia Library Co.;* A. R. SPOFFORD, *Library of Congress;*
J. EATON, *Bureau of Education;* J. S. BILLINGS, *National Medical Library;*
WM. F. POOLE, *Chicago Public Library;* CHAS. EVANS, *Indianapolis
Public Library;* THOMAS VICKERS, *Cincinnati Public Library;*
W. T. HARRIS, *St. Louis;* J. J. BAILEY, *St. Louis Public School
Library;* A. E. WHITAKER, *San Francisco Mercantile Library.*

Managing Editor : MELVIL DEWEY, *13 Tremont Place, Boston.*

VOL. I. NO. I.

[SEPTEMBER 30, 1876.]

Contents:

PUBLISHER : F. LEYPOLDT, 37 Park Row, New York.

YEARLY SUBSCRIPTION, $5.00.   SINGLE NUMBERS, 50 CENTS.

of education, gave hearty co-operation. Only William F. Poole exhibited alarm at the presumption of such unknown nobodies, especially ones connected with the book trade. On May 20, the *Publishers' Weekly* proudly announced the success of its preparations: the preliminary call for a conference was being signed and the basis had been laid for a library journal to be published by Leypoldt, endorsed by leading librarians, and conducted under a consulting editorial board of the latter.[11] The first number, under the name *The American Library Journal,* was dated September 30 and was available for distribution at the conference of librarians which convened on October 4. Its spirit and contents were admirably practical and international and thus prophetic of the *Journal's* continuing character.

The Philadelphia conference of librarians was composed of ninety men and thirteen women. Its accomplishments were notable. By special arrangement, advance copies of the first historic *Report on Libraries* of the Bureau of Education were furnished the convention, so that its work might supplement and not duplicate that of the *Report.* In addition to discussing problems of buying, binding, cataloguing, and indexing, the conference pressed for the completion of Poole's *Index to Periodical Literature,* the securing of larger discounts for libraries from booksellers, the preparation of uniform catalogue title-slips to be supplied from some central cataloguing bureau and the issuance of monthly or quarterly general indexes to periodicals.[12] It also set up an important Co-operation Committee which was destined to make some valuable reports and encouraged Melvil Dewey to start a library supply house, which became, eventually, the Library Bureau.[13] Finally, on October 6, the work of the conference culminated in a resolution forming the American Library Association. Justin Winsor was its first president, Melvil Dewey its first secretary, and the *Library Journal* its official organ. Its motto, suggested by Dewey, was a magnificent one: "The best reading for the greatest number at the least cost."[14]

"The time has come," Bowker chronicled in a *Library Journal* advertisement, "when the librarian, with his books, must take his place beside the teacher and the school, and the four thousand libraries of the country, that have till now worked almost entirely alone, each independent of the rest, must from this time go rapidly forward in a constantly increasing usefulness, by means of thoroughly organized effort and co-operation."

11 "Library Co-operation," *Publishers' Weekly,* May 20, 1876.

12 *Library Journal,* undated advertisement.

13 R. R. B., "The Library and Library Organization," *Library Journal,* January, 1896.

14 R. R. B., "Seed Time and Harvest," *Library Journal,* October 15, 1926.

The staff of the new library journal consisted of Leypoldt, publisher; Bowker, general editor; Dewey, managing editor; and Charles A. Cutter, bibliographical editor. Leypoldt was to assume the entire financial risk for the first issue. Dewey was to assume editorial management in Boston, as well as responsibility for promoting subscriptions and advertising. Bowker was expected only to edit Dewey's copy and supervise its actual publication, and this duty was not intended to add substantially to his responsibilities on the *Weekly*. The names of twenty-one prominent librarians from Boston to San Francisco adorned the title pages as "associate editors," but the office was purely honorary and these men took no part whatever in the actual editorial work. Henry R. Tedder, librarian of the London *Athenaeum,* was to serve as English editor, and when the Library Association of the United Kingdom adopted the *American Library Journal* as its official organ in 1877, its name became, in more cosmopolitan spirit, the *Library Journal.* The *Journal's* features were to include editorials, signed articles, communications, foreign correspondence, notes and queries, general notes, a department of bibliography prepared by C. A. Cutter, and one on pseudonyms and anonyms by J. L. Whitney.[15]

The *Journal* was a financial liability from the start. Bowker once referred to "the roseate hopes for its pecuniary success,"[16] but if he and Leypoldt ever entertained such expectations, they were promptly disillusioned. They may have felt that there were intangible benefits to be derived in good will and the further centralization of book matters in the *Publishers' Weekly* office, but so far as material compensation was concerned the *Journal* proved to be a labor of professional love. The fact that Dewey's library plans had already gathered momentum in Boston enabled him to drive a hard bargain. In lieu of salary, he insisted on being paid 20 per cent, not of the net, but of the gross returns from both subscriptions and advertising.[17] Leypoldt and Bowker were to get nothing for their services, but these were not intended to be heavy.

The expected arrangement for running the *Journal* collapsed completely. Dewey's considerable talents were best displayed in bold planning, and there his creative vision did the young library profession a great service. As a responsible wheel-horse to be depended on in getting specific work done, at least as far as the *Library Journal* was concerned, he proved an almost total failure. A mercurial egotist, fiery and

[15] *Library Journal,* September 30, 1876, pp. 12–13.

[16] R. R. B., "The *Library Journal* and Library Organization," *Library Journal,* January, 1896, p. 5.

[17] See Mrs. Leypoldt to R. R. B., September 18, 1880; R. R. B., "The *Library Journal* and Library Organization," *Library Journal,* January, 1896; R. R. B. to W. E. Foster, July 1, 1927.

lovable, Dewey charmed some persons and dismayed others. Mrs. Leypoldt from the first considered him "as miserable a specimen of a gabbling idiot as I had ever beheld."[18] It became Bowker's unpleasant task to deal with Dewey,[19] and the way in which he discharged this task shows as clearly as anything the temper of the young editor.

At first, the Bowker-Dewey relations were cordial enough.[20] Dewey admitted his letters were "wholly without organization" and confessed to tardiness and blunders in getting copy to Bowker, but he invited criticism, and described himself as a willing pupil in the new art of journalism. "Don't be at all afraid to give me a blowing up for my weakness," he insisted. "I like it as I do a cold bath. . . . I will try to be docile, if I can't be an apt pupil." By April, 1877, however, when subscriptions totaled only three hundred, Bowker prodded Dewey sharply into a more realistic approach to the promotion program. Nevertheless, the balance at the end of the first year was a disheartening one: a total return on subscriptions and advertising of slightly over $3,000, but a deficit, still without entering any charge for the services of Leypoldt and Bowker, of over $1,800 which had to be carried by Leypoldt and his other publications. The next year, though the *Journal* continued to be owned by Leypoldt, its management was given to Bowker in hope of recouping the loss, and it showed a balance of $207.[21]

These developments suggested the need of reviewing the initial contract. A good deal more business responsibility had now fallen on Leypoldt's shoulders and a good deal more editorial and managerial work on Bowker's than either of them had expected. Moreover, Dewey alone was being compensated, at what seemed an almost exorbitant rate, for work that was erratic, undependable, and frequently subordinated to his parallel interests in metric and spelling reform. Leypoldt was for breaking the contract altogether, but Bowker counseled patience and a modification. Dewey on his part was induced to promise that his other interests would not interfere with work for the *Journal*.[22]

Soon, however, matters again reached an impasse. There was a clash over the handling of the title-slip project. Dewey continued to excuse his chronic delays by claiming that each of his "three wives," (metric, spelling, and library reform) was demanding all of his time. No new returns were coming in. By the date that Bowker had set for the acqui-

18 Mrs. A. Leypoldt to R. R. B., September 18, 1880.

19 See Dawe, *Melvil Dewey*, 118; R. R. B., "The *Library Journal* and Library Organization," *Library Journal*, January, 1896, p. 8.

20 M. Dewey to R. R. B., November 9, 20, 1876; R. R. B. to M. Dewey, April 9, 1877.

21 R. R. B., MS draft letter to A. L. A., 1880.

22 R. R. B. to C. Cutter, January 3, 1879; R. R. B. to M. Dewey, April 18, 1878.

sition of fifty new subscriptions, there was actually a loss of sixty-five. On top of this, Dewey mailed out without Bowker's knowledge or approval an advertising circular which was wildly irresponsible. When surprised businessmen first called this circular to Bowker's attention, he was indignant and alarmed, and immediately wrote Dewey a stiff letter of rebuke and admonition. "I should write," he admitted, "as a businessman, with as much indignation as distress, but I feel the matter more and otherwise as counting you a personal friend." He proceeded to deliver a fatherly lecture:

> Statements of that sort to businessmen arraign either one's honesty or one's business common sense: in either case it is a direct blow at our, as well as your, standing and financial credit. Business can only proceed on a basis of trust,—and what are we to do if you warn everybody not to trust you?
>
> I am writing strongly, not in anger, but really in great grief. This is no everyday matter of business,—it seems to imply a habit of mind in you, a recklessness of true thinking and speaking that makes us doubt your relations towards us. . . . My dear Dewey, you are too valuable a man to wreck your own future in the way this sort of thing is sure to do. . . . The times are hard enough, without such difficulties added. The safety of the *Journal* demands that you put all the force you can concentrate—certainly half your time,— on bringing up its direct pecuniary returns.
>
> You must put this thing before yourself very clearly. It is a question of personal and business morals. May we trust you and will you stand by your promises—and be regardful of the truth?[23]

Relations with Dewey sputtered through 1878 and toward the end of the year exploded. Dewey felt that he was not receiving enough financial return from the *Journal;* Bowker agreed, but insisted that since the *Journal* was losing money, it could not possibly pay him more. Dewey wished to charge the expenses of his Boston office to the *Journal;* Bowker claimed that, since this office was very directly serving the interests of the A.L.A., that organization should pay part of the expenses. Dewey wished to bring the *Journal* to Boston; Bowker thought this unfair since he and Leypoldt had "shown fairly what we can do with it." Finally, Dewey claimed that he alone had originated the *Journal;* Bowker would acknowledge only his editorial equality, claiming that the *Journal* was an old idea of his and Leypoldt's.[24]

23 *Ibid.*, Bowker was equally firm with William F. Poole (R. R. B. to W. F. Poole, June 29, 1878).

24 R. R. B. to C. Cutter, January 3, 1879; R. R. B. to Justin Winsor, January 15, 1879.

The crisis was reached when Dewey threatened to withhold copy from the January, 1879, number, to place this material in a new, low-priced, opposition periodical to be started in Boston, and to bid for the *Journal's* subscribers.[25] Bowker, holding this action to constitute a "breach of faith," wrote directly to Charles Cutter to find out what semiofficial support there might be for Dewey's action, and to Dewey to assert his faith that fair-minded people in the A.L.A. would not support him, to insist that he would not negotiate on the basis of a threat, and to declare that he and Leypoldt would discuss a new contract, but would not renew the old one or be browbeaten.[26] Leypoldt and Bowker then offered to have the Executive Board of the A.L.A. arbitrate the matter. The canvass of subscriptions, however, had been interrupted by the dispute, and financial distress threatened the *Journal*. As it was, the loss on Volume IV (1879–80) was $766, making a total loss of nearly $2,400.[27]

When in the early winter of 1878, Bowker rescued the *Publishers' Weekly* from Leypoldt's financial mismanagement, he also decided to assume responsibility for the deficit, the management, and the editorial supervision of the *Journal*. In a printed statement to subscribers, Bowker and Leypoldt cited the *Journal's* record of financial deficits indicating that the reason for it was lack of support by the library movement. Nevertheless, despite continued loss in 1879, they declared their belief that the *Journal* could be made "a self-supporting permanency," and that in this hope they planned to continue it through 1880. At the same time an appeal was made to the A..L.A. to reconsider its decision against defraying the expense of printing its annual Proceedings in the *Journal*.[28] The unfortunate misunderstanding with Dewey was shelved for the time being and was not finally settled until 1886, but personal ties were not broken.[29]

In the summer of 1880 there occurred, within three months, the *Journal's* death and resurrection, the former due to Bowker's hard-headed business realism, the latter to Leypoldt's softhearted humanitarianism. The story is rather dramatic. Late in May, 1880, Bowker advised Leypoldt to discontinue the *Journal* on the ground that it was a financial liability. Dewey promptly concurred since his Boston assistant had just left him for California, Bowker would be absent in London, and he, along with Leypoldt, was "so overworked as to fear a complete

25 R. R. B. to C. Cutter, January 3, 1879; R. R. B. to M. Dewey, January 10, 1879.
26 R. R. B. to C. Cutter, January 3, 1879; R. R. B. to M. Dewey, January 9, 1879.
27 R. R. B. to C. Cutter, January 10, 13, 1879; to J. Winsor and M. Dewey, January 15, 1879; R. R. B., MS draft letter to the A. L. A., 1880.
28 R. R. B., MS draft letter to the A. L. A., 1880.
29 See M. Dewey to R. R. B., June, 1880.

breakdown."[30] The June issue of the *Journal* announced this decision, along with a plan to combine its main features with the *Weekly* and to return half of the subscription price to dissatisfied subscribers.[31] Since the *Journal* was costing Leypoldt and Bowker several thousands of dollars, since the A.L.A., though informed of the facts, did not make any move to come to its rescue, since the *Journal* was under no obligation to the A.L.A. in any case, and since the subscribers had been given more than fair treatment, Bowker was confident that this move was not only necessary but honorable.

The library world, however, was not reconciled to the suspension of the periodical it had been unwilling to support. Dewey, claiming that it was "a disgrace to the profession to have the *Journal* stopped in the middle of a volume," sought subscriptions to a sinking fund of $2,000 to enable it to continue. W. F. Poole, however, was incensed, and declared that it was "more of a disgrace to the publishers, who have got our money, to stop in the middle of a volume." When he learned of the merger of the *Journal* with the *Weekly*, Poole described the move as "the 'dog in the manger' way, keeping the matter so that nobody else can continue the work."[32] In letters to the American Library Association, to the Library Association of the United Kingdom, and to Leypoldt, he charged that the entire action was "discreditable." When Bowker learned of this, he felt that he had been "stabbed in the back."[33]

The resulting situation proved too much for Leypoldt. The first week in August he announced the resumption of the *Journal* as a separate publication.[34] Leypoldt took this action against his own better judgment, and certainly against Bowker's, and the shame-faced letter in which he rationalized his softheartedness to Bowker is the very picture of a guilty conscience:

> I know you are shaking your fists at the latest perjury of your incorrigible renegade. But I could no more help it than the cow jumping over the moon; . . . It happened in a paroxism of fever. . . . I was . . . completely routed, and short-staffed. . . . In the con-

30 M. Dewey, "Past, Present, and Future of the A. L. A.," *Library Journal*, September–October, 1880, p. 275.

31 *Library Journal*, June, 1880, pp. 168, 169, 192. The five issues of the *Publishers' Weekly* starting with July 3 bore the title *The Publishers' Weekly and the Library Journal*.

32 W. F. Poole to M. Dewey, July 2, 6, 1880; in Dewey files, Bowker Papers, New York Public Library.

33 R. R. B., Journal, October 5–11, 1880; MS Memoir; *Library Journal*, November, 1886, p. 437; January, 1896, p. 8.

34 *Publishers' Weekly*, August 7, 1880, p. 157; *Library Journal*, July–August, 1880, p. 207.

dition I was, and worried to death by the letters from discontented librarians, also feeling rather mean at the sudden wind-up in the middle of the volume, I staggered. And Miss Sophistry, watching her opportunity, kept on pushing me . . . with her whisper, "it won't cost you a cent more."[35]

Bowker was dismayed by this further lapse of business judgment in the well-meaning but impractical Leypoldt, and his letters to the latter so hurt the harassed bibliographer that he did not reply to Bowker for a year, and then continued to protest pathetically that he had "tried so honestly to do the right thing." As a matter of fact Leypoldt announced, at the end of 1881, that the *Journal* had become self-supporting, but Bowker frequently stated in later years that this condition was not reached until the mid eighteen nineties.[36] In view of these circumstances, it is clear that the continuation of the *Journal* from 1880–84 was Leypoldt's doing, and in spite of Bowker's judgment; and that its continuation after 1884 by Bowker was due as much to his loyalty to Leypoldt and the profession as to anything else.

During all this time, Bowker was entering as fully into the developments and problems of the library profession as he was into those of the book trade. The titles of some of his library articles suggest his range of interest: "The People's University" for the *Tribune,* "Learning to Read in College" and "On a Co-operative Scheme of Subject Entry, With a Key to Catalogue Heading" for the *Journal.*[37] In 1878 he prepared an authoritative summary of the entire American library system for the Catalogue of the *Collective Exhibit of the American Booktrade at Paris.* While Bowker could not accompany Winsor, Cutter, Poole, and Dewey in attending the historic London meeting of the first International Library Conference in 1877, he took pride in the fact that the Library Association of the United Kingdom was there organized on the strength of the American example and that similar steps were being taken in France and Germany. As for his month-to-month editing of the *Journal,* he made it what an eminent librarian in 1933 declared it always to have been: "the best and, on account of its good indexing, the most accessible body of source material for library experience in the world . . . an achievement in public service for the highest national welfare unequalled in its field in any other country."[38]

[35] F. Leypoldt to R. R. B., August 11, 1880.

[36] *Library Journal,* December, 1881, p. 328; R. R. B. in *Library Journal,* January, 1896, p. 8.

[37] R. R. B., "The People's University," *Tribune,* July 9, 1877, September 4, 1877; *Library Journal,* October, 1877, pp. 60–62; November, 1878, pp. 326–29.

[38] E. C. Richardson to R. R. B., August 15, 1933.

VI

A Yankee Puritan and His Friends

To see Rogers Bowker striding down the street in the early eighteen seventies was to see a young man who appeared to know exactly where he was going, and why. A pink in his lapel, neatly dressed, erect, a picture of trim, brisk self-assurance, he was all health and bustle. "A bright, red-cheeked young man," one friend remembered him. "A handsome fellow," recalled another, "with lustrous eyes . . . heavy eye lashes . . . a large and shapely nose . . . and such a complexion as a woman might long to possess." He was five feet, nine inches tall. His manner already suggested a gentleman of the old school, noticeably courteous and attentive.

Bowker was an ambitious young man in an age of energy and bounce. His daily program was strenuous, but it must have been rewarding. Perhaps the best picture of his activities can be gained by following him through a typical day:

In his Brooklyn home where he is supporting two parents and a sister, Rogers Bowker leaps out of bed to write an editorial or two for the *Press* and the *Jeweler's Circular* before taking the ferry across the East River to commence the day's work as literary editor of the *Evening Mail*. After delegating the daily correspondence and filing to his assistant, he writes a column of book reviews, throws into another column a round-up of publishers' announcements, current magazine articles, and foreign book movements, and works up odds and ends of news for the chit-chat columns of the paper. In the afternoon he sets off briskly for the *Publishers' Weekly,* which he serves as an editorial assistant. Here he answers correspondence and composes an editorial. More than likely he manages to squeeze in a few notes on current publishing developments for the Boston *Daily Globe* and the London *Publishers' Circular*. Back in the *Mail* rooms late in the afternoon, he notifies members of the reform group of the next meeting of the Brooklyn Free Trade League, of which he is secretary, or of a planning session for the Liberal Republican convention to be held at Cincinnati. Riding home on the ferry, he relaxes by scribbling down the first draft of a manuscript to be sent to the magazines. He is publishing religious verse and prose in the *Independent* and *Christian Union,* and light verse in *Old and New* and *Scribner's.* He is writing vigorous, meaty articles on poor relief, prison reform, the servant problem, psychic phenomena, mental health, and camping for such magazines as *Appleton's* and the *Herald of Health.* After dining at home, he is off to a meeting of the New York Prison Association or the American Free Trade League, or drops in for a musical program at the Aldine Club, a literary soiree at the Gilder home, or a reception at the Century Club as a guest of E. C. Stedman.

By 1876, at the age of twenty-eight, Bowker had achieved maturity, and during the Centennial year, he certainly won his spurs. He gave an important oration at the annual convention of his college fraternity on invitation from the national committee. He provided real leadership in the free trade movement by helping to launch the American Free Trade Alliance and editing its journal, *The New Century.* He matured his own political philosophy, gave it expression in writing and speaking, and did his part in shaping the liberal Republican protest against the presidential aspirations of Grant, Blaine, and Conkling. He achieved a position of leadership in the book trade, performing several notable services for the American Book Trade Association, becoming indispensable to Leypoldt in editing the *Publishers' Weekly,* and carrying on with credit his literary work for the *Tribune.* In the same year he became a leader in a new field by helping to found the *Library Journal* and the American Library Association. On top of this, he published ten literary pieces in five magazines. Anyone watching this young man was bound to be impressed by three qualities in particular: a passion for getting things done, moral earnestness, and a genuine interest in people.

"You are the practical half of the great public," a novelist once wrote Bowker while commending his managerial proficiency.[1] According to his friend Werner he belonged to the tribe of "the practical Yankee" which was characterized by "insight, quickness, determination, ingenuity."[2] He delighted in bringing together ideas, men, materials, and money; in planning and executing, co-ordinating and organizing.

1 Margaret Veley to R. R. B., March 22, 1882.
2 Adolph Werner to R. R. B., August 18, 1884.

By native gift and temperament, Bowker represented what he later called "the executive profession," which included lawyers, corporation managers, and heads of business and educational institutions.

The particular quality which Bowker coupled with his managerial ability was "push." To his sister he once wrote of "that fierce desire to show by doing that things can be done, which rages within me when you, for instance, cry 'cant's.'" Bowker was a dynamo. He not only loved work but was addicted to it. Family, friends, and associates continually urged him not to work so hard. Shepard described him as "amazingly industrious" and agreed that few people had "Bowkerian powers."

This capacity for sustained concentration and hard work was partly the result of his attention to the conditions of physical and mental health. In an *Evening Mail* editorial he urged that employees be given two weeks' vacation with pay in order to maintain their efficiency.[3] In a national health magazine he denounced the American sin of overwork, pleaded for the practice of common-sense hygiene, and argued that sensible habits should enable a man to work for forty years at a much higher average activity than the burning-out process would yield for twenty.[4] "The art of living is indeed a new-found art," he wrote, "but it is worth all the 'lost arts' together. . . . There is a very great waste of human life which is entirely unnecessary." In his review of Hinton's *Physiology for Practical Use,* Bowker underlined the teaching that "good thinking and good willing conduce as directly as diet and exercise to length and effectiveness of life."

Bowker preached and practiced the gospel of hiking and camping. He urged American youth to emulate German youth in this regard. He deplored the fact that on Mountain Day at Williams College most of the students went down to North Adams to play billiards instead of climbing Greylock. He became an early member of the Appalachian Mountain Club and took many trips along the Palisades, into the Catskills, the Berkshires, and the Adirondacks which he described for the magazines. For fifty years he was a leader in getting his fraternity brothers out for their annual summer pilgrimage to Lake George, with its tradition of boating, swimming, and climbing. He wrote one article crammed with practical suggestions for the prospective hiker, and another giving full and explicit directions for overnight excursions.[5] Again and again he eulogized the recreational resources of Lake George

---

[3] "The Economy of Vacation," *Evening Mail,* August 5, 1869.

[4] "Hot House Brains," *Herald of Health,* May, 1870.

[5] "On the Tramp," *Herald of Health,* September, 1873, pp. 102–104; "Camping Out," *Appleton's Summer Book,* 1880, pp. 95–99.

as both summer resort and camping spot.[6] Bowker himself loved the
mountains, the trail-sharpened appetite, the songs around the fire, the
sense of freedom which came when city restraints were left behind.
He remained a conscientious walker all his life. Though not endowed
by nature with the robustness and animal vitality of Teddy Roosevelt,
the most famous exponent of the strenuous life, Bowker nevertheless
maintained an exceptional record of good health and vigorous activity.

Bowker's industry, however, was only in part the result of his attention to health. To a greater extent it was the result of his creed. His
executive "push," his passion for work, his compulsion to fill the passing moment with good works were accompanied by a moral earnestness
and ascetic sense of duty well expressed in the classical Puritan faith.
Bowker himself referred to his creed as having come "from Salem thinking," and he listed John Bunyan as one of the three most important religious writers for a young man's library. He might have added a book
of devotion which he and his friend Everett P. Wheeler made their
constant companion: *De Imitatione Christi* by Thomas a Kempis. Bowker's copy—coverless, battered, dog-eared, with passages frequently
underlined in pencil—confirms the basically religious character of his
thought and action. For Bowker, indeed, faith in the fact of God was
a necessity of the mind and of the will if man was to understand, accept,
and work in this world.[7]

Bowker was a Yankee, but first of all a Puritan. The world was
important because God was in it, and the individual was important because he was the instrument of God's will in history. It was thus clear
to Bowker that human life was purposeful, that man's time and energies were not his own to squander because he held them in trust.[8] Like
an athlete or a soldier, man must keep the discipline of training. If this
meant a measure of asceticism, Bowker would accept it: he did not
drink, smoke, or keep late hours. "A man must find out where his little
corner is," he once wrote in the *Mail,* "and just what bit of the world's
work he wants to do, and just how much knowledge he must covet and
plan for to work out that bit—if he is to work out his work at all."[9] In
the effort to subordinate impulse to principle, he was conscious of the
moral struggle between the lower and the higher self. "So far as we
surrender to the lower nature," Bowker wrote, "we link ourselves day
by day to the savage and the brute—sinning in the light, we are worse

6 "Summering at Lake George," *Appleton's Journal,* October 7, 1871; "A College
Camp at Lake George," *Scribner's Monthly,* March, 1879, pp. 617–31.

7 See his poem, "Toll Then No More," *Christian Union,* April 9, 1870.

8 See "The Master's Work," *Independent,* May 25, 1876; "An Humble Spirit,"
Sunday School Times, July 13, 1878.

9 "The Economy of Vacation," *Evening Mail,* August 5, 1869.

than the heathen."[10] He also knew the Puritan's kinship with the Stoic, and his writings frequently express the Stoic's stern sense of life as duty, of life as work, of life as a battle against great odds.[11]

This dash of the Old Roman in Bowker helped to make him a "man of character" who believed in character. Vague sentimentality and utopian optimism had no place in his scheme. "I don't want any Pollyana business," he would frequently say in later years. But the weakness that to him was anathema was self-pity. Though at an early age he was obliged to support himself, his parents, and his sister, and in time a number of relatives and classmates as well; though he committed himself to political crusades that failed and to business causes that lost money; and though he completely lost his eyesight in the prime of life, Bowker was never once guilty of self-pity. He preached the importance of courage and faith on many occasions, and he practiced what he preached. "Nothing can be done without faith," he told the Hamilton College undergraduates on one occasion. "It does move mountains, and without it you cannot move even yourselves. There is nothing more melancholy than a young man with the cynicism of blasé age. In the name of all that is good, keep this spirit of hopelessness out of our American colleges."[12] In the mood of national soul-searching prompted by the Centennial, Bowker declared to his fellow citizens that "Character, whether in a man or in a people, is the main thing, and of all forces in the universe, character is that which sums up everything."[13]

Every man suffers the defects of his virtues, and Bowker was no exception. The compulsion to plan every hour and every day undercut the play of creative spontaneity. The drive toward work and results produced a tenseness inimical to relaxed enjoyment. The temperamental preference for intellect over feeling tended to result in a thinness of emotional experience. Devotion to principle was accompanied by an austere conscience. It is hard to know whether Cousin William Savory intended a compliment or not when he remarked, "Rogers . . . is perfection itself, and nothing bad can live in his presence." Some of his associates felt, occasionally, that in Bowker's character the Puritan's humility before God was accompanied by the Puritan's pride of self-righteousness before men.

Whatever these faults may have been, there was one virtue which no one could fail to observe and respect: Bowker's practical helpfulness. The brotherhood of man came near to being the heart of Bowker's

10 "Of Sin as Death and Rightness as Life," an unpublished MS.

11 See "In Memoriam, L. D., died February 9, 1871"; *"Finis Coronat Opus," Scribner's Monthly*, December, 1872.

12 *Morning Herald* and *Daily Observer*, Utica, New York, May 25, 1876.

13 "True Usefulness of the Centennial," *Christian Union*, April 5, 1876.

religion. When in 1870 Edward Everett Hale started the "Ten Times One Is Ten" clubs with their motto, "To look up and not down, to look forward and not back, to look out and not in,—and to lend a hand," Bowker responded heart and soul, and was the first of the second ten in the country to enroll. Lending a hand became a skillful art with Bowker, as natural and as effortless as an instinct. To sense a human need was for him to act, without a moment's hesitation and without a trace of self-consciousness.[14] Nor was his action confined to private need. His creed took him into the thick of the political battles of his day. Bowker's Calvinism was enriched by the humanitarianism of the "social gospel." It was also liberalized by the scientific rationalism of the Enlightenment.

The major premise of Bowker's creed and three important corollaries of it deserve to be stressed. Behind everything else was the conviction that reality was spiritual, was characterized by meaning and unity, and was expressed as law. Since spirit was indestructible, the Resurrection was a universal truth certified by revelation, science, and intuition. Out of death, life! Here was for Bowker the archetype of the whole process of existence. One corollary had to do with the infinite worth of every human life. This was crucial. When a theological work denying immortality to all men was reprinted in this country, Bowker immediately recognized it as an antidemocratic and antihumanitarian doctrine, and publicly demolished it argument by argument in a vigorous counterattack.[15] When championing greater social justice for domestic servants, he emphasized the respect due all persons as spiritual beings.[16] This led to an invincible trust that the native good in every individual could overcome the evil if adequately encouraged. It also led to a firm conviction that man was morally free and responsible. What most impressed Bowker in George Eliot's *Daniel Deronda* was the affirmation that "There are men not 'tangled in the fold of dire necessity' but able to control circumstance, who 'stand for a fact,' and are a superior part of the law." Bowker's democratic liberalism was rooted in his Hebrew-Christian faith.

A second corollary of Bowker's belief in the prime fact of God was the second-placeness of man. Meditation on the *Imitatione* reinforced a natural self-effacement. It was one of Bowker's conspicuous traits that he avoided publicity, and was content to exercise leadership in the

14 See R. R. B., "The Shower of Gold," *St. Nicholas*, February, 1876.

15 "Eternal Death," *The Golden Age*, September 16, 1871. The book was the Reverend Henry Constable's *Duration and Nature of Future Punishment* (New York, 1871).

16 See "In Re Bridget,—the Defence," *Old and New*, October, 1871.

17 "Preaching Up and Preaching Down," *Christian Union*, June 4, 1870.

background and let credit fall to others. He deliberately remained anonymous in innumerable charities.

A third corollary was that the world was one world. There was no place in Bowker's thinking for otherworldliness. "We no longer believe religion a matter of the hereafter only," he wrote in the *Christian Union.* "That faith which makes men lead the best life in this world is the faith which best fits them for the other."[17] He had no use for people who "make a mummy-case of their religion, belittle themselves to fit it, and wrap themselves away from the wicked world until it shall be time for them to leave it." For the same reason, Bowker firmly believed that body, mind, and spirit were always to be integrated into a functioning unity, and therefore also the work of medical science, education, and religion.

> A man worried with the ills of the body is the less likely to have a healthful soul. That preaching is best whose result is a congregation of Christian men and women whose appetite, thought, and faith are equally hearty and healthy. . . . The sanitary inspector, the school teacher, and the city missionary are three points of a triangle, each of almost equal importance.[18]

Similarly, he urged, religion, morality, and art are interrelated and interdependent.

> We may not be a people great in Art until we be a religious folk, and so much, as we attain in Art, in so much shall we be the more righteous, and religious. It is all one. . . . It is His providence that in seeking the things which are higher, we fulfil also the lower at their best. The spiritual uplifts the material into ever finer enjoyment. . . . No, we have not to reject, but to redeem, the material.[19]

Throughout his life Bowker preached "the needful view of the wholeness of life," and finally wrote a book on this theme.[20]

Bowker's attitude toward formal religion perfectly expressed the facts of his religious belief. In thought and practice he was probably more devout than most of the intellectuals of his generation. All his life he served as a kind of lay preacher, presenting his faith in both prose and verse and finding a ready pulpit in the religious press.[21] Because

18 "Getting at the Masses," *Christian Union,* June 4, 1870.

19 "Art Education," *Evening Mail,* October 30, November 6, 1872.

20 R. R. B., *The Arts of Life* (Boston, Houghton Mifflin, 1900). See Chapter XVIII.

21 See the two "Lay Sermons" entitled "On Good Resolutions" and "On Keeping at It," over the signature "The Gentile Optimist," in the *Evening Mail,* January 7 and 21, 1871. The second was reprinted in the *Cosmopolitan,* January 28, 1871.

of his hearty belief in the social importance of the churches, he took the trouble to offer them his constructive criticism. In one article he denounced those preachers who sought to change men by preaching the gospel of fear rather than the gospel of love; on another occasion he criticized the bombast and rhetoric used in the pulpits.[22] Indeed, Bowker was all his life a conscientious pew-holder,[23] took pains to get acquainted with local ministers, and gave them the benefit of his lay reactions and observations. Nevertheless, he was too conscientiously liberal and too honest to become a member of any sect or to become a communicant: the church creeds, he felt, were too iron-bound, tended to "promote verbal immorality by the use of language which no longer represents belief," and distressed true spirituality with "wasteful contention of doctrine."

Hard work and moral earnestness did not preclude an interest in people. Bowker's capacity for making friendships was striking. Wherever he went, whatever he did, Bowker was immediately aware of the human beings near him, learning their names, discovering their enthusiasms, instantly finding ways of serving them. College alumni, business associates in journalism, the book trade, the library field, the Edison Company, fellow liberal reformers, traveling companions, children—scores of people knew Bowker as one who cared about them and who would give generously of his time and substance to help them. Moreover, to Bowker a friendship made was a friendship to be preserved. He cultivated his friends through the years, writing to them faithfully, remembering their birthdays and anniversaries, sending them books, recommendations, and suggestions appropriate to their interests. If he did not have the gift of conviviality or even of intimacy, no one could surpass him in thoughtfulness. "Others' burdens have a way, even here, of piling upon his shoulders," wrote Shepard after visiting Bowker in London, "far more, I think, than they ought. If gratitude remains an active virtue, Rogers has accumulated an enormous capital." There was about this more than friendliness. It was loyalty. One of Bowker's most marked qualities was his capacity for personal loyalty—to friends, institutions, and causes.

Loyalty to family was central. Bowker's parents were financially stricken and helpless; he supported father, mother, and sister, moved the family to a new house, and furnished it. They had few friends;

22 "Preaching Up and Preaching Down," *Christian Union,* August 9, 1871; book review of R. Palmer's *Earnest Words on True Success in Life,* in the *Christian Leader,* July 26, 1873.

23 On first coming to New York, Bowker attended the Episcopal services at St. Bartholomew's in Washington Square, and on moving to Brooklyn, he regularly attended the Church of the Messiah.

Rogers brought his fraternity brothers and college professors home to dinner and made their families the intimates of his family. They did not read books and provided no library in the meager New York home, disliked going out, and lacked the means or will to attend the theater or concerts; Rogers succeeded in getting both his mother and sister to read, took his sister on many of his trips, and brought the outside world to both of them through his conversation, his friends, and his letters. They had lost courage for the present and hope in the future; he undergirded their lives with cheer, with new interests, with faith. He particularly took pains to make Thanksgiving, Christmas, and Easter significant family festivals. It was an absorbing devotion, but one which he never dreamed of shirking.

The disaster to the family business had crushed both parents. Daniel Bowker was still a handsome man, but he was a pathetic figure. As long as he had had the backing of his own father in Salem, he had done well, but the first business reverses in New York had destroyed his self-confidence. Thereafter he showed neither initiative nor perseverance, but stumbled from position to position, impatient of the long way to success, ever dreaming of sudden fortune, several times risking and losing his diminishing capital in unwise speculation,[24] busying himself with wonderful patents which would restore the family to affluence. In 1878 his son arranged a clerkship for him in the *Publishers' Weekly* office, a position which he held for three years as a refuge where he might recover his morale. In the nineties he again became his son's employee for a number of years. By nature lacking in creative imagination and intellectual force, he remained all his life poorly educated, uninterested in books, unable to write anything but a childish letter filled with errors in spelling and punctuation. In the home he was a sweet, gentle, simple man, a good storyteller, and liked by everyone. Young Bowker felt pity, never bitterness, for his father.[25]

It was Daniel's wife who should have worn the trousers, according to one irreverent family friend. Theresa Savory Bowker was a small, pretty, bright-eyed woman who, at her best, possessed gaiety and charm. Used to comfort in her youth, surrounded by doting older brothers, she had made what seemed a good match in marrying Daniel Bowker and had cherished bright dreams for the future. The business collapse proved as tragic for her as for her husband, and she never quite managed to rise above it. It hurt her family pride and seemed to paralyze her will. She drew into herself, gave herself up to almost constant worry,

[24] See R. R. B. to Daniel Bowker, September 1, 1881.

[25] R. R. B. to his mother, September 5, 1881. He was undoubtedly thinking of his father when, in his lay sermon "On Keeping at It," he described the tragedy of drift.

and became a chronic invalid. Carrie, on returning from a visit away, would always look up at her mother's windows: drawn blinds would mean another spell of illness. Rogers, whenever he left town, would wire for news. It was seldom that his mother was well enough to go to church, and seldom that she did go to church without catching a cold. At home she sewed quilts, mended Rogers' clothes, and played cribbage and whist.

During his college years, young Bowker had to sell part of his stamp collection to secure money for books and laboratory fees. In his senior year he moved the family from the Jamaica boardinghouse to a new home at 147 Washington Avenue, Brooklyn. He provided his sister with a small allowance and paid all the household bills. To the few pieces of furniture which his mother had kept, Bowker gradually made additions, carefully selected in Boston and Philadelphia during business trips and paid for with what he made from magazine articles. From London he later sent home furniture, rugs, curtains, brass, and chinaware, meanwhile dreaming of a corner-house patterned on homes he had seen in Kent, with a maid to serve at afternoon tea and dinner.[26]

It was not an easy situation. To his sister the move out of the city seemed a cruel humiliation, and hurt pride resulted in dropping former friends. To Bowker, living in a small house with a dependent family meant a host of petty distractions and inconveniences. "If they knew what I knew," Carrie wrote her mother after hearing people remark how much Bowker managed to get done, "they would wonder still more how he accomplishes so much." The family became absorbed in Rogers. Perhaps it was inevitable that the mother should idolize the son who provided the material security her husband was unable to provide. It was less inevitable, but true, that the father thanked his stars for a son who retrieved him from total disgrace and permitted him a quiet, sheltered life of semi-genteel inactivity.

It was not inevitable, however, or too healthy that the sister should come to look on her brother as not only benefactor and hero but life-companion as well. Like all the other members of the family, Carolyn had attractive features, an earnest, sweet, even charming personality, a disposition that was somewhat sentimental though never narrow. Out of loyalty Rogers took her to parties, outings, meetings, on vacation excursions, and business trips. In hundreds of letters he gave her the excitement of living his life with him. She never married, and when Rogers finally took a wife, Carolyn would not speak to her for months. But Bowker did not marry until he was fifty-four. In spite of the fact that several match-makers did their best, that he professed to envy the

26 R. R. B. to his mother, January 26, February 13, 1881.

love-making of his friends, that he frequently expressed the hope that he might fall in love and marry, and that he had many feminine acquaintances, his conspicuous gallantry toward the ladies was slow to ripen into a romantic attachment. Bowker wrote of his bachelor state to his sister with a mixture of humor and stoicism:

> It does seem rather hard on you and me that so much good material for home-making should be wasted; it would be so unkind in fate to retort that we had so many friends we couldn't expect to have one in particular. . . . As for me, it's the same old story,— many friends . . . but not a flutter of the real article. . . . If it must be, I think you and I can play Darby and Joan as well as most people.[27]

This absorbing loyalty to his family did not keep Bowker from enjoying many associations with men whom he had met at college or was getting to know in business. His closest friends at this time included Edward Morse Shepard, Everett P. Wheeler, Adolf Werner, A. D. F. Randolph, and George Haven Putnam. He was always a leader in keeping his fraternity circle together and rarely missed a meeting, dinner, or outing. At the same time he had quite a social fling as a bright young man at a number of salons and soirees.

The longest and most intimate friendship of Bowker's life was with Edward Morse Shepard, a college fraternity brother one class behind his own. He was a man of marked integrity and force of character, blessed with an exceptionally vigorous mind, and it was the freely expressed opinion of Bowker, Crawford, and other alumni that he was perhaps the most brilliant of all the graduates of the College of the City of New York.[28] His father, Lorenzo B. Shepard, was a leading northern Democrat and an honored Sachem of Tammany Hall with a brilliant record as district attorney. At the father's death, when young Shepard was only six, the family's close friend Abram S. Hewitt was appointed guardian of the Shepard family. Morse Shepard entered the law and soon proved himself a competent executive, later gaining a reputation as chairman of the Brooklyn Civil Service Commission, drafter of the New York subway contracts, special district attorney in the brilliant prosecution of the McKane election frauds, candidate for mayor, and president of the City College board of trustees.

Bowker's friendship with Shepard was blessed in a number of ways. The two young men talked over their many common interests on free

[27] R. R. B. to his sister, November 6, 1881.
[28] R. R. B., MS; G. H. Crawford to Bowker, January 8, 1912; see R. R. B., "Edward Morse Shepard," *City College Quarterly*, December, 1911.

evenings, Sunday afternoon walks, and on week-end tramping trips in the Catskills. They saw eye to eye on civil service, tariff reform, currency problems, and social work. Shepard's strong Democratic background, inherited from his father and strengthened by association with Hewitt, prevented him from ever becoming as enthusiastic an Independent as Bowker, but he was always sympathetic to the ideal and came to be the Brooklyn leader of the antimachine element in his party. The two households also became intimate with each other. Shepard's younger sister Agnes became a special friend of Bowker's mother. Agnes Shepard married Charles B. Hewitt,[29] and during the summer when the Bowkers lived with the Shepards at Westerly, New York, Agnes Hewitt's children came to be almost as close to Bowker as if they had been his own.

Another lifelong friend whose family became intimate with the Bowkers was Everett Pepperrell Wheeler, also a fraternity brother, who had graduated from City College eleven years before Rogers. When Bowker came to know him, Wheeler was president of the City College Alumni Association, had already helped to found the Association of the Bar of the City of New York, and was serving on its executive committee. He was even then an eminent young lawyer being put forward by his friends as candidate for the Superior Court, and was soon to be appointed a member of the elevated-railroad commission and the Board of Education. To his friends he was a man of unquenchable optimism, genuine humility, and exquisite tact, with a genius for friendship. To his fellow lawyers and political opponents he was outspoken, firm in asserting his rights, sometimes seeming arrogant, a man who could not be intimidated or imposed upon. Scrupulous, courageous, unyielding in moral and ethical questions, he was found fighting for every cause that promised civic betterment.[30] In the seventies, Wheeler lived with his delightful family of five on Staten Island, and here as well as at the summer home at New Hamburg, Bowker, his sister, and his mother came to be frequent guests.

The Shepard–C. B. Hewitt–Wheeler–Bowker circle was a close and happy one, and Rogers was a prime favorite with them all. He deeply prized the informal intimacy which permitted him to drop into these households at any time for a friendly visit. "I begin to think I should insist on finding some such place," he later wrote home from London, "if I settled down in Kamchatka or Timbuctoo." He also enjoyed the choice associations that came through these households. He especially

29 R. R. B. to Mrs. Lucy Leffingwell, June 21, 1926.
30 R. R. B., *City College Quarterly*, April, 1925, p. 103; *D. A. B.*; D. S. Alexander, *A Political History of the State of New York*, IV, 225.

relished the private receptions given by Mrs. William Cooper at Gramercy Square and by Mrs. Peter Cooper at the great house near by. He gladly accepted invitations to join the several households for excursions on Peter Cooper's fine yacht, "Orion," and for years enjoyed telling of one such trip to William Cullen Bryant's home at Roslyn, Long Island, when the yacht ran aground on a shoal and Commodore William Cooper stood in the bow of his craft warning the big steamers away with his tin horn while Peter Cooper led the company in singing hymns.[31]

Another close friend and fraternity brother was "golden-hearted Werner," beloved German professor. He was buoyant, philosophically reflective, civic-minded, and blessed with the gift of friendship. Bowker enjoyed being one of a circle of loyal alumni who found in Werner's hospitable home a happy tie with a popular teacher and their alma mater. Even more, he prized his charter membership in a select group which read German literature with Werner on Saturdays. Here he so improved his proficiency in the language that he was emboldened to offer several German translations to the press which were printed and favorably noticed. Through the decades the two men discussed orally and by letter the problems of the College and the fraternity they both loved, Bowker honoring the gallant and mellow spirit of his senior, Werner prizing the friendship of the young man whose career he was proud to follow.

Two warm friends whom Bowker brought into the family circle from his business associations were A. D. F. Randolph and George Haven Putnam. Randolph was an honored bookseller, a writer and editor of religious verse, and several times president of the American Book Trade Union. Bowker felt toward this older man the affection of a son for a father and prized his wide humanism, his high purpose, and his happy play of humor.[32] For his part, Randolph greatly admired young Bowker, whom he called "my boy." He became a frequent caller at the Bowker household, and his two daughters the good friends of Carolyn, the elder traveling with her to Europe in 1880. He and Bowker shared not only common interests in the book-trade field, but in various liberal reform movements such as free trade.

George Haven Putnam made a prince of a companion. Four years Bowker's senior, he had studied at the Sorbonne, the University of Berlin, and Göttingen, had become a partner of his father's publishing house in 1866, and on his father's death in 1872 became head of G. P. Putnam's Sons. Of slight stature but of immense vitality and, like

31 R. R. B., MS, and R. R. B. to Burton Hendrick, November 25, 1927.
32 See R. R. B. to F. A. Stokes, February 3, 1925.

Shepard and Bowker, enjoying brisk exercise, Putnam was an alert, clean-cut young man with an orderly, vigorous mind. Bowker's book-trade work for the *Mail* and the *Publishers' Weekly* brought him into frequent and important professional relations with Putnam, and this business association soon ripened into a warm personal friendship which lasted a lifetime. Both men were liberals, and during their walking trips discussed new books, literary critics, the problems of copyright, free trade, and political reform.[33]

Putnam was solicitous when Bowker fell ill. "We have missed you in more ways than one," he wrote. "I for one have grown right lonely for want of the sight of your cheering face, and am glad enough to hear that the doctors are soon going to permit you to cross the icy channel, and resume your supervision of us publishers." When Bowker left for London in 1880, Putnam again expressed his sense of loss. "I shall miss you not only in my capacity as a publisher," he wrote, "but in all the matters in which we have been interested together, for I have found in you the most praiseworthy quality of being in accord with me on most subjects." Bowker was equally affectionate. "You have been to me," he wrote Putnam, "my *Fidus Achates*. . . . One of the pleasantest remembrances that I take abroad is your patient and modest service for all good things, heretic as you are. I hope that no distance, and no time can make any breach in so dear a friendship."[34] For several years Putnam had been an intimate of the Bowker household, where his charm and courtesy had made a deep impression.

For the rest, Bowker saw a great deal of his college and fraternity friends. There were the singing bouts in which Shepard, Frank L. Wing, and Graham McAdam particularly distinguished themselves, with Bowker a rather silent participant. There was a literary club in which lively papers were read. There were pleasant Sunday evenings of spirited talk with Henry T. Patterson, George Holmes Crawford, and Charles F. Wingate; and the Saturday evening fraternity gatherings at the lodgings of Henry Chapman when coffee or chocolate prepared on the gas stove and tobacco aplenty assisted the informal symposiums. There were national fraternity conventions at which he came to know John Jay, Edward Everett Hale, George William Curtis, Joseph Hodges Choate, Talcott Williams, and, less well, Phillips Brooks.

The most cherished fraternity experience, however, was the annual summer pilgrimage to a camp on Lake George. Bowker had helped

33 See G. H. Putnam to R. R. B., August 14, October 21, 1871; February 18, March 11, May 11, November 8, November 29, 1873.

34 G. H. Putnam to R. R. B., June 28, 1880; R. R. B. to G. H. Putnam, June 30, 1880.

Literary Associates of the Seventies: *(Top, left)* J. M. Bundy in 1873; *(Top, right)* Richard Watson Gilder at the age of forty; *(Bottom, left)* Edward Everett Hale; *(Bottom, right)* Edmund Clarence Stedman

Book Trade and Copyright Associates: *(Top, left)* A. D. F. Randolph; *(Top, right)* J. Henry Harper; *(Bottom, left)* W. H. Appleton; *(Bottom, right)* Charles Scribner (1854–1930)

to inaugurate "Camp Manhattan" in the summer of 1869 and was a prime moving spirit in maintaining an amazing record of attendance by the original group through fifty years. Beginning at Sheldon's Point and later moving to Little Green Island, the campers, numbering fifteen or so, would each summer pitch the old "Crimson Tent" and the "Gospel Tent" and tents for the kitchen and the Negro cook. The two weeks would rush by in a spirited program of boating, fishing, baseball, hiking, public receptions held on the island, and visiting with a growing circle of summer-resident friends, including the Candace Wheelers, the Randolphs, Bishop Williams, and soon the Shepard family. Military discipline and singing were special features in a round of beloved traditions which accumulated through the decades. This experience of beautiful Adirondack scenery, healthy exercise, and loyal companionship, excitedly renewed each summer and lovingly re-collected at the monthly reunions during the winter, is one of the brightest threads in Bowker's life, and it is questionable whether any other college camp in the country was more talked about and written about than this one.[35]

Young Bowker not only maintained strong personal ties with his seniors and his contemporaries, but with small children as well. His love of children, which he once playfully described as a "passion," was a lifelong characteristic. He liked to play games with them, to invent outlandish nicknames for them, to send them little inconsequential but exciting souvenirs from his trips, and to tell them stories and compose for them fables and phantasies like "The Ballad of a Gruesome Butcher" which was printed in *Scribner's*.[36] He never made the mistake of underestimating them.

> It is no use trying to write down to the level of children, for they are a great sight above us, and there are few who can write up to them. Happily the era of baby twaddle and Sunday School namby-pambyism is fast going by, and at last we have the very best writers of the country doing some of their best work for children.[37]

35 A surprisingly large literature developed about Camp Manhattan: R. R. B., "Lake George, A Newspaper Route Book," I, II, *Evening Mail*, August 12, 1869; "Lake George: A Reminiscence," *Old and New*, September, 1870; "Summering at Lake George," *Appleton's Magazine*, October 7, 1871; "A College Camp at Lake George," *Scribner's Monthly*, March, 1879; "Camping Out," *Appleton's Summer Book*, 1880. G. A. Baker, "The Trials and Triumphs of a College Camp," *Evening Mail*, September 27, 1870. Daniel K. Young, article in *Journal of Commerce*, September 11, 1878. Article in *Tribune*, August 18, 1879. *Camp Manhattan, Memoranda, 1860–1908* (New York, privately printed. 1908). W. M. Murray, *Camp Manhattan* (New York, 1911).

36 January, 1876.

37 *Evening Mail*, October 14, 1874.

In turn, children trusted him, loved him, and wrote him long letters in their labored script. He was, indeed, an ideal and fabulous uncle, following his little friends as they grew up, counseling with them, and encouraging their particular interests, which he never forgot.

His prime favorites, among the younger generation, were undoubtedly the Hewitt and Wheeler children, who regarded him as a sort of divinely appointed playfellow. When he went to London in 1880, they sorely missed him. "I was at the Wheeler's yesterday," Shepard wrote Bowker. "They were as charming as ever and as devoted to their patron saint across the water as ever. The children really give me a little vicarious devotion." And again, "You are the first and chief subject of conversation, being a sort of loved and revered household god of whom I am a priest."[38] Bowker also loved to play with the children of his classmate, E. T. Hiscox, the three charming little daughters of his Brooklyn neighbor and classmate, Miner Knowlton,[39] and a special little companion whom he called Mabel Mollie Midget Peppermint Stockings Larramore.

It is evident that young Bowker liked people and that people liked him. He was known as "Proge" to his sister, "Dick" to his college friends, and "Rogers" to his relatives. Yet no one ever thought of describing him as a "jolly fellow." "I was never much of a club man," Bowker once said of himself, and on another occasion told a prospective employer that he hadn't "the taste for conviviality to be a 'popular' man, though I think I can win confidence and reasonable liking." To his close friends he was a thoroughly good companion—genial, thoughtful, and enterprising. Bowker's friends were not confined to his private life. All his civic and business activities were built upon the solid foundation of personal friendship, and this was early remarked by others. "We are not many of us so fortunate," young George Haven Putnam wrote Bowker in 1877, "as to make, while discharging official or business duties, warm personal friends of those with whom we come in contact. From what I hear from others, that has certainly been *your* lot to an exceptional extent."

Bowker, then, had a passion for getting things done, moral earnestness, and an interest in people. He was also intelligent, ambitious, and persistent. The career resulting from these traits was intense, yet perhaps too diversified. Managerial ability promised success in business, and his ten years at the end of the century as general manager of the Edison Electric Illuminating Company were to show that he could be

[38] Shepard to Bowker, February 14, March 6, 1881.

[39] Bowker described their antics in his poem "My Maidens," published in the *Independent*, January 20, 1876.

brilliant when given a proper chance. Moral earnestness meant that he would be a persistent crusader, and in fact Bowker chose to fight all his life in the company of small minorities for unpopular causes which to him represented true social justice and progress. Perhaps it was the great defect of his career that he was not able to combine, as Godkin and Curtis did, his bread-winning and reforming interests in one journalistic endeavor. This was his hope, but it was never realized. The result was an unremunerative compromise between business and crusading. He started a career in journalism, and from 1868 to 1875 was underpaid in it. He then shifted over to the book trade and became involved in extremely demanding and completely unremunerative library and bibliography enterprises. Meanwhile, he did join the liberal crusade and gave to it more and more of his energies.

Bowker was much more concerned to be doing something useful than something financially profitable. He had no desire to become rich, and business was for him a means rather than an end. He understood the importance of politics, but it was an importance which was secondary. What he really wanted to be was a kind of social architect and engineer. And in this role he lived an enormously useful life which left a strong mark at a surprising number of different places. That his name today is not known to many in either business, politics, or the social sciences would be to him irrelevant. "Many have learned in their reading of history," he once wrote, "that it is work rather than noise that counts, and are content to fight without carrying the flag."[40] Indeed, one might say of Bowker's life what he, during the Centennial year, declared of another's:

> I do not know that he was a great man; I do not know that he would have been a great man had not disease . . . fastened so early upon him. There are not many great men; there would not be room for many. . . . But he was just the kind of man we most need, which the country most needs. He was a man who could get along without being great, but who could not get along without being right and true and without actively doing something for what is right and true. If we are to tell among our fellows . . . this is what most of us must be content to be.[41]

40 R. R. B., unpublished MS, "The AB in Politics," 1874.
41 R. R. B., address at dedication of a memorial to Samuel Eells in Utica, New York, May 25, 1876.

VII

Joining the Liberal Crusade

BOWKER'S CENTRAL CONCERN in life was not with journalism, the book trade, or the library movement, but with something which might be called social engineering. It is what he considered to be the true function of the scholar, and it is a function he probably deemed more important than any other. The concept reappears in his writings from his college days on, but receives clearest expression in the *Arts of Life* of 1900:

> This is the business in the world of the scholar, to divert men from the discouragement and waste of ill-directed effort and to enlist them in line with the co-ordinating forces of nature and human development; to reduce the useless and destructive activity thrown ignorantly or carelessly counter to progress, and to stimulate common endeavor in the line of ascertainable advance. . . . In educing these ideas and bringing them into the domain of will, he . . . performs a work with which that of the politician does not compare. He is the true leader,—not statesman only, but worlds-man.[1]

Bowker does not use the term "worlds-man" very often. He certainly never applied it to himself. This concept of the role of the scholar, however, is certainly an important clue to the central concern of his life. It is this which most clearly underlies his introduction to McAdam's *Alphabet of Finance* and his articles interpreting the "true usefulness of the Centennial" in 1876, the birthday resolutions of 1878 reviewed below, the organization of the Society for Political Education in 1880, the succession of pamphlets, tracts, and booklets in the field of the social sciences, and the devotion to the cause of books, the book trade,

[1] R. R. B., *The Arts of Life*, 18.

and the library. To discover true knowledge, to organize it, to communicate it, to put it to work for the improvement of society, this is the key to much that is dominant in Bowker's life. This was the function of the scholar. This was the role of the worlds-man. This was the real vocation to which Bowker consciously or unconsciously committed himself.

A private memorandum written on his thirtieth birthday, September 4, 1878, affords an interesting clue to this vocational commitment:

> 1. The permanent adoption, in this country particularly, of free trade principles,—the principle that every citizen must be free to earn his living without help or hindrance from the government, which does not deny mutual help and co-operation and does, it seems to me, provide the only remedy against the evils threatening a free state.
>
> These principles can be permanently adopted only through an educational process, which shall teach the people that communism, "protection," and the like are not permanently possible and are presently of great wrong, and that national, like individual, success can be had only by looking facts (and taxes) in the face, obeying natural laws, accepting responsibility and doing the most and best work we can. . . .
>
> 2. To be at the head, or managing desk, of a New York evening paper like the old *Mail*, combining Sweetser's liveliness with the strength of Bundy's old political writing, at a salary covering comfortable living and proprietary interest assuring the future. Its principles should be free trade; honest money; political, and not partisan, responsibility.
>
> 3. To be a careful student of, and make myself an authority on, social science, including especially political economy, charities, and education, for its utterances on which topics the above paper should be notable.
>
> These three aims are but divisions of a single purpose, toward which, if I am to succeed, I must thoroughly concentrate my life.

In Bowker's thinking, an age is fashioned in its ideas.

> Commonly at the root of these there may be found, in a great age, a leading thought, which produces the ruling motive. This is the soul of the age, and moulds its life and history. . . . It may be the splendid inspiration of one great man; it may be the out-

growth of a school; it may be the voicing of the vague yearnings of the mass; it may be unvoiced, yet potent. However it be produced, it gives to the age its *character*. . . .

The thinker who can reach the ideas which sway his time, to the correction of those which are ill and the promotion and diffusion of those which are good in tendency, gives to progress an intelligent impetus that speeds the world.[2]

The "leading thought" of the nineteenth century, for Bowker, was liberalism, and the way to discharge the "business of the scholar" in his time was to clarify and promote the liberal program. Thus while earning his living in journalism and the book trade, Bowker became deeply committed to one of the most notable social movements of his age—the great liberal crusade. From his college days during the Civil War to the end of his life when the storm clouds of World War II were gathering, he was a staunch, aggressive representative of the liberal faith.

The liberal faith and the liberal crusade, indeed, since they constituted the materials for his vocation of social engineering, became the central faith and fact of Bowker's life. All his other concerns—libraries, the book trade, bibliography, and copyright—had their justification in their contribution to this central cause. Such interests as science, business management, journalism, and travel were but facets of this great adventure. In the greatest crisis of his life he promptly abandoned a brilliant business career rather than compromise his liberal creed. Bowker's life exhibits extreme diversity of interest and activity until one senses the basic liberalism that tied the whole together. In that light, his life assumes a remarkable unity.

With a clear-cut grasp of the fundamental principles involved, a passion for putting those principles into practice and an unusual persistence in hewing to the line despite all discouragements, Bowker was able to employ his managerial skill and journalistic experience with great effectiveness to the cause. He did not make the headlines. His role did not turn out to be that of a prominent journalist like Godkin or Curtis, nor that of a great orator like Beecher or Lowell, nor yet that of a public officeholder like Schurz or Cleveland. But he was one of the men that every movement must have if it is to keep going: an indefatigable committeeman, willing to lavish time and energy behind the scenes, organizing capable men into working groups, co-ordinating related groups into united fronts, promoting public meetings, composing manifestoes and platforms, and endlessly circularizing congressmen, governors, and public leaders. In free trade, civil service reform, bal-

2 *Ibid.*, 18-19.

lot reform, political independency, anti-imperialism, scientific taxation, social control of franchises, adult civic education, prison reform, settlement-house programs, and housing for workers, he was, at one time or another and in some cases continuously, working in the front rank. More than most liberals, moreover, he kept the entire philosophy constantly before him, saw the interrelationship of its scattered fronts, and forever sought to unify them into a single continuing force.

The liberal crusade which Bowker joined while still in college was the heir to a goodly heritage of ideas. Rooted in the social idealism of the Hebrew-Christian tradition, enriched by the humanism of the Renaissance and the rationalism of the Enlightenment, it borrowed heavily from English Whig theorists like Locke and French Romanticists like Rousseau, was shaped by the utilitarianism of Bentham and Mill and the Manchester school of economics, and was profoundly influenced by Darwinism and the Spencerian gospel of social evolution. It was an international movement, proud of such heroes and martyrs as Mazzini, Kossuth, Cobden, Bright, and Lincoln. Its great battles for national self-determination, constitutionalism, civil liberties, toleration, democracy, free trade, pacifism, and humanitarian reform were among the glories of the nineteenth century. Here in the United States the liberal crusade gathered its first momentum in the Jeffersonian-Jacksonian tradition and in the abolitionist fervor. It was then captained by the Mugwumps, was strengthened by elements of the Populist movement, expanded from the trust-busting days of the Square Deal and the Muckraking movement through the New Nationalism, the New Freedom, and the farmer-labor program into the New Deal.

At the end of the Civil War, however, the movement found the going hard. Postwar America was weary of crusading. Most of the brains and energies of Bowker's generation poured lustily into the exploitation of the continent. What Mark Twain called "The Gilded Age," and Vernon Louis Parrington "The Great Barbecue"[3] generated currents of popular thinking and practical politics which ran strongly against the liberal movement and reduced it, with few exceptions, to an ineffectual role. Moreover, in spite of many fine individual leaders, the liberals too often differed among themselves on minor issues and failed to become fused into a stable, effective bloc. The movement gathered momentum from 1868 until 1872, but then received a staggering blow from the Liberal Republican fiasco. It again showed vitality and leadership in the elections of 1876 and 1880 and reached a high point of effectiveness in the Mugwump triumph of 1884. It then rallied behind Cleveland, but was eventually routed by the same forces which overwhelmed him. In

[3] Vernon Louis Parrington, *Main Currents of American Thought*, III, 23.

spite of almost constant reverses, however, the liberal crusade never lost its vitality. In numerous committees and organizations such as those on which Bowker served, the faith was kept alive.

The liberal crusade in the United States enrolled an outstanding company of men. Among the journalists were E. L. Godkin of the *Nation,* G. W. Curtis of *Harper's Weekly,* W. C. Bryant and Charles Nordhoff of the *Evening Post,* Horace White of the *Chicago Tribune,* and Henry Watterson of the Louisville *Courier-Journal.* Among the economists were David A. Wells, Edward Atkinson, and F. A. Walker. There were such educators as Theodore Woolsey and W. G. Sumner of Yale, James Russell Lowell and Charles W. Eliot of Harvard, and A. L. Perry of Williams. The lawyers included Charles Francis Adams, Henry Cabot Lodge, and E. P. Wheeler. At least two statesmen attained national prominence: Carl Schurz and Grover Cleveland.

The American liberals who had the most influence on Bowker were such publicists as Schurz, Godkin, Curtis, and Bryant, such religious leaders as Henry Ward Beecher, Washington Gladden, and Edward Everett Hale, and among the economists, Perry, Wells, and Atkinson. In political theory he owed much to Charles Nordhoff's little volume, *Politics for Young Americans,* and Alexander Johnston's *History of American Politics.* Moreover, Bowker belonged to that American generation whose intellectual maturity coincided with their country's discovery of the great English liberal writers. One thinks of the excitement with which young Henry Holt came upon Spencer's *First Principles* in 1865, and the revolutionary effect which John Stuart Mill's essay on Comte had on young Charles Francis Adams, Jr., as he left the Union Army for civilian life. These writers, with Darwin, Tyndall, Huxley, and Arnold, had already become familiar authorities to college seniors in Bowker's graduating class.[4] In addition to John Stuart Mill and Herbert Spencer, the liberal authorities most often mentioned by Bowker include Adam Smith, John Bright, W. S. Jevons, Claude Frédéric Bastiat, J. A. Blanqui, and Luigi Cossa. Through his book reviewing for the *Mail* he was reading widely in the representative Victorians, and much of his thinking showed the impress of Ruskin, Carlyle, and Morris.

Though deriving his chief inspiration and doctrine from such figures, Bowker was fortunate in being closely associated with men who shared his liberal sympathies. Of the City College group, Werner, Wheeler, and Shepard were strong in the faith; amongst the publishers and editors, there were in particular Major Bundy, Frederick Leypoldt, A. D. F. Randolph, and George Haven Putnam. Other liberals

4 See Nevins, *The Emergence of Modern America,* 231–32.

of Bowker's own generation with whom he came into close association at this time were Henry Demarest Lloyd, Arthur W. Milbury, Watson R. Sperry, and Frederick W. Whitridge.

Through these various influences, Bowker evolved a clear-cut liberal philosophy of history and a precise program of action. It was the "chief work of the Christ spirit in history," he believed, "to develop humanity into fullness of life, to bring the mass of men out of that mere existence which is scarcely more than a living death; to bring each man, high or low, out into a greater life than the men of his place in the world enjoyed before him."[5] The meaning of history was the growth of freedom. American history had shown three great stages in this struggle: the establishment of religious freedom by the early colonial settlements, of commercial freedom by the American revolution against British mercantilism in 1776, of social freedom by the defeat of the Southern "slaveocracy" in 1865. The Civil War had only closed one chapter to open another: the attainment of full economic freedom.

In two articles for the *Christian Union* Bowker thoroughly analyzed the demoralizing "legacy of ills" left by the war.[6] Nevertheless he felt, like everyone else, a great optimism about the country's future. He maintained that its basic spirituality was sound, that it was producing a great literature, and that the Centennial celebration of 1876 might well serve to recall the nation to its great ideals.[7] He hoped, indeed, that the Centennial era might be in the history of this nation what the Reformation had been to Christian civilization. New times demanded new policies. The war issues were dead. A great nation faced a new future of industrial expansion. For this new role the country must be put upon a sound basis. According to Bowker this meant, first and foremost, thoroughgoing administrative reform. It also meant reorganization of the civil service, tariff revision, currency reform, and a return to specie payments. Finally, it meant a conscientious program of social reform to improve the lot of the underprivileged. With Lincoln, indeed, Bowker was determined that "this nation, under God, shall have a new birth of freedom."

Free trade was one of the greatest of the international liberal causes. It was the first to claim Bowker's loyalty, and it was one to which he was devoted until his death.

In the United States the protectionist issue became acute after

[5] MS, "Of Sin as Death," 1870.

[6] R. R. B., "The Usefulness of the Centennial," "The Centennial and Citizenship," *Christian Union*, April 5, 26, 1876.

[7] R. R. B., "Easter-Tide," *Evening Mail*, April 16, 1873; R. R. B., *Evening Mail*, September 5, 1870.

1865. The country's moderate tariff structure had been greatly increased during the war. What had begun as a temporary war expedient to help save the Union, however, now came to be demanded as a permanent policy.[8] To a small but influential body of American liberals, this constituted a real threat to a free society. In 1866 they organized the American Free Trade League.

Either during his senior year at college or immediately following his graduation, Bowker attended one of the League's monthly meetings and joined in the public discussion. The initiative he showed so favorably impressed the officers that they invited him to join the ranks. Membership immediately brought acquaintance with a splendid group of intelligent, civic-minded men. The officers included William C. Bryant and zealous young Henry Demarest Lloyd. The ranks were filled with influential publicists, economists, and statesmen, including Carl Schurz, Samuel J. Tilden, Horace White, William Lloyd Garrison, and Henry George.[9] Moreover, American members returning from abroad would bring "fervent wishes of God speed" from Gladstone, Mill, Cobden, Bright, and Herbert Spencer, as well as distinguished French and German economists.[10] It is small wonder that the cause of free trade impressed Bowker as the great issue of his generation.

The attack on the protective tariff by the American Free Trade League made a powerful appeal to logic, to interest, and to conscience. The tariff, it insisted, was "legally organized class discrimination" whereby "adventurers and monopolists can absorb the earnings of the masses by means of special legislation"; it was thus demoralizing to the lawmaker, the manufacturer, the customs official, and the whole mercantile community. It did an injury and injustice to the consumer by raising the price; it represented taxation which did not yield a cent of revenue to the government. By means of it, "capital is diverted from profitable to unprofitable occupations, labor massed in large towns and manufacturing districts instead of being naturally distributed and devoted to the development of our mining and agricultural resources, smuggling called into being and maintained, official corruption fostered, the profits of a few increased at the expense of the many, and our whole people restrained in the rights of property and forced to submit

8 G. H. Putnam, *Memories of a Publisher*, 43; F. W. Taussig, *The Tariff History of the United States*, 174.

9 Others included E. L. Godkin of the *Nation*, Charles Nordhoff of the *Evening Post*, Judge Hoadley, former Governor Jacob D. Cox of Ohio, David A. Wells, Edward Atkinson, William M. Grosvenor, former Governor Randolph of New Jersey, David Dudley Field, O. B. Frothingham, Howard Potter, Caro Lloyd, *Henry Demarest Lloyd*, I, 24–25.

10 Chevalier, Bernard, Demolinari, Wolowski, and Garnier of France; Shutz-Delitch, Rosher, and Prince Smith of Germany. See *Free Trader*, July, 1868.

to a modified form of slavery." Finally, high tariffs were an obstacle to the most efficient international distribution of goods, a barrier to the unity of nations, and a breeder of nationalistic rivalry and war. The League's statement of purpose rang like a clarion call: "To abolish this iniquitous system, to inaugurate a new anti-slavery movement, and unite the whole civilized world into one great commercial and social community, which in all respects save that of government shall be as closely allied as the states of our Union."[11]

The strategy of the League was to force the tariff question into the arena of politics and have it fought out as a national issue. It was certain that, once the issue was squarely before the electorate, the League's campaign of education would lead to tariff reform. To advance this object, a vigorous program was adopted: a headquarters office, two monthly periodicals, lecture tours, branch organizations called the Young Men's Free Trade Clubs, and free distribution of pamphlets and tracts.[12]

In the first period of free-trade activity from 1868 to 1872, Bowker worked as a yeoman in the ranks. With Washington Gladden, William Hayes Ward, and Justin McCarthy, he helped to found the Brooklyn Free Trade League, with Dr. Joshua Leavitt, the capable editor of the *Independent,* as president. Bowker himself became the efficient secretary.[13] He edited a pamphlet giving the organization's platform, constitution, and officers; and he was soon reporting to H. D. Lloyd its ambitious plans for a reference library, reading room, mass meetings, publication of documents, and organization of branch associations. He saw that the *Evening Mail* printed notices of the *Free Trader* issues, and wrote strong reviews of such publications as Bastiat's *Sophisms of Protection.*[14]

From this outpost, Bowker followed closely the varied fortunes of the movement. He deplored the triumph of the wool and copper lobbies in 1868 and the passage of the distasteful Schenck tariff in 1870 in spite of the League's expenditure of $40,000 in a campaign of education. He decried the dangerous protectionist propaganda of the *Tribune's* Horace Greeley and scholarly Henry Carey, and the dismissal of David A. Wells, the capable special commissioner of revenue whose *Report* was becoming a bible for free traders. On the other hand he cheered

11 A.F.T.L. printed notice, April 21, 1869; Brooklyn Free Trade League, printed constitution, etc., 1869.

12 Lloyd, *H. D. Lloyd,* I, 25; preface to second edition of Bastiat's *Sophisms of Protection* (New York, 1870); Fred B. Joyner, *David Ames Wells,* 143.

13 R. R. B., MS Memoir.

14 R. R. B. to H. D. Lloyd, January 5, 1870; H. D. Lloyd to R. R. B., July 13, 1870, February 2, 1872, etc. R. R. B., "Bastiat Americanized," *Free Trader,* November, 1869.

the success of the League in defeating a dozen protectionist Republican congressmen for re-election and in scaring James G. Blaine into a bargain that would give the free traders a majority in the new Committee of Ways and Means in return for supporting his re-election as speaker.

By 1872 the liberal cause reached a high tide. There seemed to be enough Republicans disgusted with Grantism, enough Democrats resentful of Tammany, Repudiation, and Copperheadism, and in both major parties enough supporters of free trade, civil service reform, and reconciliation with the South to justify launching a third party. A Liberal Republican convention was called for May in Cincinnati. Bowker joined the New York and Brooklyn free traders in their running analysis of sources of support and opposition, candidates, and platform planks. He attended the Fifth Avenue Hotel conference to complete pre-cenvention plans, joined in the battle cry, "On to Cincinnati!"

What happened to the free traders was tragedy compounded by fiasco. At Cincinnati they were outmaneuvered in their plans to nominate Charles Francis Adams and were compelled to watch the convention select Horace Greeley, archenemy of free trade. Unable to stomach Greeley, they held a post-cenvention bolt in Steinway Hall at the end of May. This meeting was followed by a bolt within a bolt in the form of a private conference at the Fifth Avenue Hotel on June 20, and when Carl Schurz counseled loyalty to Greeley, twenty-five last-ditchers held "a bolt from a bolt from a bolt" and nominated W. S. Groesbeck of Ohio and Frederick Law Olmstead of New York as their candidates.[15] Bowker, in despair, voted for Grant "under protest" as probably the lesser of two evils, as did Atkinson and others. The dismal frustration of the Liberal Republican movement seemed to deal a paralyzing blow to the liberal program for the duration of Grant's second administration. As for the Free Trade League, its books were closed. "It went to Cincinnati," Bowker declared, "but it never came back," and the Panic of 1873 guaranteed that it would not come back for some time to come. By 1875, tariff reform had lost almost all the ground it had gained in an eight-year fight.[16]

The Centennial year, however, witnessed not only the recovery of the movement from the Liberal Republican debacle, but also the beginning of Bowker's leadership within it. For one thing, new warriors were attracted to the cause—such men as William Graham Sumner at Yale; Isaac Sherman, a leading merchant of the New York Produce Ex-

15 New York *Evening Post*, June 20, 1872; Lloyd, *H. D. Lloyd*, I, 25–38.
16 R. R. B. to A. L. Earle, October 11, 1875.

92

change; Watson R. Sperry, managing editor of the *Evening Post;* the young publisher George Haven Putnam; and Edward H. Van Ingen.[17] A good deal of initiative in the New York group was taken by Abram L. Earle, then serving as New York City comptroller, whom Bowker later described as "my father in the faith of free trade." For another thing, a new strategy was dictated by an analysis of the failure of the old Free Trade League. In Bowker's opinion it had made two mistakes: proposing a revenue reform tariff instead of the principle of free trade and "trying its skill at wire-pulling with the politicians."[18] What was now needed was a patient educational program. Young Henry Demarest Lloyd expressed a similar conviction. "You will never see this Free Trade party of the future coqueting with its enemies. . . . We must have a new party, and new men to run it."[19] The place to begin was a new organization and a new periodical. Bowker helped materially in providing both.

The new organization which Bowker and Earle set up in October, 1875, was the Free Trade Alliance, with the motto "The Field Is the World." F. H. Harrison, a New York merchant resident in Brooklyn, was elected president, A. D. F. Randolph, treasurer, and Earle, secretary. Bowker was given the key post of chairman of the executive committee, on which also served his friend E. M. Shepard. The twenty advisory members included David A. Wells, William Cullen Bryant, Parke Godwin, Anson Phelps Stokes, Robert B. Roosevelt, Dorman B. Eaton, and Thomas Holland. The new free-trade journal which Bowker created was the *New Century,* official organ of the Alliance. Of this interesting journalistic venture, which ran for seven numbers until December, 1876, young Bowker was the managing editor and his friend George Haven Putnam the publisher.

The keynote of the Alliance program was what Bowker described to Wells as "the steady education of the public mind." This meant dissemination of the *New Century,* the publication of useful pamphlets, press appeals, public lectures, and the encouragement of local free-trade units throughout the country. On Bowker's initiative, Sumner was kept busy giving lectures which were then issued in pamphlet form, a publications committee distributed a leaflet recommending titles on political economy which Bowker induced Putnam to carry, and one hundred corresponding members of the Alliance were secured in more than half the states of the Union to act as "apostles of its doctrines, and col-

---

17 Putnam, *Memories of a Publisher,* 40–41.
18 R. R. B., "Education and Free Trade," New York *World,* April 17, 1876.
19 H. D. Lloyd to Henry F. Keenan, June 24, 1872, in Lloyd, *H. D. Lloyd.*

porteurs in distributing its publications."[20] Meanwhile there was direct communication with college professors, librarians, and students.

Bowker was tireless. He stirred up his friends to help win new recruits, sought financial contributions, prepared occasional newspaper articles, and counseled branch associations on organizing tactics. From the beginning of the Centennial year he urged a great free-trade dinner to mark the centenary of the publication of Adam Smith's *Wealth of Nations* in order to "show the public how strong our general movement is, both in argument and in men of character, and in that indirect way influence the conventions."[21] The dinner came off at Delmonico's in December and was a very grand affair. Speeches delivered by Godwin, Bryant, Wells, Sumner, and Atkinson, and letters read from leaders of thought the country over supported the principles of Adam Smith. Bowker's own faith in the appeal to reason was complete. "If the advocates of Free Trade," he wrote in the *World*, "would put half the effort into the education of the American people in political economy that the interested Protectionists have spent in their perversion, we should soon witness the triumph of the cause. And, once triumphant, no interest would dare to ask for the return of a system which will then be seen to be as traitorous to the cause of liberty as it is false to the principles of justice."[22]

During 1877, Bowker promoted two new free-trade organizations to take full tactical advantage of the diverse elements of the movement. In the spring, he and Earle launched the New York Free Trade Club as an association of young reformers to work locally with the International Free Trade Alliance.[23] Francis O. French, a leading banker, was elected president; Graham McAdam, secretary; Bowker served on the executive committee. Putnam, Wheeler, A. P. Stokes, Abram S. Hewitt, Henry Ward Beecher, and S. S. Cox were soon added to the roll. That fall Bowker took the next step of organizing a Council for Tariff Reform to unite the younger elements and the older men still loyal to the almost moribund American Free Trade League. This merger was accomplished at a conference which he caused the Free Trade Club to convene at Saratoga. The meeting proved premature, but the objective was

20 W. G. Sumner to R. R. B., July 24, 1876; see H. E. Starr, *William Graham Sumner,* 234; Putnam, *Memories of a Publisher,* 40; G. H. Putnam to R. R. B., May 8, 1876.
21 R. R. B. to Wells, January 11, 1876; A. L. Earle to R. R. B., April 19, 1876. See R. R. B., MS Memoir.
22 R. R. B., "Education and Free Trade," New York *World,* April 17, 1876.
23 A. L. Earle to R. R. B., May 3, 12, 1877. Others helping Earle and Bowker were a young Springfield lawyer named Pratt, Francis O. French, F. H. Harrison, former president of the Alliance, and W. R. Sperry. The club was incorporated on February 7, 1878.

gained.[24] A council of thirteen was constituted with Wells as chairman, Earle as secretary, and Mahlon Sands as treasurer, while Bowker and Sperry represented the younger men on the executive committee. Actually, Bowker handled the accounts of both the Council and the Free Trade Club since Sands could not spare the time.

With this emplacement on which to mount his artillery, Bowker then fired a mighty salvo for the cause. It took the form of an "Address" to the nation on New Year's Day, 1878, issued in the name of the Council for Tariff Reform. It is an excellent expression of the creed and program of the young liberals, and Bowker must have poured his heart into the stirring words which linked the cause of free trade with the whole American crusade for freedom which had begun in 1776 and had continued through 1812 and 1861.

> Fellow Citizens: . . . Parties have lost their significance and vitality in the confusion of politics; patriotism wanes . . . solid sectionalism opposes in self-defense a party oligarchy. . . . Platforms on both sides truckle to demagogues and betray the real interests of the people, insulting the classes they pretend to favor. Principles no longer inspire parties nor aim ballots. Voters stay away from the polls; our young men, who have come into political life since the war, find nothing to fight for. Political apathy threatens a state that can live only through the energy of self-government. . . .

> We propose to uplift political discussion to pressing issues on which the country, not sections, will divide, believing that patriotic trust over old issues will assure a wider and safe patriotism the country through. We do not propose a third party which shall make votes for its opponents. We do not propose to surrender our forces to either existing party. . . . We do propose to set up, on economic questions, a standard of principles which shall rally a party of honesty, in or from both parties, a party which shall say what it means and do what it says, about which political action shall shape itself as need comes, and which shall call forth an opposition equally avowed.

The "Address" contained an analysis and refutation of the common arguments advanced against honest money and commercial freedom, and an appeal to every citizen to join actively in the crusade.

In addition to creating new machinery for organization and a fresh banner under which to march, Bowker also worked ceaselessly to

24 R. R. B. to M. Sands, December 31, 1877.

press the "steady education of the public mind." He helped to see that cogently-reasoned lectures were given and published.[25] With Putnam, he supervised the planning, publication, and sale of literature.[26] He lent a hand to the distinguished Boston Free Trade League.[27] He proposed a loan fund of $100,000 to support the educational drive, inaugurated a three-year plan of expansion for the club, and raised $6,000.[28] He particularly took pains to prevent friction between the older and less active membership of the American Free Trade League and the younger men, and between the absolute free traders and the moderate revenue reformers. In this last matter Bowker was a practical gradualist, and definitely preferred to get strong support behind a program of moderate next-steps rather than to confine the program to a few purists.[29] Indeed, at this time, as a few years later when the issue became more bitter, Bowker was peculiarly fitted by temperament to reconcile extremes.

Nothing, however, could conceal the fact that the public was indifferent. During 1879 only fifteen new members had been admitted to the Free Trade Club to make a total of forty-six; there was a treasury deficit, and several worthy projects had to be abandoned for lack of funds.[30] It was clear that free trade could not be made a national issue in the election of 1880. Therefore, Bowker and his friends set themselves to work for 1884, when they hoped the nation would elect a president committed to this cause.

At the same time that young Bowker enlisted in the liberal crusade for economic freedom, he became profoundly interested in the liberal concern for a more responsible political democracy. Ideally, government should be the wise use of political power to promote the general welfare. However, as they watched Congress succumb to the protectionists and the Liberal Republican movement die away, as they studied the methods of Tammany in New York and of the "Canal Ring" in Albany and followed the sickening story of graft, corruption and fraud in the second Grant administration, liberals could see that the ideal

25 New York Free Trade Club to Wells, September 26, 1878, Wells Papers, Library of Congress.

26 Putnam, *Memories of a Publisher*, 42–43.

27 R. R. B. to A. Milbury, June 30, 1880; A. B. Mason to R. R. B., December 22, 28, October 2, 8, 1876.

28 Memorandum, September 4, 1878; G. H. Putnam to R. R. B., February 20, March 19, April 23, 1880; R. R. B. to D. A. Wells, June 12, 1880. Wells Papers, Library of Congress.

29 R. R. B. to D. A. Wells, December 28, 31, 1877; to M. Sands, December 31, 1877; to A. L. Earle, June 30, 1880; to A. W. Milbury, June 30, 1880.

30 New York Free Trade Club Report, December 18, 1879.

was not working out in practice. Bowker offered a diagnosis of the causes for this breakdown of American democracy in two Centennial articles for the *Christian Union* which identified three demoralizing consequences of the Civil War.[31]

The first was military habits of mind, such as the transfer of the sense of personal responsibility to impersonal organizations, unthinking obedience to superiors, stubborn partisanship, and the military glamour that could place a soldier in the White House and cloak the misdeeds of the Republican party in the national flag. The second was the wave of greedy speculation which had popularized "the earning of money without equivalent work." The third was a mood of apathy, aggravated in the South by "the reckless use of the Negro vote by irresponsible carpet-baggers" and in the North by the exploitation of the immigrant vote by the city machine. Interwoven with these evils was the fact that the tremendous extension of the powers and machinery of federal, state, and municipal government had not only made office-holding a profession of large extent and power, but had served to confuse the voter in his choice of candidates. At the same time, the diversion of public attention from local to national issues had given the local and state "rings" their opportunity for plunder.

Bowker's prescription of what was needed to make democracy work followed from the diagnosis. First, every individual must be taught to assume moral responsibility for his daily acts; second, issues must be clarified for the average voter, and the voter must be educated to grasp the essential principles involved in national problems; third, leadership must be enlightened and responsible; fourth, the power of the political machine must be broken by a reform of the civil service and the organization of the liberal "conscience vote" into a bloc which would be independent of parties.

Bowker's preachment and practice of the political responsibility of the individual was continuous. The salvation of a country, he insisted in the Centennial articles, depended on the moral quality of its actions not alone at great moments of crisis, but in the hourly, daily routines of ordinary civilian life. The central thing was "the feeling of personal, continuous and absolute responsibility" doing "what comes to hand from day to day with the highest motives in the pettiest work . . . when no drums beat nor are flags flying."

Strange as it may seem at first sight, it is commonly more easy to men to die for a principle than to live for it. The basest clay

[31] R. R. B., "The Usefulness of the Centennial," "The Centennial and Citizenship," *Christian Union,* April 5, 26, 1876.

may be kindled to heroic glow in the heat of a nation's patriotic ardor, but the light which shines of its own shining, surely, day by day, amid the quenching discouragements of years that demand commonplace duty in lieu of heroic achievement, it is that, after all, which makes history splendid. A country has even more need of steadfast citizens than of great soldiers. . . . Out of the daily duty of a people—and of all the people—grows the vigor and endurance of their nation.

"The *daily* duty of *all* the people"—this is the clue to Bowker's conception of what must characterize a democracy if it is going to survive.[32]

The second point, namely, the need for civic education on basic principles, led Bowker to the varied activities which culminated in his organization of the Society for Political Education, discussed later. The third point was the need for enlightened and responsible leadership, and this Bowker took to heart. The people, he wrote, must voice themselves and act through leaders; if not good ones, then bad ones. This means that, if "the men they have trained for the work in their free schools and their colleges will not come forward, they must take those who offer."

A visit to Congress in 1874, which he described in the *Evening Mail,* stirred his scorn for the ignorance and provincialism of the legislators he listened to.[33] It was necessary that college graduates who had studied the basic principles of social science and had the perspective of history should assume political responsibility. This was a recurring plea with Bowker and his circle. In his fraternity convention address at Utica in 1876, he vigorously presented the need to put action into scholarship. "The scholar is not the social force he should be," he warned. "It is because [he] has too often lacked faith in himself, faith in the people, faith in the progress of right, that he fails to do his full part to help forward that right. . . . Let him show the qualities of leadership, and the people will hear him eagerly, follow him gladly."[34] Bowker had absolutely no sympathy with the argument that a suffrage limited to the educated would be better than universal suffrage. If democracy has failed, Bowker insisted, "it is not because of the ignorant, but because of the educated; not because the people would not learn, but because the teachers would not teach. It is the educated citizen, indignant at

32 See also R. R. B., "The Political Responsibilities of the Individual," *Atlantic Monthly,* September, 1880, pp. 320–28.
33 R. R. B., "The Nation's Library," *Evening Mail,* February 17, 1874.
34 Utica *Morning Herald* and *Daily Observer,* May 25, 1876.

the demoralization of 'democracy'—which he looks upon as something apart from himself—that we must cry out: 'Thou art the man.' "[35]

Bowker's fourth point had to do with civil service reform, which became an increasingly important plank in the liberal platform. The existing political system meant inadequate and irresponsible data for appointments, complete distraction in Washington after a change of administration, political demoralization, public corruption, and the discouragement of the best men from going into politics. The liberals wished to make the civil service efficient, clean, reasonably economical, and an honorable career for honorable men. In such figures as Schurz, Cox, Godkin, Curtis, and Horace White, the cause had excellent leadership. Bowker and his friends Shepard, Wheeler, Putnam, and Whitridge worked in the ranks. They hailed the passage in 1871 of a Senate bill introduced by Schurz providing a civil service commission to draw up rules and regulations for the service, and they hailed Grant's appointment of Curtis as chairman of the first commission. But in spite of strong planks in the Liberal Republican and regular Republican platforms of 1872, the politicians in Congress strangled the Civil Service Commission by refusing it funds. Not until 1877 was the cause revived.

Bowker's interest was continuous. In 1878 he discussed with Curtis the organization of a National Civil Service Reform League, actually launched three years later.[36] In 1879 he tried to have introduced into the House a simple bill that would do no more than provide for an examination and period of probation similar to the new regime in the New York Post Office. He investigated reforms inaugurated by Silas W. Burt, who had been appointed naval officer of the Port of New York by President Hayes to replace Cornell.[37] In the spring of 1880 he wrote the civil service plank of the national Republican platform adopted by the Chicago convention. He induced Curtis to write a pamphlet on the subject for his new Society for Political Education and urged him to push a bill in Congress.[38] In 1883, the cause finally triumphed.

Bowker's belief in democracy rested on a solid liberal conviction: people can be trusted to make right decisions when issues are clearly and simply presented to them.

> Most men have fair common sense, that is, the power to make a right judgment on simple questions clearly presented. Most men

[35] R. R. B., Introduction to *Alphabet of Finance*, by Graham McAdam (first published in 1876; reprinted in 1880).

[36] G. W. Curtis to R. R. B., November 4, 1878.

[37] Silas W. Burt to R. R. B., January 13, 1880.

[38] R. R. B. to G. W. Curtis, June 30, 1880.

have also common honesty, that is, the will to act as their judgment tells them is right. These are the chief grounds of faith in democracy. . . . It is on such political optimism that our theory of government is based, nor is any system of government, or social machinery of any sort possible, except with some belief in humanity. Every organization presupposes true men, somewhere.[39]

A basic need, therefore, was to educate the voter.

Many liberals recognized the need. *Nation* editor E. L. Godkin in New York and Special Commissioner of Revenue David A. Wells in Washington were each impressed by American ignorance of political economy and determined to educate the public on the subject. President M. B. Anderson of Rochester University wrote Wells that rich businessmen should be induced to endow chairs for political education. President Seelye of Amherst and President White of Cornell made similar statements.[40] The wave of strikes and "radicalism" that swept the country in 1877 and 1878 confirmed the belief. When Bowker pondered the arguments used by a Greenback-labor candidate, he found himself impressed less by the speaker's class consciousness than by the heretical nature of his economics. In an *Evening Post* article Bowker called them "effectively specious," filled with "vapid omniscience" and "astounding dogmatics."[41] The moral was clear: the "thinking" classes had better educate the voters in sound theory.

Bowker was constantly associated with individuals and enterprises interested in educating the voters on public issues. The American Free Trade League, the Brooklyn Free Trade League, the International Free Trade Alliance, and the New York Free Trade Club had each disseminated "sound" information by lectures, pamphlets, and books. As editor of the *New Century* and a member, with George Haven Putnam, of the Free Trade Club's literature committee, he had organized bibliographies and reviews. In 1875 he became a member of the Brooklyn Social Science Association and the following year became one of the original signers of a declaration inaugurating the Political Science Association. In the Centennial year, he printed in the *Publishers' Weekly* a full-page "List of Works on Finance and Political Science" because, so the notice stated, the national elections for some years would turn on issues in these fields. With Leypoldt, he offered in the same year a prize for the best bibliography in political science.[42]

[39] R. R. B., Introduction to *Alphabet of Finance.*

[40] M. B. Anderson to D. A. Wells, May 20, 1879; Wells Papers, Library of Congress; J. H. Seelye to James Buell, October 31, 1879, Wells Papers. *loc. cit.*

[41] "The Greenback Orator," *Evening Post*, October 24, 1878.

[42] *Publishers' Weekly*, March 11, 1876; *ibid.*, January 15, February 19, March 18, 1876.

One of Bowker's pet schemes was to organize a New York reform club to push the entire liberal program. "The important thing," he wrote to Wells, "is to get all thinkers and workers toward our end together for talk and work." He would build the club around an easily accessible lecture hall, a general reading room, and a committee on publications. "It is of the utmost importance," he urged, "to lay hold on the college men whose faith is all right but who need to be committed to good works, and quite as much on a still wider public, those who are thinking and reading on the subject of their own motion, business and working men who should see this thing as a question of bread and butter, etc. These are now only atoms; brought together they would make a strong working force to disseminate our ideas. You can't reach them by tracts as you can by voice; you want to get face to face with them." Bowker tried to launch such an organization in 1875, but Wells and the others were "too busy," and the matter was dropped.[43] This scheme, however, was a precedent for the New York Reform Club, which Bowker helped to found in 1888.

A second pet project of Bowker's was to found a liberal newspaper that would push the cause. In his birthday memorandum of 1878 he recorded his ambition to head such an enterprise. He even went so far as to broach the scheme to a friend who he thought would make a proper editor. "It seems to me," Bowker wrote, the times call for a cheap weekly People's Paper,—using simple phrases made to take among workingmen and there to throw its force against the semi-communistic notions which are growing dangerously. . . . I mean to push this plan through at some time."[44] Nothing was to come of this scheme, however, until 1888.

Bowker's third project was equally practical and was immediately realized: a national organization, nonpartisan and nonpolitical, to publish and distribute selected works bearing on political problems and to promote the reading, study, and discussion of these works. By November, 1879, he was planning it with his friends; by the following spring it was organized and incorporated as the Society for Political Education. Turning to Independents among both Republicans and Democrats in working out the preliminary plan of organization, Bowker kept in continuous touch with Wells and secured useful suggestions from Curtis, Shepard, Putnam, Sumner, and M. L. Scudder. One of his most helpful collaborators proved to be Richard Dugdale, an Englishman who had inherited a small competency providing freedom for

43 R. R. B. to D. A. Wells, January 11, 1876; D. A. Wells to R. R. B., January 13, 1876.

44 R. R. B. Letter Book, addressee illegible, October 7, 1878.

various humanitarian researches such as the pioneering work in the study of criminal inheritance, "The Jukes," which made him famous. Dugdale was a gentle, conscientious apostle of reform whom Bowker had known as a co-worker on the executive committee of the Prison Association, had befriended, and had drawn into the circle of Independents.[45]

As finally decided upon, the Society was to be as simple and as national in representation as possible. There was to be no president, so that it would not be known or judged by the beliefs of any one person. Of the executive committee of twenty-five, Bowker became the chairman, Dugdale the first hard-working secretary, and Shepard the treasurer. Wells headed a finance subcommittee including Horace White and George S. Coe, president of the American Exchange National Bank of New York. Sumner gladly accepted a post, C. F. Adams was "very happy" to be added,[46] and Atkinson was willing to serve. Others who joined the executive committee included Worthington C. Ford, Franklin MacVeagh, and President A. D. White of Cornell. Five members of the executive committee served as regional secretaries for the sections into which the country was divided.

Bowker prepared a statement of principles on which the organizers were agreed, but which were not necessarily binding on the members. An admirable summary of the Independent creed, it included such objectives as the secret ballot, civil service reform, the divorce of local government from national party issues, sound money, free bargaining for labor, tariff for revenue only, control of corporations, and freedom of the press. Forty years later Bowker wrote of these principles: "It is interesting to note how many of these have been accepted as axiomatic, while on others, the battle is still to be fought and won. They are, in fact, landmarks from which political progress may be calculated."[47]

The Society sponsored two publication enterprises. Each year it was to select and publish in a uniform edition and at cost price a series of three or four basic works which would constitute a growing *Library of Political Education* which active members would pledge themselves to read. In the second place, it would publish and distribute to its members each year four *Economic Tracts*. Lists of additional books on current topics would be circulated from time to time, and the Society would assist in the formation of "reading and corresponding circles and

45 W. C. Ford, *Library Journal*, December 1, 1933, Part II; Putnam, *Memories of a Publisher*, 171.

46 W. G. Sumner to R. R. B., April 5, 1880; C. F. Adams to R. R. B., April 27, 1880.

47 R. R. B., "Mugwump Retrospect and Prospect," New York *Evening Post*, September 5, 1919.

clubs." For the first series of books in the *Library*,[48] the Society published Charles Nordhoff's *Politics for Young Americans,* Alexander Johnston's *History of American Politics,* A. L. Perry's *Introduction to Political Economy,* and Graham McAdam's *Alphabet of Finance.* Of the four *Economic Tracts* published, the most important was a priced and classified bibliography of books on political economy, taxation, currency, land tenure, free trade, and protection, the Constitution, civil service, and co-operation. This tract was the result of an interesting collaboration between Bowker and Sumner, who wrote that he had long needed, and long contemplated, a list of this kind. It was completed by Dugdale with the help of Wells, Putnam, and W. E. Foster.

Bowker left for London before the Society's first year of work was fairly begun, but the reports were quite encouraging. Before the second year was over, the Society had acquired fifteen hundred active members, had launched six auxiliary societies, distributed six thousand copies of the *Tracts,* encouraged the formation of reading circles, lecture series, and political forums. Dugdale wrote that he was receiving ten to thirty letters of inquiry and three memberships a day, that the newspapermen had treated the Society "magnificently," and that it had a list of over 400 papers on which it could rely for notices. W. P. Garrison, Putnam, Shepard, and Wells, all wrote Bowker that the Society was a "practical success" and thriving. A proposal to merge the revived Civil Service Reform Association with the Society was considered and rejected, although Dugdale became the secretary of both organizations.[49]

The Society, which kept up its program until 1891,[50] could not have had a very great effect on American opinion. Its appeal was too little to self-interest, its membership was neither wealthy nor organized, and its opponents were far too powerful. The "easy money" cause enjoyed a much more dramatic presentation through the disciples of Ben Butler, Wendell Phillips, Peter Cooper, D. P. Morton, and Ignatius Donnelly. The high-tariff cause was made respectable and politically formidable by such well-financed and ably conducted lobbies as the Pennsylvania Industrial League, the American Iron and Steel Association, the Republican League, and the Protective Tariff League. Nevertheless, Bowker's Society performed a useful service in pioneering the composition and dissemination of popular books on the social sciences.

It was certainly important to make the machinery of American democracy work, but the crux of the problem for liberals was how to influence

48 See Bibliography for the full list of publications by the Society.
49 G. H. Putnam to R. R. B., November 14, 1880; E. M. Shepard to R. R. B., January 5, 1881.
50 See chapter XIII below.

the national parties which controlled the government machinery. Referred to variously as "the intelligent vote," the "educated vote," "the conscience vote," supposedly the vote that put principle above narrow self-interest, Bowker's element was always in a small minority. How could they make their influence count? Bowker was deeply interested in the problem and gradually matured his answer. In the first place, liberals must become independents, ready to switch their support from one party to another as circumstances of leadership and platforms dictated. (Such a proposition was politically scandalous at any time in the nineteenth century, but from 1868 to 1884 is was commonly thought to be close to political treason.) In the second place, they must learn the dangers of third-party politics, the possibilities of "scratching" the names of undesirable candidates from the ballot, and threatening the party managers with a bolt if conventions did not nominate good men. Above all, they must learn to work together as a bloc, for, as Bowker was to point out, they could actually constitute a balance-of-power vote. These techniques had a considerable success in 1876, 1879, 1880, and 1884.

The first lesson in Bowker's political education was that liberals could not hope to influence the local ward and district organizations or the primary vote. He joined his local Republican ward association and discovered the worst. He found a closed corporation meeting first in a stable loft, next in the back of a saloon, which resented his presence as an outsider. He found that there were too many candidates to know without more steady attendance at "the political purgatory of the ward meeting" than amateurs were able to afford.[51] He found that, when he did try to "defeat the machine at the primaries," he could be completely bamboozled out of his vote by clever organization men.

Bowker's second lesson was that the Republican party was not divinely inspired. He had grown up with an intense assurance that the principles of freedom were embodied in the Republican party, and in 1868 he had, with many other liberals, confidently placed his faith in Grant. But before the new administration was a year old, he lost faith in both President and party. A third lesson was learned in 1872 in observing the fate of the Liberal Republican movement and realizing how impractical third-party politics could be. The alternative seemed to be the development of a cohesive liberal bloc which would stand ready to shift its support from one party to another.

On Independence Day, 1870, Bowker drew up a memorandum of "Party Ultimates" which contrasted the two major parties in parallel

[51] Bowker, "The Republican Party for 1880," New York *Evening Post,* December 12, 1879; "Scratch and Bolt," New York *Daily Tribune,* April 29, 1876.

columns as to origins, principles, methods, and purposes. It is highly interesting evidence of Bowker's early political seriousness. Condensed and paraphrased, it contains the following ideas:

The Democratic Party:

> The one continuous party. The party in practice, of the past; in ideal, of the future. The party of principle, representing the sovereignty and entire personal freedom of the individual; radical in its principles, conservative and even stationary in its actions; its weakness the inadaptability of perfect principles to an imperfect state. A party based on the unstable combination of the landed gentry and the urban lower classes; the party of decentralization, state sovereignty, individualism, centrifugal; symbolized by Manton Marble's *World,* by Douglas.

The Republican Party:

> The party of the present, pragmatic, opportunistic, without first principles; radical in its actions, "but in ultimates, less so than the Democrats"; its failure the result of attempts to perpetuate itself by dead issues, to render everlasting an ephemeracy. A party based on the unity of the great middle class; the party of centralization, union; centripetal; symbolized by Greeley's *Tribune,* Lincoln.

The conclusion of such an analysis was that each party had its assets and its liabilities, and that a conscientious voter could not afford to tie himself up permanently to either party, a conclusion given strong impetus by the thought and example of Carl Schurz. Bowker's Centennial article in the *Christian Union* made his new gospel of independency explicit:

> The party that is the honest one in the nation may be practically the dishonest one in the state or city issues. . . . The independent voter may be a Republican in a national, a Democrat in a state, and a third party reformer in a city issue, and *therefore* be the one consistent man in the crowd!
>
> The independent voter of today is the independent soldier of a hundred years ago. His ballot is the bullet of the bloodless revolution for which we must hope and work. He has had for some time a guerrilla fight, like the farmers who popped away at the British, each for himself, from behind the stone walls of the Concord turnpike, but the force is now getting to be pretty strong.[52]

The election of 1876 seemed to call for just the kind of political in-

[52] R. R. B., "The Centennial and Citizenship," *Christian Union,* April 26, 1876.

dependence on the part of liberals to which Bowker was now committed. The scandalous corruption of federal officers, congressmen, cabinet officers, and foreign ministers during the Grant regime made it imperative to get the government into new hands. The Democratic party had disqualified itself with liberals when it failed to repudiate its inflationist wing. A third party was not practicable. The only course left was to put pressure on the Republican national convention to defeat all the Old Guard contenders: Grant himself, who was being boomed for a third term, Oliver P. Morton, James G. Blaine, and that archenemy of all New York liberals, Roscoe Conkling. The movement steadily gained strength and was climaxed by the Independent Reform Conference held at the Fifth Avenue Hotel in New York on May 15. Persistent pressure at the Cincinnati convention capped the climax. The Old Guard was defeated, Hayes was nominated, and the civil service plank in the platform was an obvious recognition of the influence of the liberals.[53] When Hayes was finally inaugurated, the Independents had further cause for satisfaction in the cabinet appointments, which placed Carl Schurz in charge of the Interior Department, Evarts in State, and completely ignored Conkling.

Bowker worked for the success of this reform campaign in many ways and enthusiastically attended the May 15 conference.[54] Most interesting, however, for the light they throw on his developing gospel of political independency were the three letters he wrote to the *Tribune*.[55] The first one, entitled "Statesman vs. Politician," declared bluntly that Bowker's generation would support the Republican party only if it were true to basic Republican principles; that if the party meant Morton, Blaine, or Conkling, then Bowker and his fellow liberals were not Republicans and would vote against the party.

Bowker's second *Tribune* letter, entitled "Scratch and Bolt," was aimed at the May 15 conference of Independent Republicans. In it he claimed that the most effective means open to liberals of controlling the party was neither the party primary nor a third party, but an advance threat delivered to nominating conventions to bolt the party whose leaders played false with them. He described the rights to scratch unpopular nominations on a ballot and to bolt an unacceptable party as "two divine rights given to the American people which I, for one, propose to exercise." He shrewdly observed that the so-called intelligent Republican voter was impotent because he was so consistently

[53] H. J. Eckenrode, *Rutherford B. Hayes,* 114–15, 128–29; *Nation,* September 25, 1879.
[54] R. R. B. to Brooklyn Seventh Ward Association, December 10, 1884.
[55] *Tribune,* April 15, 29, June 10, 1876.

partisan. The politician knew that, "talk as he will before the election, there is no one less likely to vote against his party when the time comes." Bowker boldly pointed to Curtis as proof:

> Mr. George William Curtis is himself the best illustration of the timidity, as of the patriotism and purity of this class, who need only bravery to give them the command they may have if they will. . . . Each year he has protested nobly; each year—until now— when the time to act came, he has "knuckled down." He didn't know he would; but the politicians did.

In spite of this rather blunt public reference to his political record, Curtis wrote Bowker a friendly word appreciating his efforts, and other letters to the press suggested that Bowker had hit a welcome note.[56]

Bowker's third *Tribune* letter appeared four days before the Cincinnati convention and sought to drive home the argument that the Independents held the balance of power. He even called the Independent vote the real party in power, for "The Democrats cannot win, the Republicans must lose without it." Pointing out that the winning majority in a presidential election was commonly about 10 per cent of the vote, he argued that "six percent of the voting citizens can smash the slate of either party and put the other in power. . . . Parties were never more nearly equal than now; the balance of power which is the real power, never resided in fewer votes; an independent single voter never counted for more." Finally, he made a passionate plea that each single independent voter do his duty.

> This six percent is made up of votes that count one. You, John Smith, at your cross-roads village, desiring to do some honest thing for your country, you are the party in power. You, Robert Doe, in your brown-stone front, lamenting that it's no use for culture to go into politics, you are the party in power. This is your year. The leaden bullet of 1776 is a paper bullet in your hands today; you also may fire a shot "heard around the world," in defense of American liberties. . . . John Smith, and Robert Doe, express your opinion. Do it by word of mouth, do it by discussions in your local newspapers, do it by letters to your representatives in Congress or in Convention. These things tell.

In the Hayes election Bowker had seen what the liberals could do when sufficiently aroused. However, he was critical of their lack of organization, and now found himself wondering how their influence could be made a more continuous and permanent factor in American

[56] G. W. Curtis to R. R. B., May 8, 1876; F. A. H. in *Tribune,* May 6, 1876.

politics. During the winter of 1876 he discussed with his friend Talcott Williams, editor of the Philadelphia *Press,* plans "by which 2,000,000 voters can be taught sound doctrine and the intelligent nucleus of a party organized whose only object should be the public good."[57] Bowker made three proposals: a public record of liberal principles and policies to be endorsed by prominent citizens having political weight; a "Postal Card Platform" by means of which voters might bring their preferences directly to the attention of their congressmen; and a "Literary Bureau" such as Tilden had so effectively used to supply general news and sound doctrine to small country newspapers, and to hold together local workers in each Congressional district. In 1878, Bowker took up the "public record" scheme with G. W. Curtis and C. F. Adams, drawing up a set of liberal principles which were finally merged with the platform of the Society for Political Education.

Between 1868 and 1878 Bowker had learned much concerning the need and the possibilities of independent political action. He had worked to secure a suitable New York delegation to the Liberal Republican convention in 1872. During the Centennial year he had preached the gospel in six articles, in the preface to McAdam's book, and in the college oration at Utica. Between 1876 and 1879 he proposed machinery to sustain Independent influence on Congress to his friends in New York, Philadelphia, and Boston. By 1879 he was ready to assume leadership of the New York Independents and organize them into an exceedingly effective campaign committee which was to make history in the state election of that year. At the height of the campaign, Bowker issued a ringing declaration that well summarizes his thought:

> We want a vigorous Protestantism in our politics, a new reformation, appealing from creeds that mean nothing in practice to the individual—to the individual conscience of right and wrong; a new emancipation from the heirarchy of office holders and the slaveocracy of party whips. There is, indeed, now a crisis in this country, which demands a new anti-slavery crusade. It is the struggle of the people against the politicians, not easy to fight, and with none of the heroics about it.[58]

Bowker shared with his fellow liberals an unshakable conviction that the world was subject to natural law, but he carried this belief further than most of them did. Each distinct area of human life, he believed, was subject to its own peculiar set of laws. The spiritual law required

[57] T. Williams to R. R. B., December 22, 1876.

[58] "Political Responsibility of the Individual," *Atlantic Monthly,* September, 1880.

that man place God and not himself at the center of the picture; the moral law required that man subordinate his lower self to his higher self and personal indulgence to the public good; the biological law required observance of the given laws of health; the economic law required free trade. Violation of natural law brought its own inevitable consequences. "Let those aspirants who disdain Nature and her laws have a care," he warned. "In the physical world, it has been well written, there is no forgiveness of sin."[59] Righteousness, whether in an individual or a nation, was thus common-sense conformity with conditions of well-being which could not be blinked away. Two corollaries were self-evident. Where the natural laws were not known, they should be discovered; where they were known, they should be applied. "What is wanted is not nostrums," he wrote of economic problems, "*our* notion, each different, but such investigation of the subject as will bring out the basic principle on which the issue must be permanently decided."

As is evident from the statement of the business of the scholar or "worlds-man" quoted at the beginning of this chapter and from his birthday resolutions of 1878, the field of Bowker's particular concern was to be the social sciences. His faith in what the scholar might do here was complete.

> By the aid of the scientific method on which he relies to verify progress, history, the study of the past, becomes to the scholar, as sociology, a science of the present which gives the key to the future. He is enabled to study and discern his own age, as he has studied those gone by. . . . And in educing these ideas and bringing them into the domain of the will, he makes sociology an art.[60]

Through much of his study and writing Bowker sought to grasp and communicate sociology as a science; through much of his reform activity he sought to use sociology as an art.

In the field of economics, Bowker early worked out an adaptation of the Manchester school and the German or historical school which stood up remarkably well during the next thirty years. He had no occasion to take back in the eighties what he had believed in the seventies. With regard to American currency, for instance, it was clear as daylight to him that the legal-tender act was contrary to natural law, so "having thrown the government, by the legal tender act, in opposition to nature, human effort must get it back into the course of nature." As a sound-money man he opposed the "heresies" of the greenbackers and the free-silver men. As a champion of the free market he attacked the

[59] *Herald of Health*, May, 1870.
[60] R. R. B., *The Arts of Life*, 17–18.

fallacy that there could be such a thing as overproduction, or that food prices could be too low for the farmers' good even during the great harvest year of 1878.[61] Similarly, Bowker never went back on what he wrote in *Economics for the People* in 1886. Moreover, the chapter on business in *The Arts of Life* of 1900 only slightly modified *Of Work and Wealth* of 1883. In his own mind, the difference between the "old" and the "new" schools of economics was slight:

> The old political economy indeed thought first of things; the new economics thinks first of men—and this is better. But there is no more need of a new economics than of a new religion. . . . True theory becomes actual practice; and an enlightened self-interest *is* altruistic in high degree. The aim of economics is gain. But greed is not gain. Selfishness and self-interest are not the same. For men cannot live to best result except in the light of the larger good. Here economics shades into ethics, and cannot be separated from it.[62]

It is clear that Bowker was no believer in simple laissez-faire. He was a strong believer in social responsibility, and would not tolerate a smug indifference to social evils. "We laissez-faire people," he told a British audience in 1880, "have to remember that we are not to let ill enough but well enough alone."[63] When the papers carried the harrowing story of a railway accident in which a derailing coach crushed more than twenty passengers and reported that "no one was to blame," Bowker wrote a satirical poem upbraiding this official attitude of indifference.[64] Improving the lot of the underprivileged and promoting social justice were from the beginning an integral part of his liberalism. In his own case this came to mean an active interest in poor relief, social settlement work, workingmen's homes, prison reform, and free public education.

Nothing is more characteristic of Bowker's liberal position than his attitude toward poor relief. He made it clear that something definitely should be done about the wretched conditions of the underprivileged, equally clear that this should not be done by the government. His own solution called for carefully planned charity by the well-to-do. In his essay "Getting at the Masses" he made three criticisms of the prevailing "city missionary" program: that it failed to co-ordinate sanitary, educational, and religious reform; that it failed to develop means whereby the "best of the common people" might them-

61 "The Great Harvest Year," *Evening Post*, December 4, 1878.
62 R. R. B., *The Arts of Life*, 102.
63 At Edinburgh Social Science Congress (London Journal, October, 1880).
64 "No One to Blame!" *Independent*, August 17, 1871.

selves be interested in helping to get at the worst; and that charity programs were not encouraged to develop naturally into self-support-ing organizations.[65] Bowker urged the kind of help that encouraged self-help. "It is much the better plan," he argued, "to lend rather than to give." The real core of Bowker's thinking was a specific plan for the formation of a society with about $5,000 capital to sponsor in various cities self-managing, and eventually self-supporting, social centers equipped with rooms for meetings, games, and reading. It was a striking anticipation of the social settlement program which years later he helped to institute.[66]

A more striking example of Bowker's liberalism in both its strong and its weak points is found in a provocative editorial he wrote for the *Christian Union* entitled "Charity,—And the Commune!"

> This is a matter of vital present importance when a political party can be built upon the principle that there is an easier way of earning a living than by working for it, or the political ideal of a bankrupt nation of government-coddled paupers. Unwise char-ity is the seed of pauperism, blossoming in the blood-red flower of the Commune. That kindly and wise helpfulness with which the rich, reverent of their responsibilities, should reach out to their needy and deserving brethren is the best remedy for the social disease of revengeful discontent."[67]

Bowker stressed the need of three reforms in the administration of char-ity: to officer the volunteer army of willing recruits by a professional staff of scientific philanthropists; to eliminate the duplication of char-ities, prevent waste, expose both fake benefactors and fake beneficiaries; and to ground charity on "sound principles" so that it would not "con-flict with the immutable laws."

> It must seek to help men to their feet, not to encourage them to lie on their backs,—to graduate them from pauperism into pro-ductive labor. This is not easy to do. . . . But it is better to have brought one man, after many years, out into the sunshine of self-support than to have helped promiscuously a dozen families who are none the better off for all the helping.

Bowker wrote an editorial for the *Tribune* commending the work of the State Charities Aid Association, and an article for the *Christian*

65 *Christian Union,* June, 1870.
66 See chapter XVI below.
67 *Christian Union,* October 9, 1878.

Union analyzing the program and accomplishments of the Brooklyn Bureau of Charities.[68]

The public conscience was as yet unaroused by the shocking slums springing up in every American city, but Bowker and his fellow liberals often discussed the problem.[69] When Shepard went abroad in 1876 he wrote Bowker that in no city of Europe had he seen, "even proportionately, half the wretchedness or apparent poverty one sees in the streets of New York." Bowker encouraged Bundy to print articles on decent low-cost housing in the *Mail,* and discussed developments in the field with his free trade friend Abram L. Earle.

Bowker wrote a scathing denunciation in *Old and New* of the average housewife's exploitation of her servant girls with a fervid plea for a more enlightened attitude.[70] He visited the Clark Institution for Deaf-Mutes and the Northampton Asylum for the Insane and pondered the hopeful achievement of the first and the tragic picture of human waste in the second.[71] He became particularly interested in prison reform, a subject which had not yet attracted much attention. In the fall of 1871 he offered the *Independent* a manuscript on the problem. In 1872 he became a member of the New York Prison Association and showed such conscientious interest in its program that he was elected to its executive committee five years later along with Dorman B. Eaton and Richard Dugdale. A characteristic concern, expressed in his essay, "Our Crimes Against Crime," published in the *Herald of Health,*[72] was that prisoners be allowed to work at trades for wages with which to help support their families and effect their own rehabilitation, and that means be found to develop such socially constructive feelings of the prisoner as home loyalty and love of independence.

Nothing, finally, better illustrates Bowker's liberal faith than his belief in experimental science and the scientific attitude. In an article for *Appleton's Journal* Bowker pleaded for observation and experimentation.[73] He deplored "the fears of timid folk" on the one hand, and the unreasoning ridicule of closed minds on the other.

It has always been the way of the world, first to be afraid of, then to pooh-pooh, then to wonder at, at last to investigate, those things which men could not explain to themselves. . . . There is no call to

68 *Tribune,* November 28, 1878; *Christian Union,* December 11, 1878.
69 E. M. Shepard to R. R. B., June 24, 1876; A. L. Earle to R. R. B., August 8, 1872.
70 *Old and New,* October, 1871.
71 See unpublished MS, "Of Sin as Death."
72 February, 1872.
73 "Science and the Spirits," *Appleton's Journal,* January 20, 1872.

fear "more light"; knowledge is power, not weakness; man has thus far profited by every new development of science. . . . We cannot afford to be laughed out of progress. Science has its grandest work before it in the investigation of the mysterious agencies which have frightened men too long.

Bowker had found a banner to fight under, and had enlisted in the ranks of the goodly company who were following where it led. He marched on with them through the years, seeing their numbers now decrease, now grow, but firm in his faith that he was fighting on the side of the right.

VIII

Fathering the Mugwumps
in 1879

LIBERALS GENERALLY AGREED that the Hayes administration had
made a good beginning toward restoring honest government after
the Grant debacle, but they felt that 1880 was a crucial year to
press forward the liberal program. Administrative reform, civil service
reform, tariff reform, and sound-money legislation were by no means
assured. Yet the old dilemma of party remained. Which party could
the liberals use to advance their cause? The Democrats had just disqualified themselves by abusing their control of Congress to repeal the
federal election law in a way that most Republicans, and not a few liberals like Curtis, immediately interpreted as tantamount to revolution
and treason. The Republican party, however, had been little changed
by the Hayes administration. Grantism still hung like a pall over the
party of Lincoln. None of the party managers, whether Stalwarts like
Conkling, Cameron, Logan, and Morton, or Half-Breeds like Blaine,
inspired confidence. Not one of them had supported President Hayes'
policy of administrative reform. Many of them seemed ready to divert
attention from reform by waving the bloody shirt and crying up Democratic treason. It seemed almost certain that they would nominate for
the presidency someone like Grant or Blaine who would have little or
no sympathy with the liberal program. This, to Bowker's thinking,
would set back both the cause and reform for a generation.[1]

Bowker clearly saw that the task confronting liberals was to prove
to the Republican managers that the Independents held the balance-
of-power vote, and then force them to make an acceptable nomination
by threatening a costly bolt if they did not. He was also convinced that

[1] R. R. B. to G. W. Curtis, October 6, 1879.

the place to begin was the New York state election of 1879, and the first person to convince was Roscoe Conkling, the Republican boss of that State.[2] Conkling was the embodiment of everything that Bowker and his friends deplored in American political life. He had declared a war to the death against President Hayes, Curtis, and reform. He was now rallying his forces throughout the state to assure the nomination of his henchman Cornell to the governorship. If the Independents could make a dent on Conkling's machine in the state election of 1879, they might impress the other state bosses. More than one political oracle held that "as New York goes, so goes the nation." *Harper's Weekly* in this case compared the New York campaign to the action at Quatre Bras before Waterloo.[3]

The first skirmish was the primary election of delegates to the state convention to be held at Saratoga on September 3. This Conkling won hands down. In Brooklyn, where Bowker lived, the local bosses astutely arranged the primaries just at the time of summer when the "brownstone fronts" were out of town. Moreover, many of these residents found, on returning to the city, that their own names had been voted by henchmen of the machine. The reform wing of the Brooklyn ward association which Bowker represented could protest, but it did them no good. A majority of pro-Cornell men was sent to Saratoga.[4]

The second engagement was the Saratoga convention itself. In it George William Curtis led a small minority of liberal delegates. Would they have the courage to face up to the machine? Letters of exhortation were sent to the delegates. Bowker publicly addressed himself to Curtis in an open letter which appeared in the *Evening Post:*

> There are two methods of bulldozing. The Democrats in the South favor the Yazoo plan of securing harmony in the party: they shoot the minority. The Republican managers at the North render it harmless by tying it hand and foot with the machine-made wires of political courtesy; they rely on your elegant politeness, sir, not to say anything acrimonious, not to make any "personal attacks," not to disturb the "harmony" of the convention. . . . Wanted, a man who dares! Who dares not only to write before the convention, but to talk in it, and to act after it! The true Republicans look to you to be that man. This is your opportunity.[5]

[2] R. R. B., "An Open Letter to Mr. Curtis" (signed "A Young Republican"), New York *Evening Post*, September 2, 1879.

[3] *Harper's Weekly*, September 20, 1879.

[4] R. R. B., "The Republican Party for 1880," New York *Evening Post*, December 12, 1879.

[5] R. R. B., "An Open Letter to Mr. Curtis," New York *Evening Post*, September 2, 1879.

Conkling, however, had everything his own way. He was elected to the chair, he shaped the convention resolutions and the convention platform. The entire ticket, with the exception of one man, was his personal selection, and he even forced through a resolution making the nomination of Cornell unanimous.[6]

Conkling's high-handed action was widely condemned. The Saratoga nominations were assailed on all sides as "a flagrant act of insubordination," "exceedingly unfortunate," and "brainless and stupid." In fact, there was hardly a Republican paper of any standing in New York City that did not treat them as unwise, and many upstate held the same view. Moreover, machine dictatorship was charged before, during, and after the convention. It was publicly stated that votes had been stolen and voting lists manipulated, that officeholders had interfered, and that support had been secured from the Tammany Ring, the Custom House Ring, the Canal Ring, and the Insurance Ring. According to the *Nation,* Republicans in New York were "as completely stript of the right of self-government as any Southern State under carpet-bag rule."[7]

Yet in spite of what was felt and known about the Conkling dictatorship, nobody in authority proposed doing anything. Not only did the journals running with the machine echo Conkling's plea for party harmony, but even the loyal representatives of Independent Republicanism, the *Evening Post,* the *Times,* the *Utica Herald,* and others, counseled the Independents not to vote against their party.[8] If there was any opposition left, it was without leadership, organization, or knowledge of its real strength. To the question asked during the summer by the *Nation, Harper's Weekly,* and the Boston *Herald* concerning what had become of the Independents of 1876, there was simply no answer.[9] Everything seemed to point to surrender.

Bowker was unwilling to accept this situation. Although the Independents had been tricked in the primaries and ignored in the convention, he now decided to rally them and make a fight of it. He would have been willing to follow the leadership of his elders, but his elders offered no leadership. Therefore he stood up and volunteered, and what he started gathered momentum. The first result was the Inde-

[6] Alexander, *A Political History of the State of New York,* III, 413–14.

[7] R. R. B., "The Republican Party for 1880." New York *Evening Post,* December 12, 1879; *Harper's Weekly,* September 27, 1879; *Nation,* September 25, 1879; George Bliss to General C. Arthur, November 29, 1879; *Nation,* December 4, 1879; *Nation,* September 25, 1879; D. B. Eaton, *The Independent Republican Movement in New York,* 37.

[8] R. R. B., "No Surrender." New York *Evening Post,* September 5, 1879; see *Nation,* September 18, 1879.

[9] Letter to the *Nation,* September 11, 1879.

pendent Republican Executive Committee and its valiant "Young Scratcher" campaign. This carried over to the "Independent Republican Committee" of 1880 which helped to nominate Garfield, then the "Brooklyn Young Republican Club" of 1882 which helped to defeat Folger, and eventually the "Mugwumps" of 1884 who helped to elect Cleveland. Bowker, indeed, came to be known as "the original Mugwump."[10]

Bowker's plan was a simple one which offered to meet simultaneously the need of conscientious liberals and of the general cause of reform. As for the former, he realized there were many thoughtful Republicans who would not want to vote the Conkling "gag" ticket or the Democratic ticket, yet who did want to vote. Certainly restlessness and revolt were in the air waiting to be given shape and direction.[11] On the other hand, what was needed to impress the party bosses was concrete evidence of the strength of the Independent vote. The solution was for conscientious Republicans to "scratch" the names of a few but not all of the Republican ticket. This would enable them to protest against the worst machine candidates and still elect most of their ticket. The difference between the votes cast for the "scratched" candidates and for the ones voted on by the Independents would be the number of Republican voters in New York who could be counted on to stand up to the machine. Two Conkling candidates to scratch were obvious: Cornell, Conkling's former naval officer of the Port of New York and treasurer of the state Republican Committee whom Hayes had removed from office for maladministration and who was now running for governor; and Soule, already convicted of guilt in certain Erie Canal frauds, now running for state engineer. To facilitate the scratching, Bowker would print and distribute at cost ballots with the spaces for governor and state engineer left blank. What if there should be a Democratic governor with a Republican administration and legislature?

Bowker moved swiftly. On September 5, two days after the Saratoga conference, he presented his plan in the *Evening Post*. Entitled "No Surrender," the pronouncement had all of Bowker's usual force and ring. "If a few thousand will adopt this course," it insisted, "the defeat of patriotic Republicanism is retrieved; if a few hundred, or a few tens

10 The term "original Mugwump" was applied to Bowker at least as early as 1897 in a biographical sketch in *Municipal Affairs*, December, 1897, p. 803; also in *Selections from the Correspondence of T. Roosevelt and H. C. Lodge, 1884–1918,* (New York, 1925), I; Brooklyn *Eagle*, September 4, 1928. He was also called "the Founder of the Mugwumps," *Tribune.* November 13, 1933; and "the Father of the Mugwumps." G. H. Putnam states that Bowker, Putnam, and Whitridge "are entitled to the credit of initiating for the State of New York, the great cause of Mugwumpery." (*Memories of a Publisher*, 181–88.)

11 *Harper's Weekly*, October 4, 1879.

only, this will be at least a conscience-vote of protest. It is time for each man to shoot from behind his own tree." The next day he issued a call through the *Post* for the names of men interested in the immediate organization of a Young Republican Committee. Six days later he brought together in his office at the *Publishers' Weekly* a representative working group of those responding. What emerged was the Independent Republican Executive Committee of nine, with Bowker as chairman, Whitridge as secretary, and A. C. Zabriskie as treasurer. The following day the Committee launched its campaign in the office of G. P. Putnam's Sons by adopting an address which Bowker had prepared and sending it out for signature by prominent New York Republicans thought to be sympathetic to the cause. From a phrase in the address, "not to bolt but to scratch," soon adopted as one of the campaign mottoes, came the nickname "Young Scratchers" by which these Independent Republicans were known.

This address, which remained the platform and creed of the Independent Republicans throughout the campaign, was a clean-cut, well-reasoned, high-principled statement of the Young Scratcher position. It included a vigorous expression of loyalty to true Republicanism, a biting arraignment of Conkling, Cornell, and Soule, a stirring rejection of the old plea for party harmony, and full particulars on the proposed plan of action.

> We have tried various methods of reform. We have attended primaries, and found there the same domination of the machine. We have expressed our protests before conventions and have found them disregarded. We have seen excellent platforms adopted only to be rejected in practice. We are convinced that the one way for the ordinary citizen to oppose the machine politician with his professional skill, is to make his trade uncertain by giving him practical notice that a bad candidate may be defeated by those independent votes within the party which he chooses to defy. We propose not to bolt but to scratch. . . . We urge true Republicans not to stay at home from the polls . . . not to desert their party but to attempt to purify it from within.

Signatures to the address soon numbered over three hundred, representing fifty-two counties; as soon as the first sixty reached Bowker on September 17, he released the document to the press.[12] Copies were im-

12 The address to which the original sixty signatures were attached is now in the Bowker Papers in the Library of Congress. Those signing include: Nelson Spencer, Edward Eggleston, Clarence Deming, Jacob Schoenhof, and F. Leypoldt. For publication of the address by the New York *Herald,* see Putnam, *Memories of a Publisher,* 183–84.

mediately mailed to 799 newspapers in the state and to 22 in other states.

The address, when noticed at all, provoked mostly disapproval, very little enthusiasm. Of the Republican papers in the city only the *Times* and the *Evening Post* published it, and only two others upstate. All were lukewarm. The usual comment was that the danger of Democratic victory was too great to permit an attack on the Republican machine. The *Tribune* treated the Young Scratchers as adolescent idealists capable of no good and much harm. The Democratic papers, following the example of the *World,* coolly assumed that they had walked into the Democratic ranks, and gave the address wide publicity.[13] The *Nation,* on the other hand, gave immediate and magnificent support.[14] It ridiculed the *Times, Post,* and *Harper's Weekly* for having followed denunciation of the machine with meek acquiescence in its nominations for fear of disrupting party harmony. It pointed out the usefulness of the scratching technique and pleaded for cash contributions. The *Evening Post* noted the address and admitted there was need for such action, but refrained from support. By September 27, *Harper's Weekly* conceded that the Independent vote in New York was large enough to be "a vital consideration in all political calculations," but still did not support the Young Scratchers.

The Young Scratchers did not wait idly for support, but set out aggressively to win it. Their public appeals to the Civil Service Reform Association and the Union League Club were made in a style so racy and vigorous that the *Nation* reported them "something new in political documents of this character."[15] Bowker himself kept after the editor of *Harper's Weekly,* urging Curtis to come out boldly for the Young Scratchers and assume the leadership of the Independents. "We consider ourselves your disciples," he pleaded in a letter of October 6, "following your lead, and we believe this is the time for you to take the lead. . . . We ask you to stand up in your place and speak out." On October 11, Curtis courageously accepted the challenge. *Harper's Weekly* came out with a vigorous, unqualified endorsement of the theory and practice of "The Bowker Movement" and of the technique of scratching in particular. The same issue included a magnificent statement by Harper and Brothers upholding the course of their editor.[16]

This accession of Curtis to the Young Scratcher ranks gave the

[13] *The Independent Republican Campaign of 1879,* a report issued by the Independent Republican Executive Committee (New York, 1879).

[14] *Nation* editorials of September 18 and October 2; "The Grounds of the Independent Revolt," *Nation,* September 25, 1879.

[15] October 16, 1879.

[16] *Harper's Weekly,* October 11, 1879; Harper, *The House of Harper,* 449–50.

movement wide publicity. The Philadelphia *Ledger* reprinted both the Curtis editorial and the Harper statement for its half-million readers. Charles Eliot Norton wrote from Cambridge that national political interest centered in the New York attempt to defeat Cornell in the interest of the Republican party at large as "our sole chance of saving the party from the ruin which overtakes every party that has lost moral convictions and personal independence."[17] John M. Forbes sent his personal check for $400 from Boston with the statement that "the question is one that in principle, at least, concerns the Republican party and the independent voters generally throughout the whole country."[18] By September hundreds of letters had commended the Young Scratchers' course of action, and by the end of the campaign these numbered over 1500.[19]

The Young Scratchers were not professional politicians, but businessmen with limited time and energy to spend on promoting a political campaign. Nevertheless, they worked hard. Bowker, as generalissimo, was, as usual, indefatigable. By October 1, a central headquarters was established at 8 Union Square. There a transparency was set up bearing the Republican ticket with the names of Cornell and Soule scratched. Envelopes were printed with the same device. Good slogans were used, such as "Not to bolt but to scratch," "The only way to obtain good candidates is to defeat bad ones," and "The deliberate selection of weak candidates is treachery to the party." Subcommittees were formed for New York County, Kings County, and Staten Island, and useful allies organized in Buffalo, Rochester, and Albany. A small campaign chest of something over $5,000 was built up, of which $275 was left as an unexpended balance at the end of the campaign. All financial offers by individual Democrats and by the state Democratic Committee were declined, as well as "offers to sell votes in small quantities at low prices."

"Bowker's party," as the Young Scratchers were sometimes called, relied chiefly on the printed word. They prepared about a dozen telling leaflets and sent them all over the state. A general mailing list was compiled from the fifteen hundred Republican correspondents who wrote to the Committee, the additional six hundred sympathizers resident in forty different counties suggested by these, special lists secured from Jefferson, Genesee, Lewis, and Allegheny counties, the six or seven thousand dissatisfied Republicans whose names were contributed by the

17 C. E. Norton to Harper and Brothers, October 15, 1879; Harper, *The House of Harper*, 453.

18 Putnam, *Memories of a Publisher*, 184–85.

19 New York *Evening Post*, September 19, 1879; *Independent Republican Campaign of 1879*.

state Democratic Committee, and from the lists of Independents which *Harper's Weekly* had gathered from various yearbooks and reports. A special mailing list of some thirty thousand clergymen, educators, and progressive businessmen was compiled. By mail and by direct hand-outs, over 72,000 pamphlets, 145,000 single documents, and 1,000,000 printed ballots were distributed.

Mailing documents, however, was not the whole of it. Government employees were exhorted through circulars not to be bullied into making campaign contributions against the President's orders. Reminders of registration were mailed out. Several public meetings were held in the New York and Brooklyn Academies of Music. Challenges to debate were hurled at the Cornell and Hoskins campaign clubs which were not accepted, though others were. Bowker took part in one Brooklyn debate in which he effectively stated that the Young Scratchers "proposed to follow the flag rather than the bloody shirt," and in which his opponent charged that Bowker had assailed Cornell "more strongly than the vilest sheets of the Democratic party."[20] Republican rallies were attended and counter-propaganda there issued, especially in the case of Secretary Evarts' Cooper Union speech and Secretary Sherman's addresses in New York, Albany, and Rochester. The *Tribune's* current attack on the Independents of 1879 was effectively countered by quotations from the *Tribune's* defense of the Independents of 1876.[21]

The Young Scratchers worked diligently up to the last minute. During the last few days of the campaign, 240 packages containing 50,000 ballots and 12,000 pamphlets were sent out, some by men employed to travel through upstate counties. Thousands of small hand-cards, containing a résumé of the Committee's arguments, were distributed at ferries, depots, and other public places. Twenty of the twenty-four Assembly Districts of New York County were covered in whole or in part, and of the 234 election districts thus covered, 45 were attended on Election Day by volunteers, while 189 were watched by men hired for the purpose. Similar zeal was shown in Brooklyn.

Nothing better indicates the effectiveness of the Young Scratcher campaign than the efforts that were made to defeat it. In Brooklyn, Henry Ward Beecher on October 8 denounced the Bowker movement. On October 21, Secretary Evarts saw fit to come to New York and publicly attack the Young Scratchers before a capacity audience at Cooper Institute.[22] A week later Secretary Sherman followed suit. The party press did its part. Not a single Republican newspaper in the state would

[20] Brooklyn *Daily Eagle*, November 2, 1879.

[21] *Nation*, October 23, 1879.

[22] *Nation*, October 23, 1879; B. Dyer, *The Public Career of W. M. Evarts* (Berkeley, 1933), 241.

publish the Young Scratcher releases in full; only two or three recognized their existence, and several, like the Buffalo *Commercial* and the Rochester *Democrat,* refused paid advertisements.[23] Curtis, after the election, referred to the "constant and persistent irritation and sneering and ridicule of Republican organs and orators."[24] Of the *Tribune's* course of vilification, Bowker wrote to Curtis: "It is simply lying right and left, without taking the least trouble to get at facts. As an old *Tribune* man, I am heartily disgusted."[25]

Some called the Scratchers "contemptible," others dubbed them "traitors"; George Bliss referred to them as "sore-headed bolters"; a southern Republican called Curtis "a sore-headed self-conceited disorganizer of the Republican party." Beecher remarked that scratching was good for cutaneous affections, while an upstate Republican observed that there was no Republican in Troy who had any disease that required scratching. Many letters were received by the Executive Committee threatening it with "oblivion" and with social suicide. Curtis himself was so bitterly attacked that he deemed it necessary to resign the chairmanship of the Richmond County Republican Convention.[26] There was even a plot, fortunately discovered in time, to destroy the entire stock of scratched ballots on the eve of the election by bribing the janitor in the headquarters building. To all attempts to belittle the movement Curtis made the obvious reply that "the incessant fusilade proves that its object is not so utterly contemptible as it is alleged to be. . . . If the thing be a mosquito, there is too much powder and ball wasted upon it."[27]

The election results clearly indicated the success of the Young Scratcher campaign. Cornell was elected governor with 418,567 votes, but since one of his Republican running mates who had not been scratched polled 438,253 votes, it was clear that 19,686 Republicans, or 5 per cent of the total voting, had followed the advice of the Young Scratchers. Secretary Sherman put the number at 30,000.[28] One of the most interesting features of the election had been the split in the Democratic ranks which resulted in two rival Democratic candidates for governor. Naturally this fact enormously strengthened Cornell. Adding up the votes received by both Democratic factions, it becomes clear

23 *Ibid.;* F. W. Whitridge, "A Brake on the Machine," *International Review,* March, 1880.

24 *Harper's Weekly,* November 8, 1879.

25 R. R. B. to Curtis, October 6, 1879.

26 *Nation,* October 16, 1879.

27 *Harper's Weekly,* November 8, 1879.

28 Independent Republican Committee Address, November 19, 1879. It is almost certain that about 14,000 Republicans, after scratching Cornell, actually voted the Democratic ticket for governor.

that, except for this intra-party squabble, Conkling's candidate would have been defeated by about 35,000 votes.[29]

Every opportunity was immediately taken by the Young Scratchers to publicize the significance of their achievement and thus impress it upon both Independents and the Republican managers. Bowker prepared an address which was adopted by the Independent Republican Committee, printed on November 19, and sent to the press. Soon after there appeared a neatly-bound pamphlet entitled *The Independent Republican Campaign of 1879,* which included the address and reports from all the committees. Bowker's address drew three conclusions from the campaign: the urgent desire of a large body of Republicans for administrative reform had been vigorously impressed on the party leaders, the administration, and Congress; the importance of the Independents as the balance-of-power vote had been established; the rank and file had shown what could be done in defiance of the machine, and established a precedent for "the next time."[30] In Bowker's thinking it was this third point which deserved the most serious study. The next spring he wrote of the Young Scratcher movement that it was "chiefly to be remembered as practical proof that in times of organized party tyranny, against all sorts of odds, and with no capital except pluck, a sense of doing the right thing, and some faith in the application of ordinary common sense even to political matters, the leadership of young men, 'unknown' and untrained in politics, was able to gather a resisting force sufficient to cope even with party 'discipline'—in a word, proof that American private citizens still possess the independence and organizing power to take care of their own affairs."[31]

[29] *Appleton's Cyclopedia* (1879), 681. See opinion of D. S. Alexander in *A Political History of the State of New York,* chapter XXXII; Eaton, *The Independent Republican Movement in New York,* 11.

[30] The *Nation* confirmed most of these conclusions in its own election review, "The National Significance of the New York Election," in the issue of November 13, 1879.

[31] R. R. B., "The Independent Republican and the Presidential Campaign," *Nation,* July 1, 1880.

IX

Leading the Independents in 1880

THE Young Scratcher campaign of 1879 was a first step by the Independents to influence the Republican presidential nomination of 1880. It was a local skirmish in a single state. The next step was to undertake the real battle on a nationwide front. The first task, so as to avoid the failure of the Fifth Avenue Hotel Conference of 1876, was to organize the Independents throughout New York and then throughout the nation. The second task was to secure properly instructed state delegations to the national Republican convention. The last task was to influence that convention. At the same time, and in order to show that they meant business, they would lay the groundwork for a post-convention meeting to launch a third party in case the Republican nominee proved unacceptable. Into this program Bowker threw himself with all the time and energy he could spare from the *Publishers' Weekly* and the *Library Journal*.

The work of organization went forward rapidly in New York. The original Independent Republican Executive Committee of nine was continued after the election, and in December was doubled by the addition of such able men as Clarence Deming, Richard Dugdale, Jacob Schoenhof, and Nelson Spencer. Soon this committee evolved into an Independent Republican State Committee whose job was to co-ordinate local county associations. Thus the Independent Republican Association of the County of New York[1] was set up, and similar associations pushed in twenty other counties.[2] In addition to these there was founded

1 Constitution and By Laws, printed by the New York *Evening Post* Steam Presses. See references in D. B. Eaton, *The Independent Republican Movement in New York*, 59.

2 R. R. B. to E. L. Godkin, February 7, 1880.

an active German-American Independent Republican Organization.

The next step was to develop and integrate the work of Independents in the several states. For this purpose there was created in mid-January of 1880 the Independent Republican Central Committee. Horace White started as chairman, but was almost immediately replaced by Bowker, who remained the responsible, executive head of the Independent effort throughout the campaign. As a working basis of unity for all Independents, the Central Committee adopted a Statement of Principles, drawn up by Bowker, Curtis, Putnam, and Whitridge, which emphasized four points: a definition of true Republicanism; the rights and duties of party members; the necessity of securing good nominations throughout the primaries and of defeating bad nominees after them; and the importance of nonpartisan, business administration of cities.[3]

On the basis of this Statement and in the name of the Central Committee, Bowker proceeded to stir up activity in neighboring states. He urged Henry C. Lea of Philadelphia to "organize in your own despotized state some significant association of protest,"[4] and was gratified to learn, a few weeks later, that the Philadelphia men had formed a National Republican league. He went to Massachusetts to confer with the Young Republican leaders there, had a cordial discussion with young Henry Cabot Lodge through Godkin's introduction, and heard reports of the thirty or forty Massachusetts clubs from various leaders. "They haven't quite the surplus vigor we have here," he observed to his New York friends, "but are entirely reliable."[5] A Young Republican Club was formed in Rhode Island which Bowker kept supplied with literature and program suggestions.[6] In Maine, he worked hard but unsuccessfully to get the Independents to demonstrate against Blaine.[7]

The first real engagement of the political battle of 1880 came when the state conventions met to elect and instruct delegates to the national Republican convention. The first was the Pennsylvania convention, meeting February 4. A simultaneous public warning of Independent intentions was issued to the party managers by the New York and Philadelphia Independents, the statement of the latter being signed by two hundred influential citizens.[8] The strategy produced re-

---

[3] Printed in single sheets by the committee. Also in *Harper's Weekly*, February 14, 1880, and in Eaton, *The Independent Republican Movement in New York*, appendix.

[4] R. R. B. to Henry C. Lea, January 10, 1880.

[5] R. R. B. to George S. Crocker, H. C. Lodge, H. C. Lea, "T" Hovery, January 27, 1880; to E. L. Godkin, February 7, 1880.

[6] J. R. Gladding to R. R. B., April 28, May 3, 10, 1880.

[7] H. W. Richardson to R. R. B., March 26, April 19, 26, 1880.

[8] *Nation*, February 5, 1880; *Harper's Weekly*, February 21, 1880.

sults: Don Cameron's support was so cut down that many observers interpreted the result as a defeat for Grant.[9]

The New York convention was held at Utica on February 25. Bowker had written a blunt, hard-boiled warning to the Republican bosses in December which had been printed and widely circulated by the Independents as a campaign document.[10] Later, when the list of delegates to the convention was made known, he sent to each one a copy of the Young Scratchers' campaign report and a new manifesto clearly indicating the line of Independent action. This was printed by the *Nation* and *Harper's Weekly* in full.[11] The Philadelphia Independents did their part by issuing a simultaneous declaration. But the machine forces at Utica were brazenly triumphant. After an exhibition of pre-convention contempt for fair play which was described by Curtis as "naked Tweedism,"[12] the Grant men railroaded through the names of Conkling, Cornell, Arthur, and Warren for delegates-at-large, and then succeeded in binding the entire delegation in a unit vote for Grant.[13] Naturally the Independents were outraged.[14] But it was not all loss. The Jamestown (New York) *Journal* and the Albany *Evening Journal* gave evidence of growing upstate support,[15] and a Massachusetts observer declared in the *Nation* that "hosts" of people outside of New York were watching the Independents "with interest and hope."[16]

The Independents had better success in Massachusetts. A month before the April meeting of the state convention, the Massachusetts Young Republicans met in convention, heard and approved the platforms of the New York and Philadelphia Independents, voted to undertake joint action with them, and passed resolutions opposing Grant and Blaine.[17] This had its effect in getting the April convention of the

9 John A. Bennett to R. R. B., February 5, 1880; Talcott Williams to R. R. B., February 6, 1880; *Harper's Weekly*, February 21, 1880. The *Tribune, Times,* and *Herald* held the same view.

10 R. R. B., "The Republican Party for 1880," New York *Evening Post*, December 12, 1879. This was prompted by a public letter from William E. Chandler defending the Cornell-Conkling machine.

11 "To Members of the Republican State Convention," from the Independent Republican Central Committee; *Nation*, March 4, 1880; *Harper's Weekly*, February 14, 1880.

12 G. F. Howe, *Chester A. Arthur*, 102; *Nation*, February 5, 1880; *Harper's Weekly*, February 28, 1880; *Nation*, February 12, 1880.

13 Howe, *Chester A. Arthur*, 102; New York State Historical Association, *History of the State of New York*, VII, 165.

14 *Harper's Weekly*, March 13; see also "The Unit Rule," *Harper's Weekly*, April 17, 1880; Eaton, *The Independent Republican Movement in New York*, 13 and chapter VIII.

15 Quoted in the New York *Evening Post*, February 3, 1880; Albany *Evening Journal*, April 1, 1880.

16 Letter to the *Nation*, February 19, 1880.

"regulars" to shelve Blaine, Grant, and Sherman in favor of Edmunds.

Good progress was made in mobilizing anti-Grant sentiment. A national anti-Grant mass meeting was called to assemble in St. Louis on May 6, and the New York Independents joined representatives of the Republican Reform League, the National Anti-Third Term Republicans and the Independent German Association at a convention in Albany on April 22 to select a strong delegation from their state.[18] They preceded this convention by a press interview with Bowker and Whitridge, they had the convention called to order by Bowker, they had it adopt an Address composed by him which vigorously expressed the Independent position and which they printed and distributed widely,[19] and they then secured a majority on the state committee with Bowker acting as prime watch dog. Bowker could not attend the St. Louis convention but sent a letter which was read into the proceedings.[20] All this helped to make the movement a success.[21] Independents agreed to an iron-clad resolution to vote against Grant and do all they could to defeat him.[22] More important, a national committee was selected to meet in New York and put a third candidate in the field in case Grant was nominated by the Republicans and the Democrats offered nothing better. Bowker was commissioned to sound out candidates in advance. One of those most favored by Independents was General J. L. Chamberlain, president of Bowdoin College,[23] and Bowker wrote him a strong letter urging him to accept this patriotic duty to country and party. In May, Bowker predicted in the *Nation* that the number of Republicans who would bolt the party if Grant were nominated could be counted "by the hundred thousands."[24]

It was somewhat harder to mobilize sentiment against Blaine. Some of the liberals hesitated about denouncing him in advance. Early in May, Bowker thought the danger of splitting Independents over the issue had diminished sufficiently to announce through the *Nation* that the Independents were only a little less opposed to Blaine than to

17 *Nation*, March 11, 1880.

18 *Tribune*, April 21, 22; New York *Evening Post*, April 22, 1880.

19 "Address of the Albany Conference of Independent and anti-Grant Republicans," printed at Independent Republican Central Committee Headquarters, 8 Union Square.

20 *Tribune*, April 23, 1880; R. R. B. to the *Nation*, May 6, 1880; R. R. B. to J. B. Barnhill, December 5, 1888.

21 *Tribune*, May 7, 1880; *Nation*, May 13, 1880; *Appleton Cyclopedia* (1880), 693.

22 Passed May 24; *Tribune*, May 25, 1880.

23 *Tribune*, May 25, 1880. Bowker had reported in January that Massachusetts men were backing Chamberlain for vice-president.

24 R. R. B., "The Opposition to General Grant, and the Opposition to Mr. Blaine," May 6, 1880.

Grant.[25] However, an anti-Blaine campaign document which he prepared for the Chicago delegates encountered some criticism and was probably not sent out.[26]

But though the immediate tactical objectives of Bowker's committee were to register an impressive anti-Grant and anti-Blaine sentiment, the basic, long-range objective was to awaken the average American citizen to the political crisis confronting the nation. The machine was obviously making a mockery of popular sovereignty. It constituted a new slavocracy. Whitridge proclaimed that between four-fifths and seven-eighths of the Republican voters in New York were as effectively disfranchised by the state electoral machinery as the Negroes in the South.[27] Curtis asserted that the machine treated the voters "as the overseers of plantations in the ante-bellum days treated the slaves."[28] To free the country from this "tyranny," Bowker appealed for "a vigorous protestantism in our politics," "a new reformation," and "a new anti-slavery crusade." The cause of the Independents in 1880 was made the cause of American democracy itself.

Week in and week out, Bowker's Central Committee worked to place the issues before the public. Several clear-cut expositions of the crisis in American political life and the Independent creed and strategy were made and widely distributed. Whitridge's article, "A Brake on the Machine" was effective.[29] Dorman B. Eaton's book, *The Independent Republican Movement in New York,* was a startling analysis of the rise of machine government in New York and its culmination under Conkling, as well as a passionate endorsement of the motives, methods, and platform of the Independents. Published by Putnam, it was mailed out in quantity as heavy campaign artillery.[30] Bowker covered similar ground in a superb tract entitled "The Political Responsibility of the Individual," which William Dean Howells was glad to print in the *Atlantic Monthly.*[31] This essay was the most ably reasoned and persuasive advocacy of the Independent cause which Bowker had made. It stung, and blazed, and soared. In addition to these writings, Bowker's committee arranged five public lectures which it immediately printed

[25] *Ibid.*

[26] J. A. Bennett to R. R. B., May 12, 1880; John R. Gadding to R. R. B., May 13, 1880; R. B. Comstock to R. R. B., May 19, 1880.

[27] F. W. Whitridge, "A Brake on the Machine," *International Review,* March, 1880, p. 242.

[28] *Harper's Weekly,* March 6, 1880.

[29] "A Brake on the Machine," *International Review,* March, 1880, p. 242.

[30] G. H. Putnam to R. R. B., May 13, 1880.

[31] The article was sent to Howells in April, but there was no room for it in the June number, and it did not appear until September: *Atlantic Monthly,* September, 1880, pp. 320–28. W. D. Howells to R. R. B., April 18, June 17, 23, 1880.

and distributed as campaign documents: Horace White on "Third Term Politics," Albert Stickney on "The Aims of Independent Republicans," Charles Francis Adams on "Individuality in Politics," Matthew Hale on "Conditions and Limits of Party Fealty," and G. W. Curtis on "Machine Politics and the Remedy." Meanwhile, from day to day and month to month, Bowker's office served as a clearinghouse for campaign materials sent in by loyal supporters or requested by harassed local organizers.[32]

Bowker suffered at least one public whipping for his pains. Whitelaw Reid, the *Tribune's* chief, had been profoundly irritated by the Young Scratchers. Their continuance as an Independent Republican Central Committee seemed a gratuitous impertinence, and their February resolutions aimed at the Utica convention the last straw. Reid finally exploded. His editorial "About the Size of It" was merciless, contemptuous, and personal.[33]

> This committee is the concern irreverently described as the Young Scratchers' party. It now consists, so far as the outside world knows, of Mr. R. R. Bowker, chairman, and Mr. Whitridge, secretary; but these have bounce enough for a regiment. . . . Mr. Bowker is an amiable and well-meaning gentleman whose greatest trouble is that his intellectual development was arrested at the Grown Boy stage. This accounts for his being so profoundly impressed with the solemnity of existence, and so profoundly ignorant of his own place in it. . . . Nothing more grotesque than his occasional pronunciamentoes as to what men and what measures he will or will not support has been heard of in American politics since General Daniel Pratt last nominated himself for the Presidency. Nobody wants to know what he will support—except, possibly, Mr. Whitridge. He represents nobody, he influences nobody, he speaks for nobody, and, if we understand his political principles, he votes for nobody.

Bowker's friends immediately rallied to his support. Curtis, Whitridge, Stedman, Putnam, and Wingate all promptly expressed their disgust.[34] Talcott Williams, himself a newspaper man, pointed out how flattering Reid's personal attack was:

[32] T. Williams to R. R. B., February 9; C. Judson to R. R. B., February 20; Jacob Schoenhof to R. R. B., March 25, 1880.

[33] *Tribune,* February 4, 1880.

[34] Letters to R. R. B. from G. W. Curtis, February 4; F. W. Whitridge, February 5; E. C. Stedman, February 8; C. F. Wingate, February 4; Talcott Williams, February 6; F. W. Whitridge, October 18, 1881.

I have been on the edge of congratulating you all the time since the *Tribune* printed its brutal attack on you. You have accomplished very much more than I imagined to make such an attack timely. A paper like the *Tribune* doesn't make an attack of this kind without being asked to do it and nothing but a clear idea that you were becoming dangerous would make it possible. You have every reason to be satisfied with the results of six months' work if it leads to this broad admission that your call has led to a formidable movement.

At last, in June, came the national convention itself. Many Independents from New York, Massachusetts, and Pennsylvania journeyed to Chicago to press home the campaign so vigorously waged the preceding months. Arthur W. Milbury, the "whirlwind member" of the Young Scratcher Committee, hired a hall for the Independent headquarters opposite the Palmer House, which was to be the Grant command post and the center of the seething Convention maelstrom. Over the headquarters was erected a huge transparency proclaiming: "Nominate Grant and lose Ohio; Nominate Grant and lose New York." With Wayne McVeagh as chairman and Jacob Schoenhof as secretary a working committee was organized to meet daily and direct the Independent strategy. According to Bowker, this strategy included three minimum objectives: to write a civil service plank into the Republican platform, to stop Grant, and to nominate a suitable vice-president.[35]

Bowker had prepared an entire arsenal of handbills and leaflets to be fired at the convention delegates. One, printed on a large yellow sheet, blazoned forth a great column of startling propositions: "Grant means Extinction of the Republican Party . . . Resurrection of the Bloody Shirt . . . The rule of public plunderers." Another handbill, entitled "Can General Grant be Elected?," presented the deadly statistics of the recorded anti-Grant votes in New York, Massachusetts, and Pennsylvania. Three thousand of these were effectively distributed.[36] A much more ambitious document was his four-page leaflet entitled "Points as to the Selection of the Republican Presidential Candidate," which was literally crammed with statistics, arguments, and quotations proving the folly of a nomination of either Grant or Blaine. Perhaps the most important tract was the "Manifesto" to fellow Republicans containing a fresh and telling statement of the Independent principles, platform, and course of action. In addition to distributing this material, the Independents divided into squads of two and three to propagan-

[35] R. R. B., "Political Nexts," November 16, 1882.
[36] F. W. Whitridge to R. R. B., May 26, 1880.

dize orally the various delegations, especially the Negro delegations from the South.[37]

The convention was one of the most brilliant and exciting ever held in American political history. At stake was the continuing power of the great bosses Cameron, Logan, and Conkling; also the hope of reform within the party held by conscientious Republicans. For Bowker, the first dramatic climax came on June 5, when it would be seen whether a civil service plank would be included in the party platform. This was a major objective of the Independents, but though official pledges had been made favoring this reform, the Republican leaders were apparently determined to do nothing.

For days Bowker had been working feverishly to prepare the ground. The Independent conference had named him chairman of a committee of three to draft a plank, with John W. Carter of Boston and Stuart Wood of Philadelphia as associates.[38] The plank, as he wrote it, emphasized three features: fitness as the basic test for appointment, good behavior as the basis of tenure, and removal only for cause.[39] This last provision, intended to prevent the spoilsman's discharge of capable civil servants, was, in Bowker's own words, "a cardinal and specific article of faith representing an especial aim of the Independents within the party, but too ideal for actual adoption."

The fate of the bill was highly dramatic.[40] Bowker's draft was entrusted to the Massachusetts delegation and there, after just barely missing outright rejection at the hands of the Grant men, underwent some watering down. It was then submitted to the Committee on Resolutions and there twice rejected, so that the platform which was read to the convention on June 5 contained no reference to civil service reform. It was largely through the pluck of Colonel Charles R. Codman that the plank was brought before the convention, but then only to be further amended from the floor. As Bowker, Carter, and Wood watched breathlessly from the galleries, the removal-only-for-cause provision was rejected on the grounds that it would promote life tenure and an office holding class. Thus amended, the plank was finally adopted, the crucial phrases stating: "The Republican party [recommends] that reform in the Civil Service shall be thorough, radical, and complete. To that end, it demands the co-operation of the Legislative with the

37 See Putnam, *Memories of a Publisher*, 188–91.

38 R. R. B., MS; R. R. B. to M. Y. Ostrogorski, January 15, 1898, gives John C. Carter and *Edward R.* Wood.

39 "Proposed Plank," printed sheet. Given also in R. R. B., "The Independent Republicans and the Presidential Campaign," *Nation*, July 1, 1880.

40 R. R. B., MS Memoir; R. R. B. to M. Y. Ostrogorski, January 15, 1898; R. R. B., "The Independent Republicans and the Presidential Campaign," *Nation*, July 1, 1880.

Executive Department of the Government, and that Congress shall so legislate that fitness, ascertained by proper practical tests, shall admit to the public service."[41] Bowker later wrote that the retention of the demand for legislative co-operation represented a decided advance in the record of the party at a point "which is the key to the final triumph of Independent principles."[42] Thus the first of the Independent objectives at Chicago was achieved, and Bowker must have felt a considerable satisfaction with the outcome.

The second objective was attained when Grant's nomination was finally defeated and Garfield was nominated. In Conkling's brilliant speech nominating Grant, the Independents were honored by a description of themselves as "charlatans, jay hawkers, tramps and guerillas—men who deploy behind the lines, and forge now on one side and then on the other."[43] The third objective of the Independents, namely, a suitable nomination for vice-president, failed to be realized. Bowker worked for General J. L. Chamberlain, and other Independents favored Washburne of Illinois; Chester A. Arthur was presented by the New York delegation, and the Ohio men, apparently willing to conciliate the Stalwarts by naming a Conkling henchman to the second office, gave support. Arthur won the nomination. The Independents were outraged, and some, including McVeagh, threatened to bolt the ticket.[44] No one could then anticipate the independence which Arthur was soon to show and which was to make him, as Bowker put it, the "Prince Hal of American politics."

Bowker was obliged to leave Chicago before the selection of Garfield's running-mate was made, but he helped to plan the resolutions which were adopted by the Independents at Chicago before they returned home.[45] These resolutions enthusiastically endorsed Garfield, reluctantly accepted Arthur, and urged the local Independent associations to conduct an educational campaign. In an article for the *Nation* Bowker reviewed the Independent campaign, analyzed their strength in New York, reviewed the Democratic platform and candidates, and made a strong plea for support of the Republican ticket. The election of Garfield, he hoped, would be "only a first step in the regeneration of the Republican party."[46]

[41] *Proceedings*, 169; *Appleton's Cyclopedia* (1880) erroneously included, also, the rejected clause (p. 695).

[42] R. R. B., "The Independent Republicans and the Presidential Campaign," *Nation*, July 1, 1880.

[43] *Proceedings*, 182.

[44] R. R. B., MS Memoir; R. R. B. to J. B. Barnhill, December 5, 1888.

[45] Two gelatin-copy drafts, in his hand, with his own corrections, are in the Bowker Collection, New York Public Library.

It would be difficult to estimate the credit that the Independents might fairly take in the outcome at Chicago. Their nine months' campaign, with its battery of lectures, pamphlets, and public addresses had been a factor, and Bowker, in his *Nation* article, could rightly claim that this was so. Of course, there were heard the old belittling phrases, that they were "the namby-pamby, goody-goody gentlemen who . . . sip cold tea," and were "in reality assistant Democrats in disguise";[47] but *Harper's Weekly* freely gave them credit for the defeat of Grant and Blaine,[48] and the *Times* admitted that they controlled New York, and were "quite numerous enough to move the balance."[49] Garfield's appointment of Wayne MacVeagh as attorney general was later taken as an acknowledgment of the Independent contribution to victory. "MacVeagh probably owes the Attorney Generalship to you," Shepard wrote Bowker in March 1881, "as much as to any man." Curtis put the matter dramatically when he said that their ranks were "dangerously large and terribly quiet. They are not of the blustering kind. They do not threaten to bolt, but they bolt. They elect and defeat Presidents. They make and unmake parties. The politicians who leave them out of calculation play with fire. They are the people who justify American institutions, and keep parties and party bosses in order."

Bowker's acceptance of the offer to become Harper's representative in London now necessitated winding up his various affairs. It was difficult to leave the country with so many projects just launched, but he was sure that he would be back soon to resume his activity in them. With $6,000 actually raised for the work of the New York Free Trade Club, with the Society for Political Education well started, with Grant and Blaine defeated, Garfield nominated, a civil service plank written into the Republican platform, and the Independent Republicans nationally organized, Bowker could feel that his efforts were bearing fruit and that the liberal crusade was off to a new start. As he wrote letters of final counsel and encouragement to his associates,[50] the note of faith and optimism sounded continuously. Well might he feel satisfied with the preliminary work just accomplished. The soil had been plowed, the seed planted. He would come back soon to help reap the harvest.

46 R. R. B., "The Independent Republicans and the Presidential Campaign," *Nation*, July 1, 1880.
47 "H. C." in the New York *Times*, June 17, 1880.
48 "The Republican Nomination," *Harper's Weekly*, June 26, 1880.
49 New York *Times*, June 13, 1880.
50 Most of these letters were written June 30, 1880.

X

The House of Harper in London
1880–1882

BOWKER'S DECISION to go to London as the representative of the House of Harper from 1880 to 1882 provided a long-cherished opportunity to travel and to grow out of merely national into international relations and activities. Instead of changing his basic interests and loyalties, travel intensified and enlarged them by enabling them to include the English scene. While in England, Bowker broadened his activity in the book trade, the literary world, the library movement, copyright, and the liberal crusade. He further proved himself an alert businessman, a man of many fine friendships, and a conscientious American citizen. He went to England with the firm intention of coming back after a short stay, and he was never tempted to revise this decision. He returned greatly enriched by his experience abroad. In addition to meeting many prominent English publishers, authors, artists, and librarians, Bowker became intimately acquainted with a society and a culture which had much to teach his generation of Americans.

In 1880 the Harpers realized that the volume of their business in England was increasing, certain emergencies had arisen, and it seemed desirable to establish an English edition of *Harper's Magazine*. They therefore decided to replace their English agent with an American representative having sufficient business and literary ability to look after their interests on the spot.[1] After first approaching James R. Osgood, the veteran Boston publisher, they turned to Bowker. The choice was a happy one. Through his literary work on the *Evening Mail* and the *Publishers' Weekly*, Bowker had been in continuous relation with the

---

1 Harper, *The House of Harper*, 475. For an interesting correspondence in which Charles Reade strongly recommended this course, see pages 340–43.

Harpers' publishing program. He was well acquainted with Henry M. Alden, the editor of *Harper's Magazine,* and had already come into pleasant personal contact with Henry Harper. His fine essay on the House of Harper in 1877 had strengthened the good will of that firm. His proven competence as a journalist, the respect in which he had been held in the Book Trade Union, his contacts with English publishing houses, and the organizing ability he had shown in launching the Young Scratcher movement and the Society for Political Education, all recommended him to their confidence. The Harpers offered Bowker a salary of $6,000, to be increased $500 annually to $8,000, with the understanding that he was subject to recall at any time to assist in any department of the business at home.

Confronted with an opportunity to go abroad, to undertake a mission of some distinction, and to become intimately associated with the largest publishing house in the world, Bowker immediately accepted. Putnam, Randolph, Stedman, and other friends congratulated him on this real compliment to his ability.[2] Mother and sister found it almost impossible to contemplate the separation, but were fortified by the knowledge that Rogers would write as regularly as clockwork. As a matter of fact, he agreed to send them a day-by-day journal as well as letters, and this resolve, carried out conscientiously, enabled the family circle to share every experience.[3]

After putting himself through a rapid apprenticeship at Franklin Square, Bowker set sail early in July. He landed in Liverpool, and after a brief visit to Chester arrived in London, where he was immediately with friends. J. Henry Harper, designated by character and ability as the future head of the Harper House in the third generation, was on hand to make the rough places smooth. Within two days Bowker recorded: "I have been very well received here, and find myself rather more known than I had supposed. . . . One or two have been rather disappointed that an American should be sent over, but have been good enough to say that they rather prefer to have me than 'most any one else.' That's very nice. I indeed feel very happy in my business relations."[4] Bowker was not only happy. He was on edge with anticipation. There he was, a literary agent, in an England where George Eliot and Carlyle, Trollope and Hardy and Black, Tennyson and Swinburne, Browning and Morris, Spencer and Tyndall and Huxley, Froude and Freeman, and Disraeli and Gladstone were living and writing.

[2] G. H. Putnam to R. R. B., June 28, November 14, 1880; A. D. F. Randolph to C. T. Bowker, July 7, 1880; E. C. Stedman to R. R. B., September 2, 1880.

[3] MS London Journal in Bowker Collection, New York Public Library. It omits business details having to do with his Harper commissions.

[4] Journal, July 21, 1880.

For many years Harper's London agent had been Sampson Low, a venerable leader of the English book trade, now eighty-three, and the Harper office had been a part of the firm of Sampson Low, Marston, Searle and Rivington. The office was located in the handsome Crown Building at 188 Fleet Street, next to St. Dunstan's Church and close by the site of Temple Bar. Historic Temple Bar was no more, but the Temple, with its venerable church, its ancient buildings, its lovely gardens and greensward sloping to the Thames embankment, remained as in older times. The Crown Building was a handsome, four-story stone structure with a beautiful façade, said to be the only example of Ruskin's work as an architect. All of it was occupied by the Low firm except the ground floor.

Bowker had pretty well sized up the task ahead of him before leaving America. "I presume," he wrote J. W. Harper,[5] "that it would be necessary, in putting American push into English methods, to be very accommodating and respectful towards those methods, and to earn good-will by working quietly rather than vehemently. That would be my first aim. One drawback I recognize. I haven't the taste for conviviality to be a 'popular' man, though I think I can win confidence and reasonable liking." Bowker's first test was to win the confidence of the elderly and touchy Sampson Low. Low's earlier comment that either he or "that young man from America" would quit the office had been repeated to him, and he determined that neither event should take place. The first personal interview was a complete success. When Bowker went into Low's office, he found a fine old English gentleman with a firm mouth, a commanding presence, and a somewhat domineering temper. But within five minutes, Bowker had touched the real sweetness beneath's Low's formidable exterior and was received very kindly. Tactfully and quietly he took his place as an affectionate grandson looking to the older man for guidance, and there was soon mutual respect and affection.[6] He very much enjoyed being invited to Mechlen Square, where was located Low's "neat English house with its solid mahogany furniture" and literary treasures, presided over by Mrs. Low, "a dear old lady, chumpy and lively as a cricket."

Bowker's new responsibilities were, first, to establish an English edition of *Harper's Magazine;* secondly, to conduct Harper's extensive business with British authors; and finally, so to keep his eyes and ears open in relations with authors and publishers that the Harper House might make the first bid for the American publication of important

5 May 8, 1880.

6 R. R. B., "Memories among English Librarians," *Library Journal*, October, 1886.

works. This meant that Bowker's day was divided between his correspondence, looking up English literary news in the papers, negotiating with publishers, conferring with authors in his office or outside, and supervising the printing of the *"Maga,"* as he called the new periodical.

Launching the London edition of *Harper's Magazine* was an interesting publishing venture. The *Magazine* was by now a veteran among American illustrated periodicals, having enjoyed thirty years of popularity. It was, moreover, thoroughly Anglo-American in its contents. Its issues often contained more articles and illustrations relating to England than most of the exclusively English magazines, and in its pages had appeared the novels of Dickens, Bulwer-Lytton, Thackeray, George Eliot, Charles Reade, and other great English writers. Nevertheless, because of copyright regulations which required a first printing of English works in England, these same novels were issued in other English periodicals, and *Harper's* could not be sold in England. The solution seemed to be to purchase the entire rights to serial publication and to make *Harper's* an international magazine with an English edition. The firm could then include in it the contributions of the most distinguished writers of both England and America and apply the best American wood engraving and printing to the original designs of both English and American artists.

The London edition was to be made up on both sides of the Atlantic. It would contain certain portions, profusely illustrated, printed in America. The editorial departments, including an "Historical Record" and "Editor's Easy Chair" were to be printed in England. By combining the two portions, the magazine would contain 160 large octavo pages with over a score of articles and three times as many illustrations, including popular descriptive sketches of men and manners, travel, literary and art papers, articles of information, short stories, and installments of novels by the leading writers. Bowker's editorial in the first issue called this "an extraordinary shilling's worth," and indeed it was. Bowker's chief assistant in getting out the London *Maga* was John Lillie, who was to do the editorial work, write the "Editor's Easy Chair," and review current English books. Bowker found his lack of promptness a sore trial, but acknowledged that his book reviews were admirable.

The first issue of the *Maga* was to be the December one, and this kept Bowker busy throughout October and November. In certain quarters failure had been predicted for the whole enterprise, and Bowker knew that the first issue was the crucial one. An appropriate cover was one of the first requirements. In place of the familiar rococo design of the American edition, two long panels across the top and bottom of the magazine were adopted, one giving the skyline of London, drawn by Alfred Parsons, and the other that of New York, drawn by Edwin A. Abbey.

This issue, with its twenty-four articles and fifty-five illustrations, took an enormous amount of American "push" and last-minute generalship. The day before the publishing deadline the pressure was increased by Bowker's ambition to secure a journalistic beat. He secured prepublication review copies of Beaconsfield's *Endymion* and Tennyson's new volume, *Ballads and Other Poems,* simultaneously with the London *Times.* By midnight Bowker had dashed off his piece on Tennyson, and by dawn Lillie had managed to get through his on Beaconsfield. That last day Bowker goaded on the printers by telling them what American printers could do, telegraphed frantically for missing advertising copy, between noon and one o'clock wrote a review of Schliemann's *Ilios,* between four and six threw together the "Historical Record" from files commandeered at the Pall Mall offices, from six to eleven read final page proof with Lillie, and a few hours later had the first copy in his hands. "It has been a dreadful rush," he wrote his sister, ". . . because the people here need more pushing. . . . We really did a remarkable thing in this European edition. . . . It rather astonished these Englishers."

The first issue was an instantaneous success. Bowker had advertised the *Maga* in every ingenious way he could invent, even considering the use of luminous paint in London's underground,[7] and had secured some friendly anticipation in the English press. The home office had decided on an edition of 10,000, but by mid-November the advance sales were going so well that Bowker joyously cabled home for an extra edition of 5,000. Actually, within the first month 16,000 copies were sold.[8] The press notices were quite friendly.

Not content with the success of the first December issue of the *Maga,* Bowker secured Harper's cautious consent to a special Christmas number in accordance with the custom of English magazines, and for this he selected a group of articles calculated to make the finest impression on the English reading public. It was a difficult task to get the English printers to bring the illustrated work up to the American standard, but Messrs. Clowes heartily co-operated, and good results were attained. Bowker now had to show his "American push" more than ever, for John Lillie had just received word that his wife was ill with typhoid and the entire burden of work suddenly fell on him. He wrote the essay for the "Editor's Easy Chair," did the "Historical Rec-

[7] R. R. B. to his mother, November 28, 1880; Journal, November 12, 13, 1880.
[8] Advance flier by Sampson Low, Marston, and Company.

CHRISTMAS N°:=1881=ONE SHILLING

HARPER'S

"A Merry Christmas!"

MAGAZINE

SAMPSON LOW, MARSTON, SEARLE AND RIVINGTON
188, FLEET STREET.——LONDON=E·C·

ord," and gave out books for review. On December 18, he worked eighteen hours steadily, caught three hours of sleep, and then worked all the next day. His efforts were rewarded. The first printing of the Christmas number was for 30,000 copies, and in all some 80,000 copies were sold.[9]

The *Maga* grew steadily, keeping the confidence and respect of its old friends, and each month making new ones. It started the year 1881 with a regular circulation above 20,000 and when Bowker figured up its accounts for the third number, he found that sales and advertising were running a full 50 per cent ahead of original expectations.[10] In April the Harpers warned of possible new competition, but as the June number went to press, Bowker again had to cable the home office to increase the standing order "by a good peg." The second Christmas number was also a success, and again gave the regular numbers a substantial pull-up for the following year.[11]

The *Maga* articles took careful planning and a good deal of negotiation. In the case of biographical essays of living persons, such as those he ran of Gladstone, Tennyson, Ruskin, and Henry Irving, Bowker would have to complete plans with the author, the subject, and the illustrator. Regional studies required the planning and financing of excursions by special artists. For example, Alden, the American editor of *Harper's,* wished a series of illustrated descriptions of Holland, and Bowker had to keep prodding the artists he selected for this assignment until the series was finally published in four parts as "Artist Strolls in Holland" in the January–April numbers of the *Maga* for 1883.[12] Bowker also put Dr. Benjamin B. Martin at work on an article, "Through London by Canal," which directly stimulated him to go on to write *In the Footprints of Charles Lamb,* and, nine years later, the two-volume work on *The Stones of Paris in History and Letters.* Articles on spectral analysis by Lockyer, on the British Navy and the Bank of England, all required special and detailed negotiations.

One of the finest features of *Harper's Magazine,* and certainly one that contributed greatly to its popularity in England, was its excellent wood engravings. English printers had not essayed the fine work required by the delicate lines which *Harper's* and *Scribner's* had made familiar in America. The art in America was at its height, and none of the English work, certainly not that of John Swain, who did Du Maurier's engravings for *Punch,* could touch the perfection achieved by

[9] Advance flier by Sampson Low, Marston, and Company, December, 1880; R. R. B., MS Memoir.
[10] Journal, February 25, 1881.
[11] R. R. B. to sister, November 5, 1881.
[12] R. R. B. to sister, October 25, 28, 1880; February 21, 1882.

Smithwick and Timothy Cole in the engraving rooms at Franklin Square.[13] Bowker visited Edmund Dalziel, an English veteran of this art, and found his work inferior.[14]

English appreciation of this American art work was readily offered. Referring to the illustrations of the *Maga's* first issue of 1880, the *St. James Gazette* said that they had "all the effect of finely-executed steel engravings without losing the richness of wood engravings." The *Ayr Observer* said that the *Maga* was "illustrated with a fullness and beauty only beginning to be known in England;" Sir Frederick Leighton told Bowker that the Harper woodcutting was "unrivalled." George Scharf of the National Portrait Gallery was most enthusiastic:[15]

> I so highly admire all the specimens of wood engraving in *Harper's Magazine* that any further example will be extremely welcome to me. . . . I have been in my wonder almost impelled to ask how I might see the technical ways by which such marvels are attained. When I drew so much myself on wood, illustrating Horace, Macaulay, and reproductions of Italian art, such delicacies and softness of tints were never dreamed of. . . . I was greatly struck with some of the woodcuts in your Christmas Number. . . . Why can we not do like it in England?

Edward Lear was also greatly interested in the *Maga's* illustrations, and deplored the problem of getting satisfactory work done in Europe at that time.[16] Photoengraving, which made possible a direct reproduction of the artist's work, was still in its infancy, but was soon to make the painstaking work of the wood engraver a lost art.

In addition to managing the *Maga*, Bowker was responsible for Harper negotiations with London publishers. The latter proved to be surprisingly friendly. Bowker first called on Frederick Macmillan, whom he already knew, and met Mr. George Lillie Craik, one of Macmillan's partners of whom he was to see a great deal. Bowker described Macmillan's handsome house near Tooting Common after a visit there:

> Their house, 150 years old, is evidently of the time of some of the old Salem and Newburyport merchants' houses which, inside, the taste of Mrs. Macmillan the second has made more than a gem. A glassed porch of flowers opens by a great mahogany door into

13 Harper, *The House of Harper*, 476–77.
14 Journal, October 15, 1880.
15 George Scharf to R. R. B., April 4, 1882; *ibid.*, April 17, 1882.
16 Edward Lear to R. R. B., June 5, 1882.

the finest hall-room I ever saw, rich in bronze-gold paper and book-cases of tulip wood (grown on the place) some of which contain rarities worth at least £1,000—Walter Scott's copy of Beaumont and Fletcher, first editions of "Elia," Tennyson, Burns, etc., etc., presentation copies to Macmillan from Thackeray, George Eliot, Tennyson, etc., unpublished drawings by Wm. Blake, one of Burns' commonplace books, the MS of "A Sea Dream," (Tennyson) etc. And the charming house contains a very charming household.[17]

It was with some misgiving that Bowker visited the publishing house of John Murray, the house royal of the English trade. The partners of the English houses had, as Bowker thought, "a rather elegant way of doing business," and most Americans, he had heard, were referred to their "managers." He was therefore pleasantly surprised by the notable cordiality shown him by Mr. Cook, the managing partner, and young John Murray, who took Bowker as his personal guest to the famous annual John Murray sales dinner held at the Albion Tavern in Oldgate Street.[18] At the firm of C. Kegan Paul and Company, Bowker greeted young Trench, the junior partner and son of Dean Trench, whom Bowker had met in America. He found Longman's publishing house in Paternoster Row behind St. Paul's Cathedral quite a palace, and there he was pleasantly received by Thomas Norton Longman, head of the firm.[19]

Bowker enjoyed meeting Professor Bartholomew Price, the secretary and executive head of the Clarendon Press at Oxford. Under his development that press had become one of the most complete establishments in the world, even making its own paper and ink. Bowker described Price as "the sharpest businessman I know in England." Price, on his side, proved "very cordial" about Bowker's coming to Oxford and invited him on several occasions to stay in his fine old home there. Bowker enjoyed meeting Elliot Stock, a "courteous and rather elegant gentleman," editor of *The Antiquary,* who described his publication of the Thomas a Kempis manuscript, a new translation of which he had fruitlessly sought to have Cardinal Newman make.[20] He also came to know William Tegg, a veteran antiquarian and publisher, who with his father had kept shop in the same spot in St. Pancras Lane for a hundred years; Charles Welford, bibliographical bookseller and resident partner in England of Scribner and Welford; and Nicholas

17 R. R. B. to his mother, November 6, 1881.
18 Journal, November 5, 1880.
19 *Ibid.,* July 23, 26, 1880.
20 *Ibid.,* September 15, 1880.

Trübner, whose warm kindliness and enormous interest in everything relating to books brought to his home in Upper Hamilton Place a varied circle of friends, including George Eliot and Bret Harte. While discharging a commission to the Leipzig Book Fair, Bowker called on Brockhaus and Tauchnitz, and studied the methods of the German book trade.

Bowker's business with publishers and illustrators sometimes involved troublesome controversies. When J. A. Froude's two-volume edition of Carlyle's *Reminiscences* appeared, Bowker found himself involved in a sharp misunderstanding over whether the Harpers or the Scribners had the right to bring out the American edition.[21] When Bowker had just rushed Moncure D. Conway's illustrated memorial to Carlyle through the press, he was confronted by an infuriated Scotch artist who roared into his office and threatened a lawsuit to confiscate the entire edition. This was Alexander Tait, whose photographs of Carlyle had been used by Conway without authorization. It took three days of Bowker's studied diplomacy to woo Tait from his scheme, but in the end the two men became friends and the *Maga* was saved.[22] Two negotiations with the Clarendon Press involved Bowker in unpleasant reminders of the bitter relations existing between American and British publishers in the absence of international copyright. The first concerned an American edition of the *Revised New Testament* and the second the *New English Dictionary on Historical Principles*. The Harpers were so nettled by the "shabby treatment" they received that, as they wrote Bowker, "We haven't just now, in the shadow of the Fourth of July, quite the flunkeyism to relish it," and they dropped both. Bowker felt that foregoing the *Dictionary* was a great mistake.

> If the house is to keep up its prestige as the greatest American house, it can't afford to let too many of the great things go, and this is the greatest possible. . . . If it would do any good I would . . . even go home and back by balloon, for this is the most important thing of the next quarter-century.[23]

In addition to the publishers, Bowker's duties required extensive negotiations with English authors. In some cases, as was typical of Bowker, these business relations developed into strong personal friendships. This was particularly true of William Black, Mrs. Anne Thackeray Ritchie, and Mrs. Mulock Craik. With others, such as Thomas Hardy,

21 J. A. Froude, *My Relations with Carlyle*, 64 ff; the Harper representative to whom Froude's assurances had been given was Moncure D. Conway. Bowker refers to the furor over the books's revelations in his Journal, April 29, May 6, 1881.
22 *Ibid.*, April 30, 1881.
23 R. R. B. to J. W. Harper, June 23, 1882.

William Blackmore, and Robert Browning, Bowker had personal associations that left vivid impressions. With many others, from Tennyson and Gladstone to Edward Lear and Lewis Carroll, Bowker had correspondence that added substance to the literary names so long familiar to him.

Of all Bowker's associations with Englishmen, the most intimate and enjoyable was probably with William Black. The two men had first met in the summer of 1880, and Bowker had immediately liked the "dapper little fellow, with reddish goatee," but the acquaintance did not ripen into friendship until the spring of 1881. Black was already a fairly well-known novelist. Harper's had brought out his *Madcap Violet* serially in 1876, the year of his visit to America, and the following year had published in its Library Edition of his works his *Kilmeny, A Daughter of Heth* and *The Strange Adventures of a Phaeton*. Bowker described him as "a man of moderate stature; lithe of figure; with face often sunburnt from outdoor life; brown eyes, grave, but with a ready twinkle in them looking from behind glasses; a sympathetic mouth, half-hidden by his brown moustache; and dark hair." Black was especially fond of American humor.

Bowker's first impression of Black was a common one: that he was a silent man, into whose silence one could find no opening for friendship. But he soon came to know Black's other side, and it was not long before the two became very close friends, Bowker coming to think of the Brighton home as his home and the family as his own kin. The two men, separated in age by only seven years, found much in common: a journalistic youth, literary interests and associations in England and America, a similar Calvinistic upbringing followed by a similar religious liberalism, a common scorn for affectation, and a love of walking.[24]

Bowker thoroughly enjoyed Black's parties in his York House chambers in London, but agreed with the others who knew him best that he was most charming at his country home in Brighton. Paston House was within sound of the sea, and on the stretch of high downs between Brighton and the nestling hamlet of Rottingdean from which one could look down and off upon the sea, Black worked out many of his novels.[25] While Bowker was supervising the text and illustrations for Black's new stories, *That Beautiful Wretch* and *Shandon Bells,* he frequently dropped down to Brighton for the weekend.

24 Wemyss Reid, *William Black,* 341–43, 339–40. This biography leaned heavily on materials loaned by Bowker, including letters and an unpublished MS memoir of Black which had been revised and amended by Mrs. Black. See R. R. B. to Sir Wemyss Reid, October 12, 1901.

25 Reid, *William Black,* 190–92, 196–210; based on Joseph Hatton, "William Black at Home," *Harper's Magazine,* December, 1882. This article was planned by Bowker.

Early Companions in the Liberal Crusade: *(Top, left)* David A. Wells; *(Top, right)* Worthington C. Ford; *(Bottom, left)* George William Curtis; *(Bottom, right)* George Haven Putnam

Some International Friendships: *(Top, left)* Lady Anne Thackeray Ritchie; *(Top, right)* Mary Anderson; *(Bottom, left)* Edwin A. Abbey; *(Bottom, right)* William Black

> To Brighton to Wm. Black's and such larks! Bret Harte was also down. . . . Mrs. Black . . . sang quantities of Scotch songs for us. There are three lovely children. . . . But the childiest children most of the time were Black and Bret Harte—and the noise, and nonsense, and all that were steady-going from Saturday to Monday morning. We kept up a triangular fire of abuse and nonsense all the time, sitting, walking, or driving,—doing nothing in particular in the most vigorous way. Finally, the drawing-room, a grand Highland-fling, and the midnight descent to the dining-room for "the banquet" of bread and cheese. . . . I came home considerably refreshed in spirit with the feeling of a new "home" opened kindly to me.[26]

The two men took many a stroll together over the downs, often in silent companionship as Black would pick up the thread of one of his stories only to burst out suddenly with fun or talk until they brought up at the little inn at Rottingdean. Here Bowker was compelled to drink "that abominable mixture shandygaff," and Black would become as pungently conversational as anyone could desire.[27]

> Went to Black's for the week-end. Black was greatly delighted with a story which had been setting Huxley wild: how when the animals came out of the ark the elephant turned around to the flea who was behind him, and said; "Don't you push!"[28]

Black's many letters to Bowker, usually brief, were always bright with a rollicking and freakish jollity, and further revealed the lightheartedness and warmth of the man.[29]

Bowker grew to be as fond of the three Black children as of their father. "The children are both lovely and lively," Bowker wrote his mother, "and we have great fun, Blindman's Buff included; and it seems very like the Wheelers."[30] When the three Wheeler children did arrive in England in the fall of 1881, Bowker took them all to Brighton.

> My visit to Black's was delightful as usual: today is his fortieth birthday, but he celebrated Sunday. Mabs was away, but Dolly was delicious, particularly as she came prattling to my room while I was dressing. . . . And you should have seen the household excitement when I got out the penny monkey I had brought and which

26 R. R. B. to mother, May 23, 1881.
27 R. R. B., MS Memoir; to Miss Pickton, September 19, 1904.
28 R. R. B. to mother, April 4, 1882.
29 See, for example, William Black to R. R. B., June 1, 1881, in Reid, *William Black*, 227; August 9, 1881, in *ibid.*, 231; March 16, 1882, in *ibid.*, 234–35; June 16, 1882, in *ibid.*, 253, 295.
30 R. R. B. to mother, October 11, 1881.

climbed all the way up to the very tip of the stair-way on its piece of string. . . . Mrs. Black was delighted with the Wheeler children.[31]

Black cordially invited Bowker to take chambers next to his overlooking the Thames embankment near York gate, and Bowker, during the summer of 1882, accepted the proposal and moved in. On his next visit to England, in 1886, Bowker joined William Black on a houseboat excursion which formed the basis of Black's *Strange Adventures of a House Boat.*

Within two days of his arrival in England, Bowker had the opportunity to meet Thomas Hardy. Hardy had already written seven novels and had just definitely made his mark with *Far From the Madding Crowd.* He had become known to American readers through the then familiar *Leisure Hour Series,* edited by Henry Holt. Harry Harper had just completed a contract for Hardy's new novel, *A Laodicean,* which gave *Harper's Magazine* the rights to its entire serial publication on both sides of the water, and awarded Hardy £100 apiece for thirteen installments. Bowker was entrusted with the negotiations where Harry Harper had left off, and went out to see the novelist at his home in the London suburb of Upper Tooting.

> I was received in a pretty parlor by Mrs. Thomas Hardy, with her Kensington-stitch work, and her pet cat; she is an agreeable young-ish English lady, immensely interested in her husband's work, and we were at once good friends. Hardy presently came down, a quiet-mannered, pleasant, modest, little man, with sandyish short beard, entirely unaffected and direct, not at all spoiled by the reputation which *Far From the Madding Crowd* and its successors have won for him. He was originally an architect, and had little thought of writing novels. Told me he had the greatest difficulty in remembering the people and incidents of his own stories so that Mrs. Hardy had to keep on the look-out for him. We three fell to discussing a title for a new story which he is writing. . . . Before I went, tea and cake were served. I came home, having made two pleasant friends, I think.[32]

While *A Laodicean* was passing through the press, Hardy was much of the time confined to his bed by illness. Bowker had occasion frequently, therefore, to visit him in his cheerful retirement, during which Hardy read proof and completed manuscript in installments.[33] Bow-

31 R. R. B. to sister, November 15, 1881.
32 Journal, July 23, 1880.
33 *Ibid.,* July, 1880–November, 1881.

ker found Hardy a painstaking workman, even in proof revision, as well as "a thoroughly good fellow, quietly companionable," and quite willing to discuss his methods of writing. This particular novel was not a great success and gave no indication of the literary power later evidenced in *Tess of the D'Urbervilles*.

Bowker first met R. D. Blackmore, the author of *Lorna Doone,* at a farewell dinner given by Edward Marston for Harry Harper at the St. Stephen's Club. Blackmore impressed Bowker as "a large, bearded (turning grey) man of near sixty, with market gardening for his hobby and part occupation, looking like anything but the typical author." Bowker had inherited a sharp dispute between Sampson Low and Harper's as to whether it was fair that the novel edition of Blackmore's *Mary Anerley* should come out in England before it had completed its run as a magazine serial in *Harper's,* and he was glad to meet the principal in the issue.

Shortly thereafter, the Harpers asked Bowker to secure a portrait of Blackmore for use in one of their editions of his books. Several times Blackmore declined the request in a delightful, bantering mood:

> It appears to me that any man sticking himself up to gaze at his own title-page, and blinking at his readers, lowers himself by his self-elevation. What can it matter to his readers whether he is gifted with two eyes and one nose, or one eye and two noses? No, no, ever so many noeses! I keep out of all such little curiosity. If I can say a thing to please the public, there is pleasure on both sides; but as for labouring to look to please them what is the wise man's dictum on the subject? "More people know Tom Fool than Tom Fool knows"; let him first know himself.[34]

Not willing to take a written "no" for an answer, Bowker took a train out to Teddington to see this modest man in person. On alighting at the station, he asked where to find Mr. Blackmore, the author. Nobody seemed to know. Eventually a townsman brighter than the rest said, "Oh, he means the fruit man!" and directed Bowker along the right path. He found Blackmore in the midst of his daytime avocation, which was that of a market gardener raising fruits, for it was by evening that he did his writing with meticulous attention to details.

> *April 4:* His house is in the midst of a fine orchard, just now lovely as are all other parts of the Thames country with the pyramids of bloom. . . . Blackmore himself, who welcomed me kindly, looks

[34] See Harper, *The House of Harper,* 411; R. D. Blackmore to R. R. B., February 16, 23, 1882.

as much like a veteran sailor as anything, in his gardening dress and with his slow rugged way of speech.

Blackmore described to Bowker his love of fishing and chess and said that he attributed the success of *Lorna Doone,* after three years of initial neglect, to the fluke of the public's hope that the story might have something to do with the Marquis of Lorne's marriage. In the end he stuck to his veto of the photograph idea.

Bowker never formed an acquaintance with Browning, but saw him on several occasions. He stood with Browning at the open grave of George Eliot, had dinner with him in Boughton's studio, and chatted with him when Browning was acting as showman for a private view of his son Pen's pictures.

> *March 27:* Browning . . . was briskly complaisant, welcoming every-one and telling each of the pictures. I think he is the last man anyone would pick out for the metaphysical word-fashioning poet, this brisk, alert, business-like gentleman, with his nicely-clipped beard and almost dapper appearance.

On another occasion Bowker said of him, "He might well have been taken for a bank president or a gentleman of leisure . . . ready and agree-able in conversation, affable, without an assumption of importance such as one might find in lesser authors."

Two great English authors whom Bowker just missed seeing were George Eliot and Thomas Carlyle. Four days after Christmas, 1880, he attended the funeral of George Eliot. The news of her death had come on December 23 and was a great shock. All through the benefit concert which Bowker attended that evening he had thought: "And George Eliot lies dead—at Christmas time!" She had married John Walter Cross only two months before Bowker arrived in England, and he found his friends discussing her "newly remade life" which had commenced on the death of George Henry Lewes. As a representative of her American publishers, Bowker had eagerly looked forward to meeting her. The splendid portrait which Blackwood had shown him in Edinburgh, one of the only two ever made, had heightened his anticipation. On October 9 he had written in his Journal:

> Thence to Blackwood's again, to see the portrait of George Eliot which they had promised to show me. It is a crayon, so far back as 1861, just after *Adam Bede.* . . . The face, then, was infinitely sad,—what must it not be now? The prominent nose and full, strong mouth, suggesting wonderful nobility, are the striking features of the picture, but her eyes are said to be not less an index of this

first of women. She is not at all beautiful, homely—but the face one would carry in memory long. Now I want to see *her*.

But it was now too late. The great woman novelist was not to be buried in the Abbey, whether because of her unorthodoxy or of the Lewes connection, no one seemed to know. The ceremony at Highgate Cemetery made a vivid impression on Bowker:

> I found my way past noon, the dreadful rain making life and the green grass seem colorless as death itself, as one by one those coming straggled up the clayey, dreary road from the cemetery gate to where the chapel bell was tolling. . . . The neighborhood of the little chapel was crowded with a great quantity of people, and a very few could get inside. . . . Presently the rites were over, the crowd made way, and in her casket of some light colored wood and covered with white flowers, she passed on her last way. . . . Not far away stood Herbert Spencer, her staunch and intimate friend, his hair showing no grey . . . and Robert Browning, business-like always, with his trim white beard, and . . . Tyndall.

A month later Bowker called at the Chelsea home of John Walter Cross, to invite him to write a biographical sketch of his great wife. It seemed a charming, warm, cozy house. Mr. Cross, a tall, scholarly man, not much over forty, received him in the study by his solitary fireside from which the great presence had gone. As he entered, Bowker received the impression that Cross had just been burning the manuscript of the unfinished work which George Eliot had asked to have destroyed.

On February 4, 1881, a little more than a month after George Eliot passed away, Thomas Carlyle died. Bowker felt as though a great literary age was passing away:

> *February 9:* His [Carlyle's] death last Saturday, following G. Eliot's, made me feel that I was come to England just as the great generation is passing off the stage, just too late to catch sight of them passing. Tennyson, Browning, Gladstone, Bright, Beaconsfield,—are all old men, and the Victorian reign itself may soon come to an end.

Two English authoresses whom Bowker met during his first summer in England and was to keep in close touch with long after returning to America, were Mrs. Anne Thackeray Ritchie and Mrs. Mulock Craik. William Makepeace Thackeray had died in 1863 leaving two daughters. One of these had married Leslie Stephens, the shy but capable editor of *Cornhill*. The other, Anne, became one of Bowker's closest friends in England. She wrote stories and magazine articles, and had already published eight pieces when Bowker met her in 1880. Married for three years to R. T. Ritchie, a civil servant in the India Office, and with two young children, she presided over her country home with a charm that quite captivated Bowker when he first became an intimate there. "The family does not run to beauty," Bowker noted, "but she is as delightful as she is homely, and that is saying a good deal. Nobody could help liking her. . . . She lives in just such a house as Miss Thackeray should live in—200 years old, grimy without, quaint enough inside, full of odd things of which many were her father's . . . the open fireplace faced with tiles of Persian red, and the white, panelled, old-fashioned walls, hung with Thackeray's own drawings . . . and a homey, sunny air about it that is quite explained when she comes into it."

Bowker enjoyed the garden at the back and the old Thackeray home across the street. He came to pay almost weekly visits. "I find she and I are quite good friends," he wrote by the end of October, "and I count it a Sunday stopping place. Mrs. Ritchie says she only blossoms out with Americans." Two weeks later: "I was at the Ritchies yesterday afternoon, met Miss Veley, and played on the floor with Hester. Next week I am to go again to dinner. Quite a crowd of nice people were in— but I see no one I like better than the hostess."[35] The invitation to Christmas luncheon was a friendly show of hospitality to a young American far from home, and Bowker much appreciated it. "I scarcely expected, a year ago," he wrote his mother, "that I would this year be spending my Christmas under the Thackeray roof, with one of the little maidens of whom he wrote so tenderly, and with her daughter on my knee."

Bowker was eager to meet the former Dinah Maria Mulock, now Mrs. George Lillie Craik. She was well known to him and to his sister, as to hundreds of other readers, as the author of *John Halifax, Gentleman,* her most successful novel. By 1880 she had published sixteen novels, eleven children's books, and eight miscellaneous works. During his first week in London Bowker had asked her husband, a "nice, oldish gentleman of courteous manners," whether he might meet Mrs. Craik. He was soon given an invitation to visit "The Corner House," Shortlands, in Kent, ten miles out of London. Bowker was much impressed by the writing nook called "Dorothy's Parlor," the mottoes in each room, the library "long and light, filled with books and looking pleasantly homey." He described Mrs. Craik as "a large, motherly woman these days, gray eyed and with gray hair,—and with her pleasant, cheerful manner, and her husband's calling her 'Dinah,' I could think

[35] Journal, October 31, November 12, 1880.

of nothing but George Eliot's Dinah in *Adam Bede.*" He came to ad-
mire her for being good at a bargain and quite a mistress of affairs, but
quite as much for her charities as for anything else.

In addition to Mrs. Ritchie and Mrs. Craik, Bowker saw a good
deal of the prolific Mrs. K. S. Macquoid at her home The Edge, overlooking Tooting Common, gave continuous business advice and encouragement to Margaret Veley, and saw a good deal of Amelia B.
Edwards, poet, novelist, artist, and well-known Egyptologist. With all
three of these writers he kept up friendly relations long after he had
returned to America. Through Mrs. Craik and William Black, Bowker
came to know Mary Anderson, for whom Mrs. Craik wrote a classical
play, which, however, was not finished.[36]

Literary commissions required a constant stream of interviews and
communications with the great and near great.[37] There were arrangements to be made with Charles Lewis, literary executor of George Eliot;
with Gustav Doré for illustrations of Poe's "Raven"; with Charles
Reade, Anthony Trollope, and Edwin Arnold, "a curious appearing
man." There were pleasant negotiations with Edward Lear, Andrew
Lang, James Payn, Austin Dobson, Edmund Gosse, and William Alling-
ham, unpleasant ones with Lewis Carroll. Bowker had to search out
Justin McCarthy, the member of Parliament whose *History of Our Own
Times* had been such a surprising success, and found him "still a quiet,
unostentatious gentleman, mild-mannered, rather genial, with a long
brown beard and wearing spectacles." He had to get an assignment from
Moncure D. Conway in Bedford Park, and found "a gray-bearded
philosopher, an entire radical, who is a great conversationalist and most
interesting in his talk." Journal and letters reflect the intensity and
variety of Bowker's literary relations:

> *October 18, 1881:* Mr. Anthony Trollope was in, a bluff, vigorous,
> whiteheaded, fine-looking man, good for half a hundred more
> books. He writes so many works that he must needs publish some
> anonymously—as a current one in *Blackwood's.* After lunch I went
> up to the Legation . . . and saw Mr. Lowell. . . . Thence, with Sted-
> man's cordial letter of introduction, I looked up Austin Dobson,
> the *vers de societé* poet, who is in the civil service, in a cellar in the

---

[36] R. R. B., "Some Reminiscences of Mrs. D. M. Craik," *Harper's Bazaar,* November 5, 1887.

[37] Bowker recorded interesting anecdotes concerning Macaulay (Journal, Oc-
tober 15, 1880); Disraeli (*ibid.,* January, 1881); George Eliot (*ibid.,* February 1, 1881);
Mrs. Craik (*ibid.,* February 8, 1881); Carlyle (*ibid.,* February 9, 1881; May 6, 1881).
Some of this material and other material gathered during the years 1880–82 is used in
R. R. B., "London as a Literary Center," *Harper's Magazine,* Part I, May, 1888, pp.
815–44; Part II, June, 1888, pp. 2–26.

Board of Trade building. . . . He is a cheerful, pleasant fellow, something under forty, and said he had just been wondering whether I would prove another of the numerous Americans as to whom he got letters but who never turned up. Thence to Smith Elder & Co's. to see Jas. Payn, the novelist, of whom I've seen a great deal. He declared that he was very mad . . . on some American literary matter . . . meanwhile overflowing with good nature, lolling about his room, and munching or sipping away from the tray of eatables which he seems always to have by his desk. We generally transact business by calling each other, or somebody else, hard names—he is great fun. Thence to Piccadilly to see Chapman, of Chapman and Hall (Dickens' publishers) where again was Mr. Anthony Trollope.

November 3, 1881: These are busy days,—what with the magazine which is promising excellently; the quantity of inquiries, negotiations and details as to fall books which require one to be all about this big city at once, and international copyright, which gives me a good deal of talking and writing to do about the proposed treaty. All morning nearly was spent at Murray's where Dr. Schliemann's *Ilios* had got in a mess again, requiring a general council of war, Mr. John Murray, the other partners, the printer, the lithographer, and myself, to get straightened out.

RBB to sister, March 16, 1882: Wednesday morning, Hardy popped in and took me off to luncheon with his wife, and himself, Mr. and Mrs. C. Carr—she is the genuine leader of the aesthetes,—and Marion Terry—who didn't come. Stopped at Fred. Macmillan's office, and had some interesting talk about "John Inglesant" and Mr. Gladstone. . . . The latest yarn is that Mr. Gladstone doesn't care any more about politics, but only about the Revised Version, which he thinks so ill done that it should be done again at once. . . .

The business of the House of Harper in England involved Bowker in almost as many important negotiations with artists as with publishers and authors. Illustrations for both books and *Maga* articles required personal conferences, tactful reminders of deadlines, a certain amount of supervisory criticism. The artists with whom Bowker had most to do were Edwin Abbey, Alfred Parsons, George Henry Boughton, William Small, and George Du Maurier, though there were many others whom he came to know.

During his first week in London, Bowker made the acquaintance of Edwin A. Abbey, perhaps the most important of the Harpers' illustrators. He immediately became one of Bowker's closest friends. Abbey was then a charming and insouciant young artist of twenty-eight, still referred to as Ned Abbey, or as "Little E. A.," and described to Bowker by Frederick Barnard as "our pocket Raphael."[38] After completing his training at the Pennsylvania Academy of Fine Arts, Abbey had been engaged by Harper and Brothers in 1871 and had come to England for them in 1878, becoming a member the following year of the Lillie household. At that moment he was engaged in illustrating an edition of Robert Herrick's poems, and he took Bowker into his studio in the back yard to show him the curious and valuable wardrobe of old costumes he had accumulated for illustrating his volume.[39] Bowker found him a unique and rather incongruous personality, short of stature, grotesquely amusing in manner and speech, the artist through and through with conscience for his art. "When they look at my work in the future," Abbey once said to Bowker, "They will see I have all the buttons right."[40]

Bowker was soon to learn at first hand of Abbey's inability to manage his financial affairs. He was always short of money, and when he did have it, he wasted it recklessly in buying costumes and paying models, some of whom played upon his generosity without conscience. In Paris, after a gay time with his brother artists, he is said on one occasion to have stood on his head in the street and let such money as he had drop out of his pockets. Harper and Brothers tried to be firm with their irresponsible artist. "Give our friend Abbey some kind and practical advice," the head of the house wrote Bowker that December.

> You know that we have a great affection for Abbey, he has always been a pet of our house and we wish him well, indebtedness or no indebtedness. I question, however, if unlimited credit is a kindness to such a man as Abbey, who is as honest as a circle is round and who frets and chafes under a debt as a young thoroughbred would when first in harness. Unfortunately, Abbey is very indiscreet in financial affairs. In fact, men constituted as he, excessively generous and sympathetic, generally are. Why, Abbey's yearly expenditures must exceed the salaries of most of our diplomatic representatives![41]

Bowker was apparently able to give the "kind and practical advice" in a thoroughly acceptable manner. On Christmas Day, Abbey expressed

38 Journal, June 3, 1881.
39 *Ibid.*, July 22, 1880.
40 *Ibid.*, June 7, 1881.
41 J. H. Harper to R. R. B., December 18, 1880.

his gratitude. "You've been very good to me, old man," he wrote, "and I hope to be able to show you one of these days how much I appreciate your thoughtfulness. I get in such snarls and so mixed up generally in my affairs that a head like yours seems little short of marvelous to me."

In Bowker's Journal, in his letters from Abbey, and in Carolyn Bowker's comments, one gets colorful little glimpses of this great American artist.

Bowker's Journal, September 6, 1880: Abbey amused us greatly by a description of his models; one of them perfectly bald and doffs his wig on coming in: his card reads, "Hair on or off."

Abbey to Bowker, June, 1881: Come in and grub with me tonight about seven. I'm really ill and lonely and mizzable generally. I'll chirk up if you'll come and bang nigger songs onto the pianner. . . . I am in a deuce of a stew about money. Shortly before I left England I had three notices from creditors that they had put their accounts in the hands of their solicitors and if I don't get some money *damsoon* there will be the deuce and all to pay and no mistake.

Abbey to Bowker, 1881 (from Holland): Thanks muchly for the magazines. I shall sow them here. I have letters to three swells (not smells) here and think perhaps it will be a good thing.

Carolyn Bowker's Journal, July 12, 1881: How charmingly he rambled on, mimicking, sketching and telling tales of himself that showed how utterly impractical and delightful he is.

A brother artist of Abbey's and another member of the Harper family was Alfred Parsons, with whom Abbey shared a studio at 54 Bedford Gardens. Abbey always needed mothering, and in Parsons, his closest English friend, he found a rare combination of feminine gentleness and masculine strength. Parsons, who had been in America, was a painter of quiet, charming, English landscapes, and one of the foremost in his field. He and Abbey not only shared quarters but sometimes pictures, for Abbey would paint in a figure or two for Parsons' foreground while the latter would sometimes furnish a background for Abbey's figures. Bowker thought it a delightful companionship, each man worthy of the other and supplementing him in character. Thus the Abbey-Parsons studio was a favorite resort of many friends.

Not far away from the Abbey-Parsons studio was West House, the residence and studio of another member of this circle, George Henry Boughton. Boughton had been taken as a child of three to Albany,

New York, where he studied through high school. After gaining a reputation in America as a painter of popular colonial subjects, he had
studied in Paris, came to London in 1862, and the very next year exhibited at the Royal Academy, being elected an Associate in 1879. When
Bowker met him, he had achieved great success, both artistic and pecuniary, as an English painter whose American origin was almost forgotten
except to his American friends. His house and studio were of fine dimensions and character and provided a formal background for the
crownless old American straw hat which he always wore at work. Bowker was always impressed by Boughton's studio and his studio parties.

> *March 27, 1881.* His house . . . is magnificent: the studio, an im-
> mense room full of picturesque things and galleried at one end,
> as most of the new large studios are, to give effects from below to
> models and accessories. The quantity (and quality) that man turns
> out is marvelous. He has six fine pictures painted since he came
> back from Holland: one painted in two days and a half—"But
> those were days!" he said,—from early in the morning till as late
> as he could see, stopping now and then to lie flat on his back for
> ten minutes and then up and at 'em. "The Rose of Plymouth"
> (Rose Standish) an exquisite girl figure, in sad yet light colors, with
> autumn setting, will probably be the picture to be engraved,
> though his finely sombre yet mellow picture of "Hester Prynne"
> with the Scarlet Letter, (knocking at a door whereon is written
> "Lord, have mercy upon us!") is as good.

Harpers' business brought Bowker into close association with
George Du Maurier. The firm was anxious that the engravings for
Hardy's *A Laodicean* should be better than the usual work of the kind
in the English magazines, and asked Hardy to suggest a first-class artist.
He selected Du Maurier, and it then became Bowker's pleasant obligation to inaugurate the relations which afterwards became so close
and so widespread between Du Maurier and his American public.[42]
Du Maurier was then at the height of his fame as the society illustrator
for *Punch.* He had also been illustrating the *Cornhill Magazine* for
over a dozen years, but his debut in literature, which was made with
Trilby, was still many years in the future. Bowker's first opportunity
to study this artist's work came at the end of July.

> Saw some drawings of Du Maurier's at the engraver's. Hardy had
> told us he knew nothing of dress, but left that to his wife, who

[42] R. R. B., "Recollections of Du Maurier," New York *Times* Supplement, October 25, 1896.

drapes all his models. This would surprise those who see his strength at toilettes. The children of his pictures are his own children. He *does* notice faces and is fond of bric-a-brac. I find he draws altogether in pen and ink, having the sight of but one eye, his engraver tells me, so that he cannot use a brush, scarcely seeing accurately where its point touches the paper.[43]

The two men soon made each other's acquaintance, but it was not until December that Bowker visited Du Maurier in his studio in the artist colony at New Grove.

> I was ushered into his studio, where he was sitting by the open fire, the great dog Chang, of the *Punch* pictures, asleep in the window recess. The dog, who is an elected member of the Arts Club, is Du Maurier's constant companion [and is] known all over London. . . . Du Maurier is really a Frenchman, born near Paris, a good, genial fellow, rather stout and jolly looking, and exceedingly agreeable. . . . These *Punch* pictures, he tells me, grow: he catches a notion, draws a figure or so, and works up his page from this, often modifying his legends (which are for the most part his) at the last moment for a finer point. A good many suggestions are sent in, and sometimes these give him a hint.[44]

Actually Bowker had become critical of Du Maurier's work on the novel and had come to say so. "I finally told him out and out that we were disappointed in his drawings for the Hardy story," Bowker wrote in the *Journal*, "whereupon he rather owned up that he was better at working his own will in social satire than under the limitations of other people's stories—though his Thackeray illustrations are among his best work. He said Hardy came up and gave him the points minutely and of course he felt constrained within these limits." A few weeks later Bowker saw fit to make further criticisms of the artist's drawings for *A Laodicean*. Du Maurier admitted the justice of these and agreed to make the corrections, on another occasion charging Bowker with having "a microscopic eye."[45] English artists were not accustomed to the American magazine art editor who often made critical suggestions which artists were glad to accept.

In addition to such *Maga* illustrators as Abbey, Parsons, Boughton, and Du Maurier, Bowker also came to know Frank D. Millet, William Small, and C. S. Reinhart, who worked for the House of Harper. Perhaps it was when Small was commissioned to illustrate Black's *Shandon*

43 Journal, July 30, 1880.
44 *Ibid.*, December 10, 1880.
45 G. Du Maurier to R. R. B., December 28, 1880; May 10, 1881.

Bells for the *Maga* that he and Black and Bowker came to be intimate friends; at any rate it is clear that Black often included the other two in his frequent house parties. Reinhart had left the New York office as senior member of Charles Parsons' staff of artists in 1878 to work abroad, and was then enjoying an enviable reputation among the American colony. Bowker first visited him in his Paris studio, which Abbey alluded to affectionately as "that sink of iniquity."

Through these artists in the Harper family, Bowker was introduced to some of the other leading English artists of the day. At Boughton's studio he first met John Pettie, R. A., whom he referred to as "the very Scotch Scotchman . . . Black's special admiration."[46] He visited the studio of Hubert Herknomer, who was not only making his mark with such great pictures as "Chelsea Pensioners in Church" and "Missing," but editing the *Graphic*.[47] He also came to know John Everett Millais, who had survived his Pre-Raphaelite apprenticeship and was painting his great pictures; Colin Hunter, whose studio he first visited in the company of the astronomer Norman Lockyer; Thomas Collier, Percy Macquoid, and Felix Moscheles. He accompanied his Brooklyn neighbors, the Wheelers, to see Sir Fredrick Leighton, president of the Royal Academy, who received them "most cordially as well as courteously." "He got so interested in the Wheelers," wrote Bowker, "that he insisted on taking us into nearly every room in his magnificent house and bringing out his pet treasures, though he rages furiously at people who come simply to see his house, as is quite right. But such a house!"

It is evident that his Harper relations afforded young Bowker an enviable opportunity to look in on several art circles in England and that he made the most of it. Referring to a visit to the Grosvenor Gallery for a private showing of pictures in the spring of 1881, he wrote in his Journal: "There were lots of people there whom I knew, for curiously enough, one of my circles is decidedly the moderate-aesthetic or Grosvenorites, though I suspect I count as a Philistine."[48]

Bowker's working day, as always, was carefully planned. It was at first hard for him to adjust to the hours of English public life. "The English world centers about Parliament." he noted in his Journal, "which has its *morning* session late in the afternoon, rises for dinner at seven, resumes at nine, and goes to bed at two to four in the morning. I perceive that, to do any study or work here, outside business, one must exercise more self-restraint than at home." The English publish-

[46] Journal, February 21, 1882.
[47] R. R. B. to sister, March 20, 1882.
[48] Journal, April 30, 1881.

ers, Bowker found, were never at their offices before ten. It was with a
guilty conscience that he now planned to go to bed at twelve and rise
at eight. He would carefully read the *Times* while eating breakfast alone
in dressing gown and slippers, served by the house "slavey." His lifelong
habit of walking for his health dictated that he leave the house at nine
for a brisk thirty-minute saunter across town to his office, possibly stopping for a shave along the way. By ten he was at his desk. Lunch came
at one, and the office closed at five. The evenings were precious. Social
calls on his friends and trips to the theater and music hall alternated
with carefully planned study at home, when, back in his room with dinner eaten by 7:30, he would be free to read until midnight, by gas if in
the sitting room, by candle if in his own chambers. Just before retiring,
he faithfully wrote the day's record in the Journal. This became a tremendous catalog of historical and literary items, hotels, meals, concert
programs, anecdotes, *bon mots,* scraps of conversation. It was written
for his family and immediate friends, and was a tribute to Bowker's
journalistic fortitude and keen observation.

Since he was getting along well with publishers, authors, and illustrators, working hard, using good business judgment, and completely loyal to the interests of his employers, it was obvious to everyone
that Bowker was making a success of his London mission. The Harpers
were well pleased. J. H. Harper wrote to Bowker on November 25, 1880:
"I am delighted, so far, with your success with the *Magazine,* as well as
with the general impetus you have already given to our foreign business." J. W. Harper wrote on December 29, 1880: "Let me tell you personally, and for my partners, that we are thoroughly well pleased with
the result thus far of your going to England. You well know that we
have had our eye on you for several years, and your action has in every
way confirmed our choice." J. H. Harper tried to induce Bowker to
extend the original two-year contract for a third year and, later, in his
published memoirs, described Bowker during these years as "an active,
diplomatic, and popular representative whose business instincts were
keen and trustworthy."[49] But Bowker was more than a business success.
He became a useful ambassador of good will from America to England.

49 J. H. Harper to R. R. B., April 27, 1882; Harper, *The House of Harper,* 475.

XI

Literary Ambassador at the Court of Fleet Street

Bowker's gift for making friends, getting things done, and seizing opportunities to promote useful causes made him an important cog in the Anglo-American publishing world of London. Increasingly, English authors, publishers, and librarians sought his aid. At the same time he was more and more importuned by Americans both at home and visiting London to dispense information and give advice, serve as guide, and act as liaison between the two countries. To a number of English literary households where he became an intimate, he symbolized the American virtues of friendliness, dispatch, and open-mindedness. In several particulars, such as international copyright, an English memorial to Garfield, the American memorial to Stanley, and Anglo-American library co-operation, he definitely promoted the relations of the two great English-speaking communities. The designation which Bowker once applied to himself was not inappropriate: "Literary Ambassador at the Court of Fleet Street."[1] Bowker's usefulness was promoted by several factors: his many, varied social contacts, his thorough knowledge of London and its environs, and his ability to keep in balanced perspective the values of American and English ways.

Bowker's role as "Literary Ambassador" was partly facilitated by his membership in an interesting Anglo-American circle of writers and illustrators who worked for Harper's in London. These men foregathered in studios, homes, or famous hostelries; they went to the theater together and took trips around London and into the country together. Because of his special role in the Harper program and because of his

[1] R. R. B., "Recollections of Du Maurier," New York *Times* Supplement, October 25, 1896.

natural friendliness, Bowker was immediately taken into this circle. He keenly relished its distinguished membership, its informal companionship, good talk, and creative interests.

Bowker's introduction to this Anglo-American circle was by way of the Lillie household. John Lillie was assistant editor of the *Maga*. His wife was a brilliant and interesting woman, who, as Lucy C. Lillie, wrote charmingly for *Harper's Young People* and so was a member of the Harper family in her own right. The English had come to like her very much, taking her into their confidence. A regular member of the Lillie household was Edwin Abbey, who, indeed, was the prime pet of the entire Anglo-American circle. Bowker saw him constantly at the Lillies, and went with the latter to the frequent parties which Abbey and Alfred Parsons gave in their joint studio at 54 Bedford Gardens. Abbey also enjoyed giving more formal dinner parties, such as the "gorgeous banquet" at the Star and Garter, Richmond, which he gave in the summer of 1882 for members of the Harper staff with "a half dozen English cusses" invited.[2]

At one of the Lillie-Abbey evenings soon after his arrival in London, Bowker discovered an old associate of *Evening Mail* days, the American dramatist Bronson Howard. Howard promptly suggested that Bowker share his lodgings in Regents Park, and Bowker as promptly accepted.[3] Howard, who was to do so much to revive American drama, had already begun to make his reputation as a playwright in England, Bowker even observing in his Journal that he seemed to be regarded there as "quite the leading man in his line." The two friends, who had separate upstairs quarters, shared the same downstairs living room. Nevertheless, since Howard was of necessity a night bird, keeping greenroom hours till the early morn and Bowker regularly retired by midnight, they seldom met except for Sunday walks together, or visits with mutual friends. Bowker observed that after Howard had roughed out his scenario of plot, people, and incidents, he would reach what he called "the hansom stage" and drive aimlessly about London in a cab, occasionally directing the driver aloft by his lifted umbrella, while the driver wondered what sort of lunatic he had below.

The Bowker-Howard bachelor ménage lasted only three months, for in October, 1880, Howard was married to the sister of Sir Charles Wyndham.

[2] Among those present were Bowker, Harry Harper, Abbey, Boughton, Du Maurier, Fred Barnard, Robert W. Macbeth, Austin Dobson, Willy Paton, "young Dave Sears of Boston," and the engraver John A. Lowell. R. R. B. to sister, July 11, 1882; Harper, *The House of Harper*, 474.

[3] Bronson Howard and R. R. B. lived at 8 Blandford Place, Upper Baker Street, Clarencegate, Regents Park, N. W.

Journal, October 26: Howard and I spent his last bachelor evening together, he coaching up from my prayerbook. He overflowed with uncalled for pity at my forlorn condition. I wish you could have seen Abbey when I told him, slapping himself at intervals with "Bronson Howard!"

Bowker was best man at the wedding and looked forward to some letters from his erstwhile fellow lodger telling of the progress of the honeymoon. When Howard returned, still trailing clouds of nuptial glory, he professed great amusement at his friend's naïveté:

I forgive you, my dear boy, for the utter ignorance which such a thought evinces. A few weeks ago I had the same ignorance. I can *now* tell you that a man on his wedding-tour has no interest, whatever, in post offices, or in any affairs which connect him with the outside world and the other individuals of his race.[4]

After Howard's marriage, Bowker roomed with a former *Evening Post* reporter named Denning.

In mid-August Bowker met other members of the Anglo-American circle at a dinner given by Bronson Howard at the famous Blue Post Tavern in Cork Street, back of the Royal Academy. The dinner was in honor of Billie Florence and a fellow American actor, who were to play to their "first night" audience at a London theater that evening. The guests included Julian Hawthorne, Joseph Hatton, Laurence Hutton, and Charles Dickens the younger. Many held that young Dickens had something of his father's look and manner, but Bowker could not see it, although he was willing to concede that the young man had succeeded his father as the best punch-maker and salad-dresser in London. After the pleasant dinner, Bowker walked through Covent Garden Market to the theater with Dickens, and the latter told him interesting stories of his father, whose readings Bowker had heard as a boy. Dickens lamented that the landmarks of his father's London had almost altogether disappeared.[5]

Bowker soon became well acquainted with both Joseph Hatton and "Larry" Hutton. Hatton was a novelist and the London correspondent for the New York *Times*. He was a good friend of the actor Henry Irving, and Bowker was particularly struck with the many interesting pictures he had in his home.[6] Hutton, then living in London with his mother, was an essayist whose books Harper's was soon to publish. Pos-

4 Bronson Howard to R. R. B., November 7, 1880.
5 Journal, August 18, 1880; R. R. B., MS Memoir.
6 Journal, December 19, 1880.

sessed of the gift of friendship, he was everybody's friend, and Bowker found him a most congenial companion. Hutton and Bowker, accompanied by Howard and others of the Anglo-American group, loved to prowl about old London streets, particularly of a Sunday. Hutton was then profusely annotating his copy of *Hare's Walks in London* for a future article on Dickens' London, and these explorations contributed to this project as well as to his excellent book, *Literary Landmarks of London*, printed in 1885, for many years one of the very best guidebooks written.

A favorite rendezvous for the Anglo-American circle was William Black's York House chambers at the foot of Buckingham Street, Strand. It was a scenic and historic spot. The windows looked out upon the old Water-gate, once alongside the Thames, and over the Embankment Gardens to the river, with a vista upstream nearly to Westminster, and downstream over the bridges, to St. Paul's in far sight. The house was said to be that occupied by Peter the Great during his London experiments, and on the top story was the "singularly desirable and compact set of chambers forming a genteel residence" which David Copperfield and Aunt Betsy Trotwood had found "the very thing." Here was also laid the scene of Black's novel *Sunrise*. In this delightful spot many a midnight literary bout was enjoyed by Abbey, Parsons, Boughton, Bowker, Osgood, Colin Hunter, Hatton, and William Small.[7]

An infrequent but colorful member of this circle was Bret Harte, then United States consul in Glasgow by appointment of President Hayes and a popular guest in many city and country houses. Bowker frequently met him at the Blacks. He was picturesque and insouciant, as usual—Bowker thinking that only George MacDonald and Ned Abbey outdid him in the latter quality. He had something of a reputation at this time for arriving at a country house without a dress suit, borrowing one from his host, taking it on with him to the next house, and then forgetting it.

A fellow American who was not a member of the Harper Anglo-American circle, but who stimulated Bowker to develop his Anglo-American relations and activities, was James Russell Lowell. On Bowker's arrival in London, Lowell had just been transferred from the American Legation at Madrid to serve as minister to the Court of St. James. During his two years in London, Bowker became a frequent visitor at the Legation and the Lowell home in Lowndes Square. The two men, so different in other ways, had certain important interests in common. Lowell had been, himself, an Independent Republican, and told Bowker that he owed his present appointment to that fact. He had

7 Reid, *William Black,* 193–95, based on R. R. B., MS Memoir.

read with approval of Bowker's activities in the Young Scratcher campaign of 1879 and the pre-convention Independent Republican movement of 1880 in the *Nation*. They were also both interested in international copyright and civil service reform. "Spain," Lowell commented,
"is about in the condition of rottenness that we shall reach fifty years
hence, if we keep on with our present civil service." For banter, the
two men kept up a running comparison of the virtues of Salem and
Boston.

The Lowells were warmly hospitable toward the homeless young
American.[8] Bowker deeply appreciated having his first Christmas dinner in England at the Lowell home. He was also invited for Thanksgiving, to a number of dinner parties, and to the intimate birthday
parties which celebrated Lowell's forty-sixth and forty-seventh anniversaries.

> *Journal, February 1882:* Wednesday evening was Washington's
> Birthday,—and Mr. Lowell's, so there was a little dinner in
> Loundes Square. There were eight at table, the others, Mr. and
> Mrs. Smalley; Miss Harriet Hosmer, the sculptress; Hoppin, Sec-
> retary of the Legation; and a Miss Calhoun, a California girl train-
> ing for the stage, whom Mrs. Lowell has much taken to. . . . It
> was a nice little dinner, and after it Miss Calhoun was made to do
> "Juliet" while Lowell read "Romeo" from the book in his quiet
> but literally honeyed speech.

Bowker thought Mrs. Lowell, who was still confined to her wheel chair,
"a quiet, pleasing woman, speaking little . . . but with a frequent and
a happy laugh,—very charming," and regarded Lowell as "delightfully
gallant" toward her.[9] But he was critical of Lowell's monopoly of the
conversation.

> *October 19, 1880:* He kept up a brilliant conversation, if so it could
> be called, being so much his own as to make one feel stupid by con-
> trast. That is perhaps the difference between a man and a woman
> in leading conversation: Mrs. Lillie is charming for her "Don't you
> think?" appeals. Lowell is host and master,—self-centered to a de-
> gree that would be vanity in a lesser man, but in him carrying its

8 See J. R. Lowell to R. R. B., December 9, 1880; R. R. B. to J. H. Choate, November 27, 1914; Journal, April 7, 1881.

9 Bowker's reminiscences of Christmas dinner in 1880, of Lowell's reading of
Romeo and Juliet, his attitude toward his wife, and his perplexities in presenting
ladies at court are included in Horace E. Scudder, *James Russell Lowell, A Biography*,
II, 267–98. See R. R. B., "Reminiscences of Lowell," New York *Evening Post* (Book
Section), March 1, 1919.

own justification. . . . Mr. Lowell thinks the world was a comparatively happy one before Watt, or rather before Gutenberg; and he knew "the heroic self-sacrifice" of the many men who must have discovered these things before, and out of kindness to posterity kept them to themselves.[10]

Lowell must have noted and approved the thoroughness with which Bowker kept himself posted on political and literary developments at home. It was not the least of the qualities that made him a valuable member of the Anglo-American circle, or popular with English hosts and American visitors. An almost weekly correspondence with Wheeler, Shepard, Dugdale, Putnam, Whitridge, Milbury, McAdam, and Wells informed him of developments in the Garfield administration and in civil service and tariff reform. From the *Publishers' Weekly* office, Growoll mailed him the *Post,* the *Nation,* the indexes to the *Tribune* and the *Literary World,* while his sister sent selected clippings from the New York *Times.*

Bowker's usefulness as a "literary ambassador" was the greater because of his extensive social connections, and it is perfectly clear that the young man from Brooklyn was a social success from the start. This was, of course, partly due to his Harper connections and the fact that he had publishing favors to grant. But it was much more due to his own friendliness and to the fact that he was interesting, well informed, intellectually curious, principled, and intelligently concerned about his world.

> *October 30, 1880:* I find myself on increasingly good terms with Lowell, and indeed with everybody—they are "awfully" good to me here.

> *November 3, 1880:* I find that I am quite coming out here . . . rather curiously, for I never expected to become "popular," but having no one to fight here yet, I suspect I must be mellowing.

> *November 6, 1881:* You needn't be afraid of my lacking Sunday friends. I am only too crowded with invitations and can drop in familiarly at the Alfords, or Howards, or the Eales, hereabouts, or the Marstons at Highbury, or at Bedford Gardens in Young Street at the other end, almost as I would at the Shepards.

This successful introduction of "folksiness" into English households is no little tribute to the young Brooklyn journalist, and he realized it was not to be taken for granted. "I am given to understand," he wrote his family, "that this home-acquaintance is rather a special privilege

10 Journal, October 19, 1880.

here, according to an American who is fond of children, and (at the Macquoid's) dogs. . . . Most of the English into whose houses I go seem to give the open sesame peculiarly to an American, apparently because we are more at ease with them than they with each other."

When Shepard visited Bowker in London and went the rounds with him, he was much impressed. "I really believe," he wrote Bowker's mother, "that Rogers has the largest collection of agreeable and interesting acquaintances in London. And the affectionate admiration in which he is held by so many and different persons is wonderful indeed."[11] There was, in truth, an impressive variety to his social relations: the homely dignity of tea with the Ritchies, the intimate informality of gatherings with the Anglo-American circle in William Black's chambers, the correct formality of dinner with William Low, Edward Marston, or Lowell. Bowker enjoyed being the guest of Walter Besant at the Rabelais Club along with Lowell, Alma-Tadema, and Sir Frederick Pollock; making a well-received after-dinner speech at the brilliant annual dinner of the Bedford Park Club when a guest of the Moncure Conways; sitting down to an elaborate dinner of "a dozen or more courses" in Boughton's studio with Lowell, Robert Browning, the Blacks, and the Kendals for fellow guests;[12] and being elected a member of the Savile Club through the offices of his friend Sir J. G. Fitch. But Bowker never acquired a taste for "society" and actually had less and less heart for the increasing round of social engagements. He preferred "the quiet, non-party-giving literary circles" which he had known in New York and Brooklyn. "I still like better to see people in their homes," he wrote, "than to wander eyeless among crowds, not knowing whom one does know."

While Bowker's social relations made him familiar with a considerable number of interesting persons in and around London, his lifelong passion for "sightseeing" soon made him something of an authority on the ways and byways of the great metropolis. Within a month of his arrival in London, he set about a systematic course of study in the city's historic sights. "I have bought a number of books about London," he wrote home, "and propose to study up each part, past and present, as I am likely to go there. I begin with the British Museum. I have also bought a copy of *Pendennis* to read again, for it is full of Fleet Street and the Temple." By night he pored over guidebooks, young Charles Dickens' *Curiosities of London,* and especially his *Dictionary of London,* which he found to be the best available guide to the street mysteries

11 E. M. Shepard to Mrs. Daniel Bowker, July 4, 1882.
12 R. R. B. to sister, July 1, 1882; to mother, February 20, 1881; Journal, March 22, 1882.

of the great city. By day he carried in his pocket the sectional maps printed in the *Dictionary*, as well as a pocket compass. There seemed to be nothing in the city or its immediate suburbs that Bowker missed. The Journal is crammed with specific comments on a thousand delightful details of familiar and unfamiliar landmarks: a balloon race at Alexandra Palace, a church service at G. H. Spurgeon's Tabernacle, the "blaze of gorgeous and ridiculous costume" at the Lord Mayor's election, tramps through Epping Forest and Hampstead Heath, a coach excursion to Brighton, a boat ride to the Greenwich observatory, a channel voyage to Margate. No opportunity to get to know and to enjoy his physical surroundings was missed, whether it was the daily, thirty-minute walk across the city from his lodgings in Regents Park to the office in Fleet Street, or the weekend excursions with Hutton and Howard. And, as usual, these walks and outings helped to keep Bowker in the perfect health he enjoyed throughout his two years abroad.

Bowker's exploration of London's resources included the stage and music and the best places to dine. On weekday evenings he went as often as possible to the theater. He saw Henry Irving and Ellen Terry in *The Bells* and *The Merchant of Venice*, and twice saw Irving in *Romeo and Juliet*, which was enough to convince him of "the total unsuitability of Irving for his part." He saw Edwin Booth in *King Lear* and *Othello*, Sarah Bernhardt in *Adrienne Lecouvre*, as well as the Bancrofts, the Kendals, Charles Wyndham, and others. For music, he would go to a choral concert at Crystal Palace, Beethoven Night at the Covent Garden Opera House, Gilbert and Sullivan at the Opera Comique, the inexpensive Promenade Concert series, the "Monday Pops" and "Saturday Pops" at St. James' Hall. He heard Wagner's *Die Walküre* and *Siegfried*, and really liked them. On the other hand, he did not have much use for Patti in *Don Giovanni* and *La Traviata*, and much preferred Tyndall's first lecture at the Royal Institute. He was deeply disappointed when certain publishing negotiations cost him a long-cherished opportunity to hear Gounod conduct his own oratorio, *The Redemption*.

Bowker did not like to attend the theater or concert hall alone, but he soon discovered that London society did not approve his taking a single lady, American style. The consequent necessity of taking *two* ladies at a time, to more expensive seats than he would have preferred for himself and by cab, was an amusing bachelor problem for this economical young man.

Finally, and not the least of his enthusiasms, were places to dine, which became a kind of hobby. The Journal is crammed with notes on well-known and less well-known hostelries and their specialties. Bowker was no epicure, but his curiosity led him to try many famous dishes at least once, and what he had found out for himself he enjoyed introducing to others. With this knowledge of London's sights, theater, music, and hostelries, Bowker became an ideal guide for American visitors to London.

Not the least important quality that helped to make Bowker a useful "literary ambassador" was his ability to remain objective about the strong and weak points of both Britain and America. Bowker was never a completely biased Yankee, nor did he become an Anglophile. It was typical of him that he found Loch Katrine less lovely than Lake George; that during a visit to Westminster Abbey he noted "some very rude and irreverent Englishmen" exhibiting what "is supposed to be an American Quality"; that when he caught the postal telegraph service in "a very bad blunder," he entered complaint expressly to test whether they really "do things better in England." His reaction to the English drawing-room code was thoroughly American.

"What struck me here," he wrote his mother after attending a big social function, "as many times before, was the isolated silence in which English 'social circles' shine. There were more women than men, but the women sat silent about the walls, and the men stood silent about the doors, in painful isolation, till one wanted to go in American fashion, and 'stir them up.' . . . It is only in theory, not in practice, that the English speak without introduction, and they never, that is hardly ever, introduce. Today I was at tea at Mrs. Smalley's and was comparing notes. . . . Her experience, of *years* here, confirms mine. She says English people seem to like it—this standing or sitting about, doing and saying nothing,—and she told of introducing people who had been revolving in the same circles and wanting to know each other for fifteen years, without finding out how. The hostess mostly does nothing, and the guests help her at it."[13]

The result of Bowker's special combination of literary relations on both sides of the Atlantic, his reputation for helpfulness, promptness, and pugnacity in carrying out assignments was a steadily increasing load of miscellaneous literary commissions. The flood of requests from Englishmen for information on American matters was so heavy that even by September, 1880, Bowker found himself "more and more regarded as a sort of general Intelligence Office for American Matters." Similarly from the American side came requests for assistance that could not be well declined. Now it was Bradstreet's asking for "an occasional letter from London regarding the financial and commercial situation and kindred matters," and sending material to be placed in

13 R. R. B. to mother, June 22, 1882.

English journals. The next moment it was the matter of preparing an introduction to an English edition of E. E. Hale's stories, assembling material for an article by E. C. Stedman on "some London Poets," or showing the superintendant of one of Harper's pressrooms at Franklin Square through the printing works of Richard Clay. A commission from *Harper's Bazaar* took Bowker to Paris to check on the delivery of fashion news, and another errand sent him to the Book Fair at Leipzig.[14]

As for the American visitors who used the office as headquarters, by 1882 Bowker was describing his Fleet Street rooms as "a sort of intermittent levee of fellow-countrymen." In February it was the Ticknors, in March the Wesley Harpers, in April the Harry Harpers and old Mrs. Fletcher Harper, with whom he spent pleasant days in Munich. Edward Everett Hale paid Bowker a second visit,[15] again staying in his chambers while his daughter Nelly exhibited a picture in the Royal Academy. When Bowker's bosom friend, Edward Morse Shepard, came over to England in May, Bowker took him on the rounds of all his London friends, including Alfred Parsons, whose studio was especially fascinating to Shepard; William Black, to whose shooting lodge in Scotland they went for a pleasant excursion; and Lowell. Then there were the Everett P. Wheelers, Professor Mitchell, E. C. Stedman and his son, Henry Train, Charles Nordhoff, Charles Dudley Warner, and Will Harper. In May, 1882, Bowker wrote to his sister:

> Tuesday, Furness, the parliamentary artist of *Punch,* and Lillie came to lunch with me to talk over an article. Presently Ives came in to say good-bye—he and his charming wife go to New York for good, as he is offered the City Editor of the *Times;* and then appeared Stedman and his son from America. . . . In the afternoon I was at Lowell's, and Henry James, Jr., came in. . . . Yesterday was the Derby. Mrs. Hearst, a millionairess of San Francisco, invited me, through Martin, to go in her drag. Took Wheelers to Ritchies, meeting [John] Pettie and the Du Mauriers.[16]

The young "Literary Ambassador to the Court of Fleet Street" found several opportunities outside of his usual office rounds to promote Anglo-American friendship. One was a proposal that an English memorial to Garfield be established in the Abbey. Bowker was deeply impressed by the unexpected extent and warmth of the sympathy which the English public expressed on the occasion of Garfield's death. He

---

14 E. E. Hale to R. R. B., November 6, 1880; Journal, December 14, 1880; E. C. Stedman to R. R. B., October 14, 1881; Journal, March 22, 1881; R. R. B., MS Memoir.
15 E. E. Hale, Jr., *The Life and Letters of Edward Everett Hale,* II.
16 R. R. B. to sister, May 25, 1882.

was similarly impressed by reports from his friends at home of the warm appreciation felt by Americans for this English sympathy, Stedman writing "that the two countries will find it hard to quarrel henceforth." In a letter to the London *Times,* Bowker proposed that "this kinship of common grief should have a visible and abiding memorial," and suggested that a simple slab of American granite, properly inscribed, be placed in Westminster Abbey, and the replaced Abbey stone brought to the capital at Washington. The Dean of Westminster encouraged the plan, but it did not gain sufficient support and had to be dropped.[17]

A more successful memorial was to A. P. Stanley, Dean of the Abbey. Stanley had made a host of American friends who were always warmly welcome in the Deanery, and Bowker had come to be one of these. On Stanley's death in the summer of 1881, it was proposed that the unadorned windows in the Chapter House of the Abbey be made a memorial to him, with one window being contributed by his American friends. In Lowell's absence, Bowker drew up a list of the leading Americans in England to be invited to a public subscription meeting. When he returned home for Christmas that year, he took with him a message to Stanley's American friends inviting their participation. Bowker immediately elicited the cordial support of Edward E. Hale and Phillips Brooks, and by March three hundred Americans had contributed to the American memorial window.[18] In 1897, Bowker had the pleasure of seeing a memorial window to Lowell from his English friends appropriately placed opposite it. Bowker, incidentally, was glad to help Stanley's successor, Dean E. T. Bradley, continue the tradition of hospitality to visiting Americans.

It was natural that Bowker should continue his efforts for international copyright on reaching London. By the summer of 1880, the "Harper draft" of an Anglo-American treaty had been approved by fifty-two leading American authors, by the American members of the International Copyright Committee, and by the great body of American publishers.[19] In September, Lowell submitted this "draft" to Earl Granville. Publishers and authors on both sides of the water expressed to Bowker their hope of early adoption. On his part, Bowker gave a

17 R. R. B. to mother, September 20, 1881; E. C. Stedman to R. R. B., October 14, 1881; R. R. B., letter in the London *Times,* September 28, 1881; E. T. Bradley to R. R. B., November 2, 1881; R. R. B. to sister, November 15, 1881. R. R. B. composed a sonnet on Garfield, "The Dead President," first published in the *Maga,* reprinted in the *Evening Post,* October 11, 1881. See Scudder, *James Russell Lowell,* II, 268–70.

18 E. T. Bradley to R. R. B., November 13, 1881; March 28, 1882; R. R. B., MS Memoir.

19 R. R. B., *Copyright, Its Law and Its Literature,* 31.

good deal of energy to speaking and writing in favor of the proposed treaty, sending around to the Englishmen he had met what Mrs. Craik described as "a great weight of literature! . . . almost frightening." In March, 1881, Lord Granville replied to Lowell that the British government favored the proposed treaty, but with one amendment. Bowker was disappointed, but he agreed with President Garfield and Secretary Blaine that the treaty with this amendment should be passed. However, differences between American publishers delayed the matter, and Garfield's death temporarily shelved it, with the result that the project was not taken up again until 1884.

While Bowker was working with English publishers and authors, he also took every opportunity to get into personal touch with English librarians.[20] Henry R. Tedder, librarian of the Athenaeum and English editor of Bowker's *Library Journal,* was his "refuge in the great unknown world of London," and under Tedder's guidance Bowker made a careful study of the Athenaeum Club library, where Macaulay and Thackeray used to write and where Mathew Arnold and Sir Henry Maine were still working. Bowker found Garnett, librarian of the British Museum, "a good-natured spider in the midst of the web of the great Rotunda reading room . . . whose build is of the loose-jointed Abraham Lincoln order." Garnett proved of invaluable help to Bowker in his many literary inquiries and made several publishing suggestions to Bowker. Through Garnett, Bowker came to know very well his fellow American, Henry Stevens, a buyer of American books for the British Museum, whom he described as "the most delightful of companions" with a knowledge of books that was "something extraordinary."

Bowker also came into pleasant relations with Cornelius Walford, whose private library of 20,000 volumes was one of the finest collections of books in London; E. B. Nicholson, one of the three founders of the L.A.U.K., then head of the Library of the London Institution and later of the Bodleian; E. C. Thomas, R. Harrison, George Bullen, J. Yates, and others. However, the English librarian who seems to have made the greatest impression on Bowker was Henry Bradshaw, head of the great Cambridge University Library and Senior Fellow at King's College. Bowker found him "as delightful and affectionate and as big-hearted as ever . . . a man of fifty, rather withdrawn, and almost shy." Bradshaw represented to Bowker a human type he always profoundly admired but could not possibly emulate, the cloistered scholar.

20 See R. R. B. to G. H. Putnam, July 3, 1916; R. R. B., "Memories among English Librarians," *Library Journal,* November, 1886; R. R. B. to sister, September 11, 1882.

Bowker's stay with Bradshaw in Cambridge proved to be a very moving experience. The English university and all that it symbolized evoked in him a sincere feeling of reverence. He had already come to know Oxford well, having frequently visited in the fine old fifteenth-century home of his friend Professor Price, of the Clarendon Press. He had also attended the Commemoration Day exercises at Oxford when James Bryce introduced Robert Browning for an honorary degree.[21] Here, at Cambridge, in Bradshaw's company, as at no other time or place, he felt the living presence of the spirit of great scholarship suffusing the fine old ivied halls, and when he left, it was with the sense that no other place in England meant more to him than this.

> It happened to be about the time of full moon, and it was, indeed, one of the most rapturous sensations possible in this world to stand on one of the bridges over the little river as the college bells were striking, while the moonlight flooded the fair meadows, beautiful with trees, with its splendor, I came away "homesick backwards," even with my face turned toward home and for good.[22]

It was natural that Bowker, as one of the founders of the American Library Association and editor of the *Library Journal*, should participate frequently in the meetings of the Library Association of the United Kingdom. He attended all three of the annual meetings held in Edinburgh, London, and Cambridge during his English sojourn, and was also invited to meet with the council of the L.A.U.K.[23] At the second meeting he responded with Greenough of the Boston Public Library to the toast, "Libraries of the Old World and the New," and read a paper entitled "The Work of the Nineteenth Century Librarian for the Librarian of the Twentieth." This paper, while it touched on a few specific problems such as the housing, noting, cataloguing, and bibliographic record of books, is notable for its broad conception of the role of the library enterprise and the relation of the nineteenth century developments to what had gone before and was to come after.

> It will be the chief glory of the nineteenth century that it has organized knowledge. . . . Knowledge increases, but there is no longer confusion. . . . [The librarian] is the merchant, the middle-

---

21 The interesting exercises are described in R. R. B., "A Commemoration Day at Oxford," *The Star and Crescent,* November, 1883, pp. 3–6.

22 R. R. B., "Memories among English Librarians," *Library Journal,* November, 1886, p. 441.

23 Journal, October 5–11, November 5, 1880; R. R. B., MS Memoir; "Memories among English Librarians," *Library Journal,* November 1886; see also issue of January, 1896, p. 8.

man of thought. . . . In this busy generation, when the hurried man grumbles that "all the time there is" is not enough for him, the librarian makes time for his fellow-mortals by saving it. . . . It is now the glory of the librarian that he is the liberator more than a *keeper:* he frees his books. The missionary relation of the librarian to his readers is one of the discoveries which the nineteenth century will hand along to the twentieth.

The paper was well received, was printed in full abstract in the *Times,* and served as a text for an editorial in the *Telegraph.*[24]

In addition to the memorials, international copyright, and the Anglo-American library movement, Bowker took pains to learn what he could from the English liberal movement for the sake of the liberal movement in America.[25] He continued his study of the free-trade program, securing materials at the British Museum, receiving and accepting an invitation to become an honorary member of the Cobden Club, and attending its meetings. In the fall of 1881 he had gone to hear the great Parnell address a Land League meeting at Cork, and saw for himself "the tremendous exaggeration which I am told clothes the whole League movement." He heard William Conway and Gladstone speak at a meeting of the Liberal Social Union held at the home of James Bryce in Bryanstone Square, and went to hear Gladstone deliver his budget speech in the House of Commons, when he proved himself to Bowker "a true orator, independent of time or circumstance in carrying with him every kind of audience." He also heard Foster, Dilke, Hartington, Chamberlain, Childers, and other liberal leaders. Through Mrs. Craik, he found opportunity to study the work done by Campbell's College for the Blind; and through his friend, Sir J. G. Fitch, he came to know Miss Martin's workingwoman's college, which he described as "a sort of feminine Cooper Union." He visited Octavia Hill's "homes for the Poor," George Peabody's housing blocks, and Sir Sydney Waterlow's "Improved Industrial Dwellings Co., Ltd.," and later wrote an article on the three experiments for *Harper's Monthly.*[26] In the spring of 1882 he went, at G. J. Holyoake's suggestion, to the Co-operative Congress at Cambridge, and had "a useful and interesting talk with

24 Monthly Note of the L.A.U.K., Vol. III, Vol. IX (September 15), 147; printed in *Library Journal,* September–October, 1883, p. 2.

25 References to the instances listed are in R. R. B. to family, February 21, March 16, 18, April 23, 1882; Cobden Club to R. R. B., August 5, 1880; R. R. B. to T. Bailey Potter, May 17, 1881; E. M. Shepard to Mrs. D. Bowker, July 4, 1884; R. R. B. mention with three Americans in "Cobden Dinner," July 1, 1882, in Special Report, p. 1; Journal, October, 1881, April 4, June 1, 1882.

26 R. R. B., "Workingmen's Homes," *Harper's Monthly Magazine,* April, 1884, pp. 769–84.

the leaders of that important movement.[27] He also took pains to study the English form of government, poring over such manuals of political information as *How We Are Governed*. "I am putting together much information as to the government of England and of London which will be useful when I come back," he wrote home. In friendly conversations, in committee discussion, in articles, Bowker was to put his knowledge of these English precedents at the service of his American friends.

Bowker characteristically made the most of his two years in England. And, characteristically, they were years of intense external activity. "The dead year has been one of strange changes and much new experience," he wrote in his Journal on New Year's Eve, 1880, "yet not of time for inward growth as I had hoped." Yet there was no danger of Bowker's needing the excellent advice which J. W. Harper gave him at this same season:

> ... As an old man of fifty, let me predict that years hence you will count these London days of yours among the happiest recollections of a life which I am sure will be always useful and honorable. ... Don't let little things worry you ... London is a gloomy place in winter, I know, but my wife and I, last night, in hunting for aphorisms appropriate to the New Year, found the following, the original of which is from Seneca: "Whatever is to make us better and happy, God has placed either openly before us or close to us." Can you see this through a London fog?[28]

Yet in spite of Bowker's solid business success with Harpers', his increasingly privileged social life, and his more and more intense activity as an influential representative of America in England, there had never been a moment during his two years in London that he had not longed to be home, that he had not been convinced that his place was at home, and that he had not assured his friends of an early and permanent return from London.

The fact is that everything drew him toward home: his family, his loyalties to the liberal crusade in America, the pleas of his erstwhile comrades in the ranks. Not a week had gone by that he had not written or received letters keeping him posted about the progress of his Society for Political Education, the Independent Republican Association, civil service and tariff reform, and the library movement. Bowker was missed. "In all these matters," wrote G. H. Putnam, "your clear-headed and unselfish co-operation have been missed not a little, and we look forward to the time when, returning with what the primadonnas call a trans-

27 Journal, June 1, 1882.
28 J. W. Harper to R. R. B., December 29, 1880.

atlantic reputation, you may be able to take hold again with renewed vigor and wider experience." Wheeler was even more insistent. "Oh how I miss you," he wrote, "we want you here. . . . Don't be like the Epicurean gods,—sitting on the serene heights of Fleet Street, and looking calmly at the sinking ship,—the brave man pierced with the arrows of the wicked,—flaunting vice, and virtue *nowhere*, oh Bowker, how can you!"[29] Certainly his sister's visit to London in the summer of 1881 in the company of A. D. F. Randolph's daughter,[30] and his own visit home at Christmas time, 1881, did not change his feelings.

By mid-August, 1882, it was decided that William M. Laffan would be Bowker's successor. Laffan was a quick-witted Irishman who had served as art and dramatic critic for the New York *Sun* before joining the literary staff of the House of Harper, and who was later to succeed Charles A. Dana as editor and proprietor of the *Sun*. By September, Bowker was busy making a round of farewell calls, "dodging good-bye dinners,—and longing for dinners at home," and clearing out his desk for his "illustrious successor."

Black professed to be unable to understand Bowker's decision. "No, you don't mean to say you are going back to America! *To America!* And I dare say you'll pretend you like the prospect. However, you won't stay long. You know better. . . . You'll *soon be back*. Take my word for it. The spell will work. New York will know him no more, and Broadway will be left desolate."[31]

Shepard knew better. "He will come back," Shepard wrote in July, 1882, "one of the very, very few Americans who, after a long foreign residence in an older and more finished country, are still as loyal to their own land as when they left her."[32] It was an understatement. As Bowker now set his face toward home he was, if anything, more completely committed to serving his own country than he could ever have been before.

29 E. P. Wheeler to R. R. B., December 10, 1880.
30 See Carolyn T. Bowker, MS Journal of European trip, in custody of the New York Public Library.
31 William Black to R. R. B., August, October 8, 1882.
32 E. M. Shepard to Mrs. Daniel Bowker, July 4, 1882.

XII

The Publishers' Weekly and the
Library Movement, 1882–1900

OWKER was thirty-four years old when he returned from London in the fall of 1882, a young man with something of a reputation and a comfortable income. "You must know that you are now a man of importance," his friend Frank Wing wrote, not altogether facetiously, "one who is not to be lightly dealt with. . . . But seriously, you can hardly imagine how much it seems as though you were a character out of *Pendennis* or some such English novel."[1] He was earning a salary of $7,000 a year from Harpers and had an income of $500 from the *Publishers' Weekly*. The capital value of the latter property and his savings made him worth about $10,000.[2] This was a commendable achievement for a young man who had been strictly on his own. Nevertheless, it fell short by five years of the schedule Bowker had set himself, and he had to find consolation in the reflection that, at any rate, his experience had been "usefully wide."

There seems little doubt that Bowker could now have doubled his earning power had this been his primary purpose. He was to be as busy as ever, and his activities were to be governed by the identical principles which had ruled his life since he had entered college; but on account of his conscience and certain business accidents, he found himself in increasingly unremunerative employment while a host of reform activities swallowed up time and energy with little return in fame or fortune. The years from 1882 to 1890 comprise the most idealistic and the least rewarding period in Bowker's career, and he was finally rescued from his own high-mindedness only by the consternation of his friends.

[1] Frank Wing to R. R. B., January 7, 1881.
[2] R. R. B. to sister, August 19, 1881.

From 1882 to 1890 Bowker continued to make his living in the field of journalism and the book trade. On returning from London, his first hope was to continue in the full-time employment of the Harper firm as one of their junior officers. He knew he had organizing and executive ability of commercial value, and he promptly outlined to the Harper house a two-year program of activities which he declared would net them $50,000 worth of business. The Harpers, however, though they would have been glad to have Bowker continue in the London office, apparently had no place for him at home, and in December they announced that his relation with the firm would terminate on March 1, 1883. Bowker thereupon proposed, and the Harpers accepted, a part-time relation as assistant to H. M. Alden, editor of *Harper's Magazine,* which lasted from March, 1883, until December 1885.[3]

Bowker's duties as Alden's assistant were thoroughly familiar. He was to systematize existing magazine material, supervise several proposed articles, give occasional attention to advertising, and take Alden's place when he was absent. The articles which Bowker wrote or reworked exhibited his characteristic combination of thorough research, clear exposition, and human interest. An essay on the Brooklyn Bridge was followed by two on Columbia University, but the most ambitious undertaking was a series of twelve articles on Great American Industries, nine of which he wrote himself. The titles suggest Bowker's approach: "A Silk Dress," "A Lump of Sugar," "A Sheet of Paper," "A Printed Book," "A Piece of Glass," "A Suit of Clothes," "A Bar of Iron," "A Steel Tool," "Electricity."[4] Bowker received from $200 to $450 apiece for these articles, and they were certainly worth it.

Two years after the termination of Bowker's formal connection with the Harpers, he successfully interested them in commissioning him to do an elaborate essay on London's literary activities. Bowker had undoubtedly been hoping for many years to write something which would utilize his earlier introduction to this subject, and keenly relished the return visits to London in 1886 and 1887 which made possible the renewing of old acquaintances. Several literary items resulted from the trip. Bowker helped William Black publish an account of a glorified houseboat trip which the two of them took. Bowker's reminiscences of Mrs. Craik appeared in *Harper's Bazaar,* of Du Maurier in the New York *Times* Sunday Supplement, his "London as a Literary Center," in *Harper's Magazine,* and a study of Toynbee Hall in the *Century Mag-*

3 R. R. B. to J. W. Harper, November 30, 1882; Harper and Brothers to R. R. B., December 27, 1882; R. R. B. to J. H. Harper, December 29, 1882; see H. M. Alden to R. R. B., August 11, 1883, December 24, 1885.

4 See bibliography.

Fellow Literary Ambassadors to England: *(Top, left)* Bronson Howard; *(Top, right)* Laurence Hutton; *(Bottom, left)* Bret Harte; *(Bottom, right)* James Russell Lowell

Publishers' Weekly Associates: *(Top, left)* Mrs. Augusta Leypoldt; *(Top, right)* Frederick Leypoldt; *(Bottom, left)* Frederic G. Melcher; *(Bottom, right)* Adolf Growoll

azine. Manuscripts on "Walks About London," and "Social Helps and Charities of London," were prepared but not published.

In March, 1884, while Bowker was still employed on a part-time basis by Harpers, a tragedy occurred which had a decisive bearing on his fortunes. Frederick Leypoldt, worn out before his time with harrowing financial strain and poor health, suddenly died. The publishing world was deeply moved. Those who knew Leypoldt best realized how unselfishly he devoted his life to a cause that had brought him neither profit nor reputation. The memorial number of the *Weekly* contained some fine tributes to the work of a great bibliographer.[5]

Leypoldt's death forced Bowker to make a decision concerning his relation to the *Publishers' Weekly* which he might have preferred to postpone. His purchase of the *Weekly* in 1878 had been prompted more by a desire to make a profitable investment than by any intention to work permanently with this book-trade organ. Throughout 1879 it was easy for Bowker to see that Leypoldt unconsciously resented the firm restraint in financial matters which he exercised in the older man's interests. On leaving for London, he fully expected that Leypoldt would buy back the *Weekly* as soon as he had the capital to do so. Evidences of Leypoldt's mismanagement, however, constantly reached Bowker in London.[6] Mrs. Leypoldt described herself as "heartily disgusted" with her husband's way of doing business. In the summer of 1881 Leypoldt himself admitted to Bowker that he was $10,000 in debt, and Bowker's father wrote that there was no cash with which to pay the office salaries. In view of these developments, Bowker decided that he would not transfer the *Weekly* back to Leypoldt unless he could recoup the $5,000 cash which he had put into it, but that on the other hand he would not sell the property to an outsider. On his return from London, he therefore anticipated continuing as owner of the *Weekly*, but not entering into active relations with it.[7]

Leypoldt's death meant that the *Weekly* was without a managing editor, and apparently there was no member of the office staff who could assume the post. Had there been no personal or special considerations involved, Bowker might have done well to sell the *Weekly* immediately and let a new editor be appointed. There was, however, one very special consideration. The *Publishers' Weekly* office intimately combined the book-trade organ with Leypoldt's whole intricate and costly biblio-

[5] *Publishers' Weekly*, April 5, 1884.

[6] Mrs. A. Leypoldt to R. R. B., September 18, 1880; F. Leypoldt to R. R. B., August 5, 1881.

[7] R. R. B. in *Library Journal*, January, 1896; R. R. B. to his father, August 22, 1881.

graphical apparatus. Together, the two enterprises could just make a living; separated, the dream of Leypoldt's life would certainly dissolve. Yet it was highly unlikely that a purchaser for the *Weekly* would be found with the idealism to undertake the burden of bibliography. There was, moreover, a personal consideration. Leypoldt's widow and three children had no inheritance but the bibliographical properties which Leypoldt left, and these would be almost worthless without sympathetic management. Bowker knew that Mrs. Leypoldt, saddled with heavy debts which her husband had not been able to pay off, was overwhelmed with a "dreadful feeling of uncertainty, ignorance, and helplessness" in regard to her future.[8]

It seems almost certain that Bowker's sense of loyalty to Leypoldt's family and bibliographical enterprises and the fact that at this very moment he was employed only half-time by the Harpers dictated his decision to keep the *Weekly,* to become once more its managing editor,[9] and to undertake responsibility for Leypoldt's various publications by leasing them from his widow. The decision was an enormous relief to Mrs. Leypoldt, who expressed her deep appreciation of Bowker's considerate action on many occasions. "Little did I think two years ago today," she wrote Bowker in 1886, "that Mr. L's name would be entirely clear from debt and that his children would be sure of a comfortable existence. And, under Heaven, I owe it all to you; for I feel day by day how little I could have struggled without your planning and the support of your position in the office."[10]

The office publications which Bowker leased from Mrs. Leypoldt included the *Literary News,* the *Library Journal, Index to Periodicals* (edited by W. I. Fletcher as a supplement to the *Journal), Monthly Reference Lists, Index Medicus, American Catalogue, Publishers Trade List Annual, The American Educational Catalogue,* and several pamphlets, including *Books of All Time, Books for the Young* (by C. M. Hewins), *Libraries and Readers,* and *Libraries and Schools.*

Certainly one of the most important activities of the entire office program was bibliography. By his decision to take up the burden of Leypoldt's publications, he became, as he put it, "unwittingly" a bibliographer, tied down to the troublesome and unprofitable routine of his profession. He immediately set to work to complete Leypoldt's bibliographical system: the weekly record of titles supplemented by the order list, a monthly and quarterly reference list, an annual catalog

8 Mrs. A. Leypoldt to R. R. B., March 31, 1885.
9 Announced in *Publishers' Weekly,* April 5, 12, 1884.
10 Mrs. A. Leypoldt to R. R. B., April 2, 1886; see also *ibid.,* March 15, 1883; April 28, July 26, 1884; June 29, 1885.

(published in January as a number of the *Weekly,* and also as a separate volume), and finally, the *American Catalogue.* Leypoldt's complete system, however, proved so unremunerative that Bowker was compelled to omit some of its features. However, he added three important features of his own and pushed through several other bibliographical projects.

The need for this service was certainly real, for in 1883 the *Weekly* was registering seventy books a week, or about 3,500 a year,[11] and the number was constantly increasing. Yet it is not at all certain that Leypoldt's bibliographical services would have been undertaken by others at this time had Bowker not stepped in. It is at least one professional opinion that "had it not been for Mr. Bowker, we might not have had the *American Catalogue* and possibly not the *Publishers' Weekly* or the *Library Journal* until more recent years."[12] If Leypoldt deserves to be honored for inaugurating his great bibliographical system, Bowker deserves to be honored no less for sticking with it through discouraging years of financial loss and providing the managerial direction to carry it to fulfillment. It is perfectly clear, indeed, that American book-trade bibliography owes a very substantial debt to Bowker.

The burden of the *American Catalogue* was a heavy one. Leypoldt had left his first two volumes showing a serious loss, but by raising the price of the remaining stock, Bowker managed to wind up the account with a debit balance of only $301.25, although this sum did not take into account the services of either man.[13] Bowker then brought out in 1885 the next volume of the *Catalogue* covering 22,000 books and 30,000 entries for the years 1876–84; in 1891 the set for 1884–90; in 1896 the set for 1890–95; and in 1901 the set for 1895–1900. The set for 1890–95 covered 1,649 publishers, 25,000 books, and 32,000 entries. The labor of preparing it involved close personal work, especially in the reading of proof, and this intensified the eyestrain from which Bowker was already suffering.

Bowker not only pushed ahead with Leypoldt's plan for the *American Catalogue* but, as has been pointed out, added three important new features on his own initiative. The first was a pioneer, systematized record of United States government publications. His plan was to include the issues of Congress and of the executive departments, court decisions, and other federal publications, and to begin with the period January 1, 1881, to June 30, 1884. The project required many trips to

11 *Publishers' Weekly,* April 5, 1884.
12 *Bulletin of Bibliography,* May–August, 1926.
13 R. R. B. to H. Putnam, July 3, 1916; *Publishers' Weekly,* September 22, 1883, p. 294.

Washington and much laborious time in the several departments and independent bureaus searching out and systematizing their "confused and confusing issues."[14]The first listing appeared as an appendix to the 1885 edition of the *American Catalogue* under the title "United States Government Publications." This undertaking was aided by the A.L.A.'s Committee on Public Documents, of which Bowker was chairman for many years. His committee report of 1891 is a statesmanlike summary of the extensive work he had done in this cause.

The second feature initiated by Bowker was a list of publications by American literary, scientific, and other societies. Librarians had expressed a desire for such a compilation as early as 1853, but the field had been left practically untouched. Bowker's work, eventually entitled *Publications of Societies*, first appeared also as an appendix to the *American Catalogue* for 1876–84, was carried forward in succeeding issues, and was published as a separate volume in 1899. Bowker admitted that it was a work which involved much more labor and cost than return either in money or appreciation.[15]

The third bibliographical contribution, a similar labor of love, was a compilation of state publications. Because of the absolute lack of material and the inadequate information possessed by state librarians, this project necessitated personal visits by Bowker to most of the state capitals of the United States. Much of the bibliographical work on the project was done by William Seaver, who had entered the office some years earlier as a personal assistant to Bowker. The first listing formed an appendix to the *American Catalogue* for 1884–90, and the completed survey was published in 1908 at a personal loss to Bowker of $5,000. These three special listings, as Bowker himself stated, added nothing to the sales value of the *American Catalogue*, but were "a free-will offering in the patriotic cause of American bibliography." They were, indeed, of increasing bibliographical value and helped to solve several problems which librarians and other research workers had faced.

Bowker accomplished two other significant bibliographical objectives and tried a third which remained incomplete. In 1893 he supplied "the one tool which the bibliographical system lacks" when he issued, with the editorial help of W. I. Fletcher, the first *Annual Literary Index*. This was to include Fletcher's annual A.L.A. *Index*, as well as an annual supplement to Poole's *Index to Periodical Literature* and other special features, and was an extension of the *Journal's* original *Quarterly Index to Periodicals*.[16] The second project was to assem-

14 R. R. B., MS Memoir; R. R. B. to sister, April 14, 1885.

15 R. R. B. to H. Putnam, July 3, 1916.

16 R. R. B., *Library Journal*, June, 1893, p. 204; R. R. B., *Library Journal*, January, 1896, p. 9.

ble a record of foreign book importations, especially English editions. The *Weekly* office thus became a headquarters for foreign importations as it had been for some time the bibliographical headquarters of America.[17] The project which Bowker especially cherished but finally had to give up was a finding list of American books in print for the period 1800–76, which, with the *American Catalogue,* would have furnished a complete American trade bibliography for the nineteenth century and would have given this country the most complete bibliography in the world. Everyone in the office took a hand in odd moments with this mammoth assignment, copying out the titles in Roorbach, Kelly, Trübner, Stevens, and Sabin on title slips, which were filed in big cardboard boxes. Aksel Josephson, a trained English bibliographer, took hold of the project, but gave it up in disgust, and the job was never completed.

The office in which these various book enterprises were carried forward had moved its location in 1882 from 13–15 to 31–32 Park Row, and in 1887 to 330 Pearl Street on Franklin Square opposite the Harper building. Soon after Bowker became vice-president of the Edison Electric Illuminating Company of New York in 1890, the office was again moved to a little brick building at 28 Elm Street directly across from the Edison offices.[18] Early one morning in the summer of 1894 a fire broke out in the building next door and spread to the *Weekly* office. Bowker and Growoll rushed down to save what they could, but most of the literary property was destroyed. "The loss of your reference library," wrote Iles, "cannot be measured in money. Your British bibliographical annuals, are, I doubt not, out of print and unpurchaseable. They were always hospitably placed at the service of inquirers, and my regrets (partly selfish) will be echoed in many quarters."[19] Temporary accommodations, and later, permanent new quarters were taken at 54 Duane Street in a large loft building on the corner of Elm Street next to the Edison building. Here the office remained until its removal in 1900 to another loft building at 298 Broadway.

These several changes of address brought little change in the personnel or the atmosphere of the *Publishers' Weekly* office.[20] Mrs. Leypoldt, who had helped her husband with the *Literary News* and managed *Books for the Young,* now took an increasingly active part on the

17 See M. Dewey to R. R. B., December 10, 1902; G. Iles to R. R. B., June 23, 1894.

18 For a description of these successive offices, see Helen E. Haines, " 'Tis Fifty Years Since: *Publishers' Weekly* Office in an Earlier Day," *Publishers' Weekly,* January 18, 1947, Section One, pp. 278–79.

19 G. Iles to R. R. B., June 23, 1894.

20 For reminiscences of the *Publishers' Weekly* office during these years, see articles by Fremont Rider, Helen E. Haines, and Marian Osborne in *Publishers' Weekly,* January 18, 1947, Section One.

staff. She was a strong-willed, sensitive, intelligent woman, possessing an abundance of courage and industry. "A Dresden marquise," one associate described her, "with her high-rolled white hair, her delicate features, and large, China-blue eyes, she had the cosmopolitan culture of her remarkable family."[21] The rest of the Old Guard had also stayed on. There was the tall, bearded Stewart, addicted to his "vegetarian luncheon" of crackers and milk, rye whiskey, and tobacco; heavy, dark, dynamic Miss Monachesi with her love of French and her gusto; and hard-working, temperamental Growoll.

Growoll was the best-known member of the staff, becoming each year more of an authority in the book trade and assuming real leadership in its ranks. His early experience as a printer and bookseller was valuable, and he was the mainstay of the *Weekly*. In 1894 he helped to organize the Booksellers' League and contributed to the *Weekly* a set of papers published as "The Profession of Bookselling." The office loved Growoll as a man of humor, loyalty, and sterling sincerity, whose German accent and gruff manner hardly concealed the real warmth and kindliness beneath. He combined German thoroughness with a devotion to the highest standards, hating sham in others and not permitting it in himself. Passionately fond of parades, a natural mimic, adorned with his little black skullcap and his cigar, he was also the center of office relaxation. There was a particularly fine comradeship between Mrs. Leypoldt and Growoll. They worked side by side. She taught him what he needed most, the English language, and encouraged him to develop his innate qualities; he taught her every detail he knew about the book trade. Other key personnel at this time included Rouse, who worked on the *Annual*, caustic, smart, and as Mrs. Leypoldt put it, "like all extra smart young people . . . often intensely disagreeable," and Miss Helen Haines, a spirited girl of twenty, who in 1892 was brought into the office family to assist with the *Journal* and the *Weekly*. She proved, in the judgment of Growoll and Mrs. Leypoldt, "quite a find."

It was an industrious, stimulating, affectionate circle. They all loved books, lived with books, and talked about books. They all had a cultivated, liberal, cosmopolitan outlook and taste. Around the corner at Zeltner's restaurant on Pearl Street, the old guard would flavor their daily lunch with spirited talk of writers, music, social movements, and politics. It was also a self-opinionated, emotional circle. "We are all rather ill-tempered," Mrs. Leypoldt once wrote Bowker, "which makes us quiet and is rather conducive to work."

21 Haines, " 'Tis Fifty Years Since: *Publishers' Weekly* Office in an Earlier Day," *Publishers' Weekly*, January 18, 1947, Section One, p. 280.

Contrasted to this close circle, especially after 1890, Bowker seemed to move in a world apart, coming in briskly from the Edison office to go over general plans and proofs, to issue pronunciamentos, and then to dash off again to lunch with tariff reformers, Gold Democrats, or civic magnates waiting for him at the Reform Club. "The office seems very quiet," Mrs. Leypoldt wrote him during one of his absences in Europe. "No Mugwumps, no free traders, no librarians, no copyright-ers, no friends."[22] There was some talk of importing certain Edison efficiency measures into the office, but Mrs. Leypoldt vetoed this plan, and the senior staff found bibliography little disturbed by electrical progress. Perhaps too little so. Of necessity the office became a marginal concern of Bowker's when possibly it should have been adjusting to meet new conditions more effectively than it did.

On the professional side, however, Growoll and Bowker kept the *Publishers' Weekly* a notable trade organ. They shared Leypoldt's con-viction that a well-developed book trade could be one of the country's most important cultural resources, and they never lost his determina-tion to provide conscientious leadership which should be practical, educational, and inspiring. The foundation service of the office con-tinued to be the bibliographical system which became "the best in any book-producing country, challenging comparison in regard to quantity, quality, and promptness of issue with any other."[23] It also provided a unique medium for the exchange of literary news of all kinds: periodi-cals and books received, forthcoming, on auction, for sale, or wanted; best-seller lists, gossip about authors at home and abroad, notes on rare books and books of the past. On the technical side, the *Weekly* consciously sought to promote "an American renascence in careful book workmanship." It printed articles on book production, paper, bindings, illustration, and repair. "From page form to the lettering of titles, from book sizes to the correct method of interleaving, from title pages to painting on edges, the *Weekly* provided a complete technical and artis-tic equipment for its subscribers."

At the same time, the *Weekly* constituted a veritable school for booksellers. "Hints to Salesmen," begun in 1891, and Growoll's "Pro-fession of Bookselling," in 1893 were only the earliest of a long series of articles which helped to give that trade a professional standing. They completely covered the field from preparatory training to learning

---

[22] See Mrs. Leypoldt to R. R. B., August 13, 1884; February 27, June 13, 1886; and in *Publishers' Weekly*, December 25, 1909, p. 1943.

[23] Stern, "The First Half-Century of *Publishers' Weekly*," *Publishers' Weekly*, January 18, 1947, p. 228. This summary is much indebted to Miss Stern's admirable analysis of the *Weekly's* services in this period. The quotations following are from her article.

stock; from the delivery, shipping, and correspondence departments to
pricing old books and cataloging incunabula; from ordering and buying stock to arranging and displaying it, from knowing customers
and selling from samples to the management of bookstores, window
dressing, and publicity devices. The annual Stationery Number of the
Weekly, begun in 1873, served the needs of the bookseller who was also
a stationer; and the Travelers' Number, begun in 1908, the needs of
book salesmen on the road. Special numbers in the fall, spring, summer,
and at Christmas served as invaluable guides for the most important
publishing seasons. The Educational Number, intended to acquaint
dealers and schools with the range of schoolbooks, eventually became
"the most comprehensive list of textbooks published in the United
States." Even after the *Library Journal* had emerged from the early
library concern of the *Weekly,* the latter continued to give space to
library news and indeed for half a century remained the best link between publishers and librarians. In 1910, 75 per cent of the total library
book-buying of the country was represented by library subscriptions
to the *Weekly,* and at the New York State Library School, the journal
was studied as a recognized part of the curriculum.

A further significant service was the *Weekly's* enthusiastic attention to the history of the book trade. All phases of book trade history
from the earliest times in the ancient world were presented. This was
supplemented by the reminiscences of prominent book-trade leaders
and histories of the great publishing houses, presented on the occasions
of anniversaries, removals, or obituaries. In addition to chronicling in
news columns, editorials, and communications all developments in the
publishing field, the *Weekly* continuously discussed the interrelations
between the book trade and contemporary events.

Finally, the *Weekly* maintained its vigorous leadership in reform.
This centered around trade organization, net price maintenance, bookstore development, and international copyright. Insisting from the start
that publishing and bookselling constituted a single trade with an iden-
tity of interest, the *Weekly* worked year in and year out to promote not
only the professional organization of each field, but the close co-operation of the two. When the American Book Trade Association, which
it had helped to organize, foundered in 1876, the *Weekly* looked hope-
fully for a successor. It heartily supported the formation of the New
York Booksellers' League in 1894, the American Publishers' Association and the American Booksellers' Association in 1900, and later the
National Association of Book Publishers. As for prices, the *Weekly*
maintained a long crusade against inflated retail prices coupled with
abnormal discounts. It fought for a reduction of fictitious retail prices

to a uniform, equitable net price reflecting the actual cost of the book. It lashed out at underselling, monopolies, and department store abuses. It fought for a bona-fide trade discount large enough to enable the bookseller to make a profit, but small enough to prevent price cutting. And after the establishment of the net price, the *Weekly* fought to maintain it.

Bowker's return to the editorship of the *Publishers' Weekly* brought him once again into close touch with the crusade for international copyright. An Anglo-American treaty on this subject had been delayed by Garfield's death, but the time seemed right for a renewed effort. Bowker worked vigorously through the American (Authors) Copyright League which was organized in 1883 by members of the Authors Club. The League believed in a law that would effect a practical compromise between the demand for international copyright pure and simple, which the typographical unions opposed, and one that completely ignored the program of the International Copyright Union then in the process of formation. This policy was distasteful to the League's first secretary, G. P. Lathrop, and on his resignation Bowker was elected to take his place on the League council. The council, which usually met at Gilder's private office in the *Century* editorial rooms, included Edmund C. Stedman, Brander Matthews, W. D. Howells, Edward Eggleston, Frank D. Millett, Robert Collier, and others.[24]

Progress in securing an international copyright law had been slow, and was to continue to be slow, but it gradually gained momentum. As during the years between 1873 and 1880, the editorial pages of the *Weekly* gave Bowker a strategic opportunity to publicize the cause. Week after week he analyzed each aspect of the copyright problem, explained its current status, and discussed desirable changes. In 1886 these brief weekly essays, along with a bibliography of copyright literature prepared by Thorvald Solberg, were published as *Copyright, Its Law and Its Literature,* an immensely useful handbook for the campaign. In 1885, Bowker secured dramatic publicity for the cause by supervising an impressive memorial to Congress bearing the facsimile signatures of 143 American authors which pleaded for an international copyright law.[25]

The next year Bowker attended all four hearings held on the copyright bill in Washington, especially enjoying the one at which James Russell Lowell and Mark Twain both appeared. Three years later, he arranged authors' readings in both Washington and Brooklyn to gain

[24] R. R. B. to B. Matthews, 1916; to T. Solberg, April 15, 1925. R. R. B., MS Memoir.

[25] R. W. Gilder to R. R. B., December 7, 1885.

publicity and funds for the campaign. Meanwhile the movement was aided by the formation, in 1887, of the American Publishers Copyright League, organized under the presidency of William H. Appleton and the crusading spirit of G. H. Putnam. Since Bowker, Henry Holt, and Putnam were members of both the authors' and the publishers' organizations, a maximum of co-operation was achieved. In 1891, Bowker contributed an essay, "The Nature and Origin of Copyright," to Putnam's volume, *The Question of Copyright.*

After innumerable delays and adversities, a copyright law was signed by President Harrison on March 4, 1891. The act was imperfect, but it was a step forward, providing that foreign authors might secure copyright on manufacture of their works in America, registration within fifteen days from publication abroad, and deposit of copies of the American edition within six months.

The second great copyright struggle came in 1905 and was fought to revise the act of 1891 toward a complete copyright code with a further step toward true international copyright. The campaign proved to be a prolonged and complicated one, with three conferences held in 1905 and 1906 to draft a bill acceptable to representatives of authors, artists, publishers, printers, lithographers, libraries, and the public; and three hearings before a joint Congressional committee in 1906 and 1908. A generally satisfactory bill was finally signed by Roosevelt on March 4, 1909.

Throughout this period Bowker was serving as chairman of the executive committee and vice-president of the American Copyright League. He gave the subject his continuous attention in the pages of the *Weekly,* which remained an official clearinghouse of information on the subject; he prepared a pamphlet comparing alternative bills presented; he repeatedly traveled to Washington to testify at the hearings, once in the jolly company of Clemens, Gilder, Howells, Paine, and Johnson;[26] and finally, to crown all his other services in behalf of the cause, he wrote the authoritative and exhaustive work on the subject, *Copyright, Its History and Its Law,* published in 1912. A third campaign which began in 1922 to enable the United States to enter the International Copyright Union found Bowker as ready as ever to enlist his energies, but he did not live to see the accomplishment of this final step. During the very last months of his life, in 1933, he was restudying copyright legislation and outlining a new draft for Congressional consideration.

Bowker's role in the copyright crusade was a crucial one. He had devoted more space to the discussion of the subject in the *Publishers'*

26 See interview with R. R. B. in Springfield *Republican,* September 2, 1928.

Weekly than had all the foreign trade journals combined, and far more than any literary journal at home or abroad.[27] He was one of a company of six, including Putnam, Appleton, Scribner, Solberg, and R. U. Johnson, to whose efforts the passage of the copyright law of 1891 and of the revised law of 1909 was largely due.[28] It has been suggested, indeed, that "no greater memorial could stand for Mr. Bowker than the one which he helped erect: the international copyright law. ... This is his great monument."[29]

These various services to book-trade bibliography, to copyright, and to the development of the *Publishers' Weekly* as a first-rate trade journal justify the recognition of Bowker's leadership which the book trade has frequently offered. In 1900, E. C. Stedman's son wrote Bowker, "Every publisher, editor, and author in the country is only too glad to serve one who has done more for the literary 'classes' than any other ten people."[30] One historian of the book trade has declared that the *Publishers' Weekly* during its first fifty years did "more than any other single instrument to keep alive the sense of trade interest and trade solidarity."[31] At Bowker's death, the president of the Booksellers' League declared, "For half a century Mr. Bowker has occupied a position of unique leadership in the book industry. . . . By his own efforts he has made for himself a secure place in the history of the trade and won the highest esteem and honor among his contemporaries."[32] In 1922 he was elected to honorary membership in the American Booksellers Association. The National Association of Book Publishers called him "The Dean of American Publishers."[33]

Bowker's interest in and loyalty to the library movement was undiminished. During these years he maintained close supervision of the *Library Journal,* took an active part in the program of the American Library Association, and helped to administer at least one large municipal library system. His loyalty was not affected by the fact that the *Journal* was just barely self-supporting.[34] He still believed heart and soul in

[27] Stern, "The First Half-Century of *Publishers' Weekly*," *Publishers' Weekly,* January 18, 1947, Section One, p. 302.
[28] Stokes, *A Publisher's Random Notes*, 3–4.
[29] Ken McCormick, "Editors Today," *Bulletin* of the New York Public Library, March, 1948.
[30] Arthur Stedman to R. R. B., February 19, 1900.
[31] Stern, "The First Half-Century of *Publishers' Weekly*," *Publishers' Weekly,* January 18, 1947, Section One, p. 304.
[32] W. R. Barnes, article in *Publishers' Weekly,* November 25, 1933.
[33] Resolution passed by the Board of Directors of the association, *Library Journal,* December 1, 1933, Part II, p. 1012.
[34] See G. Iles to R. R. B., September 2, 1892.

the work it was doing, and he prized the many friendships it brought him. Relief from the details of managing the *Journal* was guaranteed by the capable editorship first of Charles A. Cutter, assisted by Paul Leicester Ford, and then of Helen Haines.

Throughout these years, however, Bowker wrote many editorials and articles for the *Journal* himself, and they maintained his usual broad liberal outlook. In 1896, for instance, he devoted successive leaders to such topics as the contribution of librarians to Anglo-American friendship, the common interests of librarians, ministers, and teachers, the need to fight the political spoilsmen in state and municipal libraries, and the interest of librarians in overcoming race antagonisms.[35] At the time of the Anglo-American friction over Cleveland's Venezuela message, he wrote:

> In such misunderstanding as has recently arisen between the mother-country and our own, librarians should be apostles of peace, and should not hesitate to use their influence for peace and good will among the nations. The two countries are in no respect knit together more strongly than in their relations as co-heirs of one literature and users of one mother-tongue. . . . The international visits of Americans and Englishmen have done much to cause a better understanding between the two people.[36]

Regarding race prejudices, he wrote:

> Probably no class of people are more desirious of putting aside questions of race and birth and breeding, in the best democratic fashion, than are librarians, for they all recognize that a great part of their mission is to make good Americans out of all classes of material, whether of bad Americans or good importations.[37]

In addition to his monthly editorials, Bowker continued to contribute informative essays on outstanding library developments.[38] In 1887 he published a paper on "The Formation and Organization of Public Libraries." In 1895 he hailed the integration of the Astor Library, Lenox Library, and Tilden Trust into one great city library system as "the finest piece of co-operation in library history," and pointed out that now, at last, New York might fairly rival Boston and Chicago as a library city. He eagerly watched developments on the Pacific Coast, and wrote an article on "Some Libraries of the North-

[35] *Library Journal*, January–August, 1896.
[36] *Ibid.*, January, 1896.
[37] *Ibid.*, August, 1896.
[38] For references, see bibliography.

west" which emphasized the tremendous progress made in that corner of the country. In 1896 he celebrated the twentieth anniversary of the *Library Journal* and the American Library Association with a fine article on "The *Library Journal* and Library Organization: A Twenty Years' Retrospect," reviewing the dramatic progress of two decades in America and Europe, in much of which he had directly participated. Two months later he made an authoritative study of "Libraries and the Library Problems in 'Greater New York' " which he presented before the New York Library Club and later published.

Bowker praised the completed plans for the new Library of Congress in an essay on "The American National Library," in which he described the new building as "the most comprehensive and fitting home for a national or government library existing in the world" and made a number of specific recommendations of policy. He followed the preparations for this great undertaking with close interest and saw to it that the A.L.A. contributed to the efforts of the Congressional Joint Committee on Library to inaugurate the new regime. In July, 1897, Bowker attended, as one of its vice-presidents, the highly successful Second International Library Conference in London, at which there were 640 librarians representing fifteen governments. His paper, "Bibliographical Endeavors in America," prompted one of the British historians to remark, "There is no department upon which we can look with more satisfaction in the world's history than upon the way in which they in America have devoted their attention to books and reading."[39] In 1887, Bowker issued *The Library List*, a directory of public libraries in the United States and Canada containing over one thousand volumes. This evolved into the *Annual Literary Index* of 1893, the *Annual Library Index* of 1906, the *American Library Annual* of 1912, and finally in 1923 became the present *American Library Directory*.[40]

From his unique observation post in the library world, Bowker was able to note and welcome the many significant developments which marked library progress during these decades: the standard catalog card, the Dewey decimal system of classification, the library school, the magnificent Carnegie library benefactions (totalling sixty million dollars for 2,200 library buildings by 1926), open shelves, card catalog cases, the Library Bureau, the Publishing Section of the American Library Association, children's departments, library work with schools, the school library, the county library, regional depositories, local library

[39] Second International Library Conference, *Transactions and Proceedings* (London, 1896), 150–53; references to R. R. B.'s participation in the program are made in the Birmingham *Mail*, July 10, 1897; Plymouth *Western Morning News*, July 21, 1897.
[40] Anne J. Richter, "Books from the Office of the *Publishers' Weekly*," *Publishers' Weekly*, January 18, 1947, Section One, pp. 339–40.

clubs and associations, international library conferences, and the increase of tax support as compared with private endowments. He also hailed the broadening of the American Library Association which came through affiliation with the Special Libraries Association, the League of Library Commissions, and the National Associations of State and Law Libraries; and through the growth of such cognate organizations as the American Association of Library Schools, the Bibliographical Society of America, the American Library Institute, the Medical Library Association, and the Library Department of the National Education Association.

It was in 1896 that the *Library Journal* encountered its first real competition in the form of a rival library periodical. Many small libraries felt that their peculiar problems were not being discussed by the *Journal,* and that five dollars was a prohibitive subscription price. With the influential advocacy of John Cotton Dana, it was definitely proposed to start a more popular, restricted, and less expensive library journal for this group. Possibly the publicity advantages offered by the new sheet to the Library Bureau made Melvil Dewey favorably disposed. But although Dewey wrote Bowker that the new venture was not intended to "rival or antagonize," the fact that it was published by the Chicago Library Bureau and received the support of the president and officers of the A.L.A. deeply distressed Bowker. In letters to a dozen leading librarians he deplored the fact that criticisms of the *Journal* had not been brought directly and openly to him. "Why wouldn't it have been more fair and friendly," he asked, "for frank consultation in advance?" He stated that, had he known a lower-priced supplement was desired, he would gladly have co-operated by supplying one himself rather than have it started as a rival periodical, although in either form it would "check the useful growth of the *Journal.*" He pointed out that the library field was too small for such competition, that the *Journal* had served library interests for years at a loss and had only recently been able to make ends meet. "I cannot but feel," he wrote with as much feeling as he ever allowed himself in writing, "that the way in which this matter has been handled is very discouraging to those who have been loyal to the library interests in the beginning as well as now in the heyday of success."[41]

Bowker's protest, however, was too late, and support of the new journal was too strong. In May there appeared the first number of *Public Libraries,* issued at one dollar a year and edited by Mary Eileen Ahern, former head of the Indiana State Library. Her quick speech,

41 R. R. B. to H. E. Davidson, March 20; to R. G. Thwaites, March 27; to president of A. L. A., April 12, April 20; to secretary of A. L. A., April 2, 1896.

direct approach, and Irish pugnacity made her a forceful character, while her irrepressible humor and warm spirit made many friends for her. She was a good reporter and succeeded in making *Public Libraries* more personal, lively, and informal, albeit less scholarly, than the *Journal*, which suffered a certain loss in circulation. The incident, which caused Bowker and his staff some chagrin, leads one to suspect that Bowker may have been too preoccupied with the larger issues of policy and his other public activities to appraise the needs and mood of the "rank and file," and too confident in his own course to imagine a serious lack of confidence in it by others. *Public Libraries* was competition which might have been prevented.

Bowker's support of the American Library Association was unflagging. Between 1882 and 1889 he attended five of its annual meetings; during the decade of the nineties he found time to be present at eight conferences in the United States and a ninth in England. Although by this time the annual conferences had grown to include four hundred delegates, they still had a family affection for each other, it was still possible "to know everybody," and the old zeal was still evident. Bowker entered fully into both the serious work of policy determination and the light side of sight-seeing and informal play, always concerned to promote the professional dignity of the field, always insisting on breadth of view, practical soundness in planning, progress in collaboration, and technical efficiency. His own particular hobbies were national bibliography and library administration, and his most important committee work was done as chairman of the standing and special committees on government publications, for which he spent many long hours in Washington with Congressional committees and made many valuable suggestions concerning the printing, classifying, binding, indexing, and distributing of public documents.

On at least three different occasions Bowker was urged to accept the presidency of the A.L.A., but he always felt that it would be inappropriate for a non-librarian to hold that position.[42] However, he was for twenty-four years a member of the council of the A.L.A. (from 1898–1902, 1907–23, and 1929–33), was elected an honorary president in 1926, and an honorary member in 1933. To many leaders in the library movement, he was a close and trusted adviser. This was particularly true of John S. Billings, the first director of The New York Public Library; E. H. Anderson, who was making a success in Pittsburgh and was to succeed Billings; E. C. Richardson, Librarian of Princeton University; charming, courtly, and erudite Charles A. Cutter of the Boston Athenaeum; Herbert Putnam, scholarly director of the Boston Public Li-

42 Frank P. Hill, in *Library Journal*, December 1, 1933, Part II, p. 1010. ,

brary; Paul Leicester Ford, novelist and editor, a warm personal friend and fellow resident of Brooklyn; Miss Mary W. Plummer, head of the pioneering library school at Pratt Institute; Frank P. Hill, Director of the Brooklyn Public Library; and the mercurial Melvil Dewey, a veritable Mephistopheles with his medium dark complexion, pointed beard, and jutting brow, pouring out his words in a torrent of persuasive intensity.

The best service which Bowker did the library profession, after helping to found the A.L.A. in 1876, was, by his own estimate, his part in the appointment of Herbert Putnam as Librarian of Congress in 1899.[43] In the spring of that year this post was unfilled, a tempting political prize in great danger of being given by the administration to someone without professional library qualifications. A meeting of prominent library leaders was promptly called in New York and acted on a plan of campaign devised by Bowker. Letters were sent by A.L.A. President W. C. Lane to President McKinley and by Bowker to Governor Theodore Roosevelt; a memorial which Bowker helped to draft was sent from the A.L.A. council; Bowker and Lane had a personal interview with McKinley in which they vigorously recommended the selection of Herbert Putnam, then director of the Boston Public Library; and finally Bowker persuaded Putnam to accept the post by calling in his three brothers to a family council at the Reform Club. The recess appointment of Putnam was made on March 13 and duly confirmed December 12. The magnificent record of the nation's foremost library during the following decades was in no small measure due to Putnam's admirable leadership, and Bowker could take just pride in the part he had played in bringing this about.

Another valuable service to the library movement was Bowker's vigorous and continuous advocacy for fourteen years of a unified public library system for Brooklyn.[44] Bowker had long been interested in the Brooklyn Mercantile Library Association which was organized in

43 The incident is fully documented. R. R. B., "The Appointment of Herbert Putnam as Librarian of Congress," *Essays Offered to Herbert Putnam* (edited by W. W. Bishop and A. Keogh, New Haven, 1929), 15–21, 188–91; W. C. Lane, "The Appointment of a Librarian of Congress," *Library Journal*, March, 1899, pp. 99–100; T. Solberg, "A Chapter in the Unwritten History of the Library of Congress from January 17 to April 5, 1899," *Library Quarterly*, July 1939; R. R. B. to T. Roosevelt, January 26, 1899; T. Solberg to R. R. B., January 27, 28, 1899; M. Dewey to R. R. B., February 7, 1899; S. J. Barrows to R. R. B., February 8, 1899; G. H. Putnam to R. R. B., February 8, 14, 1899; R. R. B. to T. Roosevelt, September 22, 1905; *Tribune*, February 2, 1899.

44 Brooklyn *Eagle*, March 30, 1888; Brooklyn Library, Annual Report, 1888, pp. 7–8; minutes of Board of Directors, March 19, 1889; Brooklyn Library, Annual Report, 1890; minutes of Board of Directors, January 26, February 23, and Annual Report, 1892, p. 20.

45 Editorial, *Library Journal*, March, 1895.

1857 and became the Brooklyn Library in 1878. In 1888 he was elected to its board of directors, and from 1890 he served as its vice-president. At the first annual meeting after becoming a director, Bowker brought up the subject of a free public library system. In 1899 he was appointed with Seth Low to a committee of six to confer with other Brooklyn libraries and report on the need and means of such a co-operative move. When Mayor Boody in 1892 proposed the establishment of such a system, Bowker secured a resolution of approval from a somewhat reluctant board, but the city's indebtedness delayed action.

With the dedication of the Pratt Institute's new Free Library in 1896 and the large-scale library plans of the Brooklyn Institute of Arts and Sciences, Bowker was disturbed by the delay in securing a consolidation of library enterprises in Brooklyn such as had taken place in New York.[45] Once more, therefore, he helped to initiate, and accepted service on, a committee of the Brooklyn Library to report on the prospects of unification. His full memorandum on the subject argued that the Brooklyn Library, already at the proper site for such an institution, "would seem to be the natural germ of the free public library system of Brooklyn provided its directors utilize the great opportunity before them." From 1896 through 1900 he assisted as he could in the slow maturing of the situation in spite of continuing coolness among many of the directors.[46] Finally, in 1902, he had the satisfaction of contributing to hearings on a bill to incorporate the Brooklyn Public Library, and the following year the gratification of seeing the Brooklyn Library consolidated with it. He then entered fully into the long public discussion of the best site for a central library.[47] Meanwhile, Bowker had served as chairman of the Brooklyn Library's lectures committee, in 1899 inducing such speakers as Charles Dudley Warner, Miss Amelia Edwards, Edward Eggleston, and Theodore Roosevelt to participate in a successful course of author's readings, and the next year persuaded James Bryce to give at the library the only public address he made during his visit to the United States.

From its incorporation in 1902 until his death in 1933, Bowker served as a trustee and director of the Brooklyn Public Library and enjoyed a close, warm friendship with its director, Frank Hill. In spite of failing eyesight and finally of total blindness, he kept fully abreast of its problems even in matters of such detail that he could only acquaint himself with them by a costly effort of mental concentration. He was deeply interested in the welfare of the library staff and worked con-

46 See R. R. B. to F. B. Pratt, June 14, 1898.
47 R. R. B. to Mayor McClellan, May 20, 1904; April 29, 1905; July 19, September 11, 24, 1906; to F. Hill, April 15, 1907.

tinually for its professional and economic advancement.[48] Meanwhile he had given much of his own private library to the institution, including 549 volumes, 1,696 pamphlets, and 90 periodicals.

There were other library organizations and libraries which benefited from Bowker's direct, personal assistance. In 1885 he helped organize and became the first president of the New York Library Club,[49] which served as a model for such local associations and thus did much to promote the profession. From 1887 on he was very much interested in the Pratt Institute in Brooklyn, being closely associated with its directors, contributing frequently to its lecture program, and offering an enthusiastic *Journal* salute on the occasion of the dedication of its Free Library in 1896. He had a deep and genuine interest in the library of the City College and became a friendly adviser to its librarians. For his fraternity at the College he established what was probably the best fraternity library in this country.[50] The Free Reference Library of the Brooklyn Museum was the result of a movement by the original Library Committee of which Bowker was an active and enthusiastic member.[51] For twenty-four years he served as president of the Stockbridge (Massachusetts) Library Association.[52] He subscribed $10,000 to the Library of Congress Trust Fund for bibliographical services. He was keenly interested in the development of the library of the League of Nations and the reorganization of the Vatican library. He took out a life membership in the American Library in Paris, sent it books, and described its work in the *Library Journal*.[53] He was also a fellow of the American Library Institute and of the Library Association of the United Kingdom. Appraising Bowker's long record of vigorous library support, Herbert Putnam made a definitive appraisal when he wrote in 1933: "Our profession has had no friend who, without the professional obligation, has aided so greatly to define its aims, maintain its dignity, and promote its fellowship.[54] Close associates, indeed, formed the impression that this contribution was the greatest single satisfaction of his long life, and some library leaders have adjudged it to be his "real life work."[55]

[48] *Library Journal*, December, 1933, Part II, p. 1010.

[49] *Library Journal*, February, 1896, p. 52.

[50] *City College Alumnus*, January, 1934, p. 6.

[51] *Bulletin* of the Brooklyn Institute of Arts and Sciences, December 2, 1933, p. 121.

[52] See Chapter XX below.

[53] Report of the Librarian of Congress for the Fiscal Year Ending June 30, 1926, pp. 1-3; R. R. B. to Herbert Putnam, January 2, 1926.

[54] *Library Journal*, 1933, Part II, p. 1007.

[55] Frederic G. Melcher, "Among tthe Founders," *Library Journal*, December 1, 1951, p. 1962; obituary, *Library Association Record*, December, 1933, p. 387.

It may have been the accidental circumstance of Leypoldt's death that kept Bowker in a proprietary relationship to the *Publishers' Weekly,* the *American Catalogue,* and possibly even to the *Library Journal.* But it was no accident that this liberal found himself deeply committed to the interests of the book-publishing field and the library movement. These social forces continued to represent for him a basic educational concern in a democratic society, an essential and irreplaceable element in the great liberal crusade in which he was so deeply engaged. "The library and the school," he once declared, "together make the safeguards of America." And this was so because of the very function of the book.

"The direction of an age," he wrote in *The Arts of Life,* "comes to it often from the closets of its students or from the graves which seem to have sealed their speech. Thence the book, the still small voice which speaks from silence to silence, carries thought into the wills of men. This is the use of a real book: it kindles a flame, that from its light other lights may be lighted forever."[56]

[56] Page 17.

XIII

The Mugwump Crusade
1880–1891

T HE EIGHTEEN EIGHTIES were to see a crescendo of activity in the liberal crusade, with Bowker in the thick of the fight. Not for a moment did the amenities of his London sojourn woo him away from the causes to which he had been committed during the seventies. During his stay abroad he had kept in constant communication with his fellow reformers at home, and on his return he plunged into the work of organizing votes, defining policy, planning campaign strategy, and promoting popular education by writing a stream of pamphlets and tracts. His central concern, indeed, continued to be social engineering, the true vocation of the scholar or "worldsman."

Bowker had a burning conviction that a crucial work remained to be done by American liberals. The crusade for freedom from the unjust and dangerous restrictions of the protective tariff, from the party machine, and from unsound finance must be completed in order that social progress might be made. To this end the machinery of democracy needed more than ever to be perfected through civil service reform and ballot reform. And, since the two major parties gave no promise of adherence to principle on important issues, political leadership must be provided through the organization of the Independents. Bowker and his friends were more than ever convinced that the Independents held the balance-of-power vote and that, if only they could be rallied to joint action, an unlimited opportunity for national service lay ahead of them. In this hope they poured out their money, time, and energy. For all their idealism, they were a tough, practical-minded group of crusaders, civic-minded men who felt it their duty to follow a hard day's work at their offices with an evening's hard work for the cause. All in all, they created a significant interlocking network of organizations and publications to accomplish their objectives.

Bowker's activity in the liberal crusade during the years 1880–91 followed exactly the pattern of his activity from 1872–80. Free trade was the chief objective. Organizing the Independents, promoting civil service reform, and educating the voters through a program of publications and study groups were the basic means to this end. The agencies through which Bowker now chiefly worked were the American Free Trade League, the New York Free Trade Club, the New York Reform Club, the Kings County Free Trade League, the New York Civil Service Reform Association, the Commonwealth Club, the Brooklyn Young Republican Club, the National Committee of Republicans and Independents, the Society for Political Education, the Economist Press, *The Million,* and *The People's Cause.*

Political developments between 1880 and 1882 convinced Bowker of the need of a new party alignment. First came disillusionment with Garfield,[1] then came dismay at the prospect of Arthur's Stalwartism in the White House and Blaine's Jingoism in the State Department at the very time when the Democrats seemed again to be branded by blundering and unprincipled party management. From London Bowker wrote two letters to Shepard intended to be read to the Independents in both parties,[2] in which he declared that when neither major party provided real leadership or represented real issues, it became necessary "to reform one or both into efficiency by the balance-of-power vote." If a new party must come, the sooner the better. As for a platform he would have it stand on civil service, revenue-reform, opposition to overcentralization in government, states rights, home rule for cities, a more direct presidential election, and elimination of the lame-duck session of Congress.

The success of the New York Independents in 1882 gave Bowker a fine opportunity to develop his strategy. In Brooklyn, the Independent Republicans had transformed their Garfield Club into the Brooklyn Young Republican Club,[3] and the independent Democrats had organized the Brooklyn Young Men's Democratic Club under Shepard's initiative and leadership. In New York City the Independent Democrats had organized the County Democracy under the leadership of Wheeler, Hewitt, Whitney, Stetson, and others as a counterweight to

1 R. R. B., London Journal, August 23, 24, September, 1880; G. H. Putnam to R. R. B., November 14, 1880, E. P. Wheeler to R. R. B., December 10, 1880.

2 R. R. B. to E. M. Shepard, March 22, April, 1882.

3 R. R. B. to J. B. Barnhill, December 5, 1888; to Ostrogorski, January 15, 1898; H. Deming to R. R. B., March 11, 1927.

Boss Kelly's Tammany Hall.[4] In the New York gubernatorial campaign of 1882, when the Arthur-Conkling machine tried to force Charles J. Folger on the Republicans, all the Independents stood together behind Democratic Grover Cleveland, with the Brooklyn Young Republican Club taking the lead in rallying 100,000 Republican voters behind his successful candidacy.[5]

Bowker promptly analyzed the significance of this victory in a brilliant and stirring essay, "Political Nexts," which was printed in both the *Evening Post* and the *Nation* and then reprinted for general distribution as a tract.[6] His warning was prophetic: the Independent Republicans who had just overwhelmed Folger in 1882 were in direct succession to the Young Scratchers who had rebuked Cornell in 1879 and the Independent Republicans who had helped to defeat Grant and nominate Garfield in 1880. If the Republican party did not take a favorable stand on civil service and tariff reform, they would go on to overwhelm the Republican nominee in 1884 either by supporting a good Democratic candidate like Cleveland, or, "If both parties continue rotten, double-faced, and blind, Independents must make up their minds to stand out by themselves, to cast a conscience vote for a third candidate in 1884, and to organize a third party, which shall eventually be one of two." In December, 1882, Bowker was elected to the executive committee of the Brooklyn Young Republican Club and then to its committee on political information. In the Brooklyn mayoralty campaign of 1883 he worked hard for the re-election of Seth Low.

The heart and soul of Bowker's reform program centered in the movement for free trade. He regarded it as his "vocation," and when in London longed to come home to rally the attack again. While there, his zeal had been strengthened by election to honorary membership in the Cobden Club in the summer of 1880, by attending its London dinners, and by talks with its leaders. He made his letter of acceptance such a ringing tract on the subject that it was immediately printed as a broadside in America.[7] It read in part:

[4] E. M. Shepard to R. R. B., January 5, May 1, 1881; Everett P. Wheeler, *Sixty Years of American Life*, 331–32.

[5] R. R. B. to J. B. Barnhill, December 5, 1888; "Political Principles," New York *Evening Post*, January 24, 1884; H. Deming to R. R. B., March 11, 1927.

[6] New York *Evening Post*, November 11; *Nation*, November 16, 1882. Putnam confirmed Bowker's analyses in his letter to R. R. B., November 11, 1882.

[7] Cobden Club to R. R. B., August 5, 1880; See Putnam, *Memories of a Publisher*, 40–41; Cobden Club, Special Report on Cobden Club dinner, July 1, 1882, p. 1. R. R. B. to Hon. T. Bailey Potter, secretary, Cobden Club, May 17, 1881; printed as "An American Free Trader to the Cobden Club," with first edition of 25,000.

American free traders have . . . reason to feel that they are avert-
ing the one danger which threatens their Republic. In teaching
an economic philosophy which refuses to set nation against nation, section against section, class against class, but sees in the good
of all the good of each, they best forestall those possible wars of
labor against capital, of tenant against owner, of agricultural
against manufacturing classes, of West against East, which, now
that slavery is swept away, loom up as the threatening danger of
the future.

In 1880 the liberal Republicans had hoped for tariff reform by the
Garfield Republicans. In 1882 they looked to the Democrats, who made
such striking gains throughout the nation that they were in a position
to control the Congress which would assemble in December, 1883. On
his return from Europe, Bowker promptly entered into the work of
unifying and enlarging the efforts of reformers to guarantee Congressional action. His leadership was immediately evident. After canvassing
the situation, Bowker urged five steps: unification of the finances of
the three free-trade agencies then overlapping in the New York area,
a financial campaign for a permanent joint endowment, a conference
to reorganize the new League on a more representative basis, the employment of a permanent staff, and the assembling of "a card list of
sympathizers all over the country" as "the protoplasm of organization
through the Congressional districts."[8]

These were excellent suggestions, and they were all adopted. A joint
"Free Trade Board of Finance" was set up with Anson Phelps Stokes
as chairman, George Foster Peabody as secretary, and Bowker as one
of the nine board members. A campaign to raise $20,000 for two years'
free-trade propaganda all over the country was carefully outlined along
lines proposed by Bowker,[9] who also tried to get Thomas Holland to
subscribe $100,000 for "Holland Professorships of Economics" in the
colleges.[10]

The American Free Trade League was revived in order to organize
associations in every state and clubs in every Congressional district, and
of this David A. Wells was induced to accept the presidency and Bowker was made honorary secretary. Within a year a New York State
Revenue Reform League was organized with Bowker on its executive
committee to co-ordinate all state activities. A free-trade journal, *The
American Free Trader,* was begun in October, 1882, and continued

8 R. R. B. to E. P. Wheeler, November 20, 1882.
9 Free Trade Board of Finance, printed notice, undated.
10 R. R. B. to T. Holland, December 4, 1882.

until 1884 with Earle as editor, but Bowker as the power behind Earle.[11] Plans were made to start clubs in Albany, Poughkeepsie, Newburgh, Buffalo, and Elmira.

In May, 1883, at Detroit, Bowker engineered a national conference which for the first time brought together all free traders, and for this he not only took charge of arrangements but wrote an address which was officially adopted.[12] The campaign was concluded in the fall with a successful rally in Cooper Union, presided over by Henry Ward Beecher and addressed by Wells and Henry Watterson. No wonder Shearman told Bowker, "You are our best executive manager."

The reformers had done their best in a twelve-month campaign of educating public opinion. Now came the final test as the Democratic Congress met in December, 1883. W. R. Morrison of Illinois, the new chairman of the Ways and Means Committee, sponsored the Democratic bill for tariff reform. Few free traders thought his bill a perfect measure, but they were determined to pass it and looked for help to such sympathetic congressmen as S. S. Cox and Abram S. Hewitt.[13] Bowker analyzed each schedule, being especially interested in the items affecting publishers. On February 22, he and T. G. Shearman appeared on behalf of the bill before the House Ways and Means Committee and presented able statements which were printed as propaganda.[14] Carlisle and Sumner made strong supporting speeches at a Delmonico dinner of the New York Free Trade Club in March. Hope was high. "Conquer we must, for our cause it is just," Wheeler confidently wrote his more skeptical friend Bowker. "It took from 1830 to 1865 to free the slaves and we shall have free trade sooner than that." Wells rejoiced that "Our worst enemy, General Apathy, is dead." Valuable moral support came at the end of April when the Massachusetts Tariff Reform League was organized with C. F. Adams as its president. The Morrison Bill, however, was doomed. On May 6, forty-one protectionist Democrats voted with Randall to strike out the enacting clause. The lesson seemed clear. For the time being, at least, the reformers could not place their faith in either major party.

Bowker had kept in close touch with the significant progress which his friends were making in civil service reform while he was in London.

11 See letters from Earle to R. R. B., 1883.

12 Report of Joint Conference, A.F.T.L., N.Y.F.T.C., K.C.F.T.L., April 3, 1883.

13 For a discussion of this bill, see D. A. Wells to R. R. B., January 1, 12, 22, February 10, 1884; R. R. B. to D. A. Wells, January 10, 1884.

14 *Free Trade Means High Wages; High Tariff Means Low Wages, etc.,* Washington, 1884. See bibliography; *The Million,* March 8, 1884.

In the fall of 1880, Godkin, Whitridge, and Putnam helped to revive the old New York Civil Service Reform Association which had dissolved during the first years of the Hayes administration. Curtis was elected president, Dugdale was made secretary, and Wheeler became chairman of the executive committee, a post he was to keep for seventeen years. The Civil Service Reform Association of Brooklyn was formed with Alfred T. White, Shepard, William Potts, and Clarence Deming among its officers, and soon similar organizations sprang up in eight other cities. In August, 1881, the National Civil Service Reform League was organized at Newport with Curtis as president and Potts as secretary. Meanwhile, the leaders of the movement were rewriting Senator George Pendleton's bill for a national civil service act which was triumphantly passed in January, 1883.[15]

With the passage of the Pendleton Act, the New York Civil Service Reform Association moved quickly to secure a state civil service law, the first in any state. In this Bowker played a leading part.[16] Wheeler and Shepard drafted a bill, which was introduced by Theodore Roosevelt, leader of the Republican minority in the state assembly. As a Republican measure, the bill was so promptly defeated by the Democratic majority that both Roosevelt and the Civil Service Association gave up hope for it.

Bowker and Shepard, however, knowing that each step of civil service reform had been won by the reformers in both parties against the regulars of both parties, planned a campaign to force the bill's passage as a nonpartisan measure. To this end they concentrated on three Independents whom they knew well: Walter Howe, Roosevelt's lieutenant on the Republican side and Bowker's City College classmate; A. C. Chapin, the Speaker of the Democratic assembly who was a Williams College graduate just completing two years as president of the Brooklyn Young Men's Democratic Club; and Talcott Williams, an Amherst man who was then the Albany correspondent of the *World* and in good standing with both sides of the legislature. The strategy succeeded. Roosevelt agreed to take up the bill again, but when it again failed, Chapin rallied the better leaders of the Democrats behind it

---

15 Edward Carey, *George William Curtis,* 272–73; Wheeler, *Sixty Years of American Life,* 276–81; F. M. Steward, *The National Civil Service Reform League* (Austin, Texas, 1929), 23–30.

16 This account is based on the following sources: Brooklyn *Daily Times,* October 22, 1883; G. W. Curtis to R. R. B., October 11, 1883; R. R. B. to T. Roosevelt, October 29, 1884; T. Roosevelt to R. R. B., October 21, 1884; R. R. B. to A. C. Chapin, October 24, 1887, to S. S. Fowler, November 11, 1907, to T. C. Sweet, April 19, 1916; Wheeler, *Sixty Years of American Life,* 281–83; *City College Quarterly,* April, 1925, p. 104; Allan Nevins, *Grover Cleveland, A Study in Courage,* 123; R. R. B., MS Memoir.

and it passed.[17] In the Senate, Governor Cleveland's hearty support helped the bill's passage, and on the last day of the session, it became law. Within twenty-four hours Cleveland appointed the first New York State Civil Service Commission.

Since Roosevelt, Chapin, Williams, Wheeler, Shepard, and Bowker were all fraternity brothers, one of the opposition New York dailies referred to the coup as a college conspiracy, and in this the "conspirators" took considerable pride. "Your success in the Civil Service Reform Bill," Williams wrote Bowker, "was admirable. After all, it is hitting at the right moment which does these things."[18] At the annual meeting of the National Civil Service Reform League held that summer at Newport, Curtis acknowledged that passage of the bill was a feather in the cap of the young Brooklyn Independents who had joined the forces of their Democratic and Republican clubs.

Bowker and his reform friends, however, did not cease their activities with the passage of this bill. In February, 1884, Bowker met with Wheeler and Schurz to consider means of amending the New York Civil Service Act,[19] and under the amended act Wheeler and Shepard were appointed to draw up rules for New York City and Brooklyn. They were then appointed chairmen, respectively, of the New York and Brooklyn civil service commissions, Wheeler serving from 1883 to 1889 and Shepard from 1883 to 1890. With Deming and Schurz, Bowker labored on the executive committee of the New York Civil Service Reform Association from 1890 to 1893.

The presidential campaign of 1884 constituted a climax to the crusade of the Independents. It provided a situation exactly to their measure, and it resulted in a victory which seemed brilliantly to confirm their theories. To Bowker it remained, through the rest of his life, *the* great demonstration of what conscientious American citizens, independent of narrow party loyalties and working together in intelligent organization, could do for the advancement of the nation. For the succeeding fifty years he waited for another such conjunction of need, candidate, and balance between the two major parties, but it never

17 A year later, in replying to a public letter of R. R. B. to him, Roosevelt denied that R. R. B.'s letter of 1883 had any effect and argued that "the Republican minority by unanimous and concerted action fairly forced the Democratic majority to pass the bill." T. Roosevelt to R. R. B., October 31, 1884. Bowker on several public occasions stated that Roosevelt had "literally been caught napping" and that the bill had passed the Assembly without his vote; but Roosevelt in the letter quoted above insisted this was due to the negligence of the Democratic clerk.

18 T. Williams to R. R. B., May 21, 1883.

19 E. P. Wheeler to R. R. B., February 14, 1884.

arrived. In 1884, Bowker was no longer fighting in a small company. Many men far more capable and influential than he devoted their energy and their brains to the election of Cleveland. Yet Bowker always felt a pride in the part he played and the fact that he came to be known as "the original Mugwump," founder of the movement that defied Conkling in 1879, helped to defeat Grant in 1880, turned away Folger in 1882, and in all likelihood elected Cleveland in 1884.

The Mugwump movement in New York really began as "the Brooklyn Movement," in which Bowker was an active leader. For two years he and his fellows had been pointing their civil service, tariff, political, and educational activities toward the presidential campaign of 1884. Toward the end of January, 1884, Bowker fired his first real shot in the form of a letter entitled "Political Principles" which appeared in the *Evening Post*. It warned the party managers that it would be political suicide to ignore the balance-of-power vote wielded by Independents; it appealed to Independents to realize their strength and league themselves together; it argued against a third party now, but asserted the possible need to "open the way for a new party long before 1888"; it sounded again a call to bold civic initiative.

> Having had some experience in the organization of the "scratching" campaign of '79, I am prepared to be called any kind of hard names or silly names; to hear the old sneer about "fighting in the air"; to be told that "the same game can't be played twice." But if a few determined people, who know what they don't want, who want nothing for themselves, and who know how to stick, will set themselves at it, something can be done to insure principle in politics in the two parties and in this city of New York.

The letter brought Bowker a number of replies supporting his position and begging him to make an announcement of Independent intentions that would attract public attention.[20]

The first objective was to compel an acceptable presidential nomination by the national Republican convention scheduled to assemble in Chicago on June 2. From February to June the Independents were active. In February, Bowker was busy with the plans of the Brooklyn Young Republican Club and the Republican Conference Committee to head delegations to the Republican convention.[21] When the Massa-

[20] D. H. Chamberlain to R. R. B., January 28, February 7; Horace Deming to R. R. B., January 30; E. J. Donnell to R. R. B., February 1, 6; Charles C. Soule to R. R. B., February 14, 1884, etc.

[21] Carey, *G. W. Curtis*, 285; Report of the National Executive Committee of Republicans and Independents (presidential campaign of 1884), pp. 2–4 (hereafter referred to as N.E.C.R.I. Report).

chusetts Reform Club suggested that Independents stand ready to convene for stock-taking after the nominating conventions, he expressed hearty support in a vigorous letter to the *Times* urging the formation of "leagues of Independents within their own party lines . . . as the nucleus of a protest party," and predicting that a post-convention conference of Independents might become "the most useful event in our politics since the war period closed."[22] A few weeks later Bowker was delegated to organize a dinner conference for New York Independents on May 28 at the Down Town Club, and his draft call was soon signed by thirty prominent Independents, including young Theodore Roosevelt.[23] As an even more practical feature of the campaign, Bowker secured signatures to a manifesto listing the following four principles as governing the Independent vote: civil service reform, cessation of silver coinage, tariff reform, and the separation of local issues from national parties.[24] Meanwhile, the New York *Sun* led the party regulars in ridiculing the Independents by dubbing them "Mugwumps." The name, originally an Indian term for one who thought highly of himself, had been used in political campaigns in 1840 and in 1872. It now caught the popular fancy and stuck.[25]

The Republican Independents failed at Chicago. Working under the leadership of Curtis, they sought the nomination of Senator Edmunds of Vermont, but to their intense disgust Blaine was nominated on the fourth ballot. The real test of independency for Republicans had now come. Could they support the man they had fought in 1880 as the symbol of political immorality, "the one man," as Curtis now put it, "who is most repugnant to the political conscience of young Republicans"?

The answer was decisive. Roosevelt and Lodge might choose to swallow Blaine and stick by the party, but scores of other influential Republicans were ready to bolt if only the Democrats would give them a strong candidate. The Massachusetts Reform Club promptly repudiated Blaine. Curtis boldly swung *Harper's Weekly* against the Republican nominee. On the very day of Blaine's nomination the Independents sent telegrams from Chicago to Boston and New York calling for immediate organization. Within a week Bowker, assisted by Shearman

22 "The Work Before Independents," letter published in the New York *Times,* dated March 4, 1884.

23 Original draft and appended signatures now in Bowker Papers, Library of Congress.

24 Original in Bowker Papers, New York Public Library.

25 New York *Sun,* March 23, 1884; newspaper contributions, undated, in Bowker files. The Connecticut State Librarian later sent Bowker a photostat copy of a deed of lands dated May 6, 1579, witnessed by "Mugwump."

and Whitridge, was seeing to the mailing of a hundred and more carefully selected invitations to Independents in New York, Boston, Philadelphia, Chicago, and St. Louis to a preliminary conference at the home of J. Henry Harper on June 17. The purpose of the conference was to impress the Democratic national convention scheduled to meet July 11 with the potential support which Independent Republicans would give a good Democratic candidate. After Curtis had been elected chairman, and Bowker's two nominees, G. W. Green and S. W. Grierson, had been elected secretaries, Moorfield Storey of Boston and Carl Schurz made ringing speeches calling on the Democrats to nominate a first-rate man. The final step was to announce a general conference of Independents to assemble after the Democratic convention had met. Bowker was elected to a committee of twenty-five to organize this important meeting.[26]

Developments were auspicious. The Democrats nominated Grover Cleveland. The general conference of Independents which met four hundred strong at the University Club Theatre on July 22 enthusiastically endorsed the Cleveland nomination.[27] To mobilize for an effective campaign, a national committee of Republicans and Independents was organized with thirty-three members representing eleven states. Curtis was elected chairman and George Walton Green secretary; Bowker was one of the seven New York committeemen along with Horace Deming, Carl Schurz, and Charles P. Miller. Bowker was also appointed to the executive committee of fourteen under Deming's chairmanship, and was made chairman of a committee to work with the Democratic National Committee through Senator A. P. Gorman of Maryland, chairman of its executive committee.

The first job had been done. The Independents had a candidate, and they had an effective organization. That there was a great and growing mass of Republicans dissatisfied with their party management and waiting to be organized for effective action became more evident every day. In every city prominent Republicans were coming out against Blaine. Leading journals, nominally Republican, swung behind Cleveland, including the *Times, Herald, Evening Post, Nation, Harper's Weekly,* Springfield *Republican,* Boston *Transcript,* and Boston *Herald.* But there remained many local skirmishes and the major campaign.

26 N.E.C.R.I. Report. See *The Million,* June 21, 28, 1884, F. W. Whitridge to R. R. B., June 10, 11, 12, 13, 1884, etc. One hundred and thirty-nine signed invitations are in the Bowker Papers, Library of Congress. *Tribune,* June 18, 1884; Harper, *The House of Harper,* 499–500; *The Million,* June 28, 1884; S. W. Grierson to R. R. B., June 19, 1884.

27 See Frederic Bancroft and W. A. Dunning, *The Reminiscences of Carl Schurz,* II, 406; N.E.C.R.I. Report, 24.

A good example of the fight which many Independent Republicans now had with the party regulars in their local associations is the one which led to Bowker's resignation from the Brooklyn Young Republican Club.[28] The club's Independents maneuvered to have the Executive Committee (of which Bowker was a member) appoint a special committee (including Bowker) to present an unfavorable report on Blaine's record, following which almost every member of the executive and advisory committees declared his opposition to Blaine. The regulars, however, then took the initiative in calling for a full meeting of the club, and when Bowker and his fellow Independents arrived at this gathering, they discovered that it had been captured by the Blaine men. It was Bowker's duty to present to the club membership the view of the executive committee, but the Blaine men would not let him speak. When the vote was at last taken, the regulars carried it for Blaine, whereupon eleven out of fifteen members of the executive committee (including Bowker, Alfred T. White, and Horace Deming) and ten out of twenty of the advisory committee resigned. It was later ascertained that 500 of the 2,500 club members shared their convictions. The club, though it kept up its organization during and after the campaign, never recovered from this split.

Bowker and his associates realized that success in the fall would depend on the preliminary work of organization during the summer, so they lost no time laying the foundation of their campaign. Since Curtis followed his usual practice of summering in Ashfield and Schurz was often out of town carrying the brunt of the speaking program, the main work of organization fell on the executive committee, and this meant Deming and Bowker. Promptly the two men built up a clerical force at headquarters, starting with three in July and ending with over seventy by election day. The campaign program was divided into three parts: preparation of publicity, distribution of publicity, and organization. On the publicity front, the National Committee issued over two million copies of fourteen documents (of which four were also duplicated in German translation), and their work was supplemented by the efforts of local committees. The second task meant compiling a mailing list of sympathizers, organizing meetings, and supplying speakers. The third task involved co-ordinating the work of local committees. These committees were particularly active in Massachusetts, Rhode Island, Connecticut, New York, New Jersey, Pennsylvania, Ohio, Indiana, Illinois, Wisconsin, and Iowa.[29] Bowker did not once leave the

28 R. R. B. to Ostrogorski, January 15, 1898; R. R. B. to T. Roosevelt in Brooklyn *Eagle*, October 29, 1884.
29 N.E.C.R.I. Report, 4–13.

office during the summer, "standing in the imminent breach," as Curtis put it to him later. Aside from his work with the liaison committee, his chief contribution was a journalistic one, writing and helping to edit the campaign documents.

Bowker and his fellow Independents might have been "amateurs," but they showed a keen sense of political strategy and fired shot after shot into the enemy camp which amazed and perplexed its managers. Colonel Brooman of the Republican State Committee later said to Bowker, "Well, you boys did keep us guessing!"[30] One of the first campaign documents Bowker issued was made up from the Brooklyn Young Republican Club's report on Blaine, which he had originally helped to edit. Five others were much more dramatic.

One was the official Independent reply to the deeply distressing charges which exploded in July to the effect that Cleveland had had immoral relations with Maria Halpin and other women. Bowker attended the Newport meeting of the National Civil Service Reform League on August 6 where the morality issue was thoroughly discussed and confidence in Cleveland's character and his political rectitude established. Bowker and his associates were now convinced that the best defense was a bold admission of the truth on this fateful issue. Careful enquiries were therefore undertaken which convinced them that all charges of immoral conduct except the original one were false. On the basis of this evidence Bowker composed an effective address entitled "The Charges Swept Away." Green was then sent with the galley proof to Cleveland to say that the Independents would not issue the address unless absolutely assured by him that there was no foundation for the other stories. This assurance was promptly and fully given, Curtis approved the draft, and it was issued. On the other hand, when evidence of Blaine's own lapse from sexual morality was brought to the attention of the committee, Bowker agreed with the others that they would absolutely not deign to use it, and Cleveland wholeheartedly adopted the same attitude.

A second dramatic journalistic contribution was in helping to prepare the second series of Mulligan letters, described by one historian as the heaviest single anti-Blaine blow of the campaign.[31] During the first week of September, Schurz received word that James Mulligan was in possession of certain letters which threw additional light on Blaine's unethical relations with the Little Rock and Fort Smith Railway securities and that these would be turned over to him for use in the campaign. Horace Deming was promptly dispatched to Boston to secure

30 R. R. B., MS Memoir.
31 Nevins, *Cleveland*, 160.

the precious documents, and a conference with Moorfield Storey and a few other Boston Independents decided on immediate and simultaneous release of the letters to the nation's press. Bowker was commissioned to get the story to the New York and Philadelphia papers and to the Associated Press.[32] Attested copies were made and a set brought to Bowker in New York by Jabez Fox, one of the Boston Mugwumps, and on September 16 the first installment appeared. The most famous letter, including the words which the campaign slogans were soon to make known from coast to coast, "Burn this letter, kind regards to Mrs. Fisher," was printed in the *Times* in facsimile on October 11.

A third effective cannonade which Bowker directed and fired made use of the Gail Hamilton letters. Bowker one day received a mysterious message through the managing editor of the *Weekly* that a certain printer in his employ wished to show him some material of interest. This man, it turned out, had been a proofreader on the *Tribune,* and it had been his practice to recover from the wastepaper basket autographs and other material of interest to keep as souvenirs.[33] Among these was the manuscript of a *Tribune* editorial written in 1880 by Gail Hamilton, a niece and home associate of Blaine, disparaging all presidential candidates but Blaine. On the reverse side of this was written in Blaine's hand, "My dear Reid—This is a timely appeal and should be printed at once. J.G.B." Bowker saw the value of this document in throwing doubt on Blaine's trustworthiness even in matters of party loyalty, so had it facsimiled and printed in the *Times* and other Independent papers on October 23, with a reprint of the article. It was also exhibited in the window of the New York *Times* office. Of course the *Tribune* promptly branded the endorsement a forgery and quoted experts to prove it,[34] but to no avail. This coup had the effect of making the Conkling and Arthur men more than ever the enemies of Blaine and alienating a number of their votes.

A fourth journalistic shot into the enemy's ranks involved the famous Burchard incident of October 29, with its fatal branding of the Democrats as the party of "rum, Romanism, and rebellion." Bowker helped to make the most of this Republican slip by promptly preparing handbills emblazoned with this phrase for distribution on the following Sunday morning in front of the Catholic churches after mass.

Bowker's most effective journalistic service to the campaign, however, was probably the supplement which he prepared for *Harper's Weekly* bringing out in deadly parallel and in black-face type the dark

32 H. Deming to R. R. B., September 12, 1884.
33 R. H. Waldron to R. R. B., October 20, 1884.
34 "Now for More Morey Forgeries," *Tribune,* October 25, 1884.

Bowker with a group of former presidents of the A.L.A., Saratoga Springs, 1918. *(Back row, left to right)* Henry J. Carr, Herbert Putnam, James I. Wyer, Jr., Clement W. Andrews, Frank P. Hill, Hiller C. Wellman; *(Front row, left to right)* Melvil Dewey, Mrs. Theresa West Elmendorf, R. R. Bowker, Thomas L. Montgomery, Arthur E. Bostwick

Fellow Captains in the Liberal Crusade: *(Top, left)* Horace E. Deming; *(Top, right)* Talcott Williams; *(Bottom, left)* Thomas G. Shearman; *(Bottom, right)* Edward Atkinson

record of Blaine's contradictions and evasions in his various letters and statements. This supplement had a circulation of close to 223,000 copies and proved a most effective campaign document.[35] In addition to these more dramatic pieces, Bowker also wrote several editorials for the *Times*.[36]

At the end of October, Bowker directly challenged young Theodore Roosevelt on his decision to remain a party regular and swallow Blaine. Bowker had invited Roosevelt to debate the issues of the campaign with Independents in Brooklyn, and Roosevelt had declined. Bowker thereupon wrote a long public letter to Roosevelt, taking him to task for supporting Blaine. It was a powerful summary of the arguments against Blaine and the importance of the Independent movement with which Roosevelt had from time to time been associated, but which he now seemed to be deserting. Bowker's conclusion expressed the feeling of many Independents:

> You are separating yourself now from great possibilities of good work. The regular Republicans do not want you any more than the regular Democrats want us Independent Republicans. Your power is gone when you forego principle for party, and those who have been associated with you have had in this campaign no more sincere sorrow than the feeling that in the hope of success "within the party" you have surrendered the one possibility of continuing the work for which your name has been respected throughout the country.[37]

Roosevelt's public reply to Bowker was equally vigorous and equally temperate. It consisted, chiefly, in questioning Bowker's faith in the Democratic party and in Cleveland's character, declaring that administrative reform would be postponed ten years by a return of the Democrats to power. He evinced, moreover, very little desire to be associated with the Independents. In a letter to Lodge a few days later, Roosevelt commented, "By the way, R. R. Bowker tackled me the other day; and I think I made mince meat of him."[38]

The glorious climax to these vigorous campaign efforts came with Cleveland's triumphant election. The vote was almost as close as in 1880, but provided more convincing evidence of the balance-of-power role of the Independents. When all the figures were finally in, it was

[35] N.E.C.R.I. Report, 26; R. R. B. to Norman Davis, January 19, 1928.

[36] " 'For President, Grover Cleveland!' Why?" New York *Times*, October 4, 1884.

[37] "To T. Roosevelt," Brooklyn *Eagle* and *Union*, October 29, 1884.

[38] T. Roosevelt to H. C. Lodge, November 11, 1884, in *Selections from the Correspondence of T. Roosevelt and H. C. Lodge, 1884–1918*, I.

perfectly clear that Cleveland's victory was largely the result of his winning New York state, and that New York state had been won with the narrow plurality of 1,149 votes. This meant, according to Bowker, that if 575 voters for Cleveland had voted for Blaine, the latter would have been elected president. Naturally the Mugwumps felt that they were entitled to considerable credit. Schurz went so far as to say that there was "no room to doubt that they determined the outcome."[39] Bowker insisted that, though "amateur politicians," the Mugwumps had really put more punch into the local campaign than the Democratic National Committee had, and that Cleveland simply would not have been elected had Gorman kept sole control of the campaign. In fact, he later charged that Gorman's committee had "neither political sagacity nor strategy nor leadership, and they left all that to us 'amateurs,'" and again that they were "lukewarm and inefficient."[40] But in view of the fact that this committee included tried managers like Whitney and Manning, the characterization must be taken as a rather subjective reflection of local conditions only.

The Cleveland victory completely demonstrated the working philosophy of the Independents, and Bowker, who wrote the official campaign report, took pains to point the moral in almost the same terms he had employed in 1879:

> It has shown once and for all how one man's voice and one man's vote and one man's work counts even among ten millions of voters. . . . It has been a splendid proof of the important fact that, in the darkest days of political corruption, party tyranny, and moral depression, there exists in the American people a reserve power, capable of organizing itself without the aid of and indeed against political leaders, competent to accomplish the most difficult undertakings in political reform.[41]

Wheeler's conclusion was equally optimistic. "So it proved to be true, as Schurz and George Haven Putnam had repeatedly claimed, that both the political organizations were 'minority parties.' Neither could succeed without the help of the independent voters."[42]

The Mugwump victory of 1884 brought no immediate or clear-cut consummation of liberal ideals. There was much frustration to be experi-

39 Bancroft and Dunning, *The Reminiscences of Carl Schurz*, III, 407.
40 R. R. B. to Norman Davis, January 18, 1927; June 25, 1930.
41 N.E.C.R.I. Report, 18.
42 Wheeler, *Sixty Years of American Life*, 128.

enced in Cleveland's administration and in developments within the Democratic party. The Mugwumps did not remain together as a cohesive organization through these years. The cause of tariff reform met defeat after defeat. Nevertheless, Mugwump hopes were never dashed, and to many the election of 1888 seemed to offer the greatest hope of several decades. During these years Bowker gave an enormous amount of his time and energy to the great crusade. Apparently content to be only half-employed in business, he kept himself fully employed in his self-appointed program of reform organization and pamphleteering. He pushed the program of the Society for Political Education. He helped to spearhead a new campaign for tariff reform. He took a leading part in launching the New York Reform Club. He was full of plans for starting a new reform journal to replace the defunct *Million* and a new publishing firm devoted to the work of the liberal crusade. He was up to his ears in work for ballot reform.

Bowker wore no golden crown in the eyes of the Republican regulars for his Mugwump activities. Following the election, the Brooklyn Seventh Ward Republican Association brought formal charges of disloyalty to the party against him and his Mugwump associates.[43] Bowker was unperturbed. In a long letter to the association he reviewed his principles, his actions, and his services to the party, warned it against the danger of forcing out the Independents, and declared his intention of remaining unfettered.

> I do not desire to remain a member of any organization in which I am regarded more or less as a traitor. And I can only say that I shall do again what I have done before, and that I am not willing to continue membership in an organization which seeks to restrain me from active action in accordance with my private judgment.[44]

When this characteristic pronouncement reached the eyes of Whitelaw Reid, there was another terrific explosion that matched the previous *Tribune* attack of February 1880.

> ... Bowker shows a disposition to brace up the country provided the country will place itself in his charge and refrain from giving him any of its "sass." ... If the Republican party will consent to Bowkerize itself, then Bowker will magnanimously consent to forgive it for running a man for President in 1884 who was merely the choice of the majority of a National Convention and not of

[43] Seventh Ward Republican Association of Brooklyn to R. R. B., November 26, 1884.

[44] R. R. B. to Brooklyn Seventh Ward Republican Association, in Brooklyn *Union*, December 10, 1884.

Bowker. . . . It is evident that he is prepared to respect the will of the majority every time, provided it is in harmony with the will of Bowker. . . . Let us trust that the Republican party will make its peace with Bowker and induce him not to cast it off. For when Mr. Lincoln advised his countrymen to see to it that government of Bowker, by Bowker, for Bowker should not perish from the earth, he spoke by the card.[45]

Others seemed to feel the same way. Another paper carried the following line: "The fact that Bismarck lately expressed his contempt for majorities may lead the Young Republicans of Brooklyn to speak of him as a German translation of R. R. Bowker."

Bowker's sterling efforts in the Cleveland campaign were naturally more appreciated among the Independents. He was made chairman of a committee to write the official report of the Mugwump executive committee, and it was presented at a final dinner of the Mugwumps in February, 1885. The Report was not only a valuable factual summary of the committee's work, but a stirring reiteration of the Independents' convictions and determination for the future.

Bowker had several interviews with Cleveland. When it was decided to urge Cleveland to strengthen himself in advance against the office-seeking politicians by issuing a specific declaration for civil service reform, Bowker was selected with Green and Deming to interview the President-elect in Albany. The mission was most successful. Cleveland agreed to a public exchange of letters on civil service reform; Bowker edited a letter in the name of the National Civil Service Reform League, received emendations from Curtis and Schurz to his original draft, secured signatures from a number of the League's leaders, and sent it to Cleveland. The planned reply, promptly made on December 25, represented a significant commitment.[46] Bowker had a second interview with Cleveland in April, 1885, which he described as "very cordial and . . . very satisfactory,"[47] and a third one in November. Meanwhile, he kept Cleveland's secretary, D. S. Lamont, informed of sundry Mugwump reactions and suggestions.[48] Bowker several times referred to "an honorary appointment" proffered him by Cleveland and "a possible nomination to Congress,"[49] but it is not clear what developments he referred to.

45 "Mr. Bowker's Threat," *Tribune*, December 12, 1884.

46 R. R. B., MS Memoir; file envelope of draft and emendations marked "Origin of Reply to Curtis," in Bowker Papers. See Nevins, *Cleveland*, 198–201.

47 R. R. B. to sister, April 14, 1885.

48 R. R. B. to D. S. Lamont, July 9, September 24, October 15, 1885, in Cleveland Papers, Library of Congress.

To Bowker's regret, the National Committee of Republicans and Independents did not long survive Cleveland's election. On the question of future action, the Massachusetts men voted to continue the Mugwump organization, but the New York men were undecided. In January, 1885, the National Committee voted to continue the existing organization, but the February dinner proved to be its last official act. In the fall of 1885, Bowker hoped to rally the old alliance to defeat David B. Hill in his campaign for governor of New York. Hill had already become a focus for the anti-Cleveland opposition in the state; in character, habits, and Tammany associations, he represented everything that the Independents abhorred. Bowker urged separate action by the Independents, and the issue of an Independent address, but Curtis strongly advised against both, and the ideas were dropped.[50] Hill's election with a strong plurality was a blow at Cleveland and thoroughly disheartening to the reformers, who were again reminded of the conflicting elements within the Democratic party. In 1887, Bowker continued his own Mugwump policy by working for the election of Alfred C. Chapin, a reform Democrat, as mayor of Brooklyn, writing a strong public letter which Chapin and Shepard thought very effective, serving on a Citizens' Committee, and giving an interview to an *Eagle* reporter that was printed as a leading campaign document.[51]

Tariff reform continued to receive Bowker's major attention. Late in May, 1884, he had been appointed to a committee of the New York Free Trade Club to press for a tariff-reform plank at the Republican national convention.[52] Throughout the fall he gave David A. Wells continuous editorial advice on his *Primer of Tariff Reform*.[53] Mugwump strategy, however, was to avoid the tariff issue, though men like Wells, Shearman, and Earle thought this a great mistake.[54]

Although Cleveland had not been elected as a tariff reformer, the free traders were hopeful that under his leadership the Democrats in Congress could be rallied to support a low-tariff bill in 1886 which would redeem their defeat of the Morrison bill in 1884. A first important move was a memorial to Cleveland signed by Bowker, Beecher, Wells, Peabody, Wheeler, Shearman, and others which had considerable in-

[49] R. R. B., "Mugwump Retrospect and Prospect," letter dated September 4, 1919, in New York *Evening Post.*

[50] G. W. Curtis to R. R. B., October 1, 20, 1885.

[51] "An Interview with an Independent Republican," in a printed leaflet from the Citizens' Committee, Brooklyn, 1887.

[52] *The Million,* June 14, 1884.

[53] See Wells–R. R. B. correspondence, September 8–October 13, 1884.

[54] A. L. Earle to R. R. B., October 15; Wells, October 20; T. G. Shearman, October 21, 1884.

fluence on Cleveland's thinking.[55] The next move was to keep Wells in close touch with the Democratic leaders while a new bill was framed. He made several trips to Washington and sent Bowker a stream of optimistic reports of long sessions with Morrison, Carlisle, and Horace White, declaring that the President and Manning treated him like a member of the Cabinet.[56] Bowker joined in sending circulars to Congress and memorials to Morrison, and in putting pressure on Cleveland for a favorable word in his annual message.

A third important step was holding a great national tariff-reform conference in Chicago in November under the auspices of the American Free Trade League. As League secretary, Bowker issued the call, took charge of arranging the program, worked hard to secure good delegations, and went to Chicago in a special car with Beecher and Captain John Codman. The *Million* pronounced it "the greatest purely free trade meeting ever gathered in America." There were representatives from fifty organizations in thirteen states, and half an hour before the opening exercises an audience of 2,800 crowded a big auditorium to the highest galleries. Bowker made a carefully prepared report on "The Political Relations of Tariff Reform," which reviewed all the aspects of the League's work, and ended with a stirring appeal:

> Gentlemen, in this cause the stars in their course fight with us— the stars of freedom, the stars of our flag. We are but working out one principle of American freedom in seeking freedom in commerce, and America must be free. . . . We believe that no one step will so help the people of this country to stand steadily on a higher plane of prosperity and of national life as the removal of the restrictions in trade. How soon that great good may come depends upon how hard we are willing to work to convince the people.

The climax of the occasion was a crowded evening meeting at which Bowker presided and introduced Wells and Beecher, who gave admirable addresses. A devastating set of antitariff resolutions was then adopted and a National Tariff Reform League organized, with Wells as president, Bowker as chairman of the national committee and later secretary, and Shearman as chairman of the executive committee.[57] The conference was deemed a great success in advertising free trade, and the reformers were hopeful. "How shameless and arrogant the Protectionists are becoming," Wells wrote Bowker in December. "Well,

55 Nevins, *Cleveland*, 280–81.
56 D. A. Wells to R. R. B., February 3, 7, 10; October 11, 1885.
57 *The Million*, October 17, November 21, 1885; R. R. B. to Ostrogorski, January 15, 1898; Wheeler, *Sixty Years of American Life*, 167. Bowker's report printed in *Conference Report of the N. Y. Free Trade Club*, 1885. See bibliography.

I am not sorry. Pride goeth before destruction."[58] Proclaimed Beecher at the January dinner of the Brooklyn Revenue Reform Club: "The great natural laws are now working in our direction."

The results of this campaign, however, were almost nil. Cleveland hardly mentioned the tariff in his annual messages of 1885 and 1886. In April, 1886, thirty-five Randall Democrats voted with the Republicans to defeat Morrison's new bill. Morrison, Cleveland, and the free traders were shocked. Obviously the Democratic party was not yet by any means a sure instrument for tariff reform.

Bowker and his fellow traders immediately set to work on the coming Congressional election of 1886. Bowker had already called upon the faithful to begin local campaigns for suitable candidates.[59] Meanwhile he prepared for the New York Free Trade Club the *Economic Fact-Book and Free-Trader's Guide,* some of the chapters of which had appeared in the free-trade journal, the *Freeman.* It was just the sort of simple, practical handbook which reformers wanted. The *Million* declared that it contained "a greater variety of facts and statistics appropriate to the occasion than we have ever seen in one volume." The free traders waged a stout campaign in Massachusetts, Pennsylvania, New York, and the West. Bowker for the Free Trade Club and the League, and Wheeler for the Young Men's Democratic Club, did steady, intelligent, well-planned work.[60] Any positive results, however, were hard to see. In the House, the Democrats lost twenty-four seats, but retained control; in the Senate, the Republicans lost six seats, but kept their majority.

Soon, however, came magnificent support for the tariff-reform cause. Cleveland's third message to Congress, in December, 1887, was devoted entirely to the one issue of tariff reduction and constituted a thorough, powerful, smashing attack against the existing high rates. Cleveland knew that the Republican Senate would never accept a tariff-reduction measure, but he hoped to rally his own party behind the principle of tariff reform, and thus force a clean-cut issue into the election of 1888.

Cleveland's bold action was a great inspiration to the liberals. Here was the national challenge they had been seeking. "It is a splendid thing," Shearman wrote Bowker of the message, "and will now force the fighting. The politicians cannot avoid our having an issue." Once more efforts were directed to securing a bill from Congress. Bowker publicized his views in a lengthy interview with Talcott Williams for the

[58] D. A. Wells to R. R. B., December 21, 1885.

[59] Bowker's call, dated February 10, reported in Chicago *Herald,* February 18, 1886; in *The Million,* March 6, 1886.

[60] Nevins, *Cleveland,* 288–96; Wheeler, *Sixty Years of American Life,* 169–77.

New York *Commercial Advertiser*,[61] initiated a memorial to Morrison, and warned Cleveland's secretary that the present Independent support of the Democratic program was "a last olive-branch" which might be followed by formation of a new party.[62] The resulting Mills Bill was adopted by the House with all but four Democrats voting for it. But as had been anticipated, the Senate would have none of it, and the campaign of 1888 began with the issue still unresolved.

While helping to lead the tariff-reform fight for the showdown of 1888 and in order to stimulate the entire liberal program in the East, Bowker realized a long-cherished dream by helping to found the New York Reform Club as a reorganization of the New York Free Trade Club. This important move combined a conviction held by John De-Witt Warner and some of the younger men that the reform program needed to be stiffened to keep pace with the formidable growth of the protectionist forces, and Bowker's long-held conviction that there was need of an organization devoted to the entire program of liberal reform. Bowker served on the committee which drew up the initial plans for the new organization, secured the adoption of the name "Reform Club," served as one of the original incorporators as well as one of the first trustees, and soon became one of the club's vice-presidents. The club opened its doors on January 13, 1888, at 12 East Thirty-third Street. Anson Phelps Stokes served as the first president and Russell Sturgis as secretary. Godkin headed the club's committee on civil service reform, Wheeler its committee on tariff reform. Bowker became chairman of three of the most important committees of the club: library, publication, and work outside of the state of New York. No wonder Wheeler wrote to Bowker, "I do not see how you can possibly undertake to run them all." Within a few months the membership reached twelve hundred. Those active in the club constituted a veritable roster of the men of civic conscience in New York.[63]

The election of 1888 was regarded by every tariff reformer as a momentous one. For the first time since the Civil War, their cause had a courageous champion who was willing to make the tariff a major issue in a national campaign. Here was the long-awaited opportunity to give the American people their first thorough education on the subject. It was the reformers' intention to keep this issue before the country as the

61 "Tariff Reduction, an Interesting Talk with R. R. Bowker," New York *Commercial Advertiser*, December 22, 1886.

62 R. R. B. to D. S. Lamont, January 3, 1887.

63 See report of provisional committee to Free Trade Club, August 1, 1887; printed circular, September 15, December, 1887; R. R. B. to Ostrogorski, January 15, 1898; R. R. B. to Windmuller, May 14, 1909; Burton J. Hendricks, *The Training of an American*, 198–201.

primary issue and thus win a clean-cut verdict from the people that might settle the question for a generation. Deming expressed the sentiments of the entire reform group in a letter to Bowker hailing "the new fight now upon us, and for which you and I have so long been praying. . . . Better defeat ten times over . . . than the old state of nerveless and invertebrated politics!" Wheeler wrote Bowker in the same vein: "You ought to feel rejoiced at the result of what you and others have been laboring at for years. The harvest has come, and you, that have sowed ought to take a hand in reaping."[64]

The Independents were not encouraged to organize as a separate group, and Bowker later wrote Cleveland that this was a serious mistake.[65] Nevertheless, under the leadership of Schurz and Curtis, they fought a good campaign. Bowker worked hard through the program of the Reform Club, which put its weight squarely behind Cleveland and tariff reform. The organizational methods which Bowker had experimented with in 1879 and improved in 1884 were brought to perfection by the club in 1888; its files of sympathizers, techniques of distributing propaganda to newspapers, and system of supplying speakers to organizations throughout the country were formidable. The tariff committee conducted a semimonthly journal, *Tariff Reform,* which sponsored valuable original research and sent an avalanche of materials in all directions.[66] Bowker edited Cleveland's tariff message of 1887 with many valuable statistical annotations as *The President's Message,* and in this work he had the cordial assent and co-operation of Cleveland and Secretary Fairchild.[67] He also took charge of all the negotiations that resulted in James Russell Lowell's celebrated address before the club on April 13, 1888, "The Place of the Independent in Politics."[68] But the activity of the former Mugwumps could hardly compensate for the mortal conflict within the Democratic ranks in the key state of New York. There Governor Hill and Tammany Hall continued their bitter opposition to Cleveland. Bowker served on the Committee of Anti-Hill Democrats and Independents in Brooklyn, and elsewhere in the state the Mugwumps sought to defeat Hill while supporting Cleveland, but it was a dangerous game.

The result of the hard-fought campaign was victory for the Re-

[64] C. Deming to R. R. B., February 24, 1885; E. P. Wheeler to R. R. B., July 5, 1888.

[65] R. R. B. to G. Cleveland, July 4, 1892.

[66] Wheeler, *Sixty Years of American Life,* 184–85, 191–94; Reform Club, Tariff Reform Committee Report, August 20, 1888.

[67] H. Deming to R. R. B., February 24, 1888; R. R. B. to G. Cleveland, February 22, 1888; Cleveland to R. R. B., March 4, 1888.

[68] R. R. B., correspondence with G. W. Curtis, J. R. Lowell, February 28–June 3, 1888; see Scudder, *James Russell Lowell,* 574–77.

publicans and protectionism. Tariff reform had lost again. Nevertheless, several factors in the picture made it difficult for anyone to prove
that the American people had clearly rejected the liberal program associated with Cleveland. Moreover, Cleveland actually secured 100,000
more popular votes than Harrison. The people had voted for him, but
in the wrong states! Bowker and his friends saw no reason to despair.

The Reform Club was certainly not daunted, and dug deep to lay
the foundation of future success in a broad campaign of education.
Hadn't the Anti-Corn Law League taken a longer time to achieve its
goal? For three years the club swept the land with printed matter and
oral exhortations.[69] The Tariff Reform League was similarly aggressive,
and Bowker attended its Chicago convention in February, 1889. The
immediate setback seemed severe when, in 1890, the Republicans produced the McKinley Tariff, with the highest duties in American history.
Bowker analyzed the implications of this legislation in a paper entitled
"Reactions From Economic Freedom in the United States" which he
read before the economic section of the British Association for the Advancement of Science at its September meeting in Toronto. But it was
soon evident, however, that the bill was a boomerang, and that the
voters intended to punish the bill's supporters. In the Congressional
elections of 1890, the Reform Club worked industriously to take advantage of the public reaction.[70] As the campaign of education drew to
its close, what had seemed a stunning defeat in 1888 was turned into a
great victory in 1890. When the returns were in, it was seen that 235
Democrats had been swept into the House and all but 86 Republicans
out of it. In state after state Democrats overwhelmed the very men who
had ridiculed Cleveland's tariff message of 1887.

The Reform Club planned a victory celebration in the Banquet
Hall of Madison Square Garden. It was a brilliant and enthusiastic
affair. At the holly-festooned guest table sat Grover Cleveland, Governor Horace Boies of Iowa, Senator John G. Carlisle, Governor William
E. Russell of Massachusetts, Tom Johnson from Ohio, William L. Wilson from West Virginia, and two Cleveland Republicans, Carl Schurz
and Horace White. E. P. Wheeler, president of the club, made a stirring
speech in which he said of Cleveland, amidst fervent cheering, "He
risked a Bunker Hill in 1888. Our defeat there has given us a Saratoga
in 1890. It insures for us a Yorktown in 1892." Cleveland responded to
the toast, "The Campaign of Education: Its Results a Signal Tribute
to the Judgment of the American People," amidst an outburst of warm
devotion. He said:

[69] See Reform Club, letter to members, January 1, 1893.
[70] Reform Club circular, October 8, 17, 1890; Wheeler, *Sixty Years of American
Life*, 144.

Let us not fail to realize the fact that our work is not done. Our enemies are still alive and have grown desperate. Human selfishness is not easily overcome, and the hope of private gain at the expense of the masses of our people is not yet abandoned. . . . As the people have trusted us, let us above all things be true to them. Let the light of our campaign be carried into every part of the land where it has not been seen, and where it has been kindled, let it keep brightly burning, still showing the way to better days for the people, and disclosing the plans of insidious foes.[71]

Actually, the hope of tariff reform was doomed for almost twenty-five years, but the reformers did not realize it and would not have admitted it had they been told. They confidently looked forward to the re-election of Cleveland in 1892, and with it, the reward of a decade of strenuous crusading.

Bowker never confused ends and means. It was clear to him that to get free trade and other desired reforms under the democratic system, it was eternally necessary not only to educate the voter but to perfect the machinery whereby the voter was able to register his will. To these ends he continued to work through his Society for Political Education and a half-dozen other reform organizations to inform and rally the average citizen, to promote ballot reform and civil service reform. In this he was, perhaps, most typically fulfilling the social-engineering mission of the scholar to which he had committed himself.

In directing the fortunes of the Society for Political Education which he had founded in 1880, Bowker had the continuous counsel of Putnam, the Society's publisher, Wells, who undertook to raise funds for its program, and Richard Dugdale, its indefatigable secretary. Its basic purpose of educating the voter through inexpensive, sound reading matter was pushed without pause. Its *Economic Tracts* contained original contributions from Horace White, A. D. White, Talcott Williams, W. C. Ford, and Shepard; the second series of its *Library of Political Education* contained works by Blanqui, Jevons, Mill, Wells, and Herbert Spencer.[72] In addition, the Society distributed gratuitously 1,700 copies of Henry George's *Progress and Poverty* and an equal number of his *Irish Question,* as well as 1,500 copies of Atkinson's pamphlet on "The Elements of National Prosperity." It then planned an "Auxiliary Series" of tracts to be given away.

Dugdale's death in 1883 was a great blow, but his work was ably taken up by Worthington C. Ford. In 1889 George Iles, an energetic

71 *Ibid.,* 144–48.
72 See bibliography.

Canadian liberal with a strong interest in bibliography became the Society's secretary. Tracts were planned to cover tariff, education, prison legislation, municipal reform, the Southern question, and Canadian relations. The Society's last publication, issued in 1891, was, perhaps, its finest, *The Reader's Guide in Economic, Social, and Political Science.* In this Bowker and Iles collaborated with the assistance of twenty-five specialists, including E. R. A. Seligman, W. C. Ford, James Bryce, Gifford Pinchot, D. R. Dewey, D. A. Wells, Andrew D. White, and Horace White. The result was a comprehensive list, not confined to the writings of any one school of economics or one nation. *The Reader's Guide* met with hearty response from both librarians and professors of economy, and by 1903 had to be reissued in a second and revised edition.

With such an admirable program of service and a membership fee of only fifty cents, the Society might have been expected to flourish, but it most emphatically did not. Nothing, perhaps, is more indicative of the basic lack of popular support for Bowker's version of the liberal program than the fact that the Society's membership never exceeded 1,000 during these years. By the end of 1890 the number of subscribers fell to 113, and income from the casual sale of its pamphlets did not exceed seventy dollars a year. Iles felt that the field which the Society had entered as a pioneer was now supplied by such organizations as the American Economic Association and the new trend toward social essays in *Century, Forum,* and *Harper's* magazines. It was therefore decided to close the Society's books.

From Bowker's own pen came several items to strengthen the cause of civic education.[73] At the end of 1883 the Society published his first popular summary of economic principles, *Of Work and Wealth.* The little volume was dedicated to Richard Dugdale, acknowledged in particular its indebtedness to such economists as Walker, Jevons, and Henry George, and deliberately steered a commonsense course between the extremes of the Manchester school and the German school. For some time Bowker had felt the need of a simple presentation of elementary economic principles for the man in the street, and this effort was a very considerable success. Professor Johnson of Princeton reported that his students were "delighted" with it, President Hadley of Yale was enthusiastic, and Wells called it "exceedingly clever."[74] At the same time Bowker wrote an extremely popular little tract, *Free Trade the Best Protection to American Industry,* published by the New York

73 See bibliography for these years.
74 A. Johnson to R. R. B., May 10, 1884; A. T. Hadley to R. R. B., August 16, 1884; D. A. Wells to R. R. B., February 27, 1884.

Free Trade Club, which eventually went into four editions, two of which were issued by the Kansas Anti-Protection League. In 1884 he wrote the introduction to Jacob Schoenhof's *Wages and Trade in Manufacturing Industries in America and Europe.* In 1886 there appeared Bowker's *Economics For the People,* a more ambitious undertaking which had a surprising life of usefulness, being published by Harper's both in New York and London, running into a third edition in 1892, and a fifth revised edition in 1902.[75] Enthusiastic letters poured in, including one from John Bright in England.

In the midst of all his other activities, Bowker had found time to participate in the launching of a new free-trade paper entitled *The Million,* an eight-page weekly whose first number was dated March 8, 1884. It was published at Des Moines, Iowa, under the editorship of Henry J. Philpott, but with preponderant financial and editorial backing coming from the New York group. The purpose of *The Million* was to present a popular discussion of the political questions "which concern the welfare of the great mass of the people—the millions who neither hold nor seek office."[76] Bowker was one of its contributing editors along with Wells, Sumner, Perry, J. G. Carlisle, Beecher, Nordhoff, Watterson, Shearman, W. C. Ford, and others. For it he wrote some thirty brief essays under the title "Plain Talks on Economics," which appeared from March 8, 1884, to February 28, 1885.[77] No paper had a more intelligent or devoted circle of consultants than the *Million.* Its articles were filled with statistics based on original and painstaking research. Financial support was readily given by its well-to-do, eastern friends. Nevertheless, it never "took hold," and its subscription list at no time came to 20,000, with an actual circulation of perhaps 5,000. It was a revelation of public apathy which was particularly disheartening to Wells. By the fall of 1885, the *Million* was dying, and by 1888 it was dead.

That some stable medium of civic education should be made to succeed was now an obsession with Bowker. At one time he thought of bringing the *Million* to New York and managing it himself. Simultaneously he tried to interest his friends in a venture which he named "The Publicist" and described as "a series of papers intended to remind the American people of the principles, political and moral, underlying a democratic republic, and to discuss the governmental needs developed in the progress of recent times." To be issued fortnightly

[75] See bibliography.
[76] Prospectus of *The Million,* printed folder, dated February 15, 1884.
[77] This was later reworked into R. R. B.'s *Economics for the People.*

until completed as a volume, it would carry unsigned articles by all the leading liberals.[78] Although several acquaintances subscribed $100 each to start the venture, it did not come off. Bowker also proposed either the same or a subsequent project to Wells under the name of "The Review," and this Wells discouraged on the grounds that the Columbia and Harvard quarterlies and the *Forum* were in the field and finding the going none too easy. "There does not seem to me to be as yet sufficient popular interest in economic matters or the tariff question," he argued, "to promise success for such a journal."

By February, 1888, Bowker felt that "the demand for a means of communication among our tariff-reform people and the need of putting the printing and supply of documents on a business footing, and my belief that with the interest since the President's Message a journal can be made to pay"[79] justified him in issuing a circular announcing a new double-barreled publishing venture consisting of a new liberal journal and a publishing house to facilitate the inexpensive issue of liberal tracts. The first enterprise, finally entitled "The People's Cause," was intended to carry on the work of Philpott's *Million*. The second scheme, named "The Economist Press," was to be a co-operative publishing venture that would issue the new journal and the many other reform documents then flowing from liberal pens. Bowker's first prospectus announced that he, Wells, Shearman, and Peabody had already subscribed $10,000 toward an operating fund of $15,000.

Bowker must have had confidence that his own journalistic management would succeed where Philpott's had failed. He was to be the editor of *The People's Cause* and Louis Howland the associate editor; most of the contributors formerly listed by the *Million* were prepared to supply copy to its successor. The first issue appeared in January, 1889, and announced itself as *the* medium for all liberal and reform causes. The journal ran for twelve issues, and then was dropped, partly because Bowker became the executive manager of the Edison Company, partly because of too much competition.[80] The Economist Press started promisingly. Bowker purchased six presses and installed them at 330 Pearl Street opposite the Harper Building. The pressroom was first placed under the direction of Arthur E. Waldradt, and later of W. W. Moore. For a while things hummed, with work for Henry George, the Reform Club, and minor jobs for Putnam's and Harper's. Two interesting books which Bowker edited, copyrighted, and published on his press were *The Cleveland Album*, described as "a memorial of four

78 Undated penscript MS and printed galley draft in R. R. B. Collection.

79 R. R. B., typescript circular, dated February, 1888.

80 T. G. Shearman to R. R. B., December 26, 1889; and D. A. Wells in several letters.

years of Democratic administration," and *The Harrison Album of Republican Leaders*. Nevertheless, the business did not prosper. The first year's returns did not cover the manager's salary, and by the end of 1889, Bowker had to borrow additional funds.

To educate the voter in basic social principles was one liberal concern. Another was publicizing and perfecting the actual machinery of voting. To help inform the voter about his political system and keep alive his civic interest, Bowker in 1885 induced W. E. Foster to write a pamphlet for the Society on *References to the History of Presidential Administrations 1789–1885*, for which he prepared an introduction; the next year he published his own admirable little *Primer for Political Education* under the Society's imprint. He also took an active interest in the Constitution Club, before which he read a well-received paper on "Party Organization and Practical Politics," and helped to found the Commonwealth Club, serving on its executive committee from 1886 to 1889. In 1886 the Society published his brochure on *Civil Service Examinations*, a set of question papers with actual answers by successful and unsuccessful candidates, of which James Bryce wrote Bowker, "I . . . have been referring frequently to them and am struck by the clearness and sharpness with which you have brought out vital points."[81]

Bowker's interest in ballot reform was continuous. When in England, he made a special study of English electoral methods. At home during the winter of 1887–88 when the Yates-Saxton Ballot Reform Bill was presented in the legislature, he served on a committee to assist its passage, representing the Commonwealth, City Reform, Constitutional, and Reform clubs as well as the County Organization of the United Labor party. In 1889, Bowker edited for the Society a pamphlet entitled *Electoral Reform*, which gave a history of the subject in both England and the United States from the time of Jeremy Bentham's Radical Reform Bill, and included the texts of the best current ballot reform bills in Massachusetts and New York. He worked on the Reform Club's committee on electoral reform, which in 1890 helped to found the New York Ballot Reform League,[82] and served on the executive committee of the Brooklyn Ballot Reform League, which rallied eight hundred members for the Australian ballot. After the successful civic revolt against Tammany in 1893, he wrote a letter to the New York *Times* on "Further Ballot Reform," urging that the New York ballot law be promptly revised.[83] Warning that the party managers favored the separate party ballot which made very difficult any irregularity, discrimi-

81 James Bryce to R. R. B., December 11, 1887.
82 Reform Club circular, January 11, 1890.
83 R. R. B., "Further Ballot Reform," New York *Times*, November 10, 1893.

nation, or scratching, he recommended a blanket ballot to be furnished in advance of Election Day to every registered voter, listing all the nominees and their party designations and providing a blank under each office for the voter's choice. Such a plan, he argued, would give a reasonable opportunity for careful discrimination among the several candidates, and would save the very large expense and great printing complications faced by the election authorities. A few years later he worked on a City Club project to develop a new kind of voting machine.[84]

Bowker's passionate interest in the liberal crusade had led him to organize almost all the elements of what might have become a cohesive, well-developed movement. There was his journal of opinion, *The People's Cause;* a publishing vehicle, the Economist Press; a social stimulus and organizing center in the Reform Club; a device for developing support all over the country in the Society for Political Education; and the pattern of bi-partisan political activity in the old Mugwump committee. The American voter, however, was not won to this program, and Bowker continued to find many of his ventures turn into lost causes.

[84] W. H. Baldwin, E. M. Shepard to R. R. B., July 3, 1903; R. R. B. to F. N. Goddard, July 9, 1903.

XIV

Edison Executive
1890–1899

BOWKER HAD GIVEN ample evidence that he belonged by temperament, ability, and experience to "the executive profession." He had started by managing a literary department on an evening newspaper and had gone on to manage three or four periodicals, the foreign business of a large American publishing house, a number of political and free-trade organizations, and several campaigns. This executive ability was to find its fullest expression, however, in the years 1890–99, and in a completely new field—the electrical industry. It is a rather striking fact that without any previous experience in industrial organization, corporation management, or engineering practice Bowker made an immediate and outstanding success as the chief executive of the largest electric lighting company in the world at the time of its greatest technical development and commercial expansion. Not less striking is the extent to which he succeeded in basing his entire administration on his liberal creed, and the fact that in the end he resigned his post rather than compromise with his ideals.

Bowker's entry into the field of industrial management came at a crucial time in his career. Since leaving the Harper office in 1883, he had not drawn a salary commensurate with his obvious abilities. Managing the *Publishers' Weekly* office took only part of his time and brought him only a slight income. *The People's Cause,* which he had begun early in 1889, was definitely not an income-producing activity, yet it consumed hours of labor. The Economist Press was actually failing. The Society for Political Education had never been intended to make money, and was steadily losing it. Perhaps Bowker was actually carrying his idealism too far for his own good. Many of his friends thought so, and Wells decided to give him some hard-headed advice.[1] "I do not want to see you loaded up at this time of life," he wrote, "when you must make hay for yourself if you are ever going to do it, with matters that are not going to result to your personal advantage. . . . Look out now for your own private interests. Now is your heyday for personal action. . . . Something will turn up before long, I am sure, for you."

Perhaps it was Wells' influence that now induced Bowker to let it be known to several of his friends in banking and business circles that he would like to take up the executive work of an industrial corporation. Once his mind had seized on the idea, he could see many reasons for pushing it. He knew that his managerial talent was worth many times more than he was earning in journalism; he wished to acquire some capital to apply to his several humanitarian and reform interests; and he was profoundly stirred by the many opportunities of his age to apply the revolutionary, new developments of technology to the needs of society. Indeed, one of the strongest motives in his final decision to go into the electrical field was the chance it presented "to contribute definitely to electrical progress and the cheapening of current until it becomes the poor man's as well as the rich man's servant."[2]

Within a week, in December, 1889, Bowker was offered three outstanding opportunities. Henry Villard, president of the Northern Pacific Railway, offered him the vacant secretaryship of that company, possibly at the suggestion of Wells and certainly with his own Reform Club relations with Bowker in mind.[3] At almost the same time Bowker's close friend George Foster Peabody, who was a director of both companies, indicated that he could probably be elected either president of the Brooklyn Edison Company or first vice-president of the Edison Electric Illuminating Company of New York. On Villard's advice, Bowker chose the latter.[4]

The Edison Electric Illuminating Company of New York needed an officer to serve as liaison between the financial interests and the practical operation of the company. Shepard, who had entered into legal relations with the same company, agreed with Peabody that Bowker was just the man. Some of the directors feared that Bowker's experience had been too limited, and one remarked that he didn't want "any of those literary fellers." Impressive testimonials to Bowker's business ability, however, were soon secured from W. L. Bull, Frank Stetson, W. H.

[1] D. A. Wells to R. R. B., March 17–December, 1889.
[2] R. R. B. to Spencer Trask, October 31, 1893.
[3] H. Villard to D. A. Wells, December 30, 1889; H. Villard to R. R. B., December 31, 1889.
[4] D. A. Wells to R. R. B., January 7, 1890; O. S. Villard to R. R. B., September 13, 1928.

Appleton, and J. W. Harper; and Villard, himself a director, by the end of January won over the doubtful.[5] Bowker suggested that he start at a salary of $6,000 and receive the vice-president's full remuneration of $10,000 only when he had shown what he could do, and this arrangement was adopted.

When Bowker joined the Edison Company of New York, electricity was just beginning to be successfully harnessed to man's needs. The electric motor, generator, telegraph, and arc light had been developed; but it was not until October, 1879, that Edison created the commercial incandescent lamp, and it required another year to place it on a sound commercial basis of quantity production. There remained a host of technical problems to be solved, such as how to generate and distribute adequate current and how to utilize the current on the consumer's premises. In 1881 alone Edison successfully obtained no less than eighty-nine patents.[6] In 1878 the first parent company was set up as the Edison Electric Light Company, and in 1880 the first corporation to supply commercial incandescent lighting was organized as the Edison Electric Illuminating Company. By 1883 the first central generating station had been constructed on Pearl Street and was supplying three hundred customers in the square mile around Broad and Wall Streets with six thousand lamps.[7]

Financial assistance as well as mechanical genius was required to make a success of the new industry. Although the financial pioneer was probably Grosvenor P. Lowrey, Henry Villard, J. P. Morgan, and Spencer Trask soon became the important financial backers. Villard was one of the first directors and in 1889 headed the $12,000,000 Edison General Electric Company. J. P. Morgan had seen from the beginning the possibilities of the electrical industry and had become a backer of Edison in organizing both the Edison General Electric Company and the several service companies. He was represented in the Illuminating Company by his partner, E. P. Fabbri, and later by C. H. Coster. In 1884, Spencer Trask was elected president of the company, supplying not only capital but unbounded faith and steadfast confidence in the future of the business. George Foster Peabody became a director in 1889.[8]

5 J. W. Harper to G. F. Peabody, January, 1890; G. F. Peabody to R. R. B., December 31, 1889; January 14, 21, 25, 27, 29, 1890; August 30, 1901.

6 R. R. B., MS Memoir, Edison Company Annual Report, 1899; S. Dana Greene, *Electrical Review*, November 27, 1895.

7 R. R. B., Edison Company Annual Report, 1893; L. A. Osborne, "The Electrical Industry," in *Representative Industries in the United States*, ed. by H. T. Warshow, 302–304; J. Wetzler, "The Edison Electric Illuminating Company of New York," *The Electrical Engineer*, January 8, 1896.

8 R. R. B., MS Memoir; Payson Jones, *A Power History of the Consolidated Edison System, 1878–1900*, 104–106, 168, 172–76.

By 1890, the experimental period of the Edison Illuminating Company's history was over. The Liberty Street Annex had been built in 1886, the twenty-sixth Street Station in 1888, and the Thirty-ninth Street Station in 1889. Thirty-one miles of mains and twenty-one miles of feeders had been laid, chiefly between Madison and Sixth Avenue from Fourteenth Street to Forty-second Street. The demand had increased about 20 per cent a year, and the company had proved itself a definite success.[9] Now the system was ready for development and expansion. The directors recommended large additional installations covering new territory and important additions to the existing plant. The capital stock was increased from $2,500,000 to $4,500,000. A greatly enlarged technical staff would now be necessary, and new administrative officers would have to be found. It was at this important turning point in the history of the electric lighting industry, as the experimental period gave way to the critical period of formative development, that Bowker joined the company. He was to resign, ten years later, at the beginning of its period of "fulfillment."[10]

It was originally intended that Bowker would look after the company's fiscal and legal concerns, with a second vice-president to care for its physical and technical problems. A few months after his appointment, however, the office of second vice-president was abolished, and the duties of that executive unexpectedly descended upon Bowker's shoulders. He was now to have charge of the entire administration, and, though holding the office of first vice-president, to be discharging the duties of the acting executive. These duties involved solving a host of problems. New operating stations were to be constructed to generate more current, new customers were to be secured, and new uses for electricity were to be developed; the engineering equipment was to be kept abreast of current developments on both sides of the Atlantic; operating economies were to be effected through the promotion of working efficiency in all departments; administrative policies were to be evolved to handle the increasing personnel, to meet increasing competition, to counteract the threat of adverse legislation in Albany, and to determine rate reductions and dividend payments; patent infringements were to be prosecuted and public complaints investigated. Bowker's role was to mediate between stockholders, managers, operators, consumers, and public officials.

Bowker proved to be no routine administrator. It is evident that he had not only ability but a passion for his work. In his Edison program he found almost unlimited opportunity to exercise his zeal for

[9] R. R. B., Edison Company Annual Report, 1899.
[10] *Ibid.;* to John Lieb, June 10, 1927.

orderliness and efficiency, the thorough mastery and co-ordination of detail, the formulation of broad policy, and the application of high ethical principle. To the host of problems which came daily to his desk he brought patience, resourcefulness, and boundless energy. Indeed, he found a welcome stimulus in the knowledge that the Edison Electric Illuminating Company of New York was intended to be an example of the best Edison theory and practice for the many rapidly developing associated companies in other cities.[11]

One of Bowker's first and most important responsibilities was new plant construction. The Pearl Street Station had just been destroyed by fire, and it was decided to build a new central generating station to the north. It was now Bowker's task to locate and purchase the property for this important unit and to supervise its construction and activation. The result was the model plant extending along Elm Street from Duane to Pearl, its eight stories planned with great thoroughness and ingenuity to yield the highest efficiency at the lowest operating cost. The lower portion of the new Pearl Street unit was completed in 1891 at a cost of $160,000, and the Duane Street portion during 1892–93 at a cost of $110,000. The Panic of 1893 prevented the completion of the upper stories until 1894.[12] Bowker also supervised the construction of one sub-station at Fifty-third Street in 1892, and a second at Twelfth Street in 1895. This expansion placed Bowker in charge of an Edison system which by 1895 fully covered New York City from the Battery to Fifty-ninth Street through the whole central portion, and from Fifty-ninth Street to Seventy-ninth Street on the east side of Central Park. It represented an extension of the total underground system from sixty-seven to almost two hundred miles, necessitating over five hundred miles of copper conductors.

It was one of Bowker's earliest hopes for the Duane Street building that it might be decorated so as to combine functional efficiency and significant ornamentation. Art decoration for industrial buildings had long been one of his special enthusiasms, and at this time he was writing on the subject. In 1895 he gave much attention to the design of the new museum façade of the Brooklyn Institute of Arts and Sciences and discussed with Shepard, counsel for the Rapid Transit Commission, the art plans for the first subway stations. His plans for the Edison building were explicit:

11 See R. R. B.'s letter to Edison employees, January 1, 1891.

12 R. R. B., Edison Company Annual Report, 1893, 1895; R. R. B. to Spencer Trask, October 31, 1893. Sketches and photographs of the building are included in R. R. B., "Electricity," *Harper's Magazine,* October, 1896, pp. 711, 721; and in Wetzler, "The Electric Illuminating Company of New York," *The Electrical Engineer,* January 8, 1896, pp. 25–45.

We desire our Edison buildings to be architecturally creditable to New York within proper limitations of cost and decorations, and particularly to have them express, as all good buildings should do, their industrial function. We have felt restrained by our industrial function from any such cost or lavish ornamentation as has become perhaps too much the custom in insurance offices and savings banks.

Although Bowker's art plans for the Duane Street unit were drawn up in 1891, he was not able to complete them until 1898. They included use of the incandescent lamp and wiring in place of the conventional egg-and-dart moulding. Spaces were designed on the main façade for portrait medallions of Franklin, Henry, Morse, and Edison, as leading American electricians; and on the Pearl Street façade of Volta, Ampere, Ohm, and Watt as representatives of Europe. Along the frieze in the central two-story hall a series of panels were painted in sepia monochrome tracing the historical development of electricity, W. B. Van Ingen, one of the artists selected to decorate the Library of Congress, being commissioned by Bowker to do the paintings. These decorations cost $5,000, and so strong was Bowker's conviction of their importance that he would gladly have covered the cost himself if the directors had objected to the expense.[13] Somehow Bowker found time to go into the most minute details of all this work, supplying portraits, drawings, and biographical details of the subjects.

One of the most difficult problems for Bowker to handle in the steady expansion of Edison power generation was that of subway conduits. He studied the underground conductor systems of London and Milan and the World's Fair grounds in Chicago, and stated that conditions in New York were more difficult and costly than in any other city in the world.[14] Another problem which became more acute with increasing expansion was whether the company should specialize in generation of power or include the several growing auxiliary services. Bowker recommended the former policy and consequently the motor inspection, repair service, and wiring department were transferred to independent companies.

Although Bowker gave careful attention to these details of plant construction, he was far more interested, personally, in the machinery which the buildings were to house. Here was the heart and soul of this

[13] R. R. B., Edison Company Annual Report, 1899; R. R. B. to Van Ingen, November 26, 1898; Van Ingen to R. R. B., November 29, 1898; S. Trask to R. R. B., November 28, 1898.

[14] R. R. B. to S. Trask, October 31, 1893; also R. R. B. to Commissioner Kearney January 14, 1898.

portentous new industry. Conditions of success were rigid: the concentration of maximum efficiency in the two or three hours of heaviest load and at maximum economy during the rest of the twenty-four hours. The rapidly growing public demand for current called for new generating units of ever increasing size more rapidly than they could be built. And these intricate mechanical giants were so costly that the first vice-president could not afford to make a mistake. Bowker stretched the technical resources of his staff to the limit, and since there were hardly any precedents to guide him, he found himself working on an engineering frontier, planning pioneer innovations with his chief electricians. By reading, observation, constant cross-examination of experts, and concentration on basic principles, he soon achieved sufficient mastery of the subject to understand significant developments.

To this technical field Bowker brought the same breadth of vision and faith in wide collaboration that had marked his other enterprises. One of the earliest of his administrative policies, indeed, was to keep thoroughly in touch with electrical developments in the United States and Europe and to utilize improved methods wherever they could be found. He was certainly not content to follow along with the engineering of the General Electric Company, which to him was insufficiently progressive to justify his sole reliance on it. Trask indicated a bit of concern over the amount of traveling abroad by the Edison executives which this policy entailed, but Bowker thoroughly justified his judgment, and his staff heartily agreed with him. As a result, the Edison Company developed almost its entire equipment along new lines, and while the direct motive was its own benefit, the results were a stimulus of very great value to Edison companies in other cities and to the General Electric Company.

In achieving this technical progress, Bowker had the services of a real inventive genius in John Van Vleck, the chief electrician and consulting engineer, whom Bowker ranked second only to Edison himself in American electrical progress. He was a man made to Bowker's order, and the two became not only close working associates but warm friends.

Bowker sent Van Vleck to Europe in the spring of 1891 on a trip of investigation which had a number of important results. First was the development of what came to be known as the Van Vleck Disconnective Engine, the best for electric lighting then developed, and ready for use at the end of 1895.[15] Second was the adoption of the multipolar dynamo, then generally in use in Europe but first built here for the

15 Engineering details of this engine are given in R. R. B. to S. Trask, October 31, 1893; R. R. B., "Electricity," *Harper's Magazine*, October, 1896, p. 720.

Edison Company in 1893.[16] Van Vleck was particularly impressed by the work of de Ferranti, a daring electrical engineer working in England. He urged Bowker to accept Ferranti's trial offer of two dozen meters; to consider building a distant supply station for high-tension transmission in line with European practice, and to push the consolidation of American and Canadian plans for utilizing de Ferranti's proposals for a Niagara power plant. Van Vleck's correspondence with Bowker well illustrates the former's alertness to electrical developments and the latter's encouragement of investigation and inquiry by his staff.[17]

In 1892, Bowker himself went to Europe on a seven weeks' intensive study of electrical development abroad. He visited all the principal electric plants in the British Isles and on the Continent, including those at Glasgow, London, Paris, Berlin, Frankfort, Heilbronn, Lauffen, the Swiss works, Vienna, Budapest, Venice, and Milan, and was everywhere given abundant information and facility for examination. Bowker found that the business of low-tension incandescent lighting had in no instance reached the development abroad that it had at home, but he did find many interesting points of comparison. In the matter of artistic designs for electrical appliances and in the development of arc lighting, he found both the Englishmen and Italians ahead of the Americans, while the Germans were safely using high-power electric transmission lines carrying 10,000 volts at a time when Americans thought 2,500 were extremely dangerous. The most important result of this trip was the introduction into the Edison system of the storage battery, a device which had not then been developed in America and of which little was thought. Bowker studied the Crompton-Howell system used in England, immediately purchased one of their large batteries, and promptly installed this in the Fifty-third Street substation, where it proved very useful.[18]

The following year Bowker pushed his policy of foreign observation in a still more dramatic way. Since neither the general superintendent nor the general manager of the high-tension subsidiaries had had the advantage of broad electrical education, Bowker thought that both would be better off for a knowledge of European practice. Consequently, to the utter astonishment of his fellow directors, the operations of the company for the summer season were left in the hands of capable under-officials, and the two managers went abroad with Bowker.[19] Bowker's main objective was to secure the services of John Lieb, a capable

16 R. R. B., Edison Company Annual Report, 1897.

17 See Van Vleck to R. R. B., May 22, September 2, 1891; May 5, 1894, etc.

18 R. R. B., Edison Company Annual Report, 1893, pp. 7–51; R. R. B., MS Memoir.

19 See R. R. B. to S. Trask, October 31, 1893.

young American engineer then working in Milan who had formerly been on Edison's staff. The appointment was successfully negotiated, and a few months later Bowker was picking Lieb's brains for improvements in Edison procedures and policies based on his European experience. After the Milan visit Bowker proceeded with his electrical tour, going as far east as Budapest, and sailing home from England after visiting many old friends there and having an especially stimulating exchange of views on electrical developments with Lord Kelvin.[20]

In 1895 Bowker made a still more profitable trip to Europe. As he wrote Peabody, he wished to study "the new use of steam turbines for generators (in a third the space and at half the cost of our 600 HPs) in Newcastle and Cambridge; the destructors for refuse as fuel; the water-towers for condensing, in Germany; and the economy of Berlin and other German stations." But chiefly his trip was to be "a turbine hunt." The Edison reciprocating engines produced so much vibration that they constituted a nuisance in residential neighborhoods and several lawsuits against the company were actually pending. Bowker felt that immediate action was necessary and that turbines might be the solution.

In England Bowker looked up several installations of the Parsons turbine before calling on the inventor in person at Newcastle-on-Tyne. Mr. Parsons had been described to him as an absolutely unapproachable individual who discouraged visitors from coming anywhere near his works. With characteristic directness, Bowker bearded the old lion in his den and found a very agreeable gentleman and a great engineer who made him perfectly welcome both to his works and his home. Bowker concluded that the Parsons turbine would be useful for Edison purposes, and, when it became evident that an order could not be manufactured in England for immediate delivery, he induced Parsons to entrust to him, without question of compensation, the option for the use of his patents in America.

Crossing the Channel, Bowker looked up an installation of Swedish turbines in the Palais Royal in Paris, and then, after a brief visit to the Siemens- Helske central station in Hamburg, went on to the De Laval Angturbin Aktiebolaget in Stockholm, where he formed a warm and lasting friendship with Daniel Norman, the Scottish-trained, English-speaking president of the company. De Laval, called the Edison of Sweden, was a more difficult person to know, but he encouraged Bowker to inspect the shop and the installations, and Bowker was glad to study not only his turbine but also his amazing steam boiler, which produced the incredible pressure of two thousand pounds, and the famous centrifugal cream separator which was already in world-wide use. Because

20 Lord Kelvin to R. R. B., May 12, 1895.

the De Laval turbine emitted a high-pitched hum audible two blocks away, Bowker knew it was not the perfect answer to the Edison problem. Nevertheless, he resolved to give it a try, and in Paris negotiated a contract with the Maison Breguet for the prompt delivery in New York of two 300-horsepower turbines. These were to be the first steam turbines used in America for public service.[21] They were immediately installed in the Twenty-sixth Street and Thirty-ninth Street stations, overcame the vibrations complained of, and were ready as evidence in court that the company was making every effort to remedy protested annoyances.

In June, 1897, Bowker made his fourth trip to Europe to consult with Lord Kelvin, Ferranti, Parshall, and Bailey on the trend of development regarding the use of alternating-current generation. The Duane Street station had now reached its capacity of 7,600 kilowatts. Since 1882 the Edison Company had clung to direct-current generation, but Bowker suspected the time had come to modify this practice. What he found in Europe was practical unanimity for a low-tension, preferably three-wire, direct-current distributing system such as the Edison system used, but complemented, in view of the difficulties of commutating direct current above 1,000 volts, by high-tension, polyphase transmission from a waterside station to transformer supply stations. This was what Van Vleck had four years been urging, and what the Brooklyn Edison Company was beginning to carry out.[22]

In accordance with these findings, Bowker, on his return, vigorously urged immediate construction of a new waterside station, reporting that the ultimate development of the company, perhaps as early as 1900, would require it.[23] The directors agreed, and within three months Bowker had selected and purchased suitable property on the East River at the foot of Thirty-eighth Street. By the spring of 1898, Van Vleck had the station plans well developed. That June, in order to utilize "every possible European improvement" for the new station, Bowker boldly sent his three chief Edison officers, General Manager John Lieb, Construction Engineer John Van Vleck, and General Inspector Arthur Williams to Europe on a three months' engineering commission "to examine and report upon, technically and in detail, present European practices." Minute and exhaustive preparations were made to guarantee maximum results from the expedition, which visited the chief electrical stations and consulted with the leading electrical experts and managers

[21] Many interesting and technical details of this trip are in Bowker's MS Memoir. A photostat of the Breguet contract is included in Edison Electric Illuminating Company of New York, Memorial Volumes presented to R. R. B., New York, 1899, Vol. I.
[22] Van Vleck to R. R. B., October 7, 1897; John Lieb to R. R. B., July 6, 1897.
[23] Payson Jones, *Power History*, 224.

of England, France, Italy, Switzerland, Austria, Germany, Denmark, and Sweden. The success of the commission was complete. With the improvements resulting from its reports, it was planned to generate current at the new station at substantially lower cost than in any electric station in the world then constructed or in process of construction. Not the least tribute to Bowker's managerial ability was the striking fact that the company's organization permitted the simultaneous absence in Europe of three chief staff officers at the very moment when it was constructing two new annex buildings, providing for large and varied additional equipment stations, and increasing its business with great rapidity.[24]

A fine tribute to Bowker's alert mind and mechanical ingenuity as well as to the value of his observations abroad was his dramatic, last-minute solution of the Fifth Avenue lighting problem. First in 1891, and again in 1892 on the occasion of the Columbus quadricentennial celebration, the city authorities asked the Edison Company to provide lighting on the Avenue that would not require the irregular wooden poles and the unsightly criss-cross of wires. Both times Bowker called a staff council of the engineers to consider the matter. Both times the problem was declared to be insoluble. As Bowker walked home from the second staff meeting musing over the arc lamps he had seen in Milan and elsewhere in Europe, the mechanical solution suddenly occured to him. His rough sketch was approved, Van Vleck rushed the plan into practicable shape, the Equipment Company hurried through the lamps and posts, and on the night of the great procession Bowker's invention lighted Fifth Avenue. It was a real triumph. The posts, more ornamental than anything seen hitherto on the streets, won such public favor that they were soon installed on Fifth Avenue from Washington Square to Seventy-ninth Street and on Madison Avenue from Twenty-third Street to Seventy-ninth. The Commissioner of Public Works, after a visit of inspection abroad, reported that "no street lighting in Paris or London excels the Edison lamps on Fifth and Madison avenues for beauty or illumination." Since the device was promptly adopted by non-Edison interests without permission, Bowker secured a patent for the "Edison-Bowker system of street lighting by twin arcs" in 1894, and soon had the satisfaction of seeing his system utilized by the Brooklyn, Rochester, Buffalo, and other electric companies.[25]

24 R. R. B., "Memorandum for Engineering Commission, 1898"; R. R. B., Edison Company Annual Report, 1899.

25 August 14, 1894. Patent No. 524,305; R. R. B., MS Memoir; undated typed memo in R. R. B. Papers; R. R. B., Edison Company Annual Report, 1893, pp. 53–54; *ibid.*, 1897; R. R. B. to S. Trask, October 31, 1893; R. R. B. to C. R. Huntley, November 28, 1898.

This, incidentally, was not the only invention for which Bowker received a patent. In 1896, he patented two devices[26] forming an electrical distributing system, making it possible for a tie-feeder extending between several generating stations and an intermediate network of street conductors to deliver current from either or both stations. He also secured a patent with Van Vleck for an "Automatic Controllable Junction Box," usually referred to as the disconnective junction box system. This device saved the Edison Company one hundred thousand dollars' worth of copper, and was soon utilized by the General Electric Company, which ultimately purchased all rights to it.[27]

A technical matter to which Bowker was obliged to give a great deal of attention was the defense of the Edison lamp patents. As was to be expected, a great variety of competing lamps appeared which involved infringements of Edison's patents and made necessary long and involved court suits. Bowker later told Edison that one of the greatest satisfactions of his life was when, after lengthy litigation, he finally compelled the Westinghouse people to pay $50,000 in his own office, and the Mt. Morris people to pay $5,000 for infringements. This was something of a personal triumph, for everyone had insisted that the penalties could never be collected.[28]

Sooner or later, almost every area of administration felt the effect of Bowker's passion for order and efficiency. He brought order into the accounting system by adapting to it the Dewey decimal system of book classification, which made possible a very rapid scanning of the total figures, yet also an instantaneous notation of any significant detail, especially normal or abnormal fluctuations of expenditures which could then be discussed in the audit council held regularly in Bowker's office. This system was pronounced by an observer familiar with American and European practice to be "the most perfect and thorough . . . here or abroad." It was adopted by Edison and non-Edison companies and was still the basis of Edison practice thirty years later.[29] Taking another leaf out of library practice, Bowker introduced a card ledger system for customers' accounts which eliminated the cumbrous books that re-

26 One issued May 26, No. 560,772; the second dated June 16, No. 562,209.

27 R. R. B., MS Memoir; General Manager, General Electric Company, to R. R. B., July 11, 1896; R. R. B. to Coffin of General Electric, February 21, March 2, 3, 1900.

28 R. R. B. to S. Trask, November, 1893. A most interesting sidelight on the status of the bulb at this time is afforded by Bowker's notice to subscribers of November 1, 1895. He made some important administrative recommendations and predictions in a letter to S. Trask, October 31, 1893.

29 R. R. B. to H. Deming, June 21, 1905. Full description in R. R. B., Edison Company Annual Report, January 20, 1898. Facsimile reprinted in Wetzler, "The Edison Electrical Illuminating Company of New York," The Electrical Engineer, January 8, 1896; S. Trask to R. R. B., January 5, 1895; H. M. Edwards to R. R. B., April 18, 1925.

quired difficult handling, much waste of space, and yearly rewriting.[30] He made the annual reports models of their kind, declaring that every business deriving its corporate powers from the state should "show its hand" for the state and the people to see.[31]

A considerable burden of public relations also fell on Bowker. To allay public fear of the dangers of electricity, he capitalized on the obvious advantages of the Edison low-tension underground system. He issued statements that the Edison current was harmless, he invited the public to see for itself by visiting the stations, and he appeared with facts and arguments before the politically controlled Board of Electrical Control.[32] Circulars were distributed pointing out that current was being supplied to many of the best houses of fashionable New York, including those of John Pierpont Morgan, Secretary Whitney, Anson Phelps Stokes, D. C. Mills, Eldridge T. Gerry, and Cornelius Vanderbilt, as well as to the ballrooms of Delmonico's and Sherry's. Impressive arguments were advanced to prove the superiority of electricity to gas in safety, health, cleanliness, and variety of usage. The new uses for current were vigorously publicized: cooking, heating, pumping, ventilating, printing, sewing, refrigeration, elevators, medical applications to surgical cautery, dental instruments, X-rays, electric blankets, curling irons, cigar lighters, and electric organs.[33] In the spring of 1896 an Electrical Exposition in New York successfully advertised the new industry, and in an outstanding article for *Harper's* Bowker gave the reading public a unique survey of the subject.

Current production was not, however, all poetry, and the residents near the various Edison stations had cause for bitter complaints. The first injunction served on Bowker was to prevent a plant's exhaust steam from shaking the upper windows of an adjoining building. Soon residents near the Twenty-sixth Street station complained to the Board of Health that showers of cinders, soot, and dust from the big chimneys made life in the vicinity unbearable, and the Board threatened an appeal to the courts.[34] Complaints were made that the rapid vibrations of the many small reciprocating engines were giving near-by residents tremors both in body and in mind, and several threatened suits on this score precipitated Bowker on his turbine hunt in Europe in 1895, which even then did not end the matter.

30 R. R. B., Edison Company Annual Report, January 20, 1898.

31 R. R. B., "Public Control of Corporations," *Municipal Affairs*, February 27, 1903, p. 844.

32 See Edison Company Annual Report, 1890; R. R. B., MS Memoir.

33 R. R. B., "Electricity," *Harper's Magazine*, October, 1896; National Electric Exposition, New York, 1896, *Catalogue;* Edison Company Annual Report, 1897.

34 New York *World,* August 10, 1894.

However, there was abundant indication that the company was prospering. Not even the Panic of 1893 seriously affected it. By that year it was the largest local electric illuminating company in the world, supplying a total installation about 50 per cent larger than that of the Berlin Company, and doing 50 per cent more business than the total of all other local electric companies in the New York area. Ten months later, its business was four times that of its Westinghouse competitor and nearly twice that of all the rival companies combined.[35] In the first four years of Bowker's supervision the number of customers had increased from 1,213 to 5,197, of incandescent lamps from 39,815 to 165,673, of arc lights from 110 to 2,242, of motors from 470 horsepower to 5,295; the total installation had increased more than fivefold, the gross earning from $327,000 to nearly $1,250,000, or approximately fourfold; the net from $124,000 to probably $600,000, or nearly fivefold.

Although much of this growth would have occurred under any administration, Bowker properly felt that his own contribution had not been negligible.[36] His record, for so short a time, was impressive. The Duane and Fifty-third Street stations had been built and an enormous construction work completed; lamp negotiations had assured the company of $55,000 which had been considered uncollectable; the administration had been completely reconstructed; the wiring department had been reorganized and the Equipment Company formed to take over this work; subway relations had been worked into final shape, and the installation company reorganized; the Manhattan and Harlem companies had been successfully purchased and administered.[37]

Bowker had thrown himself vigorously into his work, and at first there had been unmistakable evidence of the appreciation of the directors. Two months after his appointment one of them moved to increase his salary from the $6,000 he had started with to $10,000. Trask wrote Bowker that it was a great comfort to know he was in control, and the first annual report expressed the "high appreciation" of the directors of his "zeal and ability."[38] By 1894, however, Bowker came to feel that the failure of the directors to vote him a further salary increase or stock issue represented a certain lack of appreciation of what he was accomplishing and the difficulties he was encountering. After a number of tactful hints had had no effect on Trask, Bowker early in 1895 bluntly

[35] Edison Company Annual Report, January, 1893, p. 13; R. R. B. to Trask, October 31, 1893.

[36] See confirmation in Wetzler, "The Edison Electric Illuminating Company of New York," *The Electrical Engineer*, January 8, 1896, p. 51.

[37] See chapter XV below.

[38] R. R. B. to G. F. Peabody, September 19, 1901; S. Trask to R. R. B., June 8, 1890; Edison Company Annual Report, January 21, 1891.

threatened to resign unless the company paid him a $20,000 recompense, voted him an increased salary, and specifically defined the limits of Trask's financial authority and his own executive authority. This ultimatum brought action, and Bowker was given two hundred shares of Edison stock as "suitable extra compensation for all the manifold and thorough work" he had done.[39] Although Trask professed surprise that Bowker felt he was being interfered with, Peabody later implied that some mistrust of Bowker's intensely idealistic policies did exist.[40] A certain tension was developing between the crusading manager and the hard-headed businessmen on the board, which, in spite of several exceedingly cordial personal friendships, led in three short years to an irreparable breach. Some of Bowker's policies which particularly startled the conservative directors must now be reviewed.

[39] R. R. B. to G. F. Peabody, January 1, 1895; S. Trask to R. R. B., June 28, 1895. Bowker transferred this stock to his sister as a family trust fund. R. R. B. to G. R. Dominick, June 28, 1901.

[40] S. Trask to R. R. B., January 2, 1895; G. F. Peabody to R. R. B., August 30, 1901.

XV

Managing a Corporation in "Rather an Ideal Way"

I T WAS DEFINITELY Bowker's hope that he would be able to combine the ideals of a liberal reformer with the duties of a corporation manager. Certainly he saw no inconsistency in being the acting executive of a public-franchise corporation and a leader of municipal reform. "I hope the time will never come," he told his employees, "when our men will not feel pride in upholding the Edison tradition that the servant of a corporation supplying the public is also a public servant."[1] Some of Bowker's fellow corporation managers expressed agreement with his view, but there were few who were willing to go the limit in putting it to the test. Bowker tried and failed, though his attempt was made in one of the most liberal companies of the country. This fact, however, was not evident during 1897 and 1898, for in several striking instances he achieved notable success in standing by his policies.

In a typically forthright manner, Bowker had laid down three basic administrative policies which he intended to follow: the open shop, equal treatment for all customers, and resistance to legislative black-mail. He made it clear that he would resign if the board of directors failed to give him support in any crisis resulting from his application of these principles.[2] He might have added a fourth policy of reducing rates and limiting dividends and a fifth of declining to create a mon-opoly instead of maintaining genuine competition. Although Bowker's firm stand led to some dramatic incidents, he always felt that it helped to save the company some costly difficulties which it might otherwise have encountered.

[1] R. R. B. to Edison employees, Christmas, 1898; see R. R. B., "The Public Control of Municipal Franchises," *Municipal Affairs*, December, 1897, p. 605.
[2] R. R. B. to S. Trask, February 13, 1894.

Associates from City College: *(Top, left)* J. Van Vechten Olcott; *(Top, right)* Ernst Eurich; *(Bottom, left)* Nelson S. Spencer; *(Bottom, right)* Adolph Werner

Associates in Electrical Progress: *(Top, left)* Spencer Trask; *(Top right)* Thomas Alva Edison; *(Bottom)* Lord Kelvin

Bowker's open-shop policy was only part of his personnel program, and no part of his administration received more serious and thoughtful attention than this. "It is my own special personal desire," he wrote in a printed letter to his employees, "to make the Company a model organization in all its relations with those whom it employs."[3] The number of employees in 1892 was over eighty, and was soon over four hundred. In dealing with these men Bowker clearly demonstrated the faith in human nature which had led him once to declare, "The economic man is an abstraction; it is the human man who exists."[4]

Bowker organized his ten executive assistants into a staff council which met weekly for lunch and discussion of company problems. Many of these men were pioneers in the field. Harry Smith, the general operating superintendent, had been trained by Edison from the mechanic's bench and was excellent within the practical field, though lacking in a broad theoretical understanding of electrical problems. In Stevens-trained John Van Vleck, as has been noted, Bowker had an ideal chief electrician and consulting engineer. John Lieb's early association with Edison, his wide European experience, his broad view of principles of administration, and his working knowledge of every detail of the business made him a highly capable assistant. His appointment not only was a source of pride to Bowker, but was regarded by him as his outstanding contribution to the electrical field.[5]

It was to the company's relations with its labor force, however, that Bowker gave his special attention. Years before he became a large employer of labor he had studied and written about wages, unions, strikes, and the general role of labor in the creation of wealth.[6] As late as 1897 he declared that the principles then outlined proved quite applicable to his Edison labor problems. Communication was maintained with the employees through an annual four page New Year letter which reviewed all developments affecting their welfare and meted out praise or criticism to specific departments. Any employee not obtaining satisfaction through his delegates had immediate access to Bowker's office. Four of Bowker's Edison labor policies deserve particular attention: the labor council, profit-sharing, high wages, and the open shop.

His labor council, inspired by Joseph D. Weeks' pamphlet of 1885 for the Society for Political Education, was a pioneering enterprise. Each employee nominated a representative by secret ballot, and from these nominations Bowker selected eleven council members to meet

3 R. R. B. to John Lieb, September 30, 1918; R. R. B., MS Memoir.

4 R. R. B., *Of Work and Wealth*, 7.

5 R. R. B. to John Lieb, September 30, 1918; R. R. B., MS Memoir.

6 R. R. B., *Of Work and Wealth* (New York, 1883); *Economics for the People* (New York, 1886).

once a month for a luncheon discussion with him and the general manager. Many directors had doubts about the labor council, but later acknowledged that the plan attained a great measure of success.[7]

The profit-sharing plan was still novel at this time. Some Edison directors thought it highly idealistic, while certain businessmen feared it would serve to confirm the Marxian thesis that labor was the source of all value. But Bowker, who had served on the executive committee of the Association for the Promotion of Profit Sharing, believed in the idea, and knew that this policy was being adopted by more and more progressive corporations. He regarded profit-sharing not at "a mere good-natured giving of gifts," or as a part of wages, but as "a direct acknowledgment and return, in addition to normal wages, for the effective co-operation of employees in operating and administering economies which resulted in increasing the company's net revenue."[8]

He outlined his plan for the Edison Company in his first New Year letter to the employees. As soon as the company should pay 5 per cent on its capital stock, there would be set up a Labor Reserve Fund for the benefit of the employees. This fund would represent the same percentage of total wages that the company paid as dividends on its stock, and would increase from year to year with any increase of dividends. Thus the wages of each man would be considered as equivalent to the investments of each stock owner.[9] The wage-dividend would be based on the value and length of each man's service, and any surplus would be used for sick benefits, death payments, or conveniences for the men "outside the ordinary relations of employers and employees." The fund was to be administered by a committee on which the employees were to be represented. The plan was introduced gradually and fully applied at the end of 1894, when a Labor Reserve Fund of $13,000 was set aside, and wage-dividends totaling $10,000 were paid out.[10]

Bowker defended high wages on practical, not humanitarian, grounds. Arguing that "the best wages get the best men and that the best men do the best and the cheapest work," Bowker consistently claimed to be paying wages that were higher than the ordinary rates, always up to and often higher than the union mark.[11] He insisted that a reduction of the price of current to the public was perfectly consistent with an increase in wages, and early proposed an extra-pay scale mod-

[7] R. R. B. to S. Trask, July 16, 1894; R. R. B. to Edison employees, October 28, 1897; R. R. B., Edison Company Annual Report, 1898, 1899; R. R. B. to O. G. Villard, October 3, 1919; to Charles M. Schwab, January 10, 1928.
[8] R. R. B. to Edison employees, Christmas, 1896.
[9] See R. R. B. to O. G. Villard, October 3, 1919.
[10] R. R. B. to S. Trask, July 16, 1894; Edison Company Annual Report, 1897.
[11] R. R. B. to Edison employees, January 1, 1892; Christmas, 1893; MS Memoir.

eled on the law for the Government Printing Office and vacation with pay for skilled workers.[12] In negotiations with various unions he made it clear that he accepted the principle of a guaranteed minimum standard of living for labor and the security of permanent employment. In May, 1892, Bowker abolished the old twelve-hour shift in the power plants and instituted the eight-hour day throughout the operating system.[13]

A fourth feature of Bowker's labor policy was a clear-cut insistence on the open shop. The second year after taking office he made a full and exact declaration of his stand:

> This Company has no desire to exert or to permit any pressure on its employees to join a labor association or to refrain from joining one. In this respect every workingman should be a free agent, without compulsion from his employers or from his associates. It is hoped, of course, that none of our men will take upon themselves obligations which involve them or their work in the conflicts of opposing labor organizations, or which require them to give over to others the freedom of opinion and action which belongs to every American citizen, or to surrender their right to earn a fair day's wages by their daily work, for themselves and their families, or to deny that right to any fellow-workingman.

Yet Bowker was a strong believer in the usefulness of unions, and once cited Typographical Union No. 6 as a good example of a union useful to both employers and employees.[14]

Bowker soon had an opportunity to put into practice his theories about how strikes should be handled. On January 1, 1892, the Brotherhood of Electrical Workers commenced a stubborn drive to secure a closed shop in the Edison Company, and soon fifty-one men were out on strike. For two months he and the Brotherhood had it out. Bowker invited a candid exchange of views, spent hours talking with the walking delegate, studied the Brotherhood's proposals with great thoroughness, and examined its constitution. He talked to his own men to ascertain their opinions and set forth his own principles and policies with vigor and precision. On February 24, the strike was called off, and every striking worker was given his old job if it had not been mean-

12 R. R. B. to Secretary, Brotherhood of Electrical Workers, February 6, 1892.

13 R. R. B. to Edison employees, Christmas, 1892; R. R. B. to S. Trask, October 31, 1893.

14 R. R. B. to Secretary, Brotherhood of Electrical Workers, February 6, 1892; to J. R. Strong, president of the Electrical Contractors Union, March 2, 1895; to Contractors Association, December 8, 1897. See Bowker's draft labor planks for Wheeler's Democratic platform of 1894 and the New York Gold Democrats, 1896.

while filled by an acceptable new worker.[15] On May 16 a second strike was called which involved thirty-five men and a loss of six thousand dollars in wages; that fall a third one was unsuccessfully attempted and in October, 1897 a fourth was averted by friendly personal conferences.[16]

A little later, when it looked as though the company would be involved in a sympathetic strike, Bowker went directly to Samuel Gompers, the labor chief, and invited him to dinner at the Reform Club to talk the matter over. Bowker took the position that the Edison Company, since it had voluntarily adopted all the principles for which the Brotherhood was contending, should not be penalized. Gompers admitted that if all companies had followed the Edison example, there would not be a strike, but insisted that this was a battle between employers and employees and that in a war those between the lines were likely to get shot. As matters turned out, the Edison Company was not affected, but Bowker always regretted that Gompers could not accept the view that responsible corporations should have the sympathy and support of labor when emergencies arose.[17]

In spite of his uncompromising opposition to the closed shop, Bowker's spirit was seen to be so scrupulously fair in negotiation that he was several times asked to serve as an arbiter in disputes. One concerned a strike of the Brotherhood of Electrical Workers and the Electrical Contractors Association in February, 1895. Bowker accepted the invitation, proposed a thoughtful basis of agreement, and showed his faith in the Brotherhood by volunteering to contribute $5,000 toward a guarantee that any understanding entered into by the Contractors Association would be kept by the men. Two years later he arranged an arbitration agreement for two years, which had such excellent results that it was proposed to make arbitration general among the building trades. In 1898 he was again importuned to act as umpire in a case involving the Doscher Sugar Refining Company.[18]

Many small policies reflected Bowker's progressive personal ideas and organizing enthusiasm. Special uniforms and an Edison button were to be worn by employees having relations with the public; special

[15] R. R. B. to Secretary, Brotherhood of Electrical Workers (Local Assembly 5468 of the Knights of Labor), February 6, 1892; Edison Company Annual Report, 1893.

[16] R. R. B. to Brotherhood of Electrical Workers No. 3, October 7. 1897.

[17] R. R. B., MS Memoir.

[18] C. W. Hoadley for the Brotherhood to R. R. B., March 1, 1895; R. J. Anslow, chairman, executive committee, Board of Delegates, Building Trades, to R. R. B., March 1, 1895; J. R. Strong to R. R. B., March 2, 1895; R. R. B. to Contractors Association, December 8, 1897; Edison Company Annual Report, 1898, 1899; minutes of Conference and Arbitration Committee, Electrical Contractors Association and Brotherhood of Electrical Workers, September 13, 14, 17, 1898.

fire badges were designed for those co-operating with the Fire Department; a general reception was proposed to employees with their families, as well as lectures and a circulating library. Following the example of his friend Waring, who had inaugurated the "white angels" in the Street Cleaning Department, Bowker had the engines and the engine-room of the Duane Street building painted white and was gratified when the employees soon asked for white uniforms.

Bowker's policy of equal treatment for all customers led to a head-on personal collision with John Pierpont Morgan, Sr. Morgan's residence had been originally supplied with current by an isolated generating plant. He had apparently consented to the removal of this plant and to the experimental wiring of his house for the first residential lighting in New York on the understanding that he would be billed at one-third discount. Bowker knew none of these details, but he did know, in 1894, that Morgan was the only customer remaining at special rates, and he consequently notified him that he would thereafter be billed like all other customers. Morgan ignored Bowker's bills and letters for four years, but in 1898 Bowker decided to get action. He credited the dividends of Mr. Morgan the stockholder to the account of Mr. Morgan the customer.

Morgan instantly called for Bowker, and when the Edison executive arrived, he found the financier in a rage. He insisted that his understanding with the company constituted a contract and said that he wanted his dividend check. Bowker replied that he had never heard of such a contract, but would of course stand by it if such could be found. A search of the files produced nothing. The two men then had a second talk. Morgan threatened to pay his bill and break off all relations with the Edison Company. Bowker, however, induced him to write out a check for $5,000 on account until the matter could be more thoroughly looked into. Morgan and Coster complained to Peabody that Bowker's attitude was "outrageous," and Peabody urged Bowker to yield.[19] Bowker declared that he would yield only if the company's legal counsel would agree that a contract did actually exist. He admitted that there was no moral reason why the company should not make as many special contracts as it pleased, but he declared that the equal-treatment policy had not only greatly helped to place and increase business on a stable foundation, but had been a chief means of holding back rival companies from rate wars and cut prices and of disarming rate-discrimination bills presented in Albany. He hinted that he was quite prepared to resign if his policy was repudiated and added with real

19 G. F. Peabody to R. R. B., September 12, 1898.

feeling, "Nothing, in fact, has been more the crumpled rose leaf in my pleasant Edison relations."[20]

Bowker's second basic policy, of resistance to legislative blackmail, led him into several tense encounters. The basis of the vicious practice by which a political machine blackmailed a corporation was simple. Almost every large business in New York could be crippled by legislation passed by the municipal Board of Aldermen or the state legislature at Albany, but the electric, gas, and insurance companies were favorite game. Croker, in control of the city, and Platt, in control of the legislature, had merely to name the price which was necessary to purchase temporary immunity from molestation, and the business heads meekly "kicked in." Legislative blackmailing proposals were known as "strike" bills. They usually took the form of mandatory price-reduction bills that would be ruinous if passed. When Wheeler H. Peckham told the Good Government Club in 1894 that the New York Telephone Company paid $50,000 a year to Tammany to avoid strike bills and that he could name a second corporation which paid a similar amount, the *Evening Post* asserted editorially that this was common knowledge. "We have been assured by the officials of many corporations," it stated, "that all give something." It quoted the estimate of competent judges that Croker had collected between two and four millions a year and asserted that Platt, using Croker's system, was employing levies as a "fertilizer of boss politics."[21]

Bowker considered this matter a "grave moral principle," determined to resist the practice stoutly, and expressed this determination repeatedly to the board of directors, the Edison employees, and the public. There were those, however, both without and within the Edison Company who assured Bowker that he could never run a business on such a lofty basis of ethical independence. One of these was his close friend, President Cutler of the same New York Telephone Company mentioned by Peckham to the Good Government Club. Peabody, whose integrity and high moral principles were beyond question, justified payments to political powers by the argument that it was better for a trustee to surrender part of the property in his charge to a highwayman than to lose it all. Bowker always regarded this as a specious argument and as an encouragement to the native industry of highway robbery, and frequently told Peabody so.[22] He grieved that he could never feel entirely sure of Peabody's support in this matter, but in general the board of directors did stand behind him.

20 R. R. B. to G. F. Peabody. The presumption is that Morgan was induced to accept the regular rate.
21 January 21, 1895.
22 R. R. B. to G. Peabody, September 24, 1898.

There were some examples of political appeasement in the Edison Company which Bowker was unable to prevent. Early in his administration a fellow director arranged for him to be presented as persona grata to Mayor Grant by a Tammany lawyer of distinction who later became a Supreme Court justice. Since this lawyer was a fellow-alumnus of City College and a personal acquaintance, Bowker regarded this act as friendly and proper. When, to his utter surprise, the company received a bill for $2,000 from the lawyer, Bowker sought vainly to prevent payment of the bill. Later a bill for $7,000 was presented for similar shadowy "services" and Trask insisted on paying it after Bowker had indignantly refused.[23] Where he was free to control the situation, however, Bowker's administrative rule was applied absolutely. He ordered his superintendent of street installation to treat Tammany card holders like any other applicants in both hiring and firing. He went directly to Commissioner (later Mayor) Gilroy to put his cards on the table and elicited from Gilroy the assurance that if any of his Tammany people overstepped the mark, he would promptly see that it did not happen again. When claims for killing strike bills introduced at Albany by Senator Owens in 1894 and 1895 were presented to him, Bowker simply declared them unauthorized and refused to consider them. In each case this blunt action caused an eruption, but the flurry blew over.[24]

Two ugly strike bills were aimed at the Edison Company in 1896,[25] one bill extending the definition of a public nuisance to include manufacturing plants in residential districts. Bowker acted with the utmost vigor, and his method seemed to work. It consisted in personal appearances before hearings, presentation of absolutely all relevant facts to the legislators, demonstrating that the Edison Company had a conscience and was giving the public a square deal, and was holding to his own faith that the honest men in the legislature could be rallied by such methods to stand up for the company against the corruptionists. The two bills were dropped. The "boys" were puzzled by this queer kind of corporation, and some businessmen were sure that such a policy would not long succeed. The showdown came in 1897.

The strike bill aimed at the Edison Company in the spring of 1897 was personally engineered by "Big Tim" Sullivan, a politician who was typical of the best and the worst in the Tammany tradition. At Albany, first as Assemblyman and then as Senator, he hunted corporations as fair game. On leaving the Assembly to take his place in the Senate, he caused "Little Tim," his nephew, to be elected in his old district, and

23 R. R. B. to Governor Charles E. Hughes. in New York *Evening Post*, April 24, 1907; memorandum by R. R. B. for S. Trask, March 8, 1899.
24 R. R. B. to Senator W. L. Brown, April 10, 1896.
25 Assembly Bill Int. No. 96, No. 1146.

the family team soon became responsible for a large share of corporation strike bills and holdups. Usually a Sullivan strike bill would be passed by the Assembly and then held up in a Senate committee until the victimized corporation made terms.

"Big Tim's" strike bill threatened to cut the price of arc lighting from nine to four cents per lamp hour, and of incandescent lighting from one to three-quarters of a cent. "Little Tim" saw that the bill was passed in the Assembly. When "Big Tim," with the cordial support of the gas companies, had steered it to a third reading in the Senate, Bowker knew that it was time for him to go directly to Albany.[26] It was late in the session. The legislators were working hard. There had been a long night sitting on the eve of the day for the committee hearing, and most of the Senators were late in arriving. Bowker noticed immediately that "Big Tim" was right on hand to watch the performance and do the steering. The two men took their places at the committee table to await the others.

"Well, Senator," remarked Bowker, "your hard work will soon be over and you will get some rest."

"Rest will it be!" said "Big Tim." "Oh, this is dead aisy and it's the hard work when I get home and have to look after me constituents."

"You've had long experience up here, Senator," Bowker replied, "and you ought to write your autobiography."

"Me aut'biography!" he said, "Yes that'd be a foin thing t'do— t'write me aut'biography. I tell ye there'd be money in it. All I'd have t'do'd be t'put it in type and send a friend o'mine to see gentlemen in Wall Street and—there'd be money in that book—not to print it." Whereupon, the other Senators still being late, Senator "Big Tim" became rollickingly confidential and garrulous. But the situation, after the hearing, seemed really dangerous. "Big Tim," indeed, seemed on the point of breaking Bowker and his policy. The bill was passed. One possibility remained. Bowker went directly to Governor Black and asked for his help. Black vetoed the bill.[27]

The immediate crisis was over, but there was no assurance that the bill would not be revived. That December, Bowker decided to appeal directly to "Big Tim." Accordingly he wrote a letter to him:

> I don't like your kind of "politics," but I must say that you put them in a straightforward and interesting way that one can't help but admire. As I told you at Albany last session, I don't mean to get into that interesting autobiography of yours and there are no "horses" to come up to Albany from this Company for I have said

26 Account in R. R. B., MS Memoir.
27 Memorandum, R. R. B. to S. Trask, March 8, 1899.

248

straight that I will get out of this Company, and give up my salary, rather than have that done. I think you like to get, as well as to give, straight talk and I would be glad to show you, before you go to Albany for the next session, that this Company is trying to act straight by the public and by its men. What I am trying to do, and am doing step by step, is to get prices down for our customers— among whom are some of your constituents—and the public. I wish to ask you, therefore, to come and lunch with me some day before the end of the month and if you could come on Friday next, we have then a Staff Council luncheon. . . .[28]

The luncheon did not come off, and when the legislature met again, Bowker's fears were realized: the bill was revived. In the end, however, it was pigeonholed by both the Assembly and the Senate committees.

On leaving the Edison administration in 1899, Bowker could state confidently that his policy regarding legislative blackmail and political contributions had not once been violated, and that the practical wisdom of his policy had been completely vindicated.[29] His own conviction was that the fault for such corruption lay with public opinion: adequate salaries were not paid to legislators, easy sanction was given to the argument that buying protection from politicians was better than risking other people's property, and large contributions by business firms to election war chests encouraged the growth of "invisible government." On several occasions he discussed this problem with Governor Theodore Roosevelt.[30]

If some of the directors had been skeptical of the labor council and the wage-dividends, incensed at the Morgan episode, and impatient with the anti-blackmail policy, they were frankly alarmed at Bowker's determination to reduce rates, limit dividends, and wipe out all margin of overcapitalization. His immediate policy was to press for a general reduction of prices as fast as the increase of business, the introduction of operating economies, and the diminution of investment charges permitted; or, more specifically, to decrease the price to the public with each increase of dividends to the stockholders. His long-range policy was to put a ceiling of 10 per cent on dividends as constituting sufficient compensation to stockholders for their investment of capital and initial risk, and thereafter steadily to reduce the price of current to the public.[31]

[28] R. R. B. to Timothy D. Sullivan, December 8, 1897.
[29] R. R. B., Edison Company Annual Report, 1899.
[30] R. R. B., "Public Control of Municipal Franchises," *Municipal Affairs*, December, 1897, pp. 629–30; R. R. B. to Governor T. Roosevelt, March 2, 1899.
[31] R. R. B., "Public Control of Corporations," *Municipal Affairs*, February 27,

The directors were induced to accept this long-range policy, but considerable difference of opinion developed about when dividend increases should be made. During the first decade of the industry, heavy capital expenditures had kept profits very low: up to 1893 no other lighting company had even earned enough to pay any dividends at all, while for the first time in that year Edison dividend payments reached 6 per cent and had not been increased since. Meanwhile the cost of current had been reduced from one and two-tenths cents per "lamp hour" in 1888 to one cent soon after Bowker took charge, and the principle of reduction for wholesale use of current had been adopted on his convincing presentation of the facts.[32] Now, in 1897, the higher earnings long anticipated by the directors began to be realized,[33] and the issue whether to reduce prices or to increase dividends became acute. In this matter Bowker found himself in sharp disagreement with his close friends Peabody and Shepard.

Bowker's insistence on restricting dividend payments and reducing prices was based on four arguments: price reduction would bring in more business and would reduce competition; it would make it easier to rally decent legislators in Albany against strike bills; it represented a broad moral obligation resting on a semi-public-service corporation; and it was a primary cause of the good will which really lay at the basis of the company's phenomenal development.[34] In his stand, Bowker had the support of Lieb and of Edison himself. Peabody, however, was flatly opposed.[35] He argued that price reduction would not bring enough new business to recoup a quarter of the net revenue sacrificed, that enormous Edison investments in plant might be jeopardized by new engineering developments, that a reduction would have no effect on strike legislation other than to invite still lower mandatory rates, that it represented unjustifiable experimentation with the stockholders' money, that the company's mounting earnings were not due to Bowker's "ideals" but to the exceptional lighting conditions in New York, and that it would harm the Brooklyn Edison Company, in which he and Trask were heavily interested.

In 1897, Bowker pressed for price reductions to the full extent of the surplus above a 6 per cent dividend payment. Peabody called for a 7 per cent dividend payment. Bowker was completely successful in winning over the directors to his position[36] and even induced the company

32 R. R. B. to Edison customers, October 28, 1897; to C. H. Jackson, December 13, to Lieb, December 27, 1897.

33 F. Enos to R. R. B., June, 1897.

34 R. R. B., Edison Company Annual Report, January, 1893, p. 14.

35 T. A. Edison to R. R. B., November 30, 1898; G. F. Peabody to R. R. B., March 3, 1897; February 4, 1898.

to go beyond all its competitors and its own practice in putting depreciation charges under operating expense, and to make a special reduction to the municipality for its public lighting, on the ground that this was a fair recognition of franchise relations and a strong argument against a municipal electric plant.[37] All in all, Bowker effected a 7 per cent reduction in prices during the year. The results were even more gratifying than he had predicted. In the case of the Harlem Lighting Company, one of the Edison subsidiaries, the lower prices effected, within two months, a 15 per cent increase in earnings, a saving of $18,000 of annual business that had threatened to go to isolated plants, and a gain of $14,000 of new business that would otherwise have installed isolated plants. Indeed, in his annual report he declared that the general results justified a further reduction.[38]

Early in 1898 Bowker again pressed for new price schedules which would increase reductions to wholesalers. To the protesting Westinghuose officers he proved that a careful study of American and European conditions demonstrated the wisdom of a reduction to wholesalers as the best way of meeting the competition of the gas companies.[39] Again Bowker had his way. The new schedules were announced in October. But even this reduction did not satisfy him. It was now his urgent desire to secure a rate of three-quarters of a cent per lamp hour to be announced not later than December 1, 1898. Peabody again objected, urging an 8 per cent dividend instead. Shepard criticized Bowker's bookkeeping method of indicating depreciation and noting assets. Bowker replied that it was precisely the depreciation reserve fund that had been made the object of legislative attack. He told Shepard that his course deserved the full support "of all good citizens" and finally made the proposed reduction a condition of his remaining in office.[40] Once again Bowker won his point. Trask agreed not to declare the 8 per cent dividend, and the reduced rate was adopted.

Thus Bowker succeeded in accomplishing one of his basic purposes in accepting the original Edison appointment—reduction of the price of current to the consumer. The kilowatt hour, which had cost twenty cents in 1890, cost eleven cents in 1899, and he had fought for every reduction along the way. In the course of these skirmishes over

36 *Ibid.*, February 11, 1900.

37 R. R. B. in Circular Letter, October 1, 1898.

38 R. R. B. to C. H. Jackson, December 13, 1897; R. R. B., Edison Company Annual Report, 1898.

39 R. R. B. to C. H. Jackson, July 29, 1898.

40 E. M. Shepard to G. F. Peabody, November 26, 1898; to R. R. B., December 8, 1898. R. R. B. to E. M. Shepard, December 10, 1898; to S. Trask, January 20, 1899; to Governor C. E. Hughes, April 19, 1907.

dividends and prices, Bowker also sought to have surplus set aside as reserve, and this principle likewise met the opposition of his more conventional associates, who argued that additional capital should be subscribed through new stock issues rather than created out of earnings.[41]

A final problem which Bowker met with a clear-cut policy not always approved by his fellow directors concerned the growing competition from other electric companies. The New York Board of Aldermen held a vigorous belief in the beneficial effect of competition and did not hesitate to issue franchises to new electricity supply companies. The Brush Electric Illuminating Company of New York and the United States Illuminating Company of New York were granted franchises a few weeks after the initial Edison franchise in 1881. Nine other companies were granted franchises in 1887, though only five of these, at most, began operation at the time.[42] In 1889 the important United Electric Light and Power Company was incorporated. By 1890 there were at least nine New York companies in rivalry with the Edison interests, all of them high-tension systems.

Bowker recognized that under certain circumstances it was necessary for a corporation to protect its property by securing control of rivals. In 1891 the East River Electric Light Company (soon to be renamed the Thomson-Houston Electric Company) maneuvered to secure control of the Manhattan Electric Light Company and the Harlem Lighting Company. To prevent the serious competition which would result from such a combination of high-tension interests and to secure a foothold in the high-tension field, the Edison Company delegated Bowker to beat the Thomson-Houston interests to this purchase. This he did, and proceeded to manage the new properties with conspicuous success.[43] Bowker also supported the Edison acquisition of the Madison Square Light Company in 1894, and the purchase of the East River Electric Light Company.[44]

From this stage of consolidation on, however, Bowker opposed every proposal for further combination, even though interest in or control of every remaining competing company was at one time or another

41 E. M. Shepard to R. R. B., February 4, 1898.

42 The East River Electric Light Company, Bell Electric Illuminating Company, Mount Morris Electric Light Company, Harlem Lighting Company, North New York Lighting Company; see M. R. Maltbie, *Franchises of Electric Corporations in Greater New York*, 30–44.

43 R. R. B. to Trask, November, 1893; Peabody to R. R. B., January 10, 1892; R. R. B. to Trask, October 31, 1893.

44 Maltbie, *Franchises of Electric Corporations in Greater New York*, 45. On September 1, 1896, the Manhattan Company and the Madison Square Company were consolidated to form the Manhattan Electric Light Company; R. R. B., "Piracy of Public Franchises," *Atlantic Monthly*, October, 1901, p. 469.

offered to him. In some cases he argued that purchasing less efficient competing companies at inflated prices represented an expensive and fruitless attempt to eliminate competition when the same capital might be invested in new plant. In other cases he insisted that a multiplication of high-tension companies actually gave the Edison system the opportunity for larger success than as a monopoly, and that reasonable competition really served both the public interest and a company as strong as his own.[45] This conviction was based chiefly on the fear of the political abuses of monopoly, not on any doubt as to its technical economies.[46]

Bowker sought to maintain relations with his competitors on a basis of "real though friendly rivalry." He could honestly say that his company had "never taken, planned, nor conceived any plan with the purpose of harming any rival company." He admitted that the Edison Company was interested in making money, but believed in the broad policy of "doing this by extending the field, and not by trying to break down the interests or decrease the value of the securities of a rival company—one result of which would be to lessen the public confidence in electrical securities in general and incidentally those of one's own company."[47] When the Westinghouse interests threatened litigation for a patent infringement, Bowker's reply was characteristic. "In that case," he declared, "I shall be prepared to fight *fortiter in re* though I trust with *suavitor en modo* on both sides."[48]

Bowker succeeded in getting considerable adhesion to a gentleman's agreement among the larger companies that the agents of one company should not be permitted to solicit customers of another company, that the published rates of a company should not be departed from in individual cases, and that fair notice should be given of any contemplated rate reductions.[49] It is not surprising that certain people began to think that competition had practically ceased to operate in the New York electrical industry. Obviously a situation had grown up that would sooner or later tempt businessmen less ethically sensitive than Bowker to create a real monopoly of electric power.

Bowker enjoyed a position of respect and honor in the growing family of Edison executives. He was elected vice-president of the Asso-

45 R. R. B., "Piracy of Public Franchises," *Atlantic Monthly*, October, 1901, p. 469; R. R. B. to S. Trask, January 20, 1898.

46 R. R. B. to C. H. Jackson, December 8, 1897; see also R. R. B., "Public Control of Corporations," *Municipal Affairs*, February 27, 1903, p. 844; R. R. B. to Governor C. E. Hughes, in New York *Evening Post*, April 24, 1907.

47 R. R. B. to C. H. Jackson, December 8, 1897; January 6, 1898.

48 R. R. B. to C. H. Jackson, September 26, 1898.

49 R. R. B. to S. Trask, January 20, 1898.

ciation of Edison Illuminating Companies for the term 1897–98 when Samuel Insull of the Chicago Edison Company was president, and succeeded him as president for 1898–99 when the Association included fifty-three member companies as far distant as Milan, Italy. On severing his Edison relations in 1899, he resigned his office in the Association, but was made one of the latter's only two honorary members, and in this capacity was glad to renew old acquaintances at the annual meetings until 1932. He was also active in the American Institute of Electrical Engineers for many years and helped to organize and manage the Institute's Edison Medal Association. Bowker was also elected a member of the Edison Pioneers, organized in 1918, rarely missed one of their annual birthday dinners for Thomas Edison, and in 1931 was elected vice-president of the organization.

During his ten years as an Edison executive, Bowker came to have a great admiration and affection for "the Chief," as Thomas A. Edison was known to his associates. Even though his official duties did not bring him into regular touch with the inventor and though Edison, albeit one of the company's directors, never attended a directors' meeting,[50] Bowker did have many occasions for friendly exchange of opinions with him about minor engineering developments and administrative principles. In 1897, Edison asked Bowker to arrange a technical and commercial survey of his magnetic-ore-separation plant at Ogden, New Jersey—familiarly known as the "Ogden Baby"—and to serve as manager of a syndicate to raise needed capital for this dramatic development, promising him handsome profits. Bowker accepted the responsibility until early in 1898 when he was obliged to give it up.[51] Edison always enthusiastically supported Bowker's administrative policies and program. "Nothing that I have ever seen in the management line goes ahead of the record shown in your last annual report," he wrote Bowker in 1898. "No management can be successful that does not *try experiments* with the public; boards of directors are never in favor of experiments." The cordial relation between the two men continued long after Bowker left the Edison Company of New York. In 1903, Bowker offered to shape the commercial development of Edison's "electrogen"; in 1914, he offered to help develop the Edison phonograph along new lines.[52] He several times visited the Edisons in their Florida home and several times invited them to visit him in Stockbridge, maintaining intimate relations until the inventor's death in 1931.

[50] R. R. B. to T. A. Edison, February 9, 1920.

[51] The Bowker Papers contain much material concerning the Ogden Baby and plans for the syndicate: letters memoranda, reports, October, 1897–December, 1898.

[52] T. A. Edison to R. R. B., February 5, 1898; R. R. B. to T. A. Edison, October 21, 1903; R. R. B. to T. A. Edison, September 30, 1914.

Meanwhile, Bowker had presided over a phenomenal growth in the New York Edison Company's business. It was still the greatest company of its kind in the world. Bowker's office staff required six stenographers to handle the 250 letters dictated daily. The personnel had increased to an executive staff of 12 and a labor force of 745. The five central stations and two annex stations with the 220 miles of underground street mains were supplying ten thousand customers with a current equivalent to a million candle-power. The progress since Bowker's assumption of the management showed six times the number of customers, seventeen times the installation, nine times the maximum output, seven times the gross income, and ten times the net on but four times the capital.[53] Meanwhile, operating improvements had reduced the cost of fuel to one-half, of labor to one-third (despite the increase in wages and decrease in hours), and the total cost to two-fifths, with every assurance that the full development of the waterside station would further cut the cost of fuel and labor by one-half.[54] As a result of this progress, the company's earnings had reached 12 per cent in 1898, and it was estimated that, at its normal ratio of growth, it would be earning 14 to 16 per cent in 1899, and 16 to 18 per cent in 1900. In Bowker's own mind, he had brought the company to an impregnable position. It need not fear the competition from new companies starting afresh with the latest machinery and without royalty charges or experimental costs. Moreover, if any corporation could withstand "politics" as a result of scrupulous policies pursued, it was this one.

Bowker had pursued an administrative policy that was liberal to a striking degree. He had assumed that one could do business and make money and yet be fair to the city, the consumer, the stockholder, and the employee, and he had proved his assumption to be correct. He had maintained the open shop, he had insisted on equal treatment for all customers, and he had resisted legislative blackmail. He had seen to it that dividend payments went up only as profit-sharing benefits to employees also went up and prices went down, and he had established the principle that there should be a ceiling on dividends of 10 per cent. He had succeeded in writing off a liberal allowance for wear and tear of equipment and in bringing physical valuation up to capital account and thus wiping out almost all margin of overcapitalization. He had established a system of employee representation and profit-sharing, he had seen to it that franchise relations were honored, and he had main-

---

53 R. R. B. to S. Trask, January 20, 1898. A formal acknowledgment of the full figures is given in the memorial adopted January 19, 1899, by the Edison Board of Directors.
54 R. R. B., MS Memoir.

tained his relations with competitors on a plane of high principle and good feeling.

When Bowker's resignation as first vice-president was finally accepted in January, 1899, the board's formal memorial closed with a tribute to "one whose unusual capacity has been admirably united to a true sense of the responsibilities of the employer, and who in his relation with the employees of the Company has demonstrated the commercial wisdom of encouraging the growth of mutuality of interest between the employer and the employed."[55] A quarter of a century later, Peabody testified that the company was still influenced by "the moral standards respecting the rights of the public and the rights of the employees" which he had inaugurated.[56]

Actually, however, there were many critics of Bowker's regime both within and without the company. His policy was financially too conservative and ethically too idealistic. It was definitely contrary to the Wall Street trend of realizing high values by paying large dividends; it kept the stock out of the market, inactive and unspeculative because held strongly by investors and ruling lower in price than its actual or potential value. When one of Trask's banking associates dubbed his policies as "rather an ideal way" of handling a corporation, Bowker was quick to turn the slur into a proud admission. "I confess that I have tried to handle the Company's business in 'rather an ideal way,'" he wrote Trask, "but the eight years have shown practical results. . . . Many of our national financial errors, especially the silver craze, and our corporation difficulties have come, I am convinced, from popular prejudice against corporations not ideally managed." But the tocsin had already sounded, and Bowker had heard it. By the end of October, 1898, he suspected that a New York power monopoly was in progress, that Tammany was behind it, and that the Edison Company was probably doomed.[57]

[55] New York *Times* and *Tribune,* January 21, 1898.
[56] G. F. Peabody to President Sidney E. Mezes, March 12, 1926.
[57] R. R. B. to G. F. Peabody, October 26, 1898.

XVI

A Mugwump in the Nineties

AT THE same time that Bowker was managing the *Publishers' Weekly* and its manifold bibliographical enterprises, the *Library Journal,* and the Edison Company, he was more than ever involved in the various concerns of the liberal crusade. During the nineties he labored to keep both the New York State and the national Democratic party faithful to Cleveland's policies; he fought the new jingoism and the new imperialism; he contributed vigorously to the study of the municipal-franchise problem, the new taxation, and the social-settlement movement. Moreover, in adjusting to the many new problems brought by the revolutionary developments in technology and industrialism at the end of the century, he achieved a constructive adaptation of liberalism to the times, while some retreated from it into an outdated rugged individualism and others deserted it for the new socialism.

Bowker's political activities during the decade 1891–1901 provide an interesting study in the problems faced by a conscientious American liberal determined to be both consistent and practical in the field of politics. The objectives to be sought were as clear as ever: tariff reform, sound money, social control of trusts without socialization, administrative honesty, rejection of boss politics, and resistance to imperialism. "More and more I feel," Bowker confided to Peabody in 1895, "that our money botherations and our labor difficulties spring from the Protectionist group and that we have to make all along the line the strongest kind of fight against Socialism, protectionism, Bimetallism, and other nostrums—all from the same bad root."[1]

The great problem, however, was to find or fashion a political instrument for the achievement of these objectives. From 1868 to 1882, Bowker had worked within the Republican party in the belief that it

[1] R. R. B. to G. F. Peabody, May 1, 1895.

was the party of true liberal principle. From 1882 until 1901 he worked within the Democratic party, believing that it was now more liberal than the Republican. First and last, however, he was an Independent, putting nation ahead of party, regarding parties as means and not ends, willing to work "within and with any party and without or against any party to assert principles," and standing ready at all times to consider the merits of a third-party movement. As he put it in a campaign speech for Democrat Shepard in 1895, recalling his support of Republican Seth Low in 1885:

> An Independent then, I am an Independent now, because to be independent is the birthright of every American and his everyday duty. A Republican then, because I believed that party the party of freedom and progress, I am a Democrat today, because I believe that my old party has passed its fruitage, and that in this Reform organization and in the party which it seeks to purify and uplift, are the seeds of liberty and progress in the future.

The Democratic party, however, was subject to such local corruption and national heresy during this decade that Bowker usually found himself occupying a very small, critical, and independent wing of it, so independent in fact as to be forever in danger of complete severance from the main body. This situation was due to three main elements: the boss-ridden machine in New York controlled by Hill in Albany, Croker in Tammany, and McLaughlin in Brooklyn; the high tariff "protectionist cabal" of Gorman and Brice in Congress; and the Bryan silver heretics in the West. The split between the free-silver and the sound-money Democrats, indeed, was to have a paralyzing effect throughout the decade. Asked to speak on the same platform with the Populist Jerry Simpson in 1891, Bowker consented to do so only on explicit assurances by the chairman that all speakers would strictly confine themselves to free trade. Bowker explained the sense in which he was a Democrat in a public letter on the eve of the election of 1900:

> I am a democrat only so far as the Democratic party is associated with Democratic principles, particularly government by the consent of the governed and the obligation upon America to right herself before she undertakes to right the other side of the world. To these principles are equally opposed Bryanism, which has cost the Democratic party defeat in the nation; Hillism, which has cost the party the state; and Crokerism, which must ultimately cost it defeat within the city; unless the Democratic ship can rid itself of these pirate crews.

What Bowker and his fellow reform Democrats sought to do was to clear the ship if possible of the pirate crews that had captured her, or at least to keep the true flag flying. They wished to keep alive within the party the great basic liberalisms of the American democratic tradition as well as the more specific Democratic ideals of Tilden and Cleveland, hoping at each major election that enough voters could be won back to the true standard to build the party into an effective force to accomplish the great work of the new century.

Since, however, Croker, Hill, and Bryan managed to control most of the Democratic votes most of the time, the role of Bowker and his friends was to be a lonely and unpopular one calling for unceasing hard work and few rewards. "It is a long and weary task we have undertaken," Wheeler wrote Bowker understandably in 1892, "and at times I shrink from it. But I feel that duty calls, and we must obey." They had few illusions about their prospects of commanding majorities. "You and I will exert influence," Shepard wrote Bowker in 1894, "but under American political conditions, we will not hold office." Bowker continued to provide tireless initiative and drive for his associates. When the program of the reform Democrats languished during his absence in Europe in 1894, the secretary wrote him, "I am afraid that those who are of a more phlegmatic disposition will drop the work and that little, if anything, effective will be accomplished until you return."[2] It was, indeed, the old story.

The two leading New York Democratic bosses, Hill at the head of the state machine and Croker in charge of Tammany Hall, represented everything that the Independents abhorred, including a readiness to knife Cleveland in the back. The Independents' task in New York, then, was to keep alive the liberal Democratic witness by a continuous challenge of Hill and Croker. In working at this, Bowker joined the "Shepard Democrats" in Brooklyn and the "State Democracy" under Fairchild and Wheeler.

In 1893, the opportunity presented by the excesses of the Democratic machine was vigorously seized in the municipal and state elections. In Brooklyn the reform Democrats published a stinging indictment of the Hill regime, and Shepard wrote a scorching article on municipal maladministration for the *Forum* and a press denunciation of Mayor Boody's sell-out to the McLaughlin machine.[3] Bowker served on a Committee of One Hundred, representing both Democrats and Republicans, which repudiated Boss McLaughlin and nominated

2 Robert Baker to R. R. B., February 27, 1895.
3 Brooklyn *Daily Eagle*, September 15, 1893.

Charles A. Schieran as a Fusion candidate for mayor. This time the protest against the machine was amazingly successful. In Brooklyn, the Fusion ticket won. In Albany, the Hill men were defeated in both houses, in the minor executive offices, and in the constitutional convention. Even the Republicans were dumfounded. Moreover, the momentum gained was kept. As a special deputy attorney-general, Shepard helped to send the notorious Gravesend boss, John Y. McKane, to Sing Sing. The Lexow Committee was appointed to investigate the New York City Police Department. In Brooklyn, Shepard and his fellow reform Democrats resigned from the Brooklyn Young Men's Democratic Club as too much identified with McLaughlin's machine, and organized the Brooklyn Democratic Club to fight the city boss. Bowker, at Shepard's personal request, joined the club immediately. In New York the anti-Tammany fusionists set up the famous Committee of Seventy. The anti-Platt Republicans organized a Committee of Thirty.

In 1894, another opportunity to challenge the Hill machine was seized. In September, the anti-Hill delegations to the Democratic state convention from Kings County and New York County, led by Shepard and Fairchild, were cynically and treacherously denied seats, and then Hill himself was nominated for governor. Promptly, on October 29, in Shepard's New York law office, the reform Democrats set up the "Democratic Party Reform Organization," nominated E. P. Wheeler for governor, and launched a campaign that came to be known as "the conscience movement."[4] Bowker and his friends did everything possible to make the demonstration a success. Shepard was named chairman of the Kings County Democratic party, Peabody chairman of the Kings County General Committee, and Bowker vice-president of the Fifteenth District organization.

Bowker organized the independent voters of his district, arranged for campaign literature, funds, and speakers.[5] His hand is especially evident in the composition of the organization's official declaration. The situation of the Democratic party in New York in 1894 was similar to that of the Republican party in New York in 1879, and it was no accident that Wheeler's opening address closely resembled Bowker's Young Scratcher Address of 1879. "We do this," it read, "in the hope . . . that . . . the success of our movement this year will compel party reorganization, and that it will be the prelude to the triumph of a united Democracy in 1896."[6] Bowker's influence is also unmistakable in the phrasing

[4] For this treatment of the Wheeler campaign see Alexander, *A Political History of the State of New York*, III, 219–20; Smith, *History of the State of New York*, III, 407; Brooklyn *Eagle*, February 24, 1895; Russell Sturgis to R. R. B., November 9, 1894; T. G. Shearman to R. R. B., May 4, 1896.

[5] See G. H. Putnam to R. R. B., October 26, 1894.

[6] October 17, 1894.

of Wheeler's platform, which exactly expressed the political creed to which he had committed the Council for Tariff Reform in 1878, the Society for Political Education in 1880, and *The People's Cause* in 1888.

The Wheeler campaign deserved greater success than it actually achieved. When the election figures were in, it was found that Wheeler had polled only 27,000 votes against Morton's 637,818 and Hill's 517,710. Of course there were comforting explanations, but the result was discouraging to many. "What a pitiful spectacle it is," Russell Sturgis wrote Bowker, "and how unripe are our people for popular government. . . . I don't know when the outlook has been so black." Bowker was particularly indignant at the part played by the Reform Club, which had been led to support Hill. He drafted a stiff letter to the club's president protesting the action of one of the trustees in refusing to let him offer a resolution of censure and charging that three of the club's vice-presidents "were prominent in betraying the Democratic party into its tremendous defeat of this year."[7]

Others, however, were not discouraged. "I believe," Wheeler wrote Bowker in thanking him for his efficient campaign work, "that our protest was useful and hope it may be of permanent value." Certainly the brilliant success of the Fusion Campaign in New York City which defeated Tammany was cause for rejoicing that the civic conscience was aroused. Following this campaign, Bowker accepted election to the Democratic General Committee for Kings County.

In 1895, it was Shepard's turn to lead the reform Democrats. That year the Brooklyn Reform Democrats organized a movement to draft him for mayor of Brooklyn. Shepard had real strength. He had a reputation as a loyal Democrat, and many regarded him as a promising leader of both the state and national party.[8] Bowker eagerly did what he could. He contributed eight hundred dollars to Shepard's campaign fund, secured the support of Schurz, and organized a public demonstration at the Criterion on October 16 which was a great success. At the Shepard rally in the Brooklyn Academy of Music on October 22, he made one of the principal addresses, which was printed as a campaign handbill, and he served as an inspector on election day.[9] Shepard lost, polling 9,510 votes, but at least his candidacy assured the defeat of the Democratic machine. In New York City, however, Tammany

---

[7] Draft, Bowker to Charles E. Fairchild, December 5, 1894. Bowker was finally persuaded not to send the letter.

[8] Robert Baker to R. M. Shepard, August 16, 1895; R. B. Smith, *History of the State of New York*, III, 415.

[9] C. J. Edwards to R. R. B., October, 1895; Henry Rohland to R. R. B., June–September, 1895; G. F. Peabody to R. R. B., October 25, 1895; address of R. R. Bowker, October 22, 1895, printed as campaign flier.

won. Shepard's independence was probably the reason why the Hill managers again excluded his Kings County liberal Democratic faction from the state convention the following year.[10]

In the municipal election of 1897, Bowker accepted appointment to Brooklyn's Committee of One Hundred to promote Seth Low's election on a Fusion ticket, but his business trip to Europe prevented him from taking active part in the campaign which ended in tragedy for the reformers and triumph for Tammany. In the gubernatorial election of the following year, Bowker joined Carl Schurz and Fulton Cutting in supporting the independent state ticket of the Citizens' Union under the fighting slogan, "Neither Platt nor Croker."[11] In 1899 he supported the Fusion campaign to elect judges and a sheriff which secured the co-operation of the Citizens' Union, the City Club, the Republican party, the Independent Labor party, and the Independents. This united effort failed to defeat Tammany, but the failure only increased the determination of Bowker and his friends to accomplish in 1901 what they had failed to do in 1897.

Bowker's Academy of Music address during the Shepard campaign of 1895 provides an interesting illustration of an issue that continued to divide Bowker and his closest friends, Shepard and Peabody: the degree of compromise which a political liberal should make. Bowker had been invited to stump for Shepard as an influential Independent, and it was understood that he would make a bid for the support of Independents in both parties. As the Shepard strategy included a bid for Hill support in the local election, there were Hill men sitting on the platform, and Bowker's sudden and studied attack on Hill filled Shepard and his managers with consternation.

> Rejected by his old allies, he comes now to you with professions of harmony and in mock championship of your rights as Democrats, a ghostly buccaneer sailing under the black flag and seeking to board your ship under a flag of truce. Gentlemen of the Reform organization . . . let his sinking craft meet its pirate's fate, let the dark waters of political oblivion close over him forever, this Jonah and this Judas of Democracy. Of such Democracy, of such non-partisanship, of bosses one and all, we want none. Whatever their name or their party—Hill or Platt, Richard Croker or Jacob

10 *History of the State of New York*, IV, 27.

11 Marvin W. Schlegel. "The Gold Democrats in the Campaign of 1896," unpublished MS (1935) in the possession of the author; Wheeler, *Sixty Years of American Life*, 387; address of E. M. Shepard, October 13, 1898, at Brooklyn Academy of Music (printed by Brooklyn Democratic Campaign Committee); R. S. Haight to R. R. B., November 4, 1898.

Worth, Boss McLaughlin or Boss McKane—out with them, down
with them, away with them all!

This may have been good crusading independency, but his friends
considered it bad politics. Peabody immediately took Bowker to task
for the anti-Hill passage.

> You surely are most fully aware of the give and take in any con-
> certed action such as politics must have,—and the utilization of
> a place on the speakers' list at a great meeting to express your own
> views as to an outside issue did not seem to me quite like you, and I
> resented the assertions of some of those who did not know you, that
> it was. . . . I am only sorry that the result of your Hill interpolation
> was to make all of our men feel that you would not work with
> anyone else,—but must have your own way.[12]

Bowker was so irked by this and other criticisms of his refusal to compromise that he determined to resign from his District Association.
Peabody strongly urged him against this, arguing that it would only
seem to confirm the criticism and that it would be unfair to Bowker
himself and to the principles they were trying to establish. Apparently
Bowker took his friend's advice. It was as well.

Yet in many circles Bowker was trusted precisely because he was
not an "extreme doctrinaire" and could mediate between those who
would not compromise at all and those who would draw no line in
compromise. Free trade was one of these circles. "I know very well that
the violent men are ready to advance sensible steps," Atkinson wrote
Bowker,[13] "but they put up such an obstruction in many instances
that the sensible step cannot be taken. I have never included you yourself among such extreme doctrinaires. I have been one of them. I have
indulged in . . . what I call the 'vituperative' method; and I have
learned better." Bowker's politics may at times have seemed too uncompromising to his friends, but did Shepard and Peabody, following other
tactics, do so much better? It may have been the observation of their
difficulties in seeking to work with the "regulars" that led Bowker to
insist, in 1896, that the Gold Democrat movement should not yield its
leadership to "half-hearted or irresolute counselors" whose compromise
had hitherto invited the defeat of reform movements within the party.[14]

While Bowker was helping to mobilize the liberal Democrats in
New York for a useful show in 1896, the national party was exhibiting

12 Peabody to R. R. B., October 25, December 27, 1895.
13 E. Atkinson to R. R. B., January 11, 1890.
14 R. R. B., memorandum for Peabody, probably August 8, 1896.

disturbing signs of apostasy and schism. The cause was saved in 1892, but lost in 1896 and in 1900.

As the presidential campaign of 1892 began, it was clear to Bowker's circle that there was only one candidate who guaranteed administrative honesty, tariff reform, and unquestionable soundness in financial matters. This was Grover Cleveland, and they determined to secure his nomination and election. Bowker was in Europe when his fellow Democratic liberals organized the "anti-snapper" convention at Syracuse which elected a contesting delegation to the Chicago convention to demonstrate the weakness of Hill and the impressive strength of Cleveland in the state.[15] He was jubilant when Cleveland finally won the nomination on a platform favoring the repeal of the Sherman Silver Purchase Act and denouncing Republican protection in general as fraud and robbery and the McKinley Tariff in particular as "the culminating atrocity of class legislation."

Bowker immediately wrote Cleveland offering to rally the Independent Republicans who had done so much to assure him victory in 1884 and who, in Bowker's opinion, had they only been organized in 1888 might then have saved the day.[16] He pointed out that they might be useful in reaching certain voters leaning to the Republican camp because of their fear of Cleveland's Tammany support and his running mate, and that as amateur politicians they might have a keener sense than "professionals" of how the *people* were actually thinking and what should be said to them. Cleveland replied to Bowker's offer with a warm and appreciative letter,[17] but did not commit himself on the matter of organizing an Independent Republican committee and, in fact, no such organization was undertaken. It is significant in this connection that William C. Whitney, who ran Cleveland's campaign, was so distrustful of the New York Reform Club that he saw to it that none of its members should have official position on the Democratic Campaign Committee.[18] Nevertheless, Bowker joined the Reform Club in working hard and effectively for Cleveland, and helped to bring ninety Brooklyn Mugwumps together for a Cleveland rally addressed by Carl Schurz.[19] Bowker also served on Wheeler's committee to issue a tariff-reform textbook for the campaign.

The tariff reformers rejoiced at Cleveland's election and now

15 J. deF. Baldwin, MS speech; Smith, *History of the State of New York*, III, 376; Reform Club circular, January 1, 1893; Nevins, *Cleveland*, 483–86; Wheeler, *Sixty Years of American Life*, 204–10.

16 R. R. B. to Grover Cleveland, July 4, 1892.

17 Grover Cleveland to R. R. B., July 15, 1892.

18 Wheeler, *Sixty Years of American Life*, 212.

19 New York *Evening Post*, September 19, 1892; C. Schurz to R. R. B., May 6, 1899.

looked forward confidently to the triumph of their long crusade. "We now see the great current flowing irresistably along the channel we so painfully scratched to guide the trickling waters," Shearman wrote Bowker.[20] "The nominal defeat of 1888 brought the glorious victory of 1892." But the "Yorktown" which Wheeler had prophesied in 1890 was not to be. The Wilson tariff reduction bill passed the House, but then in the Senate there occurred what Bowker and his friends always referred to later as "the great betrayal"; eight Democratic senators organized by Gorman of Maryland and including Smith of New Jersey, Brice of Ohio, and Murphy of New York, united to kill the reform features of the bill. Cleveland thought the final measure, with all its six hundred emendations, better than the McKinley tariff, but such a wretched fulfillment of party pledges that he allowed the bill to become a law without his signature. Bowker never forgave the "treachery" of Gorman, Brice, Hill, and the others who "practically betrayed the cause of tariff reform."[21]

The "great betrayal" proved to be not only the end of the long tariff-reform effort, but the end of the faith which many liberals had put in the Democratic party. The Springfield *Republican* feared that the tariff fiasco had already "cost the Democracy its place for years as a majority party, if not the very life of the organization."[22] C. E. Russell was outspoken in urging Bowker to assume leadership in an independent movement.[23] "I suggest to your good judgment whether this is not a good time to begin independent action. You are the man who can best start such a movement." Bowker was ready to start all over again. He chided the Reform Club for giving up the fight for tariff reform, declaring it was an issue "as to which boldness is now if ever needed."[24] He completely agreed with Grover Cleveland and J. G. Carlisle, secretary of the treasury, that the battle was not yet lost.[25] The Democrats, however, were not to have another opportunity to revise the tariff for eighteen years.

The "great betrayal" of liberal tariff-reform hopes in 1894 was only a prelude to the still greater betrayal of liberal sound-money hopes in 1896. The West was in bitter and open revolt against the deflationary policies of the East, and its representatives in the Democratic party now repudiated all the measures that had won for Cleveland and the

20 T. Shearman to R. R. B., January 10, 1893.

21 R. R. B. to Ostrogorski, January 15, 1898.

22 Nevins, *Cleveland*, 584.

23 C. E. Russell to R. R. B., March 10, 1894.

24 R. R. B. to S. Fairchild, December 5, 1894.

25 Nevins, *Cleveland*, 586; Carlisle to E. P. Wheeler, in Wheeler, *Sixty Years of American Life*, 217.

party the loyalty of Bowker and his fellow liberals: the repeal of the Sherman Silver Purchase Act, the veto of a bill to coin the silver seigniorage, the successive bond issues to preserve the gold standard, and federal intervention in the Pullman strike to enforce delivery of the United States mails. The Reform Club launched a great avalanche of educational material to teach the inflationists the error of their ways, but by June of 1896, it was apparent to even the most optimistic Cleveland men that the silver forces would rule the national Democratic convention at Chicago.[26] Indeed, Bryan's great speech made him the master of the convention and its candidate for president on a platform that utterly repudiated the Cleveland administration.

To Bowker and his fellow liberals this was not merely a revolt but a revolution: the Democratic party had been captured by new men for new purposes; the party of Tilden and Cleveland had disappeared in all but name. Peabody expressed a typical reaction when he described the Bryan coup as "unspeakably disappointing and exasperating . . . a stunning blow," and the proposed program as "completely revolutionary and threatening the very continuance of our civilization." Prominent Democrats everywhere promptly denounced the Chicago platform and candidate. New York's leading Democrats bolted in a body: Abram S. Hewitt, Roswell P. Flower, Frederick R. Coudert, W. C. Whitney, and Charles S. Fairchild. The *World* and the *Evening Post* joined in. In Cleveland's cabinet, Secretaries Olney, Herbert, and Morton repudiated Bryan a few days after the Chicago convention closed, while another was known to favor voting with the Republicans.[27]

Bolting was one thing; what to do next was quite a different problem. There were only three courses open to the Gold Democrats: to remain silent, to support McKinley, or to organize a third ticket. Bowker and his fellow Cleveland Democrats in New York were associated together as the Democratic Reform Organization. Anticipating the worst, they held themselves in readiness for joint action following the national convention.[28] Once Bryan was nominated, Bowker's ideas about what should be done were clear. In a memorandum to Peabody he presented his analysis, his suggested strategy, and his faith.[29] The true Democratic party had been betrayed, but it might be that this had finally freed the real Democracy "for the great work of freedom that may come to it with the new century." A third ticket should be organized, and its leadership in New York should be kept in the hands

26 Wheeler, *Sixty Years of American Life*, 252–53; Schlegel MS, "The Gold Democrats in the Campaign of 1896," pp. 14, 15.

27 *Ibid.*, 38.

28 R. A. Widenmann to R. R. B., June 15, July 3, 1896.

29 First page with date and addressee missing, probably written August 8, 1896.

of those who had worked for Wheeler in 1894 and for Shepard in 1895. Candidates should be picked by such men as Peabody to represent the Reform Democrats, Whitney the regulars, and Schurz the Independents, and they might consider either Secretary Carlisle or Sterling Morton. As for the platform, Bowker preferred gold-and-free-trade, but was ready to compromise on the single gold plank. He realized that the electors for such a ticket would not be elected in any state, but hoped that some Republican sound-money candidates might be elected "by distinctively Democratic protest action."

Momentum for a third party quickly developed. Atkinson, who like Bowker held a vision of a reformed Democracy that would play the role of the Republicans in 1856 and eventually lead the country, wired Governor W. E. Russell on July 10 while the latter was still at the Chicago convention to call a third-party rally.[30] Four days later sixteen prominent party leaders in Illinois published the first important Gold Democratic manifesto, and, on the seventeenth, fifty representative Pennsylvania Democrats met in Philadelphia to sign a similar proclamation. On the same day, Bowker, Widenmann, and Baker took the initiative in calling a meeting of the New York Reform Democratic Committee for July 22 at the Reform Club, when the same position was affirmed in a resolution drawn up by Bowker with Wheeler's counsel. Bowker had already taken pains to establish the continuity of the Wheeler organization of 1894 and the Shepard organization of 1895 with the proposed Gold Democrat movement by having their ship emblem registered for the coming elections. He was now appointed to a committee on organization, busied himself mobilizing delegates from his assembly, senatorial, and Congressional districts to the state convention to be held at Syracuse August 31, and was asked by the state committee to attend both the state convention and the national nominating convention in Indianapolis on September 2. Business kept him from the first, but he did attend the latter as an observer and supported the adoption of the official name "National Democratic party," the nomination of John M. Palmer and Simon B. Buckner, and the approval of a platform favoring the gold standard, tariff for revenue only, and civil service reform.

Bowker's heavy Edison duties could hardly be put off during the campaign, but as usual he found many ways of promoting the Gold Democrat cause. He co-ordinated the publicity work of the Reform Club's Sound Currency Committee and the National Democratic party headquarters; he gave editorial attention to many campaign docu-

[30] H. F. Williamson, *Edward Atkinson, the Biography of an American Liberal*, 210.

ments, advised speakers, kept in close touch with Atkinson's "question clubs" in Massachusetts,[31] and worked hard to make a success of the Gold Democrat state convention held in Brooklyn on September 24. On October 26 he journeyed to Boston to speak at the well-publicized National Ratification Rally held in Music Hall, and there pleaded that votes be not thrown away on either "the already defeated Bryan" or "the too triumphant McKinley," but that they be cast "for the men who have the making of the future in their hands." On this point Bowker was eloquent. "The National Democratic party," he assured his audience, "sets itself for the future. In 1896 it is the king of 1900. And the strength which the votes of the Democrats of Massachusetts gives it today is the strength needed when the twentieth century comes to make sure of the Democratic principles, principles that shall rule America when the new era opens. It is for that that the old Democratic party is new born in the shape of the National Democratic organization. Will you stand by it, young Massachusetts?"[32]

Bowker's two most important contributions to the Gold Democrat campaign were writing a series of currency articles for the New York *World* and editing the official campaign textbook of the National Democratic party. It was Joseph Pulitzer's own idea to feature a series of "lessons" on sound economic principles pitched to the twelve-year-old intelligence level and aimed especially at farmers, and he personally asked Bowker to write these. Bowker had to agree that it was important to get the basic truths of economics before the 750,000 buyers of the *World,* and he finally gave in,[33] though the only time he could find for writing the articles was the early morning before starting for the *Publishers' Weekly* and Edison offices.

The series eventually ran to forty-one "lessons," and appeared from September 21 to October 30 under the title "The World's Schoolhouse." Their purpose was to expose the silver heresy and especially to show that free silver would chiefly hurt the poor. Each lesson was clear, brief, compact, and pointed, effectively utilizing such charged phrases as "A boom is always a boomerang," "The silver prophets are fake fortune-tellers," "Free silver would be like cheap whiskey, first a burn in the vitals, then uproarious jimjams, then a wreck." Bowker's knack for getting down to the popular level was telling. "Silver men say this country is so big," he wrote, "that it can stand the strain of free coinage. This is like saying that if a small boy tumbles off a roof it will kill him, but if a big man tumbles off it won't hurt him. The facts are generally the

[31] R. R. B. to W. B. Bynum, September 25, October 2, 1896; G. F. Peabody to R. R. B., September 13, 1896; *Literary News*, September, 1896, pp. 273-79.

[32] Boston *Herald*, etc., October 27, 1896.

[33] G. C. Eggleston to R. R. B., September 5, 1896.

other way. The bigger the man, the harder the hit." The editor in charge thought the series "admirably put and calculated to do much good," and sent Bowker a check which he described as "the highest rate I have ever paid for contributions to the *World*."[34]

Editing the party's official campaign textbook was both more important and more exacting, even though Bowker had the assistance of an experienced journalist and the co-operation of many leading Gold Democrats. Characteristically he was determined to make the compilation "an important confirmative influence on the future of the party . . . not a campaign document in the ordinary sense."[35] In addition to the customary collection of addresses, biographies, and arguments, there were extracts from articles and speeches embodying the liberal interpretation of the history and basic principles of the Democratic party. One of Shepard's best speeches was included, and, on the insistence of Peabody, several chapters from Bowker's *Economics for the People*. By September 25 the five thousand copies of the first edition had been followed by fifteen hundred of the second revised edition, and by early October a third edition of five thousand was issued.

A few Gold Democrats made a vigorous campaign, especially in the border states where the vote was likely to be close, but in general the party suffered from the closeness of the contest. A rumor on election eve that labor was swinging heavily to Bryan led many thousands of Democrats to shift their votes from Palmer to McKinley. Cleveland advised Gold Democrats to support Republican electors in doubtful states; and Palmer declared publicly that he did not consider it "any very great fault" if his hearers voted for McKinley. The result was a pitiful 131,000 votes for Palmer, less than 1 per cent of the total and 10,000 fewer than the Prohibition party polled. Even so, many Gold Democrats were well satisfied. Atkinson claimed it as an acknowledged fact that McKinley had been elected by the Gold Democrats.[36] Wheeler insisted that they had polled enough votes in Indiana, Kentucky, and Maryland to give those states and a majority in the electoral college to McKinley, though others have doubted whether this was true in any state but Kentucky.[37] Certainly a nucleus of "true" Democracy had been preserved for 1900. Leaders like Atkinson were sanguine. "Heretofore," he wrote, "both the old political parties have truckled to the

[34] W. H. Merrill to R. R. B., October 28, 1896.

[35] R. R. B. to E. M. Shepard, Peabody, September 16, 1896; R. R. B. to C. Vey Holman, September 24, 1896.

[36] Atkinson to Lord Farrer, November 23, 1896, in Williamson, *Edward Atkinson*, 212.

[37] Wheeler, *Sixty Years of American Life*, 259; Schlegel, "The Gold Democrats in the Campaign of 1896," p. 46.

silver states; hereafter, the National Democratic party will, like the old Free Soil party, hold the balance of power, and although small in number, they will in a forceful manner control events."

The Gold Democrats had been badly defeated in 1896, but for a short while they were able to enjoy the illusion of having a party that would be a factor in 1900. The executive committee of the national organization decided to maintain its structure of national and local units, set up new units where needed, and undertake a program of publicity. There were several encouraging signs. The spring elections in Michigan and the May primaries in New York showed gains. Carl Schurz offered the party the prospect of becoming "a great political force in the country," and possibly even electing enough members to wield the decisive vote in the next House of Representatives. Cleveland stated that the party split did not represent the wishes of the rank and file. Bowker shared the faith of Schurz and Cleveland. He was convinced that the country needed a permanent third party. Since the Republicans were committed to protectionism and the silver Democrats to an essentially "socialistic" scheme, the National Democratic party was the only organization that could work on true lines; it could "give to many Democrats their true political home and to many Republicans a needed refuge."[38]

Although Bowker and Peabody helped Atkinson edit, finance, and distribute the anti-silver letters he had written for the campaign,[39] and Peabody accepted the chairmanship of the national committee, they saw fewer and fewer encouraging prospects for the new party. The Bryan men remained implacable. In only five of the ten states having state-wide elections in 1897 were Independent tickets presented, and in these the Gold Democrat vote was less than in 1896. The following year, in Maine, the party candidate for governor received only 315 votes. In New York, a tentative move under Shepard to run a Gold Democrat candidate for governor was soon dropped for lack of support.

The new issue of imperialism which the Spanish-American War injected into the presidential campaign of 1900 strengthened Bowker's conviction that a third party was the only consistently liberal way out of the party dilemma. The Bryan Democrats stood for the desirable principles of resistance to imperialism and protectionism, but also for the undesirable principle of inflation. The McKinley Republicans stood for the desirable principle of sound money, but for the undesirable principles of imperialism and protectionism. Shepard and Peabody

38 G. F. Peabody to R. R. B., April 5, 1897; R. R. B. to Peabody, April 24, 1897.
39 Peabody to R. R. B., June 16, 1897; *ibid.*, March 13, 1897; E. Atkinson to R. R. B., December 12, 1898.

tended to believe that imperialism was so much more important an issue than the gold standard that anti-imperialists should work together regardless of currency differences.[40] Bowker, however, emphatically disagreed. In a public letter to Shepard he conceded that the Democratic party's one hope of success was "a rigid insistence upon a single and concentrated campaign of education" against imperialism, but warned that the party would go down to "overwhelming defeat" if it opposed sound money.[41] Since there seemed no chance of wooing Bryan from the silver issue, Bowker concluded that the revival of the National Democratic party was "never more urgent than now," and he indicated an intention to stir it up out of its "innocuous desuetude."

While Bowker sought to revive the National Democratic party with an addition to its 1896 platform of a strong anti-imperialist plank and a plank demanding publicity for corporation affairs, Peabody decided to join a few others in organizing a new third party which would not be related to the Gold Democratic organization or call itself Democratic. Its strategy would be to nominate in each state all the McKinley electors but one, making a vigorous campaign to secure one million votes with which to form the nucleus of a new party, and at the same time give "emphatic notice to McKinley" that his re-election did not mean the endorsement of his imperialistic, protectionist, and anti-civil-service policies. Peabody insisted that it was Bowker's duty to launch this new third party, writing, "I think you are the ideal man to put it through."[42]

Such a party was actually organized, but Bowker did not take a hand in the work, and it is not clear what relation he had to it. His friends Thomas M. Osborne, R. A. Widenmann, Cutting, and Peabody supplied a good deal of the initiative. Preliminary organization meetings were held, the name "National party" adopted, headquarters set up at 141 Broadway, and a national convention called for September 5, at which a strong platform was adopted and nominations were made for president and vice-president.[43] In October the Gold Democrats met in Indianapolis to adopt an address demanding the defeat of Bryan, but saying absolutely nothing about how this was to be done. In the end, McKinley won an overwhelming victory. If this meant anything, it meant that the country approved both imperialism and a high protective tariff.

40 Peabody to R. R. B., February 11, 1900.
41 R. R. B. to E. M. Shepard, printed sheet dated February 5, 1900.
42 Peabody to R. R. B., July 24, July 27, 1900.
43 E. B. Smith to R. R. B., August 20, 1900; R. A. Widenmann to R. R. B., August 23, 28, 1900; see Thomas M. Osborne, "Address before the Convention of the National Party," September 5, 1900, p. 10.

The end of the decade again saw the temporary defeat of the Mugwump leader's hopes. A reform wing had been faithfully kept alive within the New York Democratic party from 1894 to 1896 in order to assure the success of Cleveland, only to have Bryan capture the party; a third party had been created in 1896 and kept alive until 1900 in order to rally a rededicated Democratic party to meet the new century, only to have the party prove itself a fiasco. Reform within the Republican party had failed. Reform within the Democratic party had failed. Reform by organizing a balance-of-power vote by Independents had failed except for a brief session. A third party had failed. When the brave new century dawned, it did not bring a glimpse of the promised land but only a further stretch of the rocky road which Bowker had been traveling.

As American industrial development gradually forced the nation at the end of the century to abandon the isolationism of the preceding eighty years, new problems of foreign relations arose which brought out clearly certain principles that had been latent in Bowker's liberal creed. The first of these problems involved the issue of war and peace. In 1895, Cleveland sought to mediate the boundary dispute between Venezuela and Great Britain. In December, however, when the British minister failed to meet the American position, Cleveland delivered a belligerent message to Congress, as a result of which, "with the suddenness of the last trump," as Bowker put it, "this Christian nation, at this Christmas tide, faces war, and war with our nearest kin." Immediately a wave of jingoism swept the country. Congress was wildly enthusiastic. Henry C. Lodge, Theodore Roosevelt, Chauncey M. Depew, W. C. Whitney, and Andrew D. White publicly applauded. Of twenty-eight governors reached by the *New York World,* twenty-six gave Cleveland their patriotic support. Civil War veterans offered their services. The *New York Sun* carried the headline: "War if Necessary." Other newspapers, including Pulitzer's *World,* Godkin's *Evening Post,* and Bowles' *Springfield Republican,* pointed out the shocking blunder.

Bowker was unable to keep silent. He was bound by many deep friendships to the English people, and he was committed by the liberal creed to international collaboration. He took the unusual step of writing a *Publishers' Weekly* editorial on the subject, which he immediately reprinted at his own expense as a little eight-page pamphlet entitled "Peace Between Kin." It was an imaginary speech that might have been delivered in Congress the day after Cleveland's special message. He pointed out the folly of those "who prate glibly that war will be a blessing; we will annex Canada, free Ireland, invade England, sweep her

A Quartet of New York Independents: *(Top, left)* R. R. Bowker; *(Top, right)* George Foster Peabody; *(Bottom, left)* Everett Pepperrell Wheeler; *(Bottom, right)* Edward Morse Shepard

Two Library Interests: *(Top)* Brooklyn Public Library; *(Bottom)* The Stockbridge Library

commerce from the seas, 'boom' at home, and be cock of the walk among the nations,—By Jingo, we will!" Victorious, he argued, the country would pay a terrific cost; beaten, an incalculable one. "The passion of war," he declared, "is the poison of a people." He did not excuse England. "It will be a blot on England's history," he made clear, "that she has on her part declined to accept and apply the very principle of peaceful arbitration of which she had been a champion and to which her Parliament has given formal and official sanction. But," he argued, "two wrongs do not make a right. Let us not confuse passion with patriotism, Jingoism with justice, hate with honor." On the last page of his little pamphlet, Bowker printed his poem, "A Hymn For English Folk."

The issue of war and peace was presented a second time in the spring of 1898 when the United States stood on the brink of war with Spain. Bowker was in Spain during the critical days before the American declaration of war, and there he had discussed the Cuban crisis with General Woodford, the able American ambassador. As a result of what he then learned, Bowker became completely convinced that Spain would have accepted the "truce of God" which Woodford had arranged, that it had been ready to free Cuba, and that the woe and the waste of war might have been avoided had McKinley not been afraid to tell Congress what it did not want to hear. In Bowker's mind, America had been "betrayed into unneeded war."[44]

Even more than our lighthearted declaration of war, Bowker deplored our readiness to take the road to imperialism. An incident involving our seizure of the Philippines dismayed him. Bowker had visited in Washington just before leaving on his trip around the world, and Mrs. Arnold Hague had quoted a comment by Admiral Dewey. The latter had breakfasted at her house the day before his sailing and had said to her casually, "Mrs. Hague, if Uncle Sam wants me to run over and take Manila before breakfast, I shall be ready."[45] Bowker was convinced that with the growing clamor for Puerto Rico, Guam, and the Philippines, the United States was being betrayed into wrongful expansion. Nothing, indeed, had impressed him so much on his trip around the world that year as the tragic evidences of the West's hungry imperialism and the fact of conqueror and conquered. He sensed that India "was in revolt under her breath," and in one of his poems he warned Britain not to "rule always with the iron hand, nor teach the Christian graces with a blow . . . lest the dumb creep and leaping lay thee low." Farther east he came upon a China being at that very mo-

[44] R. R. B., in New York *Times*, January 28, 1916; to W. Wilson, July 3, 1916.
[45] R. R. B., MS Memoir.

ment partitioned between England, France, Germany, and Russia: "Bear, lion, eagle, watch the gates beneath, eager to paw the prey, in ravenous strife."

Bowker immediately identified himself with the Anti-Imperialist League which was founded in Boston in November, 1898, with such good men as Edward Atkinson, C. F. Adams, Jr., J. G. Carlisle, Grover Cleveland, Andrew Carnegie, and David Starr Jordan. He heartily approved the League's condemnation of imperialism as "a policy of political dishonor, economic folly, and moral delinquency," and he added, for himself, that it was "equally unDemocratic, unRepublican, and unAmerican." He joined in the pamphleteering conducted by such old companions-in-arms as W. G. Sumner, Carl Schurz, and Moorfield Storey. He served on a committee of the New York Reform Club to stimulate public opinion against the new imperialism. On January 22, while the terms of the peace treaty were being debated before the Senate, he and his friends arranged a crowded meeting of protest at the Academy of Music. Charles Francis Adams was invited down from Boston to speak, and Bowker dined with Adams and Carl Schurz to discuss joint efforts in opposition to the expansion policy.[46]

In the spring of 1899, Bowker was one of the first ten persons asked by Edward Atkinson to "suggest, amend, or to suppress if not timely" his prospectus of a new periodical to be called "The Anti-Imperialist." Bowker backed the idea heartily, suggested some practical changes which Atkinson thought "Excellent," and sent along two poems on the subject which Atkinson thought were "the best that I have seen." These were printed in the fourth number of the *Anti-Imperialist*,[47] and express, better than anything else can, Bowker's convictions as to where his country's duty lay.

The True America
Be not thy drum-beats heard around the world.
A mightier mission hath been given thee
Than war or spoils, conquest or colony.
Only for peace be thy great flag unfurled,
In freedom's cause be thy just thunders hurled,
That to all nations thy sure gospel be
In paths of peace to teach men to be free—
The harvest-homed, the peace-pipe's smoke upcurled.
Firm as thy hills, free as thy plains, prove thou
The might of right, in panoply of peace,

46 C. Schurz to R. R. B., January 21, 1899.
47 August 20, 1899.

A Mugwump in the Nineties

That those who toil, free from greed and hate
And armed wrong, reap surely what they plow.
So shalt thou speed the day when war shall cease,
And be of nations greatest of the great.

What America Should Say
to the Philippines

I broke the power of thy tyrant, Spain,
Dashed loose thy chains, and paid thy ransom fee.
Now, like a captive on the slave-mart's block,
Dost thou crouch weeping, trembling, doubting me,
As a new master alien to thy race?
Nay, nay, poor Sister, lift thy head. Take heart.
I traffic not in birthrights. Where I come,
There freedom comes. Be free. Now do thy part.
Learn in Time's school. Be patient. Rule thyself.
So, in the darkened East, the dawn shall clear.

Till then—I wait. From far, I watch and ward.
No ravening wolf will my swift vengeance dare.
Nor dare I other than to make thee free,
Lest with His scourge of woe the Lord, who saves,
Who smites, shall smite again His land redeemed.
The land of Lincoln nevermore holds slaves.

It is a striking characteristic of Bowker's liberalism that he distinguished clearly between unchanging ends and changing means and that he found little difficulty, at the turn of the century, in shifting from the old liberalism with its almost unlimited emphasis on laissez faire to the new liberalism with its emphasis on the public assumption of responsibility for the irresponsibilities of private enterprise. For thirty years he had held on to a formula which enabled him to steer a middle course between the old rugged individualism and the still new socialism. "Laissez-faire," he had said over and over again, "means to let well enough alone, but not to let ill alone."

No one was more aware of the abuses of monopoly and the social injustices which had driven some liberals to adopt the panacea of socialism. Foremost among these evils Bowker listed the fact "that the social increment goes chiefly to the making of colossal private fortunes, which in turn dominate government," the "conscienceless greed" of large corporations, and "the overweening fortunes which have been made and used so unwarrantably." "I am thoroughly an individualist," he once wrote, "but it seems to me that arrogant individualism has much to answer for." It was this line of thought which gradually reconciled him to what was loosely called "the socialized state" as the lesser of evils. This was the state which "does not interfere with individualism, but does regulate and control those affairs in which society and the individual have especial inter-action." "I think we are all socialists in a degree," he wrote Peabody in 1917, "and that the 'socialized state' and the socialized city have come to stay. These I think are the happy mean between individualism . . . and the socialism which would wipe out the individual and make him a puppet of the state."[48] When in the mayoralty campaign of 1917 it became clear that Mitchell's reform ticket could not win, Bowker infinitely preferred the victory of the Socialists under Morris Hillquit to that of Tammany under Hylan.

However, Bowker remained uncompromising where real socialism was concerned. He watched its growth throughout the world and came to believe that the issue between "collectivist socialism and individualist democracy" was the great "world issue in politics," whether in England, France, Germany, Russia, or the United States.[49] He spoke of "the new industrial slavery of state socialism" as a dangerous poison spreading in western Europe. For forty years he consistently spoke and wrote against socialism as a direct denial of the liberal values he cherished. "The government of Lincoln," he wrote in 1907, "meant a democratic republic, not a populistic socialism. . . . The American theory of government is based on individual freedom, the right of an individual to manage his own affairs without interference, unless he interferes with his neighbor. Democracy and socialism are in this sense absolute contraries."[50] "Socialism," he had written in 1900, "is the offer of a social Catholic and infallible church to give peace of mind to the perplexed Protestant willing to surrender his liberty of action to a state Pope called the People. It transfers tyranny from monarchy to democracy. It is the backward swing of the pendulum."[51]

The two means of correcting the abuses of unrestricted laissez faire, and therefore the spread of socialism, in which Bowker came to have the most interest were a liberalized tax structure and public control of public-franchise corporations. In his thinking about taxes, Bowker was much indebted to Henry George. He gave hearty support to the Henry

48 R. R. B. to E. M. Shepard, undated, 1902; R. R. B. to Miss Picton, December 21, 1905; R. R. B. to Dr. G. E. Vincent, July 13, 1907; R. R. B. to E. J. Clapp, November 13, 1917; R. R. B. to G. F. Peabody, November 16, 1917.

49 R. R. B. to Miss Picton, May 17, 1906.

50 R. R. B., "Public Control, Ownership or Operation of Municipal Franchises?" *Municipal Affairs*, December 1897, pp. 605, 630.

51 R. R. B., *The Arts of Life*, 209.

George movement, was once asked to manage the single tax periodical *The Standard*,[52] attended the Henry George dinners, and in 1914 applied for membership in the New York Single Tax League. He argued that George was "the most pronounced individualist after John Stuart Mill and Herbert Spencer," but he also argued that if George had used his wonderful powers to secure the general principle of the social increment instead of concentrating so exclusively on land values, "we might have been much further ahead today in our system of taxation toward a logical and social, not socialistic, method of taxation."[53] In discussions with his friends, he found himself to the left of Wells, Putnam, and Shepard, but to the right of Peabody, Shearman, and Atkinson. For this reason Bowker was often thought of as a "Henry George man," though more accurately as "a limited single-taxer."

Bowker was convinced that the largest incomes were made possible "only by an enforced social co-operation practically in the nature of a social increment"; that the American people were not socialists, but meant to have and should have a large part of that social increment; and that emphasis on the social ownership of the unearned increment was thoroughly compatible with individualism.[54] Therefore Bowker favored taxing the whole amount of the social increment and doing it not only by land taxes, but also by income, inheritance, and corporation taxes. In this he thought he perceived a just principle: the return to the community of a fair share of what comes to the individual from the unearned benefits of social co-operation by tax exemption at the minimum representing normal returns and progressive taxation of returns above normal. His was a somewhat novel view, but Bowker felt it to be such a useful clue that he tried hard to get an adequate hearing for it. He spoke informally on the subject at the December, 1909, meeting of the American Economic Association and developed his thesis in a paper called "The New Taxation," which he offered unsuccessfully over a period of years to the *Review of Reviews,* the *Atlantic Monthly,* the *Review* of the American Economic Association, and the *Independent.*[55] However unorthodox his theory, it was a good example of Bowker's synthesizing mind working on a major social problem.

When it came to tax administration, Bowker had many practical convictions. He believed earnestly in direct taxation "as the one means

[52] T. G. Shearman to R. R. B., August 13, 1889.

[53] R. R. B. to E. M. Shepard, undated letter, probably 1902.

[54] Bowker took active part in the discussions of the American Economic Association on such topics as the rising cost of living and the effect of inheritance and income taxes on the distribution of wealth. See its *Proceedings* for 1909, 1913, 1914, 1916.

[55] R. R. B. to Albert Shaw, March 1, 1910; to Ellery Sedgwick, January 3, March 18, 1914; to D. R. Dewey, March 26, 1915; to Hamilton Holt, February 14, 1916.

by which a self-governing community can look facts in the face, can control public expenditure, and can make sure that every dollar goes where it is meant to go."[56] Therefore he believed that the great work before constructive statesmen was "to build a bridge from our present protective tariff through a tariff for revenue only, toward the better system of direct taxation." He believed in progressive tax rates. He believed that one of the most important reforms of the future would be the abolition of taxes on personal property, "which are notoriously difficult to collect fairly and justly and thus become extremely unequal burdens."[57]

Finally, he believed that "in place of our crooked and complicated tax system, we need to look forward to a method of taxation which shall be modern, simple, just, and comprehensive." With this in mind, he proposed to the Secretary of the Treasury in 1915, W. G. McAdoo, that he and possibly the President encourage the American Economic Association to appoint a commission on co-ordination, efficiency, and economy in taxation, "with the purpose of submitting a plan or alternative plans which would result in the maximum of needed revenue with the minimum of cost, complexity, and annoyance in collection."[58] Bowker had pressed a similar suggestion on President Cleveland in 1892, urging him to appoint competent specialists "to go thoroughly into our national resources, conditions, etc., and develop a permanent plan," including a budget and "a systematic scheme of taxation."[59] This time the suggestion was taken up, and the following year the Association appointed a committee on Co-ordination in Taxation with Bowker as chairman. The committee made a preliminary report in 1917 and a final report two years later which was reprinted in a slightly revised form as a separate pamphlet by the Princeton University Press.

The second program to prevent socialism which most interested Bowker was public control, without operation, of public-franchise corporations. To preserve political freedom, he insisted, business and politics should be kept as far apart as possible: the public should not undertake what private enterprise can do as well, and the function of the municipality should be limited at the point where democracy becomes socialism.

> Now the first practical result ... of ... socialism ... will be to put the posts of honor in government into the hands of trained

56 R. R. B., "The Political Relations of Tariff Reform," address of November 11, 1885.

57 R. R. B., typescript memo on taxation, May 25, 1895.

58 R. R. B. to Hon. W. G. McAdoo, December 16, 1915.

59 R. R. B. to Grover Cleveland, July 4, 1892.

business executives of large ability who are capable of handling large business interests, and I do not think that experience has shown that these men should also have given to them the trust of government. . . . When we cross the dividing line and mix politics with business, and business with politics, we are introducing the worst political poison into the community."[60]

It was a creditable record which this veteran Mugwump left behind him in the nineties. Although he did not hold public office or lend his name to a reform movement, he did one of the next best things in keeping himself available at all times to help with the hard work of planning, organizing, and pamphleteering which was necessary to get things done. Worthington C. Ford, a fellow crusader who shared in many of these battles of the nineties and who knew him intimately, described Bowker's role during these years as an indispensable one:

> In all this Bowker was a directing force. He was usually on the leading committees and was regarded as a wise counsellor. Quietly receptive of suggestion from others, he would allow the discussion to continue until he as quickly gave his opinion, eminently practical in its bearing. For he was a fine organizer and judge of the ability of other men, of the part each one could play in the program. Looking back, after a half century, we seem often to have been tilting at windmills; . . . [yet] there were the joy of conflict, the question of conscience, the winning or losing points and the gathering of young and earnest workers. . . .

> For this kind of service, self-sacrificing, disappointing in successes though measuring slow advance in educating public opinion, and wholly disinterested, Bowker was an ideal colleague. He was incorruptible, convinced of the right of the cause he supported and intelligent on the limits of possibility in urging changes. His patience was inexhaustible and it was sorely tried, as there was ever present the too eager and over anxious worker, as well as that indestructible fringe of cranks that is attached to any movement. His catholicity and generous sympathies took him far. . . . he had an unusual capacity for making friends and creating zealous workers in the cause, and, as he never sought benefit to himself, he offered a wholesome example to the reformers, so liable to win a success and to throw it away in disputing the manner of holding it.[61]

[60] R. R. B., "Public Control of Corporations," *Municipal Affairs*, February 27, 1903, pp. 843–44.

[61] Worthington C. Ford, in a tribute to R. R. B. in *Library Journal*, December 1, 1933, Part II.

XVII

Promoting New York's
Civic Renaissance

Bowker and his friends were intensely alive to the ground swell of civic pride and awakened responsibility that produced at the end of the century what came to be known as New York's "civic renaissance." A growing concern with the new problems and opportunities of American urban life in general was here intensified by the formation of "Greater New York" under a new charter. An aroused civic conscience which rose up to overcome Tammany was part of the story. Godkin declared the Fusion victory of 1894 "likely to prove the harbinger of a great change for the better in all the great cities of the continent, [which] will end in wiping out what has been for fifty years the greatest stain on democratic government—the gross corruption of our municipalities."[1] Political reform, however, was only part of the story. Equally important was public-spirited support of the cultural and welfare services of the modern city. Bowker's contributions were notable. He helped to give the city a new liberal newspaper of real distinction; he made his mark in constructive service for the City College, the Brooklyn Institute of Arts and Sciences, the Brooklyn Public Library and the University Settlement, meanwhile entering vigorously into the discussion of the municipal-franchise problem.

The new municipal consciousness was partly reflected in new civic organizations. In 1888, Bowker and his friends had organized the New York Reform Club. In 1890 the People's Municipal League was formed to spread the proposition that municipal government was business and not politics. In the fall of 1892, Bowker helped to organize the City Club to give to civic reform efforts permanency of policy, a head-

1 E. L. Godkin, Introduction to *The Triumph of Reform* (New York, 1895).

quarters, and a continuing organization which would parallel the Tammany district associations with a network of "Good Government Clubs."[2] In 1896 the Reform Club created a new Committee on Municipal Administration which sponsored a research staff, a special library, public lectures, and a new quarterly, *Municipal Affairs*.[3] In 1897 the Citizens Union was launched as a permanent municipal reform party,[4] and Bowker helped to found the Association for the Public Control of Franchises and the Brooklyn National Civic Club.

Bowker supported these organizations as fully as his extremely busy program would allow. Of the Reform Club he was a director, vice-president, and chairman of numerous committees. He served as vice-president of the National Civic Club of Brooklyn during 1899 and 1900 and on the Advisory Council of the National Civic Federation. In 1896 he was appointed to a City Club committee to organize a course of lectures on municipal education and a little later he was appointed chairman of its Franchise Committee. In 1899 he was elected a member of the City Club's Council and almost immediately its vice-president; in June, 1900, he was made chairman of the Council to succeed Nicholas Murray Butler, and in 1902 a trustee. He served on several committees of the Citizens' Union, and on a number of committees co-ordinating the work of the Citizens' Union, the City Club, and the Reform Club. In fact, he tried to get the City Club and the Reform Club to merge for their mutual advantage,[5] and likewise the City Club and the Citizens' Union. In later years he helped to underwrite the Civic Forum and followed with keen interest the work of the Town Hall Club.

In 1897, Bowker was appointed by Mayor Strong to an advisory committee to promote the cultivation of vacant lots by the unemployed. In 1901 he was appointed to the executive committee of a Committee of 250 to promote the enactment of the new city charter. He took his turn in accepting speaking engagements. Now it was participation with Jacob Riis and Judge White in a series of talks at the Brooklyn Y.M.C.A. on "Christian Sociology and Civil Government";[6] again it was participation with Waring, Wingate, and Shaw on a program to discuss "the Street and Park System of New York." In December, 1896, he gave at Columbia College the fourth of the City Lectures sponsored by the City Club on "The City's Traffic," later published. The piece was crammed with useful statistics, comparisons with European practices, a

2 Putnam, *Memories of a Publisher*, 333–39; Wheeler, *Sixty Years of American Life*, 338.

3 Reform Club, printed circulars, January 11, March 9, 1897.

4 Putnam, *Memories of a Publisher*, 339–44.

5 R. R. B. to J. W. Pryor, July 9, 1903.

6 See *Library Journal*, March, 1895, p. 95.

thorough analysis of administrative problems, and the moral note characteristic of all Bowker's thinking.

Bowker's liberal concern with education in general, plus his own natural loyalties as an alumnus and a New Yorker, combined to keep him an active supporter of his alma mater from the year he received his diploma. He wrote to students on the question of discipline in the classroom and helped to recruit new members of the faculty.[7] He took the initiative in defending the college from public attacks on free higher education.[8] He discussed the need of keeping the College abreast of new developments in American higher education and of raising admission requirements.[9] He contributed frequently to the Graduates' Association, of which he was a mainstay, and the Associate Alumni, of which he served on the executive committee. He kept in close touch with the activities of his fraternity, spoke in a symposium of its united chapters at Hartford along with Phillips Brooks and Edward Everett Hale, and wrote a lead article for its new publication.[10]

When in 1890 the City College undertook a major program of reorganization and modernization, Bowker was in the thick of it along with Wheeler and Shepard. He was appointed to a committee of the Associate Alumni on the progress of the College and drew up an important report which examined courses, curriculum, teaching, library, and discipline.[11] The following year he gladly served on a small alumni committee to spearhead a drive for a new site and a new building, then cheerfully served on a committee to win over the mayor and the legislature, and finally worked hard for the resulting bill by organizing pressure behind the mayor, the comptroller, and members of the Assembly by attending more hearings, getting out petitions, answering criticisms, writing several articles which helped to rally public opinion, and conferring on architectural design.[12]

7 A. G. Compton to R. R. B., June 24, 1876; W. G. Sumner to R. R. B., July 10, 1876; R. R. B. to J. B. McMaster, June 26, 1883.

8 A. G. Compton to R. R. B., November 10, 1877; C. H. Kitchel to R. R. B., February 8, 1878; "Justice to the Free College," *Tribune*, March 9, 1878; "The City College," New York *Evening Post*, January 8, 1879.

9 A. Werner to R. R. B., October 24, 1881, January 18, 1887, July 20, 1889; see G. H. Crawford to R. R. B., January 7, 1888.

10 R. R. B. to E. P. Wheeler, January 20, March 31, 1879; Amherst chapter, A.D.P., to R. R. B., October 7, 1876; R. R. B., "The Star and Crescent," *The Star and Crescent*, May, 1889, pp. 4–5.

11 Committee on the Progress of the College, Report, June 19, 1890.

12 A. G. Compton to R. R. B., December 12, 1891; R. R. B., "The College of the City of New York," *University Magazine*, November, 1892, pp. 358–67; December, 1892, pp. 507–15; January, 1893, pp. 70–82; A. G. Compton to R. R. B., January 30, 1893; *ibid.*, letters from January 30, 1893–June, 1896; R. R. B., "New Site for the City College," letter to Hon. Asbel P. Fitch in the New York *Times*, March 4, 1894; Wheeler, *Sixty Years of American Life*, 356.

These efforts were successful. In 1895, with the help of Mayor Strong's reform administration, the legislature was induced to pass a bill authorizing the purchase of new grounds and the erection of new buildings. A magnificent site was selected on St. Nicholas Heights south of 139th Street, and English Collegiate Gothic was chosen for the architecture. The program was obstructed under Mayor van Wyck's Tammany rule, but finally in September, 1903, the cornerstone of the new building was laid. Two years later the transfer of classes from the old site was begun, and by the fall of 1906 the entire academic department was accommodated in the handsome new quarters. To commemorate the occasion, the Associate Alumni voted to publish a memorial volume which Bowker helped to edit with three others, and to which he contributed a long essay himself.[13] In addition to these larger services, Bowker kept a benevolent eye on the College library, became a friend and counsellor of its librarians, and served on a number of special committees.[14]

In 1902, Bowker was asked to accept the presidency of his alma mater. President Webb had just resigned, and several prominent alumni thought that Bowker would make a fine successor. Wheeler, at their head, was particularly insistent:

> Naturally men are looking for a President, and our thoughts naturally turn to you. Would you accept? It is an office of great usefulness, and would, I should think, be congenial to you. . . . I am sure you would make a great success, and render a most important service to the City—one which would be of more permanent value than any that a Mayor can render. You have many qualifications for this position that would be hard to find in anyone else. You have always been successful in dealing with men, and that, after all, is the first qualification in a college President. You have all the qualifications and literary taste required, and you would bring an element of friendliness and sympathy with the students in your dealings with them that it not common, to say the least.[15]

The idea did very definitely appeal to Bowker. He had always been interested in educational administration, and his article, "The College of Today," written in 1884 for the *Princeton Review,* and the chapter

[13] R. R. B., "The College of the Past," in Mosenthal and Horne, *The City College,* 3–63.

[14] E.g., on the Special Committee of Seven to get more favorable status from the Board of Regents, 1902; on the Committee on Political Economy, 1907, etc.

[15] E. P. Wheeler to R. R. B., October 15, November 14, 1902; R. R .B. to E. P. Wheeler, October 21, 23, November 17, 1902; S. W. Rudy, *The College of the City of New York: A History,* 242–43.

"Of Education," in his recent *Arts of Life* showed how thoughtfully he had pondered educational trends. But Bowker wished leisure to finish writing postponed for many years, and his eyesight was so poor that, as he put it, he would not be able to tell a senior from a sophomore, and so he declined the suggestion. He was very gratified when John H. Finley accepted the office.[16]

Bowker's loyalty to the City College and his own thoroughgoing liberalism were again demonstrated in 1912 when a movement developed in his national fraternity to deprive the City College chapter of its charter because of the increasing proportion of Jewish students in the student body. Along with Shepard, Wheeler, Nelson Spencer, and others, Bowker indignantly denounced this proposal as a deplorable outbreak of "Judenhetze, significant of a snobbishness quite unworthy of a body of American scholars," and "a blot on the escutcheon" of the fraternity. Over against this anti-Semitic prejudice, Bowker asserted that "it was greatly to our credit that the schools, colleges, and universities of New York are doing so much for this new class of citizens . . . who are now coming to our shores so avid for education."[17] When the charter was revoked, Bowker characteristically hoped that the move to continue the chapter as a separate organization would not add just one more Greek-letter secret fraternity of local character and emphasis on getting "a clubable set," but would constitute "a great opportunity for leadership in the college world . . . by drafting and making public a covenant which would be a clarion call to young men of high ideals." In the end the Manhattan chapter was maintained as a separate organization under a new constitution and covenant prepared by Bowker, Eurich, and Spencer. Bowker always took special pride in the social role of his alma mater and the civic leadership of its alumni. "I have always been glad to count myself a graduate of City College," he wrote in 1899, "because there the rich and the poor did meet together, particularly in my own time, with very happy results."

At the same time that he was promoting the rehabilitation of City College, Bowker became associated with the Brooklyn Institute of Arts and Sciences. Already in 1889 he had served on one of its committees to organize a Department of Political and Economic Science which conducted courses of lectures, but his formal relation began in 1890. In that year the Washington Street headquarters of the Institute was destroyed by fire and a general reorganization seemed appropriate. Bowker became one of the new incorporators as well as a life member, was

16 R. R. B. to President John Finley, May 9, 1903.
17 R. R. B. to E. P. Wheeler, June 18, 1912; to N. M. Butler, November 12, 1912; to Dr. L. Perry, September 2, 1932.

elected to the board of trustees, and retained all of these three offices throughout the decade. The Institute had an excellent director in Franklin W. Hooper, and Bowker became his close personal friend and confidant, frequently counseling with him concerning money-raising, programs, and appointments. It was an exacting responsibility. In addition to the weekly meetings of the executive committee, the monthly meetings of the library committee of which he took his turn as chairman, and the board of trustees, there were frequent lectures and ceremonies at which Bowker's presence was expected. It was, indeed, not only exacting but frequently uphill work, for not all the trustees put work first and social prestige second.[18]

Bowker heartily relished his work for the Institute. It was a perfect embodiment of his conception of civic initiative in a democracy: a focus of broad educational service organized, financed, and administered by private individuals. The program which he helped Hooper inaugurate was an ambitious one. At the bottom of it was a membership campaign which brought in 312 new members in 1890, 632 in 1891, and 940 in 1892. The lecture committee was always busy. In 1894 it invited such speakers as William Dean Howells, Thomas Bailey Aldrich, Charles Dudley Warner, Rudyard Kipling, Mrs. Julia W. Howe, Mrs. Frances Hodgson Burnett, and Mark Twain, and, Bowker appropriately planned the topics for each.[19] The most important feature of the program, however, was the construction of a new museum building, planned to be the finest in America. In September, 1895, work was commenced, in 1897 the first unit was dedicated, and in 1900 the second. Bowker pored over architect's drawings and plans. The best example of his meticulous interest was the exhaustive pains he took in helping to select the proper names to be inscribed on the Graeco-Roman façade of the museum. For this purpose he read carefully his Plutarch, Mommsen, and Liddell, and he consulted the classical scholars at Harvard, the Harvard Law School, Cornell, Yale, Brooklyn Polytechnic, and many others.[20] When the museum was well under way, Bowker cordially supported the Institute's plans to develop a Botanical Garden and Arboretum, a series of Brighton Beach concerts, and a children's museum.

In the spring of 1896, Bowker participated in a movement to launch a new liberal newspaper which involved him in the reorganization of the New York *Times* and brought him an opportunity to become its

18 See Hooper to R. R. B., December 9, 1897.
19 Hooper to R. R. B., June 21, 28, 1894.
20 R. R. B. to Hooper, February 15, 1896.

editor. A number of people had become interested in setting up a new morning paper for the city which would espouse the principles of the Reform Democrats and Independents. Informal discussions of the subject were held at the City Club.[21] A printed draft of a circular outlining editorial policies and a plan of financial management was passed around among Bowker's friends in February, which bears every mark of his own composition. By the end of that month, Spencer Trask forwarded to Bowker and E. L. Godkin a prospectus prepared by Schurz and Kelly which closely followed the first one outlined by Bowker.

At this very moment the New York *Times* was forced into receivership. The paper was a decrepit, losing proposition, running behind $1,000 a day, and having a circulation of only 18,900.[22] A committee chaired by Spencer Trask was now appointed from the stockholders of the New York Times Publishing Company to plan a sorely needed reorganization. Trask found that the bookkeeping of the Jones administration was so obscure that he asked Bowker to undertake an audit, which he did promptly. Adolph Ochs later told Bowker that this plan of audit was his only chart for two years after his purchase of the paper.[23] In April, Trask wrote Bowker that "somebody with discretion and judgment should superintend the payment of the moneys" for the account of the *Times,* and asked whether he could "give a little time to its affairs with full authority." It seems likely that the two projects of launching a new journal and reorganizing the *Times* were now merged. The director of the University Settlement Society wrote Bowker in May asking the news regarding "our modern Newspaper," saying he would "look forward with great expectancy to the work of such a journal," and sincerely trusting that "the present opportunity to buy the *Times* and 'snatch the day' will not be lost."

Almost every newspaperman of any standing was given the opportunity of accepting the management and the responsibility of the reorganized New York *Times*. Bowker was one of these and found the offer a real temptation; but since he had not brought the Edison Company to the thoroughness of organization which he had planned and since he felt that he could neither give up the Edison Company nor run the two enterprises together, he declined the offer.[24] Trask wrote his regrets at this decision,[25] since it looked as though a rival faction of stockholders might succeed in consolidating the *Times* with the New

21 J. B. Reynolds to R. R. B., May 7, 1896.
22 O. G. Villard, in the *Nation*, August 31, 1921.
23 S. Trask to R. R. B., March 10, 1896; R. R. B., memoranda for Trask, March 12, 19, 1896; G. F. Peabody to R. R. B., no date; R. R. B., MS Memoir.
24 E. Davis, *History of the New York Times*, 178–86; R. R. B., MS Memoir.
25 S. Trask to R. R. B., April 20, 1896.

York *Recorder* and turn the paper over, "Oh horrors—to the wildest Republicanism and high tariff." Trask's fears were not realized. The rival plan was frustrated by the appointment of Alfred Ely, one of the original Mugwump committee, as a friendly receiver, and by the acceptance of the management offer by a loyal Cleveland man, A. S. Ochs. Ochs gratified Bowker and his friends by immediately committing the paper to sound money, tariff reform, administrative reform,[26] and the Gold Democrats.

A few years later Bowker half-regretted his decision not to manage the *Times*. After he had resigned from the Edison Company in protest against its sale to the Whitney-Brady interests, he wrote Peabody that he certainly would have seized the *Times* opportunity had he had the "slightest supposition" of the fate of the company. And, he added, since Ochs had given his support to McKinley in 1900, this "might have resulted in better editorial inspiration according to your and my ways of thinking."[27] Bowker always felt that he "could have made a good paper," but he gladly conceded that he could not have accomplished Ochs' result at the business end and that, indeed, Ochs proved himself a financial and journalistic genius. The incident is an interesting point in Bowker's career. Never did he come closer to a post which might have united all his talents into one single major effort.

The problem that most exercised Bowker in the course of New York's "civic renaissance" was the problem whether and how municipalities should control their public-franchise corporations. Prior to 1890, comparatively few persons had appreciated the great importance of the franchises which were being given away by city authorities in perpetuity and for an infinitesimal compensation. Those few who pointed out the folly of such a course and who argued in favor of municipal ownership were called theorists and dreamers; the franchise problem was declared an academic one, and very little was written on the subject. During the nineties, however, as the value of public franchises constantly increased, the subject became a burning one. People began asking whether the methods of granting rights to use public property, the compensation exacted, and the restrictions imposed had been such as to preserve and protect the rights of the public. The feeling had grown in some quarters that franchises should not be granted to private companies at all, but that the city itself should construct and operate its system of water supply, its gas and electric-lighting plants, its street railways, and its telephones.

[26] Elmer Davis, *History of the New York Times*, xxii.
[27] R. R. B. to Peabody, September 19, 1901.

It was natural that Bowker should be intensely interested in this problem. For years he had been a pioneer in educating public opinion to a sense of civic responsibility in this general area. Now, as the general manager of a public-franchise corporation that was also the largest electric supply house in the world, he enjoyed an inside approach to the problems concerned. The problem of combining the efficiencies to be gained in the business field from centralization with the freedoms to be found in the political world only from decentralization occupied much of his attention. On his trips abroad he took every opportunity to secure information concerning the way foreign countries were solving this problem, requesting data particularly from his acquaintances among public-services managers such as Emil Rathenau of the Berlin Electricity works and E. Thurnauer of the Paris Gas Company, and studying the English experience with particular care.[28]

There were several ways in which Bowker worked for this new cause. He encouraged his friends to organize the Association for the Public Control of Franchises in 1897.[29] He induced the City Club to appoint a franchise committee and immediately became its hard-working chairman. He helped the Reform Club and the Citizens' Union with meetings and declarations. He repeatedly joined in civic demonstrations to check the franchise acquisitions of the Metropolitan Traction Company, serving as a vice-president of one mass meeting sponsored by the People's Institute.[30] He served on a joint committee of the Citizens' Union, the City Club, and the Reform Club to suggest amendments on public-franchise corporations to the City Charter Commission.[31]

Bowker's most important contributions were to the literature on the subject. The first was a thorough, painstaking study entitled "Public Control, Ownership, or Operation of Municipal Franchises?" It appeared in the December issue of *Municipal Affairs* for 1897. After a careful analysis of the problem and an authoritative, up-to-date, twelve-page summary of public-service programs in the major cities of Europe, he offered four general principles that should underlie a solution: that social increment belonged to the people; that a municipality was equally a big business and a body politic; that the public was best served by consolidation rather than competition where public services were con-

28 R. R. B., "Public Control of Corporations," *Municipal Affairs*, February 27, 1903, p. 843.

29 *Tribune*, May 10, 1897; M. M. Miller to R. R. B., May 17, 1897; New York *Journal*, May 12, 1897.

30 City Club, printed circular, April, 1900; People's Institute to R. R. B., April 7, 1899.

31 R. F. Cutting to R. R. B., May 2, 1899.

cerned; and that municipalization and socialism were "political poison" for many general and specific reasons which he carefully detailed. Bowker's own solution was a compromise between outright municipalization, on the one hand, and unlimited private appropriation of the social increment on the other. This meant a policy of control and often ownership, but rarely operation of public-service corporations. He insisted:

> The modern city should own and control its streets, including, as far as possible, both sub-soil and surface facilities of distribution; should itself provide sewerage and water supply, but leave to private companies the operation of industries which involve manufacture or complex administration. The city should receive adequate rent for the use of its street facilities, should obtain for the people the social increment by limitations of profit or price, and should give to the private companies every economic advantage of tenure, centralization, etc., possible to a municipalized industry. . . . Under these conditions the public should get the surest and best service at the lowest price, and the few advantages of a municipalized industry with the many advantages of a privately managed industry.

Bowker frequently recommended such further ways of protecting the public interest as limiting the duration of franchises, enforcing publicity of accounts, preventing overcapitalization, imposing a limit on earnings, and providing a competent system of inspection by offering salaries that would attract experts.

Bowker's second contribution to the literature was the fine report of his City Club franchise committee. He organized an exhaustive investigation of the transportation, electric, and gas companies: the origin and legal history of their franchises and particularly any use of corrupt methods in their private or municipal management. Keeping a small staff of researchers busy, he was able to prepare a draft of the final report late in August, 1901, in time for use in the mayoralty campaign of that year.[32] A third contribution was made in the spring of 1899 when Bowker's well-known interest in the subject prompted Gustavus Myers to seek his aid in publishing a manuscript on New York franchises. Myers' facts were startling to say the least.[33] Bowker made several thoughtful suggestions on the text which led to an elaboration and rearrangement of it, and then saw that the Reform Club Committee on

[32] R. R. B. to B. W. Holt, May 20, 1899; "Memorandum on Franchise Investigation," 1899; B. W. Holt to R. R. B., November 9, 15, 1899; R. R. B. to Clarence Deming, November–December, 1899; see R. R. B. to E. W. Bemis, from October, 1900, to June, 1901; R. R. B. to R. F. Cutting, September 5, 1901.

[33] R. F. Cutting to R. R. B., May 2, 1899.

City Affairs sponsored it. The article finally appeared in the March, 1900, issue of *Municipal Affairs* as "The History of Public Franchises in New York City," and was immediately reprinted in a separate edition. Myers was very grateful for Bowker's help.

It was precisely while Bowker was thus studying and writing about the general problem of municipal-franchise control that he was personally engaged in one of the bitterest fights of his life to keep Tammany from taking over the public-franchise corporation nearest and dearest to him, the Edison Electric Illuminating Company of New York of which he was the first vice-president.[34] This first-hand experience with the methods and consequences of political seizure of these corporations provided the basis for his most dramatic and stirring contribution to the subject. This was his article, "The Piracy of Public Franchises," which first appeared in the *Atlantic Monthly* in October, 1901, and was immediately reprinted in *Municipal Affairs*. In letters to the former Edison directors, Bowker declared this his purpose was

> To aid in bringing about, not a municipalization of industries, in which I do not believe, for that seems to me a step towards socialism, but such limitation and control of franchise corporations as will safeguard the interests of the public while permitting to private capital full opportunity of reasonable return.

The article was typical of Bowker's journalism at its best; the selection of an outstanding current public problem, a completely clear analysis utilizing historical perspective and bristling with facts secured by painstaking research, a carefully considered, constructive solution, and a final appeal to moral idealism. Hamilton Holt called the article "fearless and frank" and insisted that Bowker write a similar one for the *Independent*. The editor of the *Engineering Magazine* pronounced it "priceless to men who are determined to do something to better municipal conditions in the United States," and it was significantly mentioned at the National Convention on Municipal Ownership and Public Franchises in 1903.[35]

Bowker made several further contributions to the franchise discussion. In 1903, the Reform Club's Committee on City Affairs called a pioneer convention on the subject, which drew representatives from every section of the United States, Canada, and a few foreign cities, and Bowker opened one of its discussions with a paper on "Public Control

---

34 See Chapter XIX.

35 H. Holt to R. R. B., November 2, 1901; John R. Dunlap to R. R. B., January 21, 1902; J. DeW. Warner, "Municipal Operation Needed to Correlate Local Franchises," *Municipal Affairs*, Winter, 1902–1903, p. 516.

of Corporations."[36] In 1904 he gave an address before the People's Institute on "Public Franchises: Their Centralization and their Control," and in 1907 before Chautauqua on "Corporations and Social Unrest." Bowker had prepared a memorandum for the investigation which Charles Evans Hughes undertook of the public utilities in New York City in 1905. When Hughes, as governor, favored a bill to provide regulation and control of public-service corporations by public-service commissions, Bowker gave vigorous support in a public letter which presented a striking review of the Edison sale to the Whitney interests.[37] This letter received considerable publicity. The *Evening Post* and the *Evening Telegram* gave it prominence, the *Herald* not only printed long extracts but sent a reporter to interview Bowker for an additional story, the *World* wrote a violent editorial on the basis of his "particularly pertinent exposure," and his friends sent enthusiastic letters of appreciation.[38]

Bowker never lost his early concern with urban housing problems or his interest in the many social services which alert citizens were organizing to alleviate the evils of urban society. It was part of the humanitarianism that was vital to his liberal creed. In April, 1884, *Harper's Magazine* printed his splendid essay, "Workingmen's Homes," which described the London work of Octavia Hill, George Peabody, and Sir Sydney H. Waterlow, the Brooklyn program of Alfred T. White, the developments of the New York Improved Dwellings Association, Philadelphia experiments, and the work of "building associations." He became an active member of the Sanitary Protective League. He also became interested in the Industrial Christian Alliance of which his friend Milbury was secretary, and with whom he co-operated in an investigation of lodging-house problems; in the East Side Co-operative House Owning Association in which Wheeler was active and in which Bowker held stock until 1917; and in the City and Suburban Homes Company, whose president was his friend E. R. L. Gould and in which Bowker held stock during the rest of his life. He sketched out a series of articles for *Harper's Weekly* on the history and activities of such charitable enterprises as the Loan Relief Association, the Charity Organization Bureau, the Children's Aid Society, the Fresh Air Fund, the

[36] *Municipal Affairs*, February 27, 1903, pp. 509–10.

[37] R. R. B. to C. E. Hughes, April 19, 1907; New York *Evening Post*, April 24, 1907.

[38] "Ammunition for Hughes," New York *Evening Post*, April 24, 1907; "Says Jobbery Made Possible Lighting Trust," New York *Evening Telegram*, April 25, 1907; "Public Paid for Financial Juggle," New York *Herald*, April 28, 1907; "Strong Arm Finance," New York *Herald*, April, 1907; letters from C. E. Hughes, H. C. Wright, O. G. Bonnell, John R. Dunlap, F. W. Hooper, A. W. Milbury, 1907.

Prison Society, the immigrant societies, the hospital and ambulance services, the soup and station houses. As a result of his visit to London in 1887, he prepared a manuscript on "Social Helps and Charities of London." In the March, 1887, issue of *Literary News* he told the remarkable story of how an 1870 magazine serial by Edward E. Hale had inspired a dozen different clusters of social-service clubs from coast to coast.[39]

Bowker's active interest in social work is best illustrated by his energetic association from 1891 on with the University Settlement Society. Inspiration for the social-settlement idea had come largely from the life of Arnold Toynbee in London, whose example led to the founding in 1885 of Toynbee Hall in Whitechapel. Bowker visited this pioneer center in 1887 and wrote an article about it for the *Century Magazine*[40] on his observations, which gave many Americans their first introduction to this significant social experiment. But he was only one of a small group of Americans deeply impressed by its example. In 1886, Stanton Coit founded the Neighborhood Guild in the slum region of New York; in 1889, Jane Addams opened Hull House in Chicago and Dr. Jane E. Robbins the College Settlement in New York; in 1891, R. A. Woods founded Andover House in Boston, and in New York the East Side House was incorporated under the leadership of E. P. Wheeler, who had visited Toynbee Hall in 1889. In 1893, Lillian Wald established her Henry Street Settlement with its visiting nurses. By 1896 there were fourteen settlement houses in New York City and twenty in the country.[41]

In 1891, the pioneering Neighborhood Guild was reorganized as the University Settlement, and Bowker was elected to its council with Professor A. G. Compton to represent the City College. He took his responsibilities very seriously. He was immediately requested to undertake, with E. C. Bernheim, a search for enlarged quarters which resulted in the rental of the rather extraordinary building at 26 Delancey Street. When, in 1895, the Settlement had clearly outgrown these rented quarters, Bowker led the council in undertaking the purchase of new property and the design of a new center. He was appointed chairman of the building committee and once more shouldered his responsibilities with great earnestness. His own preference was for a series of small buildings which should have a homey appearance rather than one institutional

[39] R. R. B., "What a Book Has Done: 'Ten Times Ten' and Its Author."

[40] "Toynbee Hall, London, an Interesting Social Experiment," *Century Magazine*, May, 1887.

[41] "Social Settlement," *Encyclopedia of the Social Sciences;* E. P. Wheeler, printed appeal for funds for East Side House, November 11, 1896; City College *Quarterly*, April, 1925, pp. 108–10.

building, and his alternative recommendation was the organization of an Industrial Dwellings Building Company in line with the report of the Tenement House Commission.[42] In the end, considerations of economy overruled Bowker's novel suggestions. Funds were soon raised, a lot purchased on the corner of Eldridge and Rivington Streets, and the architectural services of Howells and Stokes secured by Bowker without pay. Between January and June, 1895, he pitched with zest into the intricate problems of plans and estimates, and that summer watched the progress not only of this building but also of the two new Edison stations which were then being constructed under his supervision.

Bowker's interest and initiative resulted in many services to the Settlement. On a second visit to Toynbee Hall with Bernheim, he saw an art exhibit which inspired the two men to undertake a brilliantly successful experiment at the Settlement. For three years they sponsored an East Side art exhibit at which all the visitors were invited to ballot for their favorite pictures. This novel feature attracted a surprising number of people: in 1893 the average daily attendance was over 1,700, and on one day reached 2,793.[43] On another occasion he assumed leadership of a scheme to have the various residential rooms at the Settlement furnished by the different college groups in the city, and saw to it that City College was well represented.[44] He gave special attention to the Settlement's library work and was proud of the influence which the librarian had on the boys and girls of the neighborhood. He himself urged many of these young people to go from the local Rivington Street public school to City College, encouraged them to found the Social, Education, and Improvement Club, and followed its members with great interest through college and after, when many of them achieved careers of great social usefulness.[45] He helped to select and to retain as head of the Settlement capable young James B. Reynolds, who in 1897 became the leader of the Citizens' Union mayoralty campaign for Seth Low and later one of President Theodore Roosevelt's "lawn tennis" cabinet. He sought to keep the Settlement Council in direct contact with the neighborhood it served, and when, in 1900, it seemed to him in danger of becoming just another financial board, he was ready to resign. The Council, he maintained, should include men who had come up through the Neighborhood Guild Clubs and had gone from

42 R. R. B. to University Settlement Council, June 5, 1895.

43 A. C. Bernheim to R. R. B., June 23, 1893; R. R. B. to president of the University Settlement, March 7, 1930.

44 Miss E. Butler to R. R. B., November 20, 1899.

45 Bowker especially mentions Dr. Henry Moskowitz, Dr. Paul Abelson, Meyer Bloomfield, Leon Schwartz, Elias Lieberman, Dr. Paul Klapper, Professor J. S. Shapiro, and Leo Margolin. R. R. B., MS Memoir.

the public schools through the City College, even though they might not be able to "come to dinner in a dress suit."

A good example of the University Settlement's influence in the social-work field and of Bowker's role in this influence is the inspiration and encouragement which Lillian Wald found there, which helped to determine her later career. She was still a young woman, disturbed, unhappy, and seeking some way to relieve her social compunctions, when she was introduced to Bowker, learned from him the varied implications of the Settlement's work, and through him and his associates found sympathy, encouragement, and a clue to a new way of life. Bowker introduced her to Honor Morton, through whom she came into a long train of English friendships; he had many conferences with her as she launched her own center in 1893 and drew up a thoughtful memorandum for the first medical and nurses' conference held for the Tenth Ward under its auspices.[46] It was this kind of influence that prompted the Municipal Administration Committee of the Reform Club to declare in 1897 that in the University Settlement were "now centered, more than at any other one point in the country, the interest and the work of those engaged upon the more pressing of the problems" of municipal betterment.[47]

These efforts to improve the cultural life of Greater New York and to give it clean government paralleled the efforts of other liberals in other cities of the United States at the turn of the century. It was this tide of progressive municipal reform which rolled "Golden Rule" Jones and Brand Whitlock into office in Toledo; Tom Johnson with his able lieutenants Newton D. Baker, Frederic C. Howe, and Peter Witt in Cleveland; J. W. Folk in St. Louis, and Ben Lindsey in Denver. Bowker was in fine company, and writing a memorable chapter in the great liberal crusade.

[46] Lillian Wald to R. R. B., September 1, 1928; memo dictated March 28, 1893; A. C. Bernheim to R. R. B., July 5, 1893.
[47] Reform Club, circular, January 4, 1897.

XVIII

The Arts of Life

A YEAR AFTER Bowker entered the Edison Company, a society column contained the following item:

> R. R. Bowker, litterateur, reformer, Mugwump, and exquisite, is now so deeply immersed in business life that he hasn't time to look out for what used to be the inevitable pink in his buttonhole. He's looking out for the Edison interests, and doing it as well as if he never had written a line in his life and never had been a reformer. He says, however, that he's just as much of a Mugwump as ever.[1]

The little sketch hardly does Bowker credit. He was living a full professional life as chief executive of the Edison Company and editor-in-chief of the *Publishers' Weekly* and the *Library Journal.* He was living an active public life as a militant Mugwump engaged in reform politics at the national, state, and local levels; working for free trade, sound money, civil service and ballot reform, and against imperialism; helping to promote New York's civic renaissance by actively supporting its libraries, colleges, museums, settlement houses, and civic clubs; meanwhile contributing vigorously to the library and copyright movements, to the discussion of public-franchise control and taxation. He was also living an active personal life, cultivating a host of splendid friendships, becoming one of the best traveled men of his circle, engaging in a number of hobbies, writing poetry, and publishing a mellow volume on the meaning of human existence. Inventor, poet, author, publisher, editor, business executive, political reformer, and world traveler, Bowker in the nineties attained the years of full tide, earning a substantial

[1] Scrapbook clipping dated July 16, 1891, source not given, possibly the New York *Post.*

income, fully engaged in useful service, and enjoying the respect and influence of a successful career.

Bowker was a man of action, plunging vigorously into the busy world of his day. But he was also a man of reflection, from his college years searching for the unifying principles behind every field he entered and seeking to understand the meaning of his life as a whole. To be active was for him not enough, but to be active in the consciousness of fulfilling laws representing the very structure and purpose of life, this was his object. Just as he once wrote of his "favorite thinking ground of fundamentals" which took him "into the heart of things," so he wrote Dr. Wilfred Grenfell of "the larger thoughts of life which are so hidden behind the perspective of the lesser things in the foreground of the workaday world."[2] And so it was that during the very years of greatest practical activity he was completing his two most theoretical and abstract works, which together embodied his philosophy of life. The first was a synthesis of the social sciences and the humanities which he published as *The Arts of Life*. The second was a synthesis of what was known about force and matter which he entitled "The Unities of Nature."

In *The Arts of Life*, however, Bowker expressed a more basic characteristic of his own life. He conceived of life as an art, indeed the supreme art, an art in which the final test was not intention or profession, but the quality of the actual life lived out. Perhaps this is, in the end, the most striking thing about Bowker's career. True, it was marked by many friendships; it was versatile and represented many specific contributions in special fields; it was an amazingly consistent expression of the liberal creed. But beyond this, it was an inspiring example of a life that was whole, uniting not only action with reflection, but also profession with practice. "In true living," Bowker wrote, "the working aim should mate the professed ideal, since in all true relations fact and theory, deed and creed, conform." The living he defined was his own.

In trying to account for Bowker's enormous output, one can identify three outstanding qualities: concern, ability, and drive. The first is stamped on everything he did. Bowker not only had opinions but convictions, and not only convictions but faiths; and he held his faiths with a passion. A value to him was a commitment, and a commitment was something worth working and fighting for. Unlike the average man with his lukewarm neutrality toward the larger issues of life, Bowker was hot with concern for causes, for ideals, for people, and he was continuously translating his concern into action. For him, to be alive was

2 November 18, 1912.

to undertake voluntary responsibility for the welfare and progress of his fellow man.

In addition to his concern, Bowker had real ability. This was a compound of a fine mind, a gift for communication, and managerial skill. His mind was a superbly tempered instrument. It could master quantities of raw facts (whether tariff schedules or corporation accounts) and cope with infinite detail (whether bibliographical entries or construction blueprints). It could make an incisive analysis penetrating to the heart of the matter at hand (such as the audit plan for the bankrupt New York *Times*), or a bold correlation of data (such as *Economics for the People* or the scientific monograph on "A Theory of Ons"). Moreover, it was a mind enriched by a creative imagination that was intensely practical, whether envisioning a pioneer college student council, an American Library Association, or a Society for Political Education; whether producing an improved bookkeeping method for the Edison Company or the solution to a problem of street lighting given up by the Edison engineers.[3] Bowker was awarded four patents and negotiated for some twelve others; he published some fifty-five poems in various periodicals and anthologies, and himself printed two collections of verse. The fact is that he had the imagination of the inventor, the poet, and the pioneer. It seemed then to be but one operation for Bowker to absorb a mass of information, order it, and then shape it into some practical form, whether a patent, a platform plank, or an editorial.

The result, moreover, would invariably be expressed in clear, logical, and effective language. It was Bowker who was called upon to draft the public addresses of reform conventions and to edit campaign circulars and personal memorials. When he spoke in committee or public meeting, it was to the point, brief, and positive. "The first time I had occasion to observe your mind in action," a stranger once wrote him, "was when a Congressional committee was in session at the Holland House to discuss second-class postage. The discussion was becoming greatly involved, and more heat than light was being developed, when you arose, and with a few words set everybody straight."[4] It was the same in library and free-trade meetings.

Productive thinking and clear communication were two important

---

[3] Examples of Bowker's practical problem-solving abound, e.g., a suggestion that New York relieve its fresh-water shortage by using salt water for fire protection and street cleaning (R. R. B. to T. R. Slicer, September 8, 1899); that the Rockefeller Foundation introduce visible speech symbols into China as a much-needed substitute for her cumbrous idiographic system (R. R. B. to Volta Bureau, August 11, 21, 1916; to Fred DeLand, August 23, 1916).

[4] F. A. Dibble to R. R. B., September 4, 1928.

gifts. Bowker's managerial skill was another. He was a keen observer. He could make plans to remedy or improve what he observed. He could organize people into working crews to accomplish what he planned, driving them hard and getting the most out of them. He knew how to judge the ability of others, and all his life showed a knack for selecting capable lieutenants, whether Dudgale and Ford in the Society for Political Education, Lieb in Edison, or Melcher in the *Publishers' Weekly*. He was economical to the point of being sometimes considered a penny pincher, and he could drive a hard bargain when he wished. He had plenty of common sense, and his sound business judgment was attested and sought by all his associates. With all this he exuded a sense of authority, decision, and command. He always knew his own mind, and usually got what he wanted. He would listen to others, but those who differed with him had to know their facts and stand their ground. He could say no. He instinctively took charge of things and expected his orders to be carried out. He was a leader in almost every field he entered.

Finally, in addition to concern and ability, Bowker had drive. He seemed to have within himself a concentration of force and will power that would brook no obstacles. He positively loved hard work and was capable of enormous quantities of it. "Life has indeed been full to the brim of duties," he wrote Peabody in 1912, "but after all it is better to die in harness. . . . I think none of our close circle could be happy without activity and work." The letter files are filled with notes from hard-working businessmen who thought Bowker worked too hard and begged him to spare himself.

This remarkable vitality was the result of the same calculated attention to efficient living which Bowker had shown as a young man. He gave considerable attention to the subject in the *Arts of Life*,[5] calling health the first art and the first moral duty, and defining health as including "mind-health and will-health, saneness of the mind and rightness of morals." On psychosomatic unity he was explicit: "A sound body is quite as much, if not more, conditioned in a sound mind, as a sound mind upon a sound body." He described himself as "one who throws off business cares and counts worry a business weakness." He believed conscientiously in knowing one's own physical limits and not working beyond them. He believed in cultivating rest. "We of today not only 'murder sleep,' but murder waking rest. The diversion of our busy thoughts into quiet is an unknown art. We cannot fold our hands or infold our spirits with quiet. The art of rest must be one of our educative arts of life."[6] Bowker's primary dependence for rest was upon

[5] Pages 57–61.
[6] *Ibid.*, 95.

travel; meanwhile, walking continued to be a favorite pastime, whether he was in London, the Adirondacks, or the Berkshires. And the regimen worked. Except for the typhoid illness of 1876, severe eyestrain in 1898, and a mild heat stroke in 1899, Bowker enjoyed almost perfect health until his death.

Concern, ability, and drive were fortified by many sterling assets. There was his stock of information. There was his wide range of acquaintances and his political sense of who could do what and how to get to them. There was his courage. "Never did he confess to being discouraged," wrote W. C. Ford, "and his quick recovery from defeat was an inspiration to those associated with him. . . . It was a rich experience to meet in committee, listen to the discouraging reports of defeat, and have the skies cleared by Bowker's immediate plans for a new attack."[7] There was his scrupulous defense of personal rights, whether his own or his neighbor's. There was his insistence on direct, above-board discussion with all cards on the table. He hated "behind the doors" arrangements; he liked to speak straight from the shoulder. "I have said *to* you and shall say *to* you," he wrote one person, "what I am likely to say *of* you in conversation with others." One always knew where Bowker stood. And finally there was his clear-cut sense of the difference between right and wrong and his refusal to compromise on matters of principle.

What made Bowker's candor the more impressive was its complete freedom from emotion. Few people felt irritability or rancor in Bowker when he differed with them. He was forthright but temperate; he could be blunt, but he was never sarcastic. There was a persistent, fearless pressing of a point, but with a genuine underlying concern for the real welfare of the other person that was over and over again perceived and appreciated by individuals who first believed themselves victims only to discover themselves beneficiaries. Some people felt in Bowker a trace of arrogance and a tendency to "know it all," but if so it was not egocentricity. All his life he made it a point to withhold pictures of himself from the press,[8] to keep his own name off the masthead of his publications, to refuse the honorary degrees tendered him from time to time,[9] to decline public office, and to give anonymously to charities. He refused to feel slighted when not given credit for work that he had done. "We must all put aside any feeling of that sort," he wrote Putnam when both men were passed over in the selection of a new Free Trade League president in 1919. "Many things in this world of countercurrents

[7] *Library Journal,* December 1, 1933, Part II.

[8] R. R. B. to New York Press Art Bureau, November 12, 1905; to Miss Crafts, May 18, 1908; to Utley, April 19, 1915.

[9] *City College Alumnus,* January, 1934, p. 6.

must be overlooked, and I do feel that we who have borne the heat and burden of the noonday should not feel hurt as the torch is passed on to others, but rather glory in whatever we have been able to do."

Bowker's private life was full to the brim with friendships, clubs, a wide range of hobbies, travel, and conscientious philanthropies. During the nineties he was at his best. About five feet, nine inches tall, weighing about 160 pounds, sturdy and erect, he gave evidence of being a good walker, with not a pound of superfluous flesh. He had a good thatch of graying hair and a full beard. He dressed meticulously and conservatively. His manner was brisk, confident, and alert. He was cordial without being genial, earnest but not severe unless provoked, far from being aloof but intimate with few, the kind of man not many called by his first name.

He was always welcomed by his friends, always recognized for his sincerity and forthrightness. "Few . . . had wider acquaintance," testified H. M. Lydenberg, "few had more lasting friendships, few were more generous in recognition of new talent, few more cherishing of old memories." People spoke of his great charm of manner and culture, his gracious thoughtfulness, and his ability to make people feel that he was interested in them. He was no snob, and his own way of life was simple and democratic, but he liked to associate with cultured people. He was an engaging conversationalist, enjoyed showing hospitality, and could be a superb host to distinguished guests. He had a profound admiration for the life of the English country squire acquired during his London years, and when he later made his home at Stockbridge, one of his neighbors who knew him best liked to think of him as a sort of American Sir Roger de Coverley.

Closest to him were his sister and parents, for whom he continued to make a home in Brooklyn, first at 283 Ryerson Street and then in a more comfortable three-story, brick-and-stone house at 274 Lafayette Avenue. Bowker's father remained an unresourceful dependent. Still handsome, with a quiet, warm, humble way about him, he also retained a Down East drawl, a weakness for profanity and tobacco-chewing which often filled the son with ill-concealed mortification. He died in 1895, at the age of seventy-five. Bowker's mother became a sort of picture-book old lady, small, frail, and dainty, with a vivacity, quick wit, and charm which made her much loved. She died in 1906, at the age of eightyone. There were a number of family relatives in Salem whom Bowker regularly visited and who became completely dependent on him for support. He still loved to play with children, whether the three daughters of Henry Mills Alden, little Marjorie Hiscox, or the Drake sisters and the de Navarro children in England. Bowker initiated an exchange of notes and gifts with the daughter of the Amherst College librarian when she was nine years old. "It is not as the great man he was that his life touched mine," she wrote fifty-eight years later, "but as one interested in such lovely fashion in numbers of young folks such as I was, stimulating our ideals, quickening our desires, opening up to us the world's treasures, talking over what made life most worth while."[10]

Bowker was fortunate in several very close friendships. One of these was a three-cornered intimacy with Edward Morse Shepard and George Foster Peabody. Shepard continued to be his oldest and warmest personal friend. The strong affection developed when they were undergraduates at City College was sustained for another forty years. The friendship with Peabody began in 1883 and continued intensively for half a century. The three had much in common. They had all risen from modest circumstances through hard work. They were all bachelors into their fifties, and handsome ones at that. Of Peabody's olympian appearance the New York *Times* declared "that Phidias would have chosen him to sit for Zeus." They all lived in Brooklyn and formed part of the distinguished circle of public-spirited citizens who made that city an outstandingly civic-minded community at the turn of the century. None of them smoked or drank; Shepard and Bowker did not dance. They were all three deeply religious men and conscientious to a fault in the use of their wealth. They enjoyed private dinners at home and at Delmonico's, a box at the Philharmonic or the Metropolitan, taking walks together, traveling together at home and abroad. Sooner or later all three established comfortable country homes—Shepard on Lake George, Bowker at Stockbridge, Peabody in Saratoga Springs. They were all "gentlemen of the old school," formal, dignified, courteous, well-dressed, and a bit class-conscious.

All three, moreover, were hard-working and successful businessmen. Shepard was legal counsel for the New York Rapid Transit Commission, the Pennsylvania Railroad, and the Edison Company. Peabody was a partner in the Wall Street banking houses of Spencer Trask and Company, and Kidder, Peabody and Company, and a member of the Stock Exchange. At the same time they were all determined to give a large margin of leisure to public service. Shepard served on the Brooklyn Civil Service Commission, the Brooklyn Water Commission, the State Forestry Commission, as special deputy attorney general, and chairman of the City College Board of Trustees. Peabody was an outstanding supporter of both Negro and white education in the South, and of many good works in the North. They all agreed that "the chief business of life in a democracy is politics." Shepard ran for mayor of

10 Elizabeth Fletcher to Rose Weinberg, August 15, 1937.

Brooklyn in 1895, for mayor of New York in 1901, and for United States Senator in 1910. Peabody served as chairman of the National Democratic party after 1896, and national treasurer of the Democratic party in 1904. The three were closely associated in such causes as free trade, civil service, sound money, tax reform, ballot reform, and anti-imperialism. Peabody helped to back the *Million* and the *People's Cause,* which Bowker edited, and the Independent Democracy of Kings County, of which Shepard was for many years the leader. Of the three, Bowker was the more radical and consistent independent.

Bowker's friendships were clustered in several overlapping circles. Oldest, perhaps, was the college fraternity circle which kept up its annual reunions faithfully year after year, until 1918 at Camp Manhattan, and thereafter at Camp Chaire (Xaipe) at Bowker's summer home in Stockbridge. The ones closest to Bowker (excluding Shepard and Wheeler) were Nelson S. Spencer, Henry F. Chapman, Adolph Werner, Van Vechten Olcott, Albert Delafield, and Ernst F. Eurich. Other City College acquaintances were maintained through the programs of the College chapter of Phi Beta Kappa, the Graduates Association, and the Associate Alumni. The next oldest circle, which included many of Bowker's best friends, was the library circle, faithfully revisited at least once a year at the annual meetings of the American Library Association.[11]

Many warm friendships were included in Bowker's literary circle, which centered in the Authors' Club, of which he served as a council member. Here he regularly saw such old friends as R. W. Gilder, E. C. Stedman, Bronson Howard, Laurence Hutton, and George Iles, as well as many newer and more famous acquaintances. He enjoyed the fortnightly Thursday evening meetings, the occasional afternoon teas, the annual New Year's Eve watch-night gatherings, and the special dinners.[12] Through the activities of the American Authors' Copyright League and the American Publishers' Copyright League, Bowker came into especially close association with Robert Underwood Johnson, G. H. Putnam, W. H. Appleton, Charles Scribner, and Thorwald Solberg. These and other book-centered friendships were kept active through the meetings of the Bibliographical Society of America, the Grolier Club to which Bowker was elected a few months after it was founded in 1884 and in which he maintained active membership until 1907, the National Press Club, the National Arts Club (to which he belonged for over thirty years), the Nineteenth Century Club, (later the Twentieth Cen-

11 See chapters XII, pp. 191–92.

12 Bowker contributed to the club's two limited-edition publications of signed, original works by club members of 1893 and 1921. D. Osborne, *The Authors' Club,* 14–15; R. R. B., MS Memoir.

tury Club), Ye Twilight Club to which he belonged for some sixteen years, and the Association for the Advancement of the Arts and Sciences.

Perhaps Bowker's circle of fellow liberal reformers was the most intense and active. Of the Brooklyn civic leaders, four were men whom he had come to know in the seventies or earlier and kept as intimate friends for at least fifty years: those two lawyers and stalwart Independents, Everett P. Wheeler and Horace Deming, publisher George Haven Putnam, and the distinguished librarian and historical editor, Worthington C. Ford, whose even more distinguished brother, Paul Leicester Ford, for several years helped to edit the *Library Journal*. Also from Brooklyn was English-born, American-bred Thomas G. Shearman, the successful lawyer and publicist who contributed leadership and funds for many of Bowker's causes. Several close reform friends lived out of town. Over in Philadelphia was Talcott Williams, a fraternity brother and fellow liberal who graduated from the New York *World* and the Springfield *Republican* to launch a career of thirty-one years as editor of the Philadelphia *Press,* and who for forty years gave Bowker excellent advice on politics. Up in Norwich, Connecticut, was Bowker's close friend David A. Wells, scholar, publicist, economic adviser to Garfield and Cleveland, who leaned heavily on Bowker's editing and publishing judgment, and in turn offered, for twenty-five years, sound, fatherly counsel on Bowker's unremunerative reform activities.[13] In Boston was Edward Atkinson, industrialist, economist, and financier, close to both Wells and Bowker, the three constantly reading each other's manuscripts and raising money to print and distribute each other's pamphlets.

Bowker frequently saw these men and other civic leaders in Brooklyn's Hamilton Club in which he was actively interested for at least fourteen years; the Arkwright Club, where he would lunch when running down to the city from Stockbridge; the Reform Club, the City Club, and the Citizens' Union. A wider circle of acquaintances interested in the social sciences was sustained through active attendance at the annual meetings of the American Social Science Association (to which he belonged for at least fifteen years), the American Economic Association (whose *Proceedings* record Bowker's frequent participation in conference discussion), the American Statistical Association (to which be belonged for a good thirty-two years), the Academy of Political Science, and the Metric Association. Meanwhile Bowker's outdoors interests were reflected in his memberships in the Appalachian Moun-

[13] One of Bowker's most delightful outings resulted from an insistent invitation from Wells in 1887 to join a company including Horace White, W. C. Ford, and Moncure Conway on a cruise to the West Indies. Bowker edited a daily newspaper chronicling the cruise, *The Occasional Barracoutean.*

tain Club, the Lenox Garden Club, and the American Forestry Association.

One of the newest circles was the Edison and engineering circle. This included the Spencer Trasks, the Thomas Edisons, and many friends made and kept through the Association of Edison Illuminating Companies, the Edison Pioneers, the American Institute of Electrical Engineers, the New York Electrical Society, and the American Association for the Advancement of Science. Particularly enjoyed were the visits to Yaddo, the lovely country home of the Spencer Trasks in Saratoga. Here Bowker formed a close friendship with Mrs. Katrina Trask, taking pains to understand and encourage her shy efforts at writing poetry, and finally arranging for the publication of her first volumes of verse.

Bowker's frequent trips abroad on Edison business were very successful in maintaining the many fine English friendships made in the first Harper days and extended during the English visits of 1886 and 1887. Perhaps the friendship he most enjoyed was with Mrs. Anne Thackeray Ritchie, in whose hospitable home he continued to feel like a member of the family for many decades. As her "literary adviser for both continents," he continued to do many favors for her, and through her he continued to meet English men of letters.[14] He similarly continued to visit in the homes of Mrs. K. S. Macquoid and William Black. The friendship with the latter was fortified by the famous houseboat trip down the Severn canal in 1886 when Black was getting material for his "Strange Adventures of a Houseboat,"[15] and by a lively correspondence in which Black waxed caustic at American tastes and manners. At Black's death, Bowker was appointed to a committee to prepare and finance a suitable memorial, and thereafter kept in close touch with his widow.

Among Bowker's English friends was Lord Kelvin who, as Sir William Thomson, had been electrician for Cyrus W. Field's first American cable. Bowker helped entertain the English scientist on his frequent trips to the United States, taking him to visit the Trasks at Yaddo and the Edison installations at Schenectady and Niagara. In England, Bowker visited with Kelvin year after year, often meeting around his dinner table such notables as Lord Lister and Becquerel. It was an association which greatly stimulated Bowker's interest in science. Another very meaningful English friendship was with Mary Anderson, who later became Madame de Navarro. It was through Mrs. Craik, but especially at William Black's Brighton household, that Bowker came to know this

14 Especially Swinburne. See R. R. B., MS Memoir.
15 R. R. B., typescript notes on the trip; Reid, *William Black*, 292–96.

gifted American when she was still in her twenties and the favorite actress and reigning beauty of London. At first sharing with her a common enthusiasm for the Black children, he later came to feel a strong affection for her own household, enjoying romps with her children and taking her younger sisters to see Buffalo Bill. Following Bowker's 1927 visit in the charming Worcestershire home, Mary Anderson wrote: "Do come over again and let us see a lot of you. You are a dear link with a dear past."

One of the finest expressions of Bowker's interest in people was his note-writing. He was a master at it. He tossed these notes off by the hundreds, on all occasions, but always aimed directly at the person and the occasion in question. They might be warm remembrances of people sick, or bereaved, or away from home. They might be cheerful greetings for birthdays and wedding anniversaries, for arrivals and departures. Many were expressions of appreciation, for Bowker was convinced it was well "to take opportunity to express outwardly the thoughts which are often kept back," and that there was little point in waiting until the death of a person to express one's admiration or gratitude. And so he would commend a group of street cleaners for their prompt action after a parade; a farmer for wood-cutting which enhanced the beauty of a woodland drive; a streetcar motorman "for clearness in calling out streets, politeness to passengers, and carefulness in warning them not to get off until the car stops."

A great many other notes represented efforts to see outstanding service recognized and, where possible, rewarded. This was a passion with Bowker. "We ought to honor our heroes of peace not less than our heroes of war," he insisted. Thus he organized a tribute to a branch train conductor on the completion of fifty years of service. He saw that a pension was voted in Congress for the widow of a former civil service official. He urged a certain chamber of commerce to organize a testimonial for a rescue at sea; he inquired into details of a fireman's prevention of an explosion in a theater, and of a policeman's rescue in a subway in order to recommend the Carnegie hero's medal.

The writing of notes merged into the doing of little favors. One day it was counseling an elderly lady burdened with a troublesome estate; the next it was getting a honeymoon cabin for a young friend at Yaddo. He wrote detailed travel instructions to house guests, speakers, and visitors. He acted as a literary scout and clipping bureau for a host of friends in their special fields of interest. He had such a knack for bringing together people with common interests that some remarked on it. "I can't help wondering," wrote authoress Margaret Veley, "whether you are in the habit of making friendships for your friends in this fashion, whether you have some gift of divination which tells you that people will fit."

The favors often became gifts. Bowker made an art of giving. In fact, he engaged in giving with so much gusto and relish that it might be described as one of his hobbies. His Christmas gift lists were extensive; he gave turkeys at Thanksgiving; he gave birthday presents and "unbirthday" presents; he gave flowers to people who weren't used to receiving flowers. To an indigent former librarian he made a typical gift in the form of an anonymous pension check. He once asked a clergyman to help him give away a hundred dollars because he was "a little behind in his benefactions" on account of the press of other matters. He was constantly making "loans" which were to be paid back if and when possible, or passed on to others. Today he might send a Victrola and records to an elderly invalid; tomorrow he might send a doll to a little girl who needed one; most often he sent books, of all kinds, for all ages. "If you send us anything again," Mrs. Anne Ritchie wrote in 1887, "I shall give up writing, for you do bestow much too much upon us and I am quite ashamed as I take up one thing after another which we owe to your kindness and remembrance." A thank-you note from an elderly couple suggests the spirit of this giving: "Somehow, we both feel that the giver is with the gift. . . . My husband remarked he thought Mr. Bowker one of the few persons who knew how and when to bestow a gift." Finally, Bowker gave constantly to public causes with intelligent interest, and with gratefulness that means enabled him to assist good works beyond the limits of personal time and energy. Increasingly after 1890 he had the means of maintaining a full list of annual charities as well as funds for emergency gifts, and at the same time that he himself gave generously, he was always happy to solicit funds from others, believing it a favor to help people with resources to find worthy causes close to their interests. "If ever there were a man of my acquaintance who comprises within himself the Christ-like spirit and epitome of the Christian beatitudes," one wrote of him, "I can recall but one, and he is R. R. Bowker."[16]

Quite apart from his friendships and his charities, Bowker was a man of many avocations. He was a collector of stamps, bells, and souvenir spoons. More important, he was a notable collector of autograph letters and of the penscript manuscripts of a wide range of literary celebrities. His favorite pastimes included talking with interesting companions, walking, playing with children, writing poetry, and attempting new syntheses of frontier scientific theories. A special set of enthusiasms related to travel, sight-seeing, and "collecting" outstanding restaurants,

16 J. F. Minturn to A. W. Milbury, February 18, 1930.

about whose specialties he came to know enough to qualify as co-author of a cook book. Increasingly after he acquired the Glendale farm in 1898, Bowker took up farming as a hobby, adding it to his love of gardening. He also had a strong and informed love of music. His wife was an accomplished pianist; he followed the opera and built a collection of recordings of "nationally characteristic music from all over the world" which taxed the gramophone makers.

Writing verse was a kind of hobby. In these years of his prime, Bowker wrote more poetry and better poetry than in his first *Evening Mail* days. On his annual trips abroad he would throw many of his most vivid impressions and feelings into verse form. Subjects ranged from places visited to patriotic and religious themes. Verse forms varied from the classic ode through lyrics and sonnets to simple quatrains. More than once his lines were selected to grace a public occasion or mark a memorial. During these later years he had twelve poems published. In 1915 he printed for private circulation a first little collection of his verse both published and unpublished, and in 1923 a second.[17] Several notebooks are filled with pieces which were rejected or which remained unfinished; fragments survive written on the backs of envelopes, hotel and steamship stationery, and office paper, suggesting a happy spontaneity of composition. Three examples of his published pieces might be quoted.

For the solemn Memorial Day ceremonies in 1897 at which General Grant's body was to be placed in the great marble tomb on Morningside Heights, Bowker wrote a formal ode, "Peace Out of War," which was printed in the New York *Times*.[18] It is a good example of Bowker's ability to combine uplifted thought and genuine feeling on a theme of social import. The following is only a fragment:

> *What hurt it were to this fair land of ours*
> *If those who from our bondage gave release,*
> *If those who braved the thorns to give us flowers,*
> *If those who died in war to give us peace,*
>   *Should thus dishonored be.*
> *And the great name of patriot be defiled*
>   *By these snarling over spoils,*
>   *By these stirring petty broils,*
> *Forgetting thee, our country. . . .*

17 *From the Pen of R. R. B.*, 1915, enlarged second edition, 1916; *From Years That Are Past*, 1923.
18 April 27, 1897.

Give answer, if ye be true,
Give answer, men of today,
Brothers who wore the blue,
Brothers who wore the gray.
True to a common country let us stand,
Forgiving and forgiven, hand in hand
And heart to heart. So shall the hero band
Look from their land of peace upon a peaceful land
And say: "Now died we not in vain. . . ."

A sonnet to Ruskin was published in the *Century Illustrated Monthly* that fall, and a few years later in the *Times* of Ceylon.[19]

Ruskin

Painter in words, on whose resplendent page
Caught from the palette of the seven-hued bow,
The colors of our English Turner glow,—
Silver of silent stars, the storm's red rage
The spray of mountain streams, rocks gray with age,
Gold of Athena, white of Alpine snow,
Cool green of forests, blue of lakes below,
And sunset-crimsoned skies,—O seer and sage,
Crowned with wild olive, fine of sense and sight
In the prophetic voice, through work, trade, strife,
The stones cry out: "By truth the nations live,
And by injustice die. Be thy weights right,
Thy measures true. These be the lamps that give
The way of beauty and the path of life."

In his little collection of poems, *From Years That are Past*, printed in 1923, Bowker included several poems composed on a trip around the world in 1898: "The World Around," "A Song of the Sea," "Atlantic," "Gibraltar," "Egypt," "Suez Canal," "Ceylon," "India," "China," "Japan," "Antipodes Day," and "Alaska."

Alaska

Alaska! Wonderland of ice and snow,
Here Winter trysts with Summer, hand in hand!
The peaceful ocean marries with the land,
And waveless seas, marged with fair islands, flow

[19] *Century Illustrated Monthly*, September, 1897, p. 715; *Times* of Ceylon, January 22, 1900.

In tides eternal, while men come and go
Nor leave firm footprints on the shifting sand.
'Midst wreathing mists, the snow-peaked mountains stand,
Ablush with morn, aflame with sunset glow;
Their rock-ribbed heights far fields of ice upbear
Whence silent rivers sweep, and front the seas
Or melt in milk-white torrents that adown
The hillsides dash, and dew the green-spired trees.
Winter, grim king, ne'er doffs the icy crown
That queenly Summer wreaths with flowers fair.

Closely linked to Bowker's love of versifying was his love of travel. Having found that travel was one of the best ways to relax and rest his eyes, he increasingly utilized annual trips overseas as a means of keeping fit. "The ocean," he maintained, was "really the one place left for real rest." Thus business, pleasure, and health were combined in an activity which became part of Bowker's way of life and which made him one of the best-traveled men in his wide circle of acquaintances.

Bowker traveled outside of the United States during thirty-one of the fifty-two years between 1880 and 1932, meanwhile journeying in every state but one in his own country. These foreign travels included one trip around the world, eighteen separate trips to Europe, and ten to Latin-American countries. They took him into every single European country, to all the continents except Australia, to all the chief Caribbean islands, to all the South American countries except three, through all the seven seas and the Arctic as well. He explored scenes as distant and different as the islands of the South Seas and the Grenfell mission in Labrador. He twice saw the Passion Play at Oberammergau; he was present at Queen Victoria's Golden and Diamond Jubilees; he saw Admiral Dewey's squadrons in the Pacific a few days before they attacked the Spanish forts in Manila, and he was in Austria when that country declared war in 1914. He made several trips through the Panama Canal and visited all the major American possessions. He loved to take out-of-the-way trips on his own initiative and was constantly looking for new fields to conquer.

Though Bowker traveled for pleasure and for rest, he must have seemed a hyperactive tourist. He would study guidebooks in advance, fixing the location of places in his mind so that he usually knew what he was going to find around the next corner; he would normally seek to organize his fellow travelers into a study circle; he was usually the first off the ship, well armed with introductions of all kinds. He always made voluminous records of all that he saw, utilizing these to instruct his friends, correct guidebook publishers, and supply detail for a string of published travel articles.[20]

Bowker was a good friend and a good neighbor, a man with a full, rich personal life. He was also a good citizen. For him the normal life was the citizen's life, and this meant public service. Over and over again he referred to himself and his close friends as "amateur politicians," and he once wrote Peabody that heavy political responsibility rested upon "our set of people." If, as Ortega y Gasset suggested, the true aristocrat is he who voluntarily assumes public burdens, then Bowker belonged to our native American aristocracy.

Bowker's citizenship was expressed in contributions to public discussion, the organization of pressure groups, and attendance at hearings. It was also expressed through constant vigilance and constant readiness to communicate suggestions, commendations, and criticism. The volume of correspondence which he addressed to newspaper editors, mayors, selectmen, judges, senators, presidents, and ambassadors must be seen in his collected papers to be appreciated. "It may be the impertinence of a layman to make any suggestions on such points to a high priest in this industry," he once wrote to an expert, "but sometimes I find it worth while to 'pass on the torch' even through ignorant hands, in the hope that some of the sparks may kindle in new directions."[21] And so he wrote letters discussing road signs, the protection of school children, and goitre cure. He wrote to protest the closing of children's rooms in public libraries, the location of a new courthouse, the way a mayor handled a strike. He wrote to the Treasury Department suggesting improvements in customs procedure; to the New York Public Service Commission proposing improved safety devices for subways; to the National Tax Association recommending a simplification of the income tax. He wrote to Governor Alfred Smith favoring an extension of the emergency rent law; to President Theodore Roosevelt volunteering a four-page report on the operation of the Panama Canal;[22] and to President Wilson suggesting how a message to Congress might be issued as an educational pamphlet. For Bowker there was a price tag attached to citizenship in a democracy, and civic alertness was part of it.

Bowker's success in expressing his citizenship at the municipal, state, and national levels has been noted. He was no less successful at the

20 R. R. B., "In the Other Half of America," "In the Continent of Opportunity," "Porto Rico's Charms for a Motorist's Eye," New York *Evening Post* Supplement, November 27, December 4, 1909, July 7, 1922.
21 R. R. B. to Babcock, July 16, 1901.
22 R. R. B. to T. Roosevelt, March 19, 28, 30, 1907.

international level. When barely in his teens, his stamp collection involved him in correspondence with persons in Canada and England, and thus began a love of maps, imaginary travel, and guidebooks. All of Bowker's professional activities reinforced this early cosmopolitan bent. Through his beloved Professor Werner he early acquired an affection for the German language and German people which was deepened by his intimate professional associations with both Leypoldt and Growoll in the *Publishers' Weekly* office. His book-reviewing for the *Evening Mail* brought him into weekly relation with the literary currents of England and the Continent, and his work in London for Harper's during 1880–82 gave him a rare opportunity to know the English people. His Edison investigations brought him repeatedly into intimate relations with businessmen and technicians in every country of Europe. His later relations with the De Laval companies meant an especially close tie with Stockholm and Swedish interests. The book trade with its international expositions, the library movement with its international conventions, the crusade for international copyright with its negotiations for an international treaty, the free-trade movement with its evangelical commitment to the economic unity of the world, all brought a close, continuous, natural intercourse with other nations. As a good liberal, Bowker repudiated the jingoism and imperialism which separated nations and deplored the preparedness programs which intensified international suspicion. In 1910, after attending several international conferences in Europe and visiting South America, he offered an article to the *Review of Reviews* on "The United States of the World." Indeed, Bowker was as nearly as possible, in fact as in spirit, a world citizen.

This commitment to the unity of mankind expressed itself in Bowker's religion. A deeply spiritual man, Bowker continued to emphasize the ethical behavior on which all faiths might agree rather than the theological propositions on which they might differ. Over and over again he made clear that the Christianity he believed in was "working Christianity, as shown in daily living,—that best of tests." To one churchman he wrote, "I agree that if we can persuade all men to live the life of Jesus, we can well afford to wait for their agreeing upon the faith of Jesus." To a bishop he declared, "For myself, I have never been a good enough churchman to draw the lines between the Episcopal Church and either the Roman Catholic on the one hand or the other Protestant denominations on the other as having any kind of monopoly of good works, and I believe good works are a very vital part of Christianity." Though an Episcopalian by choice, Bowker was always clear that "we [also] need the freer form of worship of the Congregationalists, the Methodists, the Baptists." He frequently defended the fine record of Christian Science. He declined to support the Y.M.C.A. because it refused membership to Unitarians and Universalists, "who are among the best Christians I know." He refused to take part in attacks on Roman Catholicism, and once went out of his way to honor a Catholic priest who was "so catholic as to recognize goodness and true religion everywhere it existed." He told Atkinson that Christians might learn a good deal from the practical relations of Buddhism. In 1902 he wrote:

> Our religious instincts and the experience of other faiths at home and in travel have led us to believe that every form of religion, every uplifting of the soul toward God, whether within the several denominations of our Christian faith or even in non-Christian religions, in which our fellow-beings are seeking to follow the light given them, should have encouragement rather than antagonism from those who are endeavoring to unite the world in a true and living Christianity.[23]

Meanwhile, Bowker continued to be, all his life, a pewholder in the Episcopal church of whatever community was his home. Until about 1910 it was the Church of the Messiah in Brooklyn, from then until 1928 the Church of the Ascension in New York, and finally St. Bartholomew's. In Stockbridge it was St. Paul's, and in Glendale the Union Chapel. Bowker generously supported church benevolences and special collections, attended services conscientiously, and kept up a friendly dialog with the ministers on their views. He cherished two prayer books which had been in his possession a long time; one, purchased in London in 1880, he used for at least thirty-five years. Nevertheless, Bowker never became a communicant. He continued to be impatient of exclusive doctrines. "There is but one God," he wrote his sister, "but many Allahs. The Allahs pass, God remains." He believed in the community church for small towns. "In the present feeling of the unity of Christians and the lessening importance of creeds and ceremonies, it does seem a waste of effort that there should be a congregation of each of these bodies (Episcopal, Congregational, Methodist, and Baptist) when the support is insufficient for more than one."

Nowhere is Bowker's inner drive to discover unities more evident than in his surprisingly aggressive interest in modern scientific theories of matter and motion. His aim was to write a volume on "The Unities of Nature," with chapters on the unity of matter and the unity of force. He did write a published address on the unity of science. He referred to

23 R. R. B. to St. Clair Hester, June 9, 1902.

"my favorite thinking ground of the fundamentals in science"; he spoke of his science studies as taking him "into the heart of things"; he was profoundly interested in the St. Louis Congress of Arts and Sciences of 1904 because he understood it would "especially consider ultimates at the base of all"; he spoke of his essays as presenting "the ultimate unity of all matter and energy." To Bowker's mind, "always fond of organization" as he put it, these were the great objectives: "fundamentals . . . ultimates at the base of all . . . unity."

Bowker's central insight or working hypothesis (less familiar then than now) was that all force could be unified in a continuous gamut of wave lengths of radiant energy, that all matter could be similarly unified in a continuous gamut of responses to radiant energy, and that thus all the problems of science could find common ground in terms of electricity.

> Accepting the view that radiant energy covers a continuous gamut of wave lengths (from the long Marconi and Hertz waves through some yet unknown octaves, to the bolometrically measured "dark heat" waves of Langley, the single octave of light waves and the ultra-violet or actinic waves with Finsen physiological effects), so there is a corresponding constitution of matter, as built up from the electron . . . through the atom and the molecule and the several organic as well as inorganic complexities, responsive to radiant energy or respective wave lengths. . . . The atom is itself perhaps only a mode of motion. . . . It seems that we may be on the brink of a discovery that physical substances are known to us only through the messages of their vibrations, which have to be translated into terms very like electricity before we recognize them at all.[24]

This insight into the unity of nature was a lifelong obsession. While still a college undergraduate, Bowker formed the hypothesis that motion, like matter, must be continuous. Consequently he prepared a table of the analogous relations of wave forces from ultraviolet waves through light and heat to longer wave lengths which he mistakenly identified with sound. Unfortunately, Professor Compton did not recognize the merit of this insight and quenched young Bowker's enthusiasm for a synthesis which, if then published, might have had some historic importance.[25] His science article in *Appleton's Journal* in 1872 reverts to the theme. Claiming Tyndall's authority for the "scientific use of the

[24] R. R. B. to G. H. Putnam, February 5, 1904; R. R. B., 'The Unity of Science," *Transactions* of the American Institute of Electrical Engineers, March, 1903, p. 282.

[25] R. R. B. to G. H. Putnam, February 17, 1904; R. R. B., "Problems of the Infinitely Little," *City College Quarterly,* June, 1910, p. 93; Alumni Address, C.C.N.Y., 1928.

imagination," Bowker threw out the suggestion that the same energy waves which science had found to be correlated and convertible as sound, heat, light, magnetism, and electricity might well extend into a still-unexplored intensity to constitute a "nerve-force, convertible, like the known forces, into physical power."[26] It was in the eighties that the paper on "the unities of nature" took shape. During his Edison years he talked with every theoretical scientist he met. His associations with Edison, Van Vleck, Lord Kelvin, and Michael Pupin were especially stimulating. The latter once remarked that Bowker was the only person whose mind seemed to have been prepared to take up the thought of his line of work in this direction.[27] The 1896 article on "Electricity" in *Harper's Magazine* repeats the theme.

Discoveries in physics, chemistry, and astral physics at the end of the century seemed to confirm Bowker's working hypothesis.[28] With increased leisure after his Edison retirement, most vigorously until 1904 but intermittently through 1926, he gave himself seriously to checking the latest developments through intensive reading and extensive correspondence with experts at the Smithsonian Institution, the Massachusetts Institute of Technology, the Harvard Observatory, the University of Pennsylvania, the University of North Carolina, and the Research Laboratory of the General Electric Company. He was particularly eager to get his paper before scientists so that, "by bringing a good many observed data into relation, as a layman is perhaps more apt to do than a technical specialist," he might "map out some lines of thought for future investigators which may prove of importance."[29]

The first fruit of this study was a paper on "The Unity of Science," read before the American Institute of Electrical Engineers in 1903. This and successive papers emphasized two original contributions by Bowker to the subject: a theory of ons and a theory of the tonality of matter. The first was more fully developed in his paper "A Theory of Ons: In Reconciliation of the Undulating Theory of Electricity With Ionization and the Electron Hypothesis," published in the *Electrical World and Engineer* in 1903.[30]

It may be supposed that homogenous ons, so infinitesimal as to be practically imponderable (which when passive and uncombined may constitute the space-medium or ether, responsive to and

26 R. R. B., "Science and the Spirits," *Appleton's Journal*, January 20, 1872.
27 R. R. B. to G. H. Putnam, February 17, 1904.
28 R. R. B. to T. C. Martin, August 25, 1903.
29 R. R. B. to E. P. Wheeler, November 17, 1902; R. R. B. to C. Baskerville, July 11, 1904.
30 September 26, 1903, p. 507.

transmitting vibrations of all wave lengths) constitute when en-
ergized and combined ponderable matter, generating or transmitting vibrations of distinctive wave lengths selectively according
to the nature of the combination . . . positive or negative according to the direction or other quality of the motion. . . .

It may be supposed that these ons constitute distinctively the
"atoms" of the several "elements" by differences of numbers or
of systems of arrangement. The distinctive groups or systems within the atom, like the strings of the piano, would give, by their different lengths or masses and thus distinctive tonalities, the characteristic spectrum lines. It is conceivable that the ons within the
atom might be associated cohesively in inert groups as rods, plates
or other solid figures, or in active vortex whirls, or in orbital rota-
tion like the solar and stellar systems of astronomy, linking the
infinitely great with the infinitely little.

It was a proposal that proved to be astonishingly in line, a few false
leads excepted, with the developments in atomic structure twenty
years later. Bowker's concept of the tonality of matter described matter's
responsiveness to "radiant energy or respective wave lengths." He became convinced that "very much is to be accomplished in extending
our knowledge of the constitution of matter by using this tonality or
responsiveness as a guide in research."[31]

Bowker's basic treatise was first called "A Theory of Matter and
Force, with an Application to Magnetism and Electricity." This was
also presented in two parts, one on matter and one on force. The paper
on "The Unity of Matter," also referred to by him as "The Tonality of
Matter," was a summary and analysis of the discoveries giving rise to
the conception of the ultimate unity of matter, especially the latest discoveries and suggestions concerning radio-active substances. Of his
paper, Bowker said flatly: "There is not elsewhere to be found so comprehensive and compact a statement of the development of this department of science, for I have had to be at infinite pains in digging out the
facts and organizing them into coherent and logical statement."[32] It
was, however, impossible to publish it. Bowker first sent it to the
Atlantic, but Bliss Perry thought it too involved; he then tried to have
it accepted as a paper to be read at the St. Louis Congress of Arts and
Sciences, but it was turned down, as Bowker felt, because of "the distrust
on the part of the professorial or professional mind of unprofessional
people whose work is naturally classed as amateurish." In 1925 he of-

[31] R. R. B. to G. H. Putnam, February 5, 1904.
[32] R. R. B. to Bliss Perry, September 26, October 5, 1903.

fered a revised version of the same basic paper, now titled "The Miracle of Matter and Motion" (subdivided into "The Infinitely Little: Chemiphysics," and "The Infinitely Great: Astrophysics"), to the *Century,* but the editors pronounced it "a bit beyond the casual reader."[33] Meanwhile, part of his manuscript, rejected by *Harper's* and the *Atlantic,* was published as an address delivered before the C.C.N.Y. chapter of Phi Beta Kappa in 1909 under the title, "Problems of the Infinitely Little With Especial Reference to Vibration Relations."[34] In this he declared,

> In closing I can only refer to that new conception of the luminiferous ether foreshadowed in Mendelieff's "Chemical Conception of the Ether," and emphasized in Sir Oliver Lodge's very recent treatise on "The Ether of Space." This is the thought which I have myself endeavored to put forward; that the ether may not be different from matter but is literally the etherealization of that of which matter is the embodiment, whether, as in Kelvin's suggestion, matter rises from vortexes in the ether, or, as in Mendelieff's view, the ether may be the infinitely tenuous condition of chemical elements or of their final constituents, or, as in the theory of Thompson and Lodge, matter may be motions of the ether, from which not only a theory of matter but a theory of gravitation may be evolved.

Blindness made it impossible for Bowker to keep up with the rapidly developing literature in this dramatic field, and he was obliged to forego the satisfaction of seeing his hypotheses published in the form he had once planned.

Bowker's alert mind led him into many applications of this central interest. He drafted brief outlines for papers on "The Search for Cold Light," "The Standardization of Electro-Chemical Terminology," and the formulation of a law of equalization:

> There seems reason to suppose that there is a general law of equalization throughout all matter which may throw some light on the problem of gravitation. The diffusion of gases, the osmosis of liquids, the tendency of metals, like silver and lead, to merge together at adjoining surfaces all point to a general law that matter

[33] Bliss Perry to R. R. B., October 10, 1903; R. R. B. to G. H. Putnam, February 5, 1904; H. H. Howland to R. R. B., December 2, 1925.

[34] R. R. B., "Problems of the Infinitely Little," *City College Quarterly,* June, 1910, pp. 89–100. Reprinted with revisions and additions. It had been rejected by *Harper's* in 1907 and by the *Atlantic* in July, 1909.

in any form tends to diffuse itself among other matter until there is equalization throughout."[35]

One of his strongest interests was the relation of electricity to the human body. In 1924 he read a paper on "Electrostatic Potential and Human Health" before the New York Electrotherapeutic Society which was published.[36] He corresponded with physicians concerning the implications of wave mechanics for human vision[37] and discoveries about the ductless glands; he prepared a lengthy paper on "Brain Deterioration as Evidence of Brain Organization."

Along more practical lines, Bowker proposed at least twelve inventions to his patent lawyer,[38] including a machine to convert heat into electricity, a battery switchboard, an electric self-starter for a gasoline engine, a clock speed recorder, a centrifugal governor for a driving wheel, a device to reverse a screw in marine work, an emergency safety apparatus for submarines, a tone-detector for wireless telegraphy, a device "for detecting from a following train or car its approach within dangerous proximity to a preceding train or car," a device for "reducing a record in three dimensions to a record of two dimensions," and a Victrola record combining voice description and musical illustration.

Bowker's lifelong compulsion to achieve "the needful view of the wholeness of life" found its fullest realization in *The Arts of Life*. The impulse that prompted him to seek a patent for an international postage stamp, to effect a completely unified bibliographical system, and to co-ordinate all tax schemes; the impulse that drove him to promote free trade as a means of establishing the "United States of the World" in the political realm, to plead for understanding and common trust among religious faiths, to search persistently for the means of demonstrating the unity of nature in the field of science, achieved here a successful integration of the humanities and the social sciences. It was the same urge to unity in the social realm which led him in the early seventies to write that "the sanitary inspector, the school teacher, and the city missionary are three points of a triangle," and that "we may not be a people great in Art until we be a religious folk."[39] He called his book, indeed, an "essay of reconciliation."

[35] MS, undated fragment in R. R. B. collection.

[36] *American Journal of Electrotherapeutics and Radiology*, January, 1925.

[37] R. R. B. to W. H. Wilmer, January 29, 1925, December 15, 1927, December 28, 1928.

[38] See correspondence between R. R. B. and Park Benjamin, 1902–14; and J. Van Vleck, 1906; and F. G. Sprague, 1928; R. R. B. to Columbia Phonograph Company, March 27, 1914.

[39] See pp. 89–90.

On the other hand, *The Arts of Life* also represents Bowker's most ambitious effort to discharge the "business of the scholar." It is here that he gives formal expression to that ideal which really formed his life vocation:

> One of the best things that a man can do for himself and for his kind is to bring clearly into his own conscious acceptance and into that of other men the ideas which should inspire and control life. ... It is the final function of the scholar to inform his fellow men how they may help or hinder progress. In those far towers of outlook whence the quiet generals of thought command the battlefields, not of war but of peace, the truest service is done.[40]

Bowker dedicated his volume "In His Name, and with the names of Paul the world-apostle, Darwin, Spencer, Gladstone, worlds-men all." It was in the spirit of the "worlds-men" that he wrote *Economics for the People* and *Of Work and Wealth;* the articles for the *World,* the *Million,* and the *Post;* that he edited *The New Century* and *The People's Cause,* and composed the manifestos of the Council on Tariff Reform in 1878, the Young Scratchers in 1879, the Independent Republicans in 1880, the Democratic reform organization in 1894, and the Friends of Freedom in 1902.

The Arts of Life was a layman's handbook of first principles for the twentieth century. It began to take shape during Bowker's college years. Even before 1883 he had selected the title, worked out the structure of the book, and sketched in some of the chapters.[41] The sections on education, business, politics and religion were written at different times, constantly reworked, and eventually reprinted separately. The whole was put into final form during the summers of the mid-nineties, the chapter on religion being written in the home of Jonathan Edwards in Stockbridge, Massachusetts. It was published by Houghton Mifflin in 1900. Bowker wrote for the modern-minded, educated man, and his style was simple, compact, forceful, full of pith and arresting insights, remindful of Emerson, as was suggested by a publisher's notice. Occasionally Bowker's thought ran the obvious danger of becoming too schematic and oversimplified, but it was at all times strong, healthy, liberal, with a clear wind of faith and courage blowing through it. Alden of *Harper's Magazine* called it "hopeful beyond any book of the kind that I have read for years." It was well received by reviewers, highly thought of by friends, and it ran into a second edition. It never, however, became popular.[42]

40 R. R. B., *The Arts of Life,* 16–17.
41 See prefatory note in R. R. B., *Of Work and Wealth.*

Of all the "ideas which should inspire and control life," Bowker emphasized one, that life was an art. His thought is explicit:

> A human life, each human life, may be and should be . . . a work of conscious and purposed art . . . and to those men and women who wish to fulfill life, to have life more abundantly for themselves and to obtain more abundant life for others, the study of the arts of life is the highest of studies.[43]

He noted how sadly this chief business of man was being neglected:

> It is the supreme defect of our civilization that we fail here. To the rearing of animals, to the perfecting of a piece of inanimate machinery, to the learning of a profession, we give time and thought and care and training which we do not give, in the highest human relations, to ourselves, or our children, or our friends, or the passing human beings who are a part of our lives and of whose lives we make part. . . . With all our learning, we have failed to learn living. With all our science, we have neglected the science of our own lives. With all our art, we have ignored the art which lifts all other arts to their supreme purpose and in which all other arts have fruit.[44]

It was clear to Bowker that this art, like all others, must be founded on science or knowledge. "Science underlies the art of living and the arts of life, as it underlies all art." In practicing this art, he recognized an initial admission: "Art presupposes . . . the original gift and the purposed training. For the gift we are not responsible, for its training we are. In this last, we make choice of means, as the artist must." The means, or arts of life, were first, *health* (wholeness of body); then *education* ("the art by which the mind is stocked with knowledges and trained in methods for its command of life"); *business* ("the art of earning a living, of applying to the affairs of every day the best equipment that can be had for it"); *government* ("the art of caring for men in their larger relations as the state"); and *religion* (the art of making the human divine"). The three basic religious virtues required were also the three scientific needs: *faith* ("the scientific use of the imagination which links the human atom in the universe" so that it vibrates in harmony with the whole); *duty* ("the rightful application of the scientific fact

42 See *Book News*, June, 1900; San Francisco *Chronicle*, May 13, 1900; E. C. Stedman to R. R. B., July 31, 1900; H. M. Alden to R. R. B., December 21, 1900; J. H. Choate to R. R. B., December 10, 1901, etc.

43 R. R. B., *The Arts of Life*, 5, 9.

44 *Ibid.*, 4, 5.

that each atom, being thus linked in the universe, counts"); and *content* ("the recognition of and reconciliation with human limitations").

Undertaking the larger responsibility of a "worlds-man," Bowker presented his guideposts for the turn of the century and the new age. According to him, modern Western history (deeply influenced by Christianity's offer of the opportunity of liberty and the responsibility of unity) had promoted the unity of mankind along four related lines: moral, material, intellectual, and social. These had combined to make the world and humankind for the first time practically one in action and in thought. The coming century, indeed, was to be a supreme age. However, social progress was a "wave line" (the drop of water goes down as well as up while motion is onward), and powerful centrifugal forces (the sundering of old ties in social, political, and religious relations) had created a dark side so as to leave mankind in "the dangerous disintegration of atoms combined only in the unstable equilibrium of explosives." Society was in "a centrifugal condition of things," a "fluent mass of individualized atoms."

In consequence, the age was actually a transitional period. The ultimate destiny of man was "from a crude, reasonless, but effective practice, an inheritance of his animal nature, through half-knowledge and groping analysis, into full knowledge and the application of science." However, this emergence from the state of nature into civilization meant passing through "a twilight time," and this is where the turn of the century had brought Western man.

> Man has been educated out of his instincts, and reason has not yet its full application. He is as a sailing vessel stripped of sails and made into a steamer, with no one on board who knows fully how to manage the new mechanism. Mankind is between lights, and twilight is the most difficult light for the eyes. . . . Man is in the dangerous domain of half-knowledge. . . . The vital progress of man has yet to come up to the progress of his intellectual and material environment.[45]

> Arrived at a great age, we are called to make ourselves great in accord with it. . . . Man is come into a high place, to which all roads of the past converge; before him all roads of the future open forth. All the kingdoms of the earth are before him. He must choose.[46]

In such a time of transition and doubt, Bowker deemed it "the question of questions whether . . . some permanent principles may be

45 *Ibid.*, 37, 38, 43.
46 *Ibid.*, 41.

discerned in social and religious relations making for progress and faith." He definitely believed that there were such principles, and that they were to be found in modern science. They were the doctrine of the conservation and correlation of forces, and "the thought that, alike in space and in time, in the material, the moral, the spiritual world, the atom is bound to every other atom by a one-law which pervades the universe."[47] This, for Bowker, was the needed centripetal force, the "central thought that marks and moulds the age." In philosophy this principle became "the necessary and eternal relation of cause and effect," and in morals, "the like doctrine of personal responsibility." He believed that it might provide a common ground for naturalists and supernaturalists.

In one respect, its application to ethics, he was confident: this idea of "the infinity of influence and eternity of duration of the effects of infinitely small cause" provided an ethical sanction which was "the most positive which man has yet discovered for himself . . . more weighty than all the awful Calvinism of an Edwards . . . the greatest sanction, to morals and right being, for earth and heaven, possible to be put before men."[48]

> We are taught that every breath alters the relations of the universe forever, and this physical parable, interpreted into ethics and made practical in life, makes each man infinitely responsible for every moment, thought, word, and act of his life. Each man is a trustee for the race, and he carries within himself the sure reward or penalty. . . . Each atom counts, everywhere, forever. . . . Nature, still more civilization, means not that men should be independent of each other, but vastly interdependent, in an infinity of relations.[49]

In the separate chapters devoted to education, business, politics, and religion, Bowker sought to present two things: the basic principles or laws involved, and a systematic overview of the field as a whole. The result is practical, inspiring, and wise. But having discovered and understood the truth, man must live it out. "The thought is not yet in our blood; it has yet to rule our life." The recurrent emphasis is on results:

> Our "higher education" should produce definite results in higher morals and higher character, and it is self-impeached when it gives us tricksters or hoodlums. . . . All religions are useless, and the exercise of religion waste, if they do not show their fruits, harvest

[47] *Ibid.*, 22, 39.
[48] *Ibid.*, 43, 44.
[49] *Ibid.*, 43–44, 40, 39.

after seedtime, in practical everyday life. . . . In all true relations fact and theory, deed and creed, conform.[50]

Bowker's final word and his vision of man's life are noble ones.

The most important fact that a man can make part of his being is this, that the first steps of right living in the personal life are in line with the ultimates of the universe.

At the last, then, a man, studying and practicing the arts of life, knows himself as a part of Man, an essential and integral unit and factor in the Universe, the master-work of Nature, the agent of God, in every act acting in unison with Universal Law. Evolved from the past, from him is to evolve the future. His Now is part of Eternity, and this earth a part of Heaven.[51]

Bowker's life was full, many-sided, and intense. It was rich in its personal, professional, and public expressions; in its local, national, and international sympathies. It was a life that combined action, reflection, and worship, and that wove the three into a pattern of meaning and unity. It was a pattern, moreover, which balanced the inner life and the outer life and which was marked by the smooth co-ordination of means to ends, the economy of time and energy, the absence of feverish rush and ragged edges. For all these qualities, Bowker was able to make his dent. Of his public service one discerning critic has fairly judged, "The immense range of his interests . . . his dominating personality . . . the expository and judicial powers of his mind, and his leadership in almost every field he entered make him a unique figure in the political, book trade and library history of the late nineteenth and twentieth centuries."[52] Of his moral achievement, the Providence *Journal* declared, "Always a leader in every cause to which he gave himself, he might well stand in bronze, with his tall, erect figure and noble head, as the typical, many-sided, idealistic, originative, executive American of the nineteenth and twentieth centuries."[53] The heading selected for the special memorial issue of the *Library Journal* was "Richard Rogers Bowker: Friend with Life."[54] Robert Underwood Johnson, a fellow-crusader, penned a fitting birthday salute in acrostic form:

[50] *Ibid.*, 92, 285, 294.
[51] *Ibid.*, 13, 305.
[52] Haines, " 'Tis Fifty Years Since: *Publishers' Weekly* Office in an Earlier Day," *Publishers' Weekly,* January 18, 1947, Section One, p. 280.
[53] November 15, 1933.
[54] *Library Journal,* December 1, 1933, Part II, p. 1001.

Rejoice, our sage of four score years and five
I, from my laggard eighty give you greeting.
Comrades of battle we, still sworn to strive,
However far may be the goal's completing.
A blot in the escutcheon of the State
Reeks like a wound to every patriotic breast.
Dawn always found your charger at the gate;
Rifle or trumpet halted not your quest.
But you are more than fighter; you do lend
Of your sweet spirit to the world's distress.
Who needs you is your neighbor and your friend;
Kin to the virtues of your kindliness,
Even are cities saved by such as you.
Receive our homage, brave and wise and true![55]

[55] "Acrostic," *City College Alumnus*, January, 1934, p. 8.

XIX

Two Last Campaigns
Against Tammany

THE YEARS 1899–1901 climaxed the period of full tide in Bowker's life during which his creed and deed attained maximum unity. It is fitting that the publication of the *Arts of Life* should coincide with the severest crises of his professional and personal relations and with his two hardest battles. Bowker had fought many a good fight year in and year out for the liberal cause, but it was now, at the turn of the century, that he made his two most courageous attacks on his old foes—corruption, monopoly, and Tammany. These two battles were not only his most stubborn and his most lonely (in the first he did stand almost alone), but they proved to be his last, for blindness was closing in upon him. In the first campaign he lost; in the second he won. But in both he fought gallantly and for the highest principles.

The summer and fall of 1898 were filled with disturbing evidence that mysterious and powerful fingers were pulling financial strings behind the electric lighting and power industry of the city of New York.[1] This field was characterized by sensational expansion and high profits, occupied by one increasingly valuable property (the Edison Company) and several moribund properties.[2] Little wonder that certain parties now secretly concluded that the latter might be bought up and used

[1] "Memo for the Appraisers," prepared by E. H. Lewis, June 4, 1902, Supreme Court, New York County; R. R. B., "Public Control of Municipal Franchises," *Municipal Affairs*, December, 1897; R. R. B., "Piracy of Public Franchises," *Atlantic Monthly*, October, 1901; R. R. B. to G. F. Peabody, October 26, 1898.

[2] The five competing systems: Edison, Westinghouse, Mount Morris, Block, and New York Light, Heat, and Power. The two independent systems: North River and Manhattan Lighting companies.

as a club to force surrender of the rich Edison interests. It was a game which several shrewd and powerful men were perfecting. In New York, Philadelphia, Chicago, Pittsburgh, and Baltimore, gas, lighting, and street-railway franchises were being cleverly consolidated by promoters who seemed to have unlimited amounts of capital, political power, and brass. The trend to mergers in the municipal utilities field was part of the merger movement evident in other fields.

The two men whose alliance was to be particularly fateful for the Edison Company were Anthony N. Brady and William C. Whitney. Brady had become interested in gas, traction, and lighting developments in several cities. In 1898 he was head of the New Amsterdam Gas Company, capitalized at $21,000,000 in stock and $20,750,000 in bonds. Florid, thick-set, and crafty, he was a successful, self-made man. Whitney was also an astute promoter, but he was equally a sportsman, society leader, and politician, serving as Secretary of the Navy under Cleveland and managing the latter's candidacy in the Democratic national convention of 1892. During the eighties, Whitney became associated with Thomas F. Ryan and Peter A. B. Widener in seeking a monopoly of New York's street-railway system, and this resulted in 1892 in the Metropolitan Traction Company, an enterprise which Brady also helped to organize. It was the Metropolitan that was now to be used as the chief instrument in effecting a gigantic combination of combinations: the gas, electric, and traction interests of Greater New York, each of which had been organized into a near monopoly.

The first move in the game was made in the spring of 1898 when the Whitney-Brady interests sought to jam the notorious Eldridge Bill through the state legislature.[3] Its essential purpose was to extend the corporate powers of Whitney's street-railway company to the lighting and power business, in which their enormous system of conduits, obviating costly subway requirements, would give them a great advantage. Here was a gun aimed at the heart of the Edison Company, and happily for it a number of civic organizations induced the governor to kill the bill.

The second maneuver, engineered by Brady a few months later, was the successful capture of the Edison Electric Illuminating Company of Brooklyn.[4] Brady had already in 1897 created the Kings County Electric Light and Power Company. By getting the newspapers to attack the Edison Company and the city machine to threaten withdrawal of its

3 Frank Enos to R. R. B., April 8, 15, 1898.

4 R. R. B., "Piracy of Public Franchises," *Atlantic Monthly*, October, 1901, p. 470; *Tribune*, December 11, 1898; R. R. B. to J. B. Henry, December 12, 1898; announced in the New York *Times*, October 4, 1898. See Peabody's reaction, in letter to R. R. B., July 14, 1898.

public-lighting contract, which accounted for 40 per cent of the company's revenue, he was able to depress the stock until the situation was untenable. The helpless victim promptly entered into negotiations with Brady, and by August the Kings County Company had purchased more than enough stock to secure control. One of the Brooklyn Edison executives later estimated that Tammany made $10,000,000 on the deal.

The third move was a carefully disguised one. On the same day that the New York *Times* reported Brady's capture of the Brooklyn Edison Company, it carried mysterious news of the incorporation at Albany by completely unknown persons of a tremendous $25,000,000 concern known as the New York Gas and Electric Light, Heat, and Power Company with the right to manufacture gas and electricity and to purchase the stocks and bonds of any domestic corporation.[5] Not until December did Bowker and his associates begin to understand the formidable nature of their secret antagonists. The actual organizer was Brady, aided on the political side by former Tammany Mayor Hugh J. Grant and former Tammany Governor Flower. Behind them stood Whitney, as the power behind the throne, with Tammany and such other members of the "Big Eight" as Widener, Elkins, and Dolan of the Philadelphia traction syndicate, and the well-known promoters Ryan and Flynn looming in the background.[6]

This powerful group was now ready to take over the New York Edison Company. The first skirmish took the form of an attempt to frighten Edison stockholders into selling their shares. Flower and Company managed to depress the Exchange value of Edison stock from 128 to 119 and keep it there for a week, but the Edison stockholders actually began to buy rather than sell, and the stock mounted steadily to 192 by mid-December.[7] The really important part of the Whitney-Brady strategy, however, was to pick up a few minor electric companies to use as a club in forcing a sale. The first acquisition was the Mount Morris Company in October; the second was the Consolidated Subway Company. Soon it was rumored that even the New York and Block companies and the Empire Subway Company with its control of all the underground conduits had been pocketed. More important still, the Power Company actually did make a contract with Whitney's Metropolitan Railway Company for the purchase of "surplus electricity" at

[5] New York *Times*, October 4, 9, 1898; *Tribune*, October 5, 7, 1898. Bowker later stated that most of this capital was never paid in. New York *Herald*, April 28, 1907.

[6] R. R. B., "Piracy of Public Franchises," *Atlantic Monthly*, October, 1901, p. 474; New York *Times*, January 3, 1899.

[7] R. R. B., "Piracy of Public Franchises," *Atlantic Monthly*, October, 1901, p. 472; *Tribune*, October 5, 1898, January 21, 1899; R. R. B. to J. B. Henry, December 12, 1898; R. R. B., "Memo of Protest," May 17, 1901.

a phenomenally low price, and finally issued $21,000,000 in 4 per cent mortgage bonds on the securities just purchased.

The stage was now set. Enough companies had been purchased and a sufficiently convincing contract signed with the Metropolitan to frighten the Edison interests into selling. Elihu Root was retained as chief legal counsel for the transaction;[8] a strong foothold was secured on the Edison board of directors in the person of W. A. Read, who had already bought enough Edison stock in Brady's interest to make trouble. Late in October, Peabody, who served as trustee for a thousand stockholders, was selected as the most suitable Edison representative with whom specific proposals might be discussed. Soon a syndicate composed of Spencer Trask and Company, Vermilye and Company, and the Central Trust Company was created to negotiate, purchase, and facilitate the transfer of securities. Shepard was retained as legal counsel for the syndicate and drew up a bond declaring that if 55 per cent of the stockholders should have agreed to the sale by February 15, the Edison shares would be purchased at 220 per cent of par in 4 per cent bonds of the Power Company. The plan meant that the Edison capital of $9,200,000 in bonds was to be represented by new bonds to the amount of $20,-240,000, with $760,000 added for expenses and profit for the syndicate. Edison himself later described this as "paying with the printing press."[9] By November, indeed, it seemed clear that the Whitney-Brady strategy was succeeding brilliantly.

Bowker did not realize the fact or the nature of the conspiracy against the Edison Company until late October when Peabody told him of the first offers being made for the Edison stock. Immediately he sensed the ominous character of the proposed deal: the company which he had worked so hard to make into a model of the highest technical efficiency and the highest administrative ethics was on the point of being surrendered to the very interests which he had most consistently fought throughout his life. Yet he also realized that opposition to this sale would entail a fearful cost: certainly fighting some of his closest and most respected business associates, possibly sacrificing the most congenial job he had ever held and the first substantial salary he had ever earned, probably forfeiting whatever usefulness and confidence he had earned with the financial community.

November, indeed, saw a crisis in Bowker's life. During long, solitary midnight walks through the deserted streets of the city he threshed the matter out in his own mind until it finally became crystal clear that

[8] R. R. B. to J. R. Dunlop, May 7, 1907.
[9] R. R. B. to Governor Charles E. Hughes, in New York *Evening Post*, April 24, 1907.

he would have to fight this surrender to the finish regardless of the consequences. The die once cast, he vigorously set forth in conversations and correspondence with his close friends, in heated discussions with the president and fellow directors of the company, in privately published memoranda to the stockholders, in newspaper and magazine articles, what for him was at stake in this proposed sale of the Edison Company to the Whitney-Brady interests.[10]

In the first place, Bowker proved that, as far as technical factors of franchise and power load were concerned, all talk of ruinous competition from the Metropolitan was sheer bluff. If directors and stockholders would only stand by the company and fight it out, there would be nothing to fear.

In the second place, Bowker argued that the proposed sale would encourage the trend toward the concentration of enormous power in the hands of irresponsible giant monopolies.

> The objections to trusts are not to their legal and economic basis, but to their usual commercial and political practices. . . . These combinations lead almost inevitably to brutal disregard of minority and public interest, to political corruption and to other obnoxious methods, as illustrated in the recent extraordinary disclosures regarding the Rubber Trusts. . . . The combination in one set of hands of most of the franchises of public supply of various sorts is fraught with grave menace to the community.[11]

For one thing, the contemplated merger represented a wholly unethical kind of financial manipulation: a thriving business was to be loaded with unnecessary and abnormal fixed charges in bond interest through the purchase of worthless securities (which Bowker had carefully shunned), thus opening the way to reckless stock-jobbing and the creation of fictitious values that would be disastrous in the long run to investors. This might be superficially a brilliant fiscal transaction, but it was fundamentally bad business practice. Worse, the enormous profits voted by the promoters to themselves really constituted a theft of public franchises. Furthermore, the deal was essentially a surrender to the Tammany school of politics, and in Bowker's opinion it was this divorce of responsibility from power under the boss system, and the political corruption made possible by corporations that were largely responsible for the curse upon municipal and national politics.

10 See especially R. R. B. to Peabody, October 26, 1898; to J. B. Henry, December 12, 1898; to Trask, January 23, March 8, 1899; R. R. B., "Piracy of Public Franchises," *Atlantic Monthly*, October, 1901.

11 Draft of a letter, R. R. B. to S. Trask, January 25, 1899.

In becoming a party to these several evils, Bowker argued that the Edison directors were endangering the future not only of the public franchise corporation but of the private corporation as well, for these evils were provoking that very defiance of the public welfare which was encouraging socialism, and thus the most serious sort of threat to private capitalism.

> The enormous combination which is throttling our city can lead only to a revolt against the "powers that be," similar to the uprising against the Tweed Ring, resulting perhaps in the municipalization of industries. . . . Much of the public protest directed against what is vaguely known as "Wall Street" and the "money power," showing itself in greenbackism, and in the silver movement, as against sound money, has come from the general revolt against the domination of legislatures and the trespass upon public and private rights on the part of such combinations as that now developing in Greater New York.[12]

With the larger implications so inescapable, the proper role of the Edison Company seemed desperately clear to Bowker. It had been made an outpost in the fight against the whole system that was now trying to engulf it: surely of all companies it should now be kept a leader in the attack on this evil in American life. The sale to the Whitney-Brady interests was unnecessary, and it was wrong. It was wrong in its objectives, its methods, and its consequences. In fact, it was not so much a sale as a surrender, "a surrender by sale to the forces of political corruption." Every drop of Bowker's fighting blood demanded that the Edison Company fight Brady to the end.

No one else, however, saw it this way. It was pointed out to Bowker that the terms of sale offered Edison stockholders a handsome profit, that the financial arrangements were perfectly normal, that he was making an ethical mountain out of an ethical molehill and reading an issue of principle into a situation where none really existed, that refusal to sell would surely bring ruinous competition and so frighten investors that capital would desert the company, that a prolonged fight against Tammany would be suicidal. It was fear, Bowker later concluded, rather than financial or engineering facts or anything else that led to the final capitulation.

Almost no one was willing to accept the gage of battle.[13] Bowker

12 *Ibid.*

13 R. R. B. to Gov. C. E. Hughes, in New York *Evening Post*, April 24, 1907; R. R. B., "Piracy of Public Franchises," *Atlantic Monthly*, October, 1901, p. 473; R. R. B. to Peabody, September 19, 1901; R. R. B., MS Memoir; R. R. B. to Peabody, September 19, 1901; R. R. B. to C. Schurz, January 25, 1899.

was told bluntly that "the game was up." The press in both New York and Philadelphia was lugubrious. Bowker tried to rally the directors, but found them resigned; Trask was deaf to all his repeated pleas and arguments. Bowker tried to rally the stockholders, but almost none of them were in a mood to take a stand. Even such public-spirited liberals as R. Fulton Cutting and Seth Low weakened and decided to sell their shares. The most discouraging development of all was to find that his closest friends, with whom he had long fought in the liberal crusade, opposed his stand and denied his logic.

Of these, Peabody was the most important. From the start he supported the sale. The two friends examined their differences in long, desperately earnest discussions. At Yaddo, Spencer Trask's beautiful estate in upper New York, they argued late into the night, each stating the other's position so clearly as to meet with no objection, and yet each unable to change his own view of duty. Mutually trusted friends were appealed to. Mrs. Trask, asked to give her judgment, decided against her intimate and trusted friend Bowker, and wrote him sharply:

> You kept saying, "It is a surrender, It is a surrender by sale," but you did not state logically, and clearly, how, where, why it is a surrender. . . . You admit it is not sold by wrong means, you do not urge that political power has been used in this case; it is not blackmail, nor coercion. It is *simply* a financial transaction with a man who *happens* to be corrupt. . . . I should like to have you set forth in a letter to me wherein this sale would be a surrender to political power. Pierpont Morgan might buy the thing, and it would simply be a sale. Wherein is this different?

Peabody and Bowker then presented the issue to R. F. Cutting, and soon to Shepard, and even Alfred White. Each one of these men opposed Bowker's position. It was a severe strain on close friendships. Both Peabody and Shepard felt that Bowker should be morally bound by these third-party verdicts, but this was not Bowker's view. "I feel in business," he later wrote Peabody in reviewing the incident, "and I think you will essentially agree with me, as we both feel in politics, that no man can rightfully subordinate his conscience or his conduct to another, and it has been to my keen regret that both you and Shepard seemed to take an attitude based on the contrary view."[14]

Bowker even turned to Carl Schurz for support, pointing out that he was acting "in the line of public service in which I have had so much of my inspiration from you," but Schurz declined to be drawn into the controversy. The irony of it rankled. "I feel disappointed beyond

[14] R. R. B. to Peabody, September 19, 1901.

words," Bowker wrote to Shepard and Theodore Roosevelt, "that in my skirmish in what I think is to be one of the great battles of the near future, I was not only without the support of my oldest personal friends and my nearest business friend, but found them, as I look upon it, not in motive but in practice, on the other side. I think there is nothing more difficult, as all experience at Albany and at Washington shows, than for a man to differ from his friends, to separate himself from his class, and to fight against his own environment. Nothing has been harder to me in all my life than this particular episode, and nothing has seemed to me more important, not in its immediate results—for that I scarcely expected,—but in making possible a good fight in the future."[15] Six years later, Bowker had not changed his mind on this point. Writing to O. G. Villard in 1905, he referred to the Edison sale as a time "when some of our friends most sincerely devoted to municipal reform failed to stand by in what was really, as has since been shown, a municipal crisis."[16]

It was certainly no part of Bowker's way to give up a fight simply because he had to fight alone. Even when he knew that his opposition was futile, he showed vigor and resourcefulness. By late October he was refuting Peabody's arguments in carefully reasoned letters. By mid-November he was in a bitter clash with Trask over the latter's autocratic exclusion of the issue from the directors' meetings. "When the Company government becomes an absolutism," he wrote Trask in indignant censure, "whether the monarchy be constitutional or otherwise, I don't fit the situation, and you would be entitled to another prime minister."[17] When, early in December, it became clear that no consultation with the stockholders was contemplated, he determined to initiate such a move himself, but was restrained by Peabody and Shepard, who convinced him that the information in his possession had been given under a seal of confidence and that he was morally obliged to withhold public comment. However, on December 10, the press carried sensational stories to the effect that Whitney's Power Company had acquired the Edison properties, and he considered himself released from his pledge, two days later mailing out printed circulars rallying the stockholders against the sale of their holdings.[18]

Ten days later, when his efforts as an Edison officer to win over the company's other officers, directors, and stockholders had clearly failed, Bowker presented his resignation as vice-president, so as to be freer to

[15] R. R. B. to Shepard, and to T. Roosevelt, March 2, 1899; R. R. B. to O. G. Villard, May 5, 1905.

[16] R. R. B. to O. G. Villard, May 5, 1905.

[17] R. R. B. to S. Trask, November 19, 1898, March 8, 1899.

[18] R. R. B. to J. B. Henry, December 12, 1898.

fight as a director and stockholder. When, on January 19, 1899, the directors issued the first formal announcement of the terms of sale to the stockholders and his plea for some further explanation to them had been voted down,[19] he sent his own statement to the *Evening Post* whence it reached the other papers.[20] In February, he reluctantly took the one step remaining and organized a stockholders' committee to protect the rights of those not wishing to enter into the proposed arrangement.[21] Already a few small stockholders had written to him for leadership. He printed a letter, and boldly asked Trask for permission to have it mailed out by the company office in the same way that the syndicate circulars had been mailed, asserting it was within his rights as a stockholder to copy a list of stockholders. This request was too much for Trask, who refused and rather bluntly invited Bowker to resign as a director. This Bowker did on March 2.

It is clear that neither the Edison directors nor the Brady interests wished Bowker to leave the company. Early in the negotiations he was offered an increase of $10,000 in his annual salary if he would remain,[22] and assurances were given him that his management would be continued and protected. On December 28 the directors received Bowker's resignation as first vice-president, but induced him to remain in office until the issue of the annual reports. On January 19 they formally accepted his resignation, but persuaded him to continue through the new year as general supervisor.[23] It was publicly declared by one of Bowker's friends that even Brady himself finally came to Bowker with a handsome proposition to induce him to remain in charge of the company. "You may name your own office," Brady said, "and your own salary." But Bowker was not moved. "Mr. Brady," he replied, "you haven't enough money to hire me!"[24] Bowker's resignation as a director was accepted on March 7.

Bowker's resignation and the protest it symbolized did not go unnoticed. He heard from strangers, from associates in the Society for Political Education and the Reform Club, from magazine editors and

19 R. R. B. to S. Trask, March 8, 1899.

20 New York *Evening Post,* January 20, 1899. Bowker apparently planned to follow this with a public letter to Spencer Trask. A draft of such a letter, dated January 25, contains a full, uncompromising attack on the proposed sale from every standpoint, but it is not clear that it was sent.

21 R. R. B. to S. Trask, February 21; to C. H. Coster, February 21; to E. Cole, March 3; to W. A. Aiken, March 7, 1899; G. K. Richards to R. R. B., March 13, 17, 1899; J. Campbell to R. R. B., March 22, 1899.

22 R. R. B. to Senator G. P. Wetmore, December 22, 1910.

23 R. R. B., "Piracy of Public Franchises," *Atlantic Monthly,* October, 1901, p. 474; R. R. B. to S. Trask, January 20, February 22, 1899.

24 Arthur W. Milbury in the Passaic *Daily News,* September 7, 1928.

managers of other public-service corporations, concurring in his analysis, praising his course of action, and thinking it well that "certain men should stand for honesty and pay the penalty publicly before the community." Testimonials to his leadership came from the New York Fire Department, from Wisconsin, from London. Undoubtedly the one that most touched Bowker was the two handsomely embossed illuminated memorial volumes containing a heart-warming acknowledgment of his efforts in their behalf from the Edison employees.[25]

The end of the Edison Company as an independent corporation came swiftly. By March 3 the stock transfer was completed. On March 21 all quotations of Edison stock were stricken from the Exchange, on May 18, Thomas Edison resigned as a director, and on May 26 all the others. Meanwhile, much that Bowker had most feared came true. The capital stock of the Power Company was increased to $36,000,000, which was paid by the promoters to themselves as clear profit except for the organization tax and the $4,000,000 cash deposit. Furthermore, no reduction of prices was made as promised,[26] and Bowker's repeated appeals to Brady were rebuffed.[27] But this was not the end of the story. By the end of 1899 the Power Company was confronted by a powerful rival in the Consolidated Gas Company, leagued with William Rockefeller.[28] A Wall Street war followed, and when the smoke cleared on January 2, 1900, the Power Company had been swallowed up by Consolidated Gas. This brought the gas, electric, and traction interests of New York City into a single great monopoly, and the electric-light companies were now swiftly amalgamated with either the Power or the Edison structures.

The final move in this game was the merger of the Power Company and the Edison Company into the New York Edison Company, a transaction which gave Bowker one final opportunity to fight what he regarded as the irresponsible manipulation of public-franchise corporations. It was a hopeless fight in every respect except the opportunity it provided to register a protest and expose what was happening, and in

25 George Iles to R. R. B., March 28, 1899; John R. Dunlop to R. R. B., September 6, 14, 17, 1899; F. Pierce to R. R. B., January 31, 1899; A. Dow to R. R. B., February 25, 1899; Alice Mitchell to R. R. B., March 3, 1899; Edison Electric Illuminating Company of New York, *Memorial Volumes* presented to R. R. Bowker, New York, 1899. Vols. I, II.

26 See interview with R. R. B. in New York *Herald*, April 28, 1907; Jones, *Power History*, 261; G. F. Peabody to R. R. B., November 10, 1928. R. R. B. to Miss Mary C. Nerney, November 14, 1928; Maltbie, *Franchises of Electric Corporations*, 44–45.

27 R. R. B. to G. F. Peabody, September 19, 1901; R. R. B. to W. A. Aiken, March 7, 1899.

28 Mark D. Hirsch, *William C. Whitney, Modern Warwick*, 542. See also p. 543, n. 5 in *ibid*.

this it was successful. On May 3, 1901, announcement was made that the merger would be effected on May 20. Bowker's first thought was to contest the legality of the consolidation in the courts, but the Tammany affiliation of the judges having jurisdiction dissuaded him from this move. His next step was to draw up a printed memorandum of protest which asserted, with characteristic vigor and statistical evidence, that the proposed merger was contrary to law and contrary to the interests of the Edison Company, the Edison stockholders, the Edison customers, and society at large. Bowker showed, for example, that within two years the original $9,200,000 of the Edison stock had been so juggled that it had come to be represented by $51,200,000 in securities, or five times its original amount, and that actually the consumer was required to pay a price that would produce earnings on three times the capitalization needed by the lighting industry.[29] Finally, on June 6, he sent a formal protest to the company against the consolidation and demanded full payment for his stock. When the company offered him three hundred dollars a share, Bowker declined the offer on the grounds that he and W. A. Shortt, another minority stockholder, were denied the information necessary to evaluate their holdings.[30] Since Bowker and Shortt refused to exchange or sell their stock, the company was finally compelled to secure a court order for the appraisal of their 216 of the 92,000 shares outstanding.[31]

The exasperation of the company was understandable. To force an appraisal of a property estimated at fifty millions of dollars or more in order to determine the exact value of ten to twenty thousand dollars of its stock seemed an outrageous position for anyone to take. "I assure you," Peabody wrote Bowker, "that there is no other person whom I would have believed to be both absolutely sane and upright in such an astonishing procedure." No wonder that strenuous efforts were made to coax, threaten, or force Bowker to accept a settlement out of court. Brady sought legal means of voiding the original stock issue made to Bowker, but the latter uncovered a technical flaw in the merger papers and intimated that if he were driven into a corner by Brady, he would take advantage of the carelessness of the lawyer who drew up the merger

29 The Stevens Report of 1905, embodying the result of an examination conducted by Charles Evans Hughes into the overcapitalization of the Consolidated Gas Company, completely justified Bowker's analysis. (See E. P. Wheeler to R. R. B., April 18, 1905; O. G. Villard to R. R. B., May 3, 1905.)

30 N. F. Brady to R. R. B., June 10, 1901; R. R. B. to N. F. Brady, June 11, 1901; R. R. B. to G. F. Dominick, June 28, 1901.

31 Supreme Court, New York County, "In the matter of the application of the New York Edison Company . . . to appraise the value of the stock . . . held by R. R. Bowker," July 12, 1901; Supreme Court, New York County, Order to Show Cause . . . , July 12, 1901.

act, and this was the end of the stock-voiding plan.[32] A number of appeals were made to Bowker's sense of honor, especially through his friend Peabody.[33] It was pointed out that it was morally inconsistent for him to have advised others not to sell their stock at the time of the Edison transfer, and yet finally to sell most of his own. It was charged that he intended to make a sensational profit on his stock at everybody's expense. It was argued that he was guilty of a straight lack of consideration for his business associates. This suspicion of his motives was a heart-breaking ordeal for Bowker, but he answered each attack, patiently clarified over and over again the real considerations which prompted him, and stuck to his guns.[34]

In the end Bowker won a complete victory. By July his first demand for information was granted in principle; by September he was supplied with a first installment of figures. In July 1902, after a full year, the appraisal was completed, and it then filled two hundred pages of printed testimony. The final judgment of the court awarded Bowker and Shortt $500 for each of their shares, plus the accrued dividends on the old Edison stock which Brady had sought to deny them. The full memorandum of the minority stockholders' case which Bowker's counsel submitted to the appraisers on June 4, 1902, was a powerful document and reviewed once more, with great skill and cogency, the entire history of the Brady-Whitney campaign against the Edison interest.

Peabody may have hoped that the Edison sale was now a closed chapter, but Bowker regarded it as "a point of departure" from which he could be "of useful public service even under present municipal conditions."[35] He had always intended to write a frank exposure of the manner of the Edison capture for some influential periodical, and in the fall of 1901, in time to swell the attack on Tammany in the New York mayoralty campaign, the *Atlantic Monthly* published his smashing essay, "The Piracy of Public Franchises,"[36] immediately reprinted in *Municipal Affairs*. Shepard tried to discourage him from this,[37] and Peabody assured him that such an article would kill any future employment as a corporation executive. Legal counsel, however, declared the manuscript to be non-liable, the *Atlantic* editors anticipated that it

32 E. M. Shepard to R. R. B., June 25, 1901; R. R. B. to E. H. Lewis, July 29, 1901; G. F. Peabody to R. R. B., August 30, 1901.

33 G. F. Peabody to R. R. B., July 21, August 30, 1901.

34 R. R. B. to G. F. Dominick, June 28, 1901; to E. H. Lewis, July 29, 1901; to G. F. Peabody, September 19, 1901; to J. W. Pryor, October 20, 1902; to T. A. Edison, October 22, 1902; to A. N. Brady, July 13, 1906.

35 R. R. B. to G. F. Peabody, September 19, 1901.

36 *Atlantic Monthly*, October, 1901, pp. 463–82; reprinted in *Municipal Affairs*, December, 1901, pp. 886–904.

37 E. M. Shepard to R. R. B., March 27, 1899.

would create a sensation in New York, the editors of *Municipal Affairs* prophesied that it would "attract wide attention and be very generally quoted," and Wheeler, reading it over in the midst of the campaign, declared that it would "stir the blood like the surrender of Fort Sumter and compel thinking men to gird up their loins for the contest this fall."[38] The remedy which Bowker prescribed for the kind of piracy of public franchises represented by the Edison capture may well have troubled the consciences of a number of his close associates:

> The remedy which will cut to the root of these evils . . . is a municipal spirit, a civic courage, a political morale, especially on the part of the well-to-do, which will overcome the timidity of capital, and stand fearlessly firm against Tammany in New York or against a Republican ring in Philadelphia. The power and danger of Tammany misrule is nowhere more strikingly shown than by the fact that such representative citizens, men of integrity, ability, and honor, as made up the Edison Boards, among them sincere and foremost leaders in altruistic enterprise, in crusades against vice, and in efforts for municipal reform, hesitate to lead in opposition to this form of Tammany domination lest they should not have the support of those for whose financial interests they are trustees.

Bowker never changed his view of the piracy of the Edison properties. In 1907 he wrote a public letter to Governor Charles E. Hughes, printed in the *Evening Post*,[39] which flatly declared that if a public service commission such as then existed in Massachusetts or such as Hughes was then favoring for New York had existed in 1899, the Edison Company would never have been captured by "politico-financial buccaneers." Bowker considered it one of the best compliments ever paid him when a former Edison official later remarked that if Bowker's policies had been generally adopted by public utility companies, there would have been no need for a public service commission.[40]

The mayoralty campaign to which Wheeler referred and for which the *Atlantic* article had been timed seemed to Bowker to involve many of the same issues and certainly the same enemy he had just been fighting on the Edison front, and an equally unhappy opposition to his close friends Peabody and Shepard.

Tammany had won a smashing victory in 1897 in electing Robert

38 R. R. B., MS Memoir; E. P. Wheeler to R. R. B., August 18, 24, 1901.
39 April 24, 1907.
40 R. R. B. to O. G. Villard, October 3, 1919.

A Camp Manhattan Reunion at Erlowest, 1908. *(Left to right)* George Jeremiah, R. R. Bowker, Carl Ludwig Jellinghaus, Albert Delafield, Carl Schurz Petrasch, Carl Frederic Jellinghaus, Nelson Stanley Spencer, Edwin Thomas Hiscox, Percy Stearns Hildreth, Edward Morse Shepard, Robert William Thompson, George Huddleston Pride

Mr. and Mrs. Richard Rogers Bowker

Van Wyck the first mayor of Greater New York and was now in full possession of the city government. Van Wyck made a clean sweep of the heads of departments appointed by Mayor Strong and even found a way to appoint notorious "Big Bill" Devery chief of police. Under Devery the city ran wide open. The East Side became what Bowker called "a seething cauldron of social iniquity and political corruption." Bishop Potter's exposures of vice conditions shocked the city to indignation. Tweed had stolen directly from the city, but Croker and his gang knew a better trick than that: they perfected the old practice of levying tribute on illegal resorts and divided it between their own pockets and the machine campaign-chest. Small wonder that every reform organization worth its salt prepared to do battle with Tammany as the mayoralty campaign of 1901 began.

Bowker's preoccupation with the Edison developments and his strained health prevented him from working as vigorously in this campaign as he had intended, but Tammany nevertheless felt his well-aimed blows. As chairman of the City Club Council, he appointed a committee to organize mass meetings in each borough before the nomination of candidates, appointed another committee on publications and records, and was commissioned by the club to support the Merchants' Association in pressing charges against the Tammany police commissioners. In the main, however, he devoted his energies to the program of the Citizens' Union, which had been preparing, ever since Seth Low's defeat in 1897, for this second municipal election.[41] First Bowker helped the Union organize a fusion Committee of One Hundred to unite Republicans, anti-Tammany Democrats, and Independents; then, as a member of this committee, he formulated and secured the adoption of a resolution aimed to guarantee the best possible nonpartisan nominations.[42] To Cutting, chairman of the committee, he gave such exhaustive recommendations on men and records as only one with a close knowledge of the situation could master, and Wheeler leaned heavily on him for advice.[43]

Nine months earlier, as chairman of the City Club Council, Bowker had sounded out Seth Low for the Fusion nomination and had received an evasive answer.[44] Consequently he promoted the candidacy of his friend Edward Morse Shepard, whose fine record of public service and leadership as a well-known Independent Democrat for many

41 Wheeler, *Sixty Years of American Life*, 385–86.

42 See R. R. B. to E. P. Wheeler, May 13, 1901.

43 R. R. B. to R. F. Cutting, August 24, 1901; E. P. Wheeler to R. R. B., August 24, October 21, 1901.

44 R. R. B. to Seth Low, November 8, 1900; Seth Low to R. R. B., November 12, 1900.

years seemed to make him an ideal choice. When definitely approached by the committee, however, Shepard declared that "he was out of politics for the campaign" and spoke of going to Europe. Bowker and others felt that, had Shepard been willing, he would have been accepted by all parties as the Fusion candidate.[45] On September 4 the committee met to draw up the Fusion ticket. It finally selected Seth Low, who was induced to accept and was formally notified by a committee of eighteen on which Bowker served. Bowker himself was nominated for comptroller, but declined because of his deteriorating eyesight. The Fusion leaders now felt absolutely confident of success. They had secured anti-Tammany unity and a leader with a brilliant reputation: Low had been for four years the successful mayor of Brooklyn and for ten years the nationally esteemed president of Columbia University; he had served on the Rapid Transit Board and the Hague Peace Conference. What could Tammany do?

It was the Fusion theory that Tammany, realizing that it stood no chance of winning the election, would put up a decorous war horse to ride before inevitable defeat, as it had in 1894, but everyone was thunderstruck at the warrior chosen. Tammany nominated Edward Morse Shepard, and Shepard accepted! It was Croker's boldest nomination since he had run Abram S. Hewitt in 1886, and it was done with the approval of the Brooklyn bosses. Wheeler called it the greatest surprise he had ever experienced in all his forty years of acquaintance with politics.[46] Bowker, like all the other Fusionists, was shocked and dismayed at Shepard's action, but with characteristic generosity he appreciated the high motives that prompted his friend.[47] Many New York Democrats were disgusted with Tammany and honestly desired to reform the city government under an anti-Tammany leader. Shepard, who had made absolutely no commitment to Croker in accepting the nomination, was sincerely convinced that he could remain clear of the bosses and possibly even win Tammany over to the higher standards of the days of his father's sachemship.

A number of Independent Democrats supported Shepard, urging him to accept the nomination and working loyally with him afterwards. Among these were Peabody, Albert Stickney, A. Augustus Healy, and other "Shepard Democrats" of Brooklyn. On the other hand, such friends of Shepard as Carl Schurz, George McAneny, Wheeler, Stetson,

45 R. R. B., "A Smashing Letter," Brooklyn *Eagle*, November 1, 1901.

46 Wheeler, *Sixty Years of American Life*, 392–93.

47 See R. R. B. to E. M. Shepard, October 4, 1901, partly quoted below; R. R. B., "Edward Morse Shepard," *City College Quarterly*, December, 1911, pp. 231–32; E. M. Shepard, "The Second Mayoralty Election in Greater New York," *Atlantic Monthly*, February, 1902, pp. 192–208.

and Bowker were obliged to do all they could to defeat him. Bowker conceded that there could be no better executive in the mayor's office than Shepard, but insisted tht he simply would not be free. "I feel as strongly as ever," he wrote a friend shortly after Shepard's nomination, "that Tammany is *the* public enemy whose defeat at the polls is the first prerequisite for a true Democracy, and I cannot let personal affection or appreciation color my sense of public duty."[48] Not only Shepard's friends but many of his foes suspected him of a major error in political judgment. The *Press* described him as "the thinnest veil ever used to mask the face of a political burglar entering a municipal household." The *Sun* declared simply that he had sacrificed his good name "for the sake of a chance to get office." Others attributed to him presidential aspirations.[49]

The Low-Shepard campaign was one of the most exciting municipal contests ever held in New York. Meetings were organized in every part of the city. Low spoke briefly when he spoke at all, but William Travers Jerome, the Fusion nominee for district attorney, was a powerhouse of oratory. Bourke Cochran was a consistently popular Tammany champion, and Shepard conducted an extremely adroit campaign. He opened it by making no apologies and asking no quarter. In fact, he carried the war to the enemy by vigorously attacking the Fusion ticket as neither competent nor nonpartisan, but designed merely to strengthen the Platt Republicans. To the Fusion demand that Shepard repeat his anti-Tammany charges of 1897, he cleverly countered with a demand that Seth Low and Carl Schurz repeat their anti-Platt speeches of 1897.[50]

Bowker threw himself into the fray. He pitched in to help organize the independent Democrats in his assembly district.[51] He induced the Brooklyn Democratic Club, founded and officered by Shepard, to adopt a position of neutrality, and resigned when this truce seemed to be violated.[52] When a Shepard movement was started by some City College alumni, Bowker wrote that Tammany was "associated not with education, but with vice and crime," and persuaded other prominent alumni to join him in organizing an opposition movement.[53] When certain Henry George followers in Brooklyn came out for Shepard, he

48 R. R. B. to H. A. Metz, October 8, 1901.

49 Alexander, *A Political History of the State of New York,* IV, 364–67.

50 "Challenge to Low Issued by Shepard," campaign flier quoting from his speech of October 30, 1901.

51 R. Baker to R. R. B., December 1, 1900.

52 Brooklyn Democratic Club, printed statement by anti-Shepard members, October 7, 1901; R. R. B. to H. Putnam, October 31, 1901.

53 R. R. B. to Hon. John Hardy, October 26, 1901; printed flier dated October 31, 1901.

wrote a strong statement for the press refuting the logic of this alliance.[54] Capitalizing on the peculiar anti-vice features of the campaign, he organized a Woman's Campaign Committee, which proved so effective that during the last two weeks the City Club Council devoted almost all its time to assisting it.[55]

Bowker's most telling contribution to the campaign was, as usual, journalistic. He had already recognized the talent which Gustavus Myers had for well-documented pamphleteering and used him actively. When Myers first showed him the manuscript of his *History of Tammany Hall* in 1899, Bowker realized its value as a campaign document, offered useful editorial suggestions, and went all out to help get it published. After eight publishers, including Putnam, had refused to touch it for fear of the political consequences, Bowker arranged to have the Reform Club underwrite the costs, supervise the revision, and publish it.[56] He put Myers to work writing such other campaign documents as *Some Facts About Unger,* exposing the Tammany candidate for district attorney; *Facts for New York Parents,* describing the system of police-protected prostitution; and *Ten Months of Tammany,* which was completed by another. Already Bowker had seen to the preparation of the pamphlet, *Some Things Richard Croker Has Said and Done.* All four tracts were printed by the City Club under Bowker's direction and proved very effective. As the City Club's official campaign address, Bowker drafted a statement "To Voters of Open Mind," incorporating suggestions made by other council members and printed over his signature.[57] It was a stirring document which cheerfully testified to Shepard's splendid character while exposing the role he had been forced into. Bowker also worked hard to publish the report of the City Club franchise committee, of which he was chairman, in time to add this artillery fire to the rest.[58] And at the end of September appeared his brilliant *Atlantic* article, "The Piracy of Public Franchises," warning against the Tammany threat to corporation property.

Bowker's chief blow, however, was a blistering attack on Shepard's candidacy that was shrewdly timed to hit the enemy on the very eve of the election. He shaped his charge in the form of an open letter addressed to the Brooklyn Democratic Club president, but he aimed it at

54 Brooklyn *Eagle,* November 1, 1901; see R. Baker to R. R. B., October 18, 23, 1901.

55 R. R. B. to W. J. Schieffelin, November 21, 1932; City Club, Report of Secretary, November 21, 1901; R. R. B., MS Memoir.

56 G. Myers, *The History of Tammany Hall, xii;* G. Myers to R. R. B., December 20, 1899; M. R. Maltbie to R. R. B., October 13, 1900, August 26, 1901, June 29, 1903.

57 The City Club, October 31, 1901.

58 R. R. B. to F. Cutting, September 5, 1901.

the Brooklyn community and especially at Democrats. He intended this to be his own personal campaign *pièce de résistance,* he hoped it would kill Shepard's chances, and he offered to pay for the printing of five thousand copies if they could be effectively circulated.[59] The Brooklyn *Eagle* published it prominently on November 1, entitled it "A Smashing Letter," added in the headlines that it came from "Mr. Shepard's most intimate personal friend," and called it "a powerful statement of facts, reasons, and conclusions." The very night it appeared, Charles Francis Adams referred to it in his anti-Shepard speech at the Brooklyn Academy. "Its shaft went home," declared one of Bowker's friends, "and cannot be extricated by sophistry or squirms of declamation. It is a trumpet-note in behalf of good government and civic duty, and its appearance is most timely."[60] Peabody rushed to defend Shepard and refute Bowker's attack, but his letter, similarly printed in the *Eagle,* was too hurried to be effective. Bowker's statement carried great weight. The cogency of its remarks, its perfect timing, and the fact that Bowker was known to be Shepard's close friend probably made it the most effective single campaign piece of his life.

Bowker's attack began with a personal tribute to Shepard's character, his record of public service, and his sincere motives. It characterized his campaign as "masterful, brilliant, and adroit . . . dignified and as fair to his opponents as they would permit." After refuting Shepard's main arguments one by one, it charged Shepard with inconsistency, and gave an explanation of his amazing change of view since 1897 and of his present position which Shepard never forgave:

> Mr. Low has not changed; his platform has not changed; Tammany has changed only for the worse; and the only change to account for Mr. Shepard's change of view is his own nomination to mask the outrageous Tammany ticket. . . . His speeches are as spotted as the tiger itself—here honest and brave words, there eloquent silences; again praise for an historic Tammany utterly contrary to the Tammany of present fact—but nowhere the ringing words of indignation which once won for him the leadership of Democrats who wished better for their party than Tammany and the Willoughby Street ring. Should he be elected, as I believe he will not, he will have made for himself an impossible situation, disastrous for good government, and for the real welfare of the Democratic party. He cannot be loyal to the city and to Tammany Hall. . . . The more intimately we know Mr. Shepard, the more

[59] R. R. B. to A. H. Eastmond; R. R. B. to G. H. Crawford, November 20, 1901.
[60] St. Clair Hester to R. R. B., November 2, 1901.

truly we believe that he could not be a traitor to good government, but good government is not possible, even with the "best of men," with the worst of tickets and the worst of forces behind him.

The election resulted in a stunning defeat for Tammany. Shepard trailed in every borough but one. It was, in fact, a great civic uprising, and the public-spirited leaders with whom Bowker had worked could justly take pride in their successful efforts to expose Tammany and organize the community conscience. For Bowker there was even a flattering move to appoint him president of the Board of Tax Commissioners, which he squelched to the dismay of his friends.[61] But his friendship with Peabody and Shepard, strained by the Edison controversy, was now broken.

Until almost the end of the campaign, Bowker was able to maintain cordial relations with the two close friends whom he was doing everything in his power to defeat. He called Peabody's anti-Low letter to Dr. Parkhurst "excellent," offered to show him the City Club's address against Shepard in advance of publication, and gladly gave him help in preparing a biographical sketch of Shepard for the *Review of Reviews*. "One of these days," he wrote Peabody in mid-October, "after both our candidates have won, I hope to remake your acquaintance, and shake hands with you over the dead past and the live future." The same trustful intimacy had existed with Shepard. Immediately after Shepard's acceptance of the Tammany nomination Bowker had written to pledge his personal friendship and respect, though opposing his political views:

> Whether the coming contest results in your success as a triumph of personal character, or the defeat of Tammany as the public enemy—for which I must still hope and work,—our city is happily certain of a chief magistrate best fitted by character, purpose, and experience, to be its worthy head. . . . Should the great burden of the administration of this great city be laid upon you . . . you will have my most earnest wishes and any help that I can give toward fulfilling the ideal which I know is in your heart.[62]

The two friends continued their usual Sunday afternoon walks and discussed frankly those features of the campaign of which they could speak freely.

To both Peabody and Shepard, however, Bowker's "smashing letter" constituted a breach of friendship in that it coupled fervid pro-

61 Robert Baker to R. R. B., November 23, 1901.
62 R. R. B. to E. M. Shepard, October 4, 1901.

testations of personal loyalty with a deliberate intent to injure. Bowker did not realize for some time how deeply he had wounded Shepard, and then was hopeful that the damage might be soon mended. "There have been indeed many wounds in the old campaign," he wrote a mutual friend, possibly for Shepard's eyes, "which perhaps only time can heal. But where friendships have been so long a-making they should be slow a-breaking."[63] When Shepard finally did put his feelings into words, they must have distressed Bowker. What had so profoundly shocked him, he wrote, was the use of a personal intimacy with a friend as a basis for a disparaging estimate of him in his public relations. "That a man having affection and respect for a friend, should do such a thing against him when he seems to be . . . in extreme personal peril, is certainly close to the incredible."[64] Shepard did not attend Bowker's wedding in 1902, but by 1907 some of the old intimacy was recovered. By then Shepard could term the break "a partial interruption," attribute it to "mistaken diction on the one side and misapprehension of feeling on the other," and judge it "one of the chief regrets of my life."[65] Time was more generous where Peabody was concerned.

[63] R. R. B. to G. H. Crawford, November 20, 1901.
[64] E. M. Shepard to R. R. B., November 30, 1901.
[65] E. M. Shepard to R. R. B., September 4, 1907.

343

XX

Finis Coronat Opus

WITH THE conclusion of the Edison fight and the mayoralty campaign of 1901, Bowker began a withdrawal from active public life which was made more and more necessary by failing eyesight. In spite of excellent health and undiminished enthusiasms, at the very prime of life and the height of his influence and ability, he had to accept an affliction which terminated the creative period of his career. Thirty very active years still lay ahead of him, but they were increasingly conditioned by the hard fact of almost total blindness. Old crusading interests were loyally maintained: copyright, the library movement, political reform, free trade, civil service, and civil liberties; but Bowker's role was to be more and more a consultative and advisory one, his influence more impersonal, more indirect. He certainly kept busy. "Tonight is the Civil Service Dinner at the City Club," he wrote of a typical week in 1917, "tomorrow DeLaval and Brooklyn Institute meetings, and Friday noon my library talk." But the opportunity for active leadership had slipped away. There were rich compensations. Marriage converted the bachelor into a family man; the new home in Stockbridge transformed the urban executive into a country squire. A comfortable income augmented by new business relations made possible more leisure for writing and the cultivation of friendships. College, fraternity, Edison, and Authors' Club associations were actively maintained. Bowker's life was never to know a winter time. What now followed was Indian summer.

The blindness which colored every detail of Bowker's life from 1900 until his death in 1933 had a long history. He had inherited myopia from his father, a condition which was noticed when he was four years old. From his early college years he wore thick glasses, and during his senior year a noted specialist predicted early blindness unless he undertook a delicate operation whose outcome seemed so problematical that Bowker refused to risk it. His professional work placed a terrible strain on already weak vision—book reviewing, proofreading, and especially the minutiae of bibliographical supervision. The first ominous signs of trouble developed in 1897. By 1903 he could not recognize individuals sitting across the aisle of a train; by 1905 he could not read for more than an hour at a time, was obliged to give up writing his own copy, and found it dangerous to move through the city alone. After 1910 he could do no more than distinguish the difference between light and darkness. Expert treatments were undertaken,[1] and in 1920 some hope was held out that an operation might restore vision, Bowker ill concealing his eager anticipation. No political defeat of his career came harder than the medical verdict, when the treatment was over, that there was now no hope.

It was typical of Bowker that he rose above this handicap and determined to live out his life as though no defect were there. He would not permit people to refer to his privation, and he became impatient when friends sent him news items concerning the blind; for years he refused to contribute to institutions caring for the blind and took no interest whatsoever in Braille, though later this was less true. In Glendale he had strings run along the trails in his woods to guide his steps, with knots placed at points where he would call the attention of visitors to views which he would then describe in detail from memory. He continued to be an inveterate traveler, and would later narrate what he had "seen" without ever betraying the fact that it had all been at secondhand. His memory was such that he could direct taxi drivers through New York traffic with exasperating exactness and indicate points of interest to his guests with infallible precision when motoring through the Berkshire country—taking his cue from road turns and differences in road surfaces. In committee meetings he utilized his acute memory for voices to recognize instantly those who gathered to greet him. His desk at the *Publishers' Weekly* office and his bookshelves at home were so arranged that he could confidently turn to the materials he wanted. His memory and mental alertness were such that he could serve as auditor of a substantial business concern with only a listener's access to figures, and the stream of editorials, letters to the press, verse, articles, and pamphlets continued without the slightest break. Throughout this trial Bowker's chief thought was that being blind was more desirable than being deaf since it was less trying on others and seemed

[1] The affliction was progressive atrophy of the nerves of the center of the retina. In 1910 Bowker placed himself in the care of Dr. W. Wilmer, who later remarked that this was just five years too late. W. W. Bishop, in the *Library Quarterly*, October, 1945, pp. 333–34.

to leave the victim more cheerful, and that his slight awareness of light was infinitely better than total blindness.

The tragedy of Bowker's blindness was partly offset by his marriage to Alice Mitchell on New Year's Day, 1902. It was a surprise to all of his friends. When one remarked to him, "I wonder that you didn't do it before," he replied, "That's what everyone says, that's what everyone says." Talcott Williams wrote, "For years you have seemed to me the one man I know who could make a perfect husband."[2] In a way it was a surprise to Bowker, also. It was on his birthday, only four months earlier, that the idea had first occurred to him, and he immediately announced it to his sister. The ceremony was performed in a private home in Brookline, Massachusetts, by Edward Everett Hale, a mutual friend who had introduced the couple to each other twenty years earlier. Bowker was now fifty-four, his bride was thirty-eight. The wedding was a small family affair and was followed by a wedding trip to Europe and Africa.

Bowker first met his bride-to-be at a house party in Normandy in 1881 when he was a Harper editor aged thirty-two and she a charming young girl of sixteen. The party was a jolly one, but devoid of romantic significance for Bowker, and indeed he did not see much of Alice Mitchell again until the nineties when she went to Cambridge to live. Her father, Edward Cushing Mitchell, was a Bowdoin graduate who had become professor of Greek at the old Theological Department of the University of Chicago and later head of the McCall mission in Paris, where Alice was the favorite piano pupil of Marmontel. Her mother, Mariah Morton, was a niece of Vice-President Morton; and one of Alice's cousins became Dean Robbins of the Cathedral of St. John the Divine. On her father's death, the young girl had a trying ordeal for a number of years, tending an invalid mother and looking out for an obstreperous younger brother on seriously limited funds. This experience put a severe strain on her health. When she moved to Cambridge on her mother's death to keep house for herself and her brother, she earned her living by giving French and music lessons.

When Bowker came to know of Alice Mitchell's plight, he was able to lend both moral and financial assistance in various ways, visiting her on his occasional trips to Boston. The friendship ripened. By 1898, Alice Mitchell had overcome her first sense of inferiority and was entering more and more fully into Bowker's thoughts and problems. As he wrote the chapters of his *Arts of Life*, he sent her the manuscript for comments; they exchanged views on art, poetry, and religion, and on his increasingly frequent visits he would take her to the opera and the

2 T. Williams to R. R. B., April 18, 1902.

symphony. She followed solicitously his world tour in 1898 to cure his eyestrain, and wrote him with pride when he resigned from the Edison Company.[3] The friendship had not been a romance, but when old ties with the Edison Company, Shepard, and Peabody snapped, Bowker suddenly realized what this friendship meant to him.

The two made a handsome couple. A friend of Bowker's had written in 1895 that Alice Mitchell was one of the most charming and beautiful women that she had ever known. Bowker himself declared that he had never seen such beauty combined with such vivacity. An old family friend who had known Bowker's wife as a girl declared that her marriage brought to her almost all the happiness she had ever known, and that due to it she really blossomed out.[4] The two had many devoted friends who filled the household for teas, dinners, and weekend visits. Mrs. Bowker, who was a bright, graceful woman, looked like a butterfly as she moved about in her flowerly dresses, but she contributed a lively knowledge of books and music to any conversation. She knew several languages, she was an accomplished pianist, and in Glendale earned a reputation as something of a practical nurse. Bowker called her "Lady Dear"; others, "The Angel." As he became increasingly deprived of sight, she served as his all-seeing eyes and constant reporter.

Bowker brought his bride to a new home which he had just built in Stockbridge, Massachusetts, as the fulfillment of a long-cherished desire for a country place. In the eighties he had taken his family to Lake George, made familiar by the continuing Camp Manhattan outings and the residence there of the Candace Wheelers and the Shepards, and in 1894 he seriously considered purchasing some property there. Bowker's mother, however, feared the unruly lake, and Stockbridge, known to Bowker since 1873, was finally chosen as a more satisfactory site. During several summers spent here from 1892 until 1898 at the Edward Arms and Red Lion Inn, Bowker looked about for a home and finally hit upon the old Caroline Dresser place in the Glendale section of Stockbridge. Made of bricks a hundred years old, the house was badly in need of repair, but the property seemed to hold infinite possibilities. Close by the house flowed the Housatonic, back of it was a fine hill, and beyond this a splendid pine wood; the property included some fifty acres of woods, hillside, and river slope. In 1898, Bowker secured title to it with the intention of giving it to his mother and sister.

He thoroughly enjoyed making over this abandoned farm. First he rebuilt the house, clearing away the old horse sheds, taking down the whole front and part of each side of the walls, overhauling and strength-

[3] Letters of Alice Mitchell to R. R. B., 1898–1902.
[4] M. B. Bruère to R. R. B., May 6, 1933.

ening the beams and floor structures. He designed a new façade with triple windows on each side of the door and extended the front pillars forward from the pilasters to make an attractive porch. The interior woodwork was excellent in design and good enough to keep, especially the mantel pieces and doors with their old-time wrought-iron latches. The blocked-up fireplaces were opened, and a wooden extension was added for the domestic service, and then an annex connected by a porte-cochere. The result was a house of an English pattern, one hundred feet long, heading the street with vastly improved respectability.

Bowker was equally ingenious in developing the possibilities of the surrounding grounds. The old cornfield was redeemed with a hedge of tamed wild roses; an old brickyard about a quarter mile from the house was turned into a flower garden entered through a Shinto gateway; a small swamp just beyond was scraped, dammed, and transformed into a small pond called "Lady's Lake," crossed by three Japanese bridges and bordered by a garden house to serve as boathouse below and summerhouse above. Along the path between house and pond was erected a sturdy rustic platform with bench, called the "Viewpoint" because it afforded a fine vista of the country across the Housatonic. Several bits of existing wood road were used in opening up a forest driveway about three quarters of a mile long which curved through the twenty-odd acres of pine, hemlock, birch, and other trees. On the hilltop was built a platform called the "Outlook," from which could be had a magnificent sweep of view into three states. On the northwestern corner of the property was constructed the "Log Cabin," with informal loft accommodations for half a dozen overnight guests and a comfortable rustic sitting room around a great stone fireplace. Down by the Housatonic was built a dock and later a boathouse where a small steel motorboat and a rowboat were kept. In 1904 an additional fifty acres came into Bowker's possession on the other side of the river. Within a few years he was keeping three cows and selling hay. He had almost become a gentleman farmer.

Stockbridge, surrounded by a picturesque circle of mountains, was a beautiful town, and Bowker came to love it deeply. He thought that its elm-shaded Main Street was the loveliest village street in America, and that no stream in the world, not excepting the Thames and the Avon, was more beautiful than its Housatonic. As one of the resident country squires he came to take a strong proprietary interest in every detail of the town's civic life. In Glendale he was a particularly alert watchdog of the public welfare, jolting the selectmen on the matter of unseemly advertising and sign posts, the placement of new buildings, saving old trees, road repair, improving recreational facilities, preventing pollution of the river, and promoting lectures and school exhibits. It was typical of him that he became chairman of a committee to make his neighbors "alive to the importance of uplifting our town life from . . . hoodlumism and intemperance," and that he hoped to "make it once again one of the loveliest villages of Berkshire and a credit to the country." In Stockbridge he launched an organization called the Stockbridge Home League with standing committees on social service, festivals and sports, and public safety and order, which would have made the town a veritable paragon of commonwealths had not human weakness terminated the organization's life within two years.

A less ambitious but more successful channel of effort was found in working with the Laurel Hill Association, oldest village-improvement society in the country, and of this he became a vice-president. He helped to launch, and served on the advisory committee of a monthly magazine, *Stockbridge,* which ran for two years in 1914–15; undertook considerable research on the early history of the Stockbridge Indians, and of the town,[5] took the initiative in maintaining old trails and opening new ones, and in agitating for improved commuting service to New York.[6] Bowker's outstanding service to the town of Stockbridge was as trustee from 1904 until 1933, and president from 1904 to 1928 of the Stockbridge Library Association.[7] In this relation he exercised his usual attention to details, taking pains with the book-purchasing policy, the selection of periodicals, personnel, and special collections; securing gifts of books and a new heating plant. In 1917 he was instrumental in arranging the purchase of a plot of land next door to the old library for expansion into an enlarged building. His hope was to include a historical museum. At his death, over eleven hundred of his personal volumes, and later a collection of eighty-five autographed first editions, were given to the Stockbridge Library.[8] Through the years he also encouraged the maintenance of a small library at Glendale and another in near-by Interlaken, making generous gifts of books to each.

Bowker entered as fully into the social life of Stockbridge as into its civic activities. The Log Cabin, with its kitchen, grand piano, full book shelves and piazza roofed each year with a fresh thatch of pine branches, became the favorite spot for afternoon teas and special enter-

[5] See "The Stockbridge Indians," by R. R. B., in Berkshire *Courier,* December 9, 1926; "Stockbridge History in Brief," *Stockbridge,* November 1, December 1, 1914; "The After History of the Stockbridge Indians," *ibid.,* April 1, May 1, 1915; and "Old Roads in Stockbridge," *ibid.,* July 1, 1915.

[6] R. R. B., "The New Haven Railroad in the Berkshires," Springfield *Republican,* October 11, 1927, etc.

[7] See *The Stockbridge Library,* his address to the association, September 30, 1905.

[8] Town of Stockbridge, Annual Report for 1933–34, p. 39; *Berkshire Eagle,* October 6, 1938, p. 2.

taining. Here the Bowkers played host to the local garden club, the Edison Association, the Massachusetts Library Club, the American Library Institute, and the Council of the National Civil Service Reform League. The old fraternity group now held its annual summer reunions here.

The most notable tradition established at the Cabin was the weekly Saturday morning gathering of neighbors for informal talk. This grew to be a well-known institution. Among the company were such Glendale neighbors as Daniel Chester French, foremost of American sculptors; Professor H. W. Farnam of Yale, and Newton Mackintosh. From Stockbridge came Bernhard Hoffmann, Alexander Sedgwick, Dr. W. Gilman Thompson, Professor William H. Carpenter, vice-president and provost of Columbia University; Congressman A. T. Treadway, and Joseph H. Choate; and in later years Lyman Beecher Stowe, Frank Parker Stockbridge, Robert Underwood Johnson, Dr. J. R. Goffe, John C. Lynch, Edwin T. Rice, Justice William P. Rudd, and Norman H. Davis, who became ambassador-at-large for Presidents Herbert Hoover and Franklin D. Roosevelt.[9] Guests were frequently invited, including such figures as Professor Woolsey of Yale, Anson Phelps Stokes, Craveth Wells, and Jay Freeman.

The origin of this well-attended gathering was in a walking club which Bowker formed to explore and reopen old paths around Stockbridge—which he had called the Pathfinders, but which Sedgwick had dubbed The Leg-It Club. Bowker led the conversation, trying to keep it on the central topics, sometimes reading news items or extracts from letters. If anyone became dogmatic about current politics, however, he would thump the arm of his rocking chair and say, "Gentlemen! Gentlemen! Not allowed here!" His tenacious memory, wide-ranging sympathies, remarkable command of facts, and exemplary English were thoroughly appreciated. The company presented him with a silver loving cup on his seventy-fifth birthday in 1923,[10] and a second handsome loving cup with a fine tribute on his eightieth.

From 1902 on, Bowker spent the warmest five months of the year in Stockbridge and the rest of the year in New York. In the years of Mrs. Bowker's last illness, after 1929, the Glendale house became an all-year residence. During the summer he would concentrate his city work into fortnightly trips of three days each. His legal residence remained until 1913 at the old Brooklyn address of 274 Lafayette Avenue, from then until 1925 at a new city home on West Twelfth Street, and

9 The history of the cabin and lists of the Log Cabin Company are given in the New York *Times*, September 5, 1923; Springfield *Republican*, September 2, 1928; *Berkshire Eagle*, October 31, 1934.

10 See tribute by A. W. Milbury in Springfield *Republican*, September, 1923.

finally on East Fifty-seventh Street, where a cheerful, sunny apartment was kept at the disposal of his friends while he was in the country. Bowker would always take a walk through his woods before commencing the day's work, a second before lunch, and a third before dinner. Usually the day began with Mrs. Bowker reading to him the morning *Springfield Republican*. Later, and throughout the day, special friends would read prose and poetry to him; indeed, he would listen as long as there was anyone with strength and time to read. All of his writing had, of course, to be dictated. In addition to daily walks, almost daily drives were taken, which Mrs. Bowker also enjoyed when she was up to them.

When Bowker left the Edison Company, a number of interesting opportunities for new service presented themselves. He was offered the presidency of the Third Avenue Elevated Company at an annual salary of $25,000, with the assurance that no money would be spent at Albany or in the city for political blackmail;[11] he was urged to serve as city comptroller in Seth Low's Fusion administration; and he was invited to permit his name to be suggested for the presidency of City College. He declined all three, explaining that he needed a period of rest before taking new burdens, that he wished leisure to complete some writing which he had at heart, and that he was limited by his failing eyesight. When, however, his old friend Daniel Norman, head of the DeLaval Steam Turbine Company, invited him to serve as president of the American branch of that company in 1901, Bowker was glad to accept the vice-presidency instead, later becoming vice-chairman of its board of directors. The following year he also accepted the vice-presidency of the DeLaval Separator Company, of which F. J. Arend was the *de facto* president, and became chairman of its board of directors. He continued with both companies until his resignation in 1931, acting as consultant and as watchdog of their interests. Both companies made good profits, though the Separator business was the more successful.[12]

From time to time Bowker was tempted to try additional forms of business promotion, as for instance the offers made to Edison and a proposal drawn up in 1909 for a Pan-American Steam Company, with himself as president of the board of directors, but nothing came of these. Meanwhile, Bowker's Edison relations had a happy ending. Until 1905 he held on to fifty shares of Edison stock belonging to his sister and twenty belonging to Thomas Edison, and was thus one of the two sole owners of the Edison Company along with the Consolidated Gas

11 R. R. B. to J. H. Schiff, January 31, February 1, 1900; J. H. Schiff to R. R. B., February 2, 1900.

12 See R. R. B., letters to Daniel Norman and R. Bernström, 1901–12, etc. R. R. B. to E. Atkinson, June 24, 1905; *Herald Tribune*, November 13, 1933.

Company. By this time he had become so assured that the administration of George B. Cortelyou could be trusted that he gladly agreed to a plan for disposing of his stock.[13] Bowker never changed his opinion of the piratical methods used by Whitney and Brady in 1898-99, but he was frequently glad to admit that the new Edison Company had made a fine record in keeping the old staff, in developing a good welfare program, and in generally wise administration.[14]

Bowker himself was the most stable fact about the *Publishers' Weekly* office from 1900 to 1933. Its location changed several times,[15] old publications were dropped and new ones taken on, old staff members passed away and new ones took their places, but through all these years Bowker remained the directing head, and never for a moment relaxed his grasp of every detail of office management.

In 1900 the staff was still very much the one that Leypoldt had originally assembled, with Augusta Leypoldt, Marian Monachesi, Adolf Growoll, William Stewart, and Helen Haines at the main desks. Several changes, however, now took place. G. D. T. Rouse was replaced as business manager, first by W. J. Bell and then in 1904 by John A. Holden, long associated with the New York office of Thomas Whittaker and thoroughly experienced in both publishing and retailing. In 1908, Helen Haines was forced by ill health to give up her work and was succeeded by her sister, Mabel R. Haines. When Miss Monachesi died the following year, the first of the old staff was gone. A few months later Growoll went, too,[16] a tragic loss to Bowker both of a valued business associate and a personal friend to whom he had given in 1907 a loving cup in recognition of thirty years of faithful service. In 1910, Fremont Rider took over Growoll's duties. The staff now consisted of five in the business department, five in the editorial department, and four in charge of bibliography.[17]

Bowker admitted that the business did not make enough to "butter my bread or buy cake." He was paying himself a salary of about $4,000, drawing 5 per cent on his capital investment of $10,000 before reckon-

[13] R. R. B. to N. F. Brady, July 13, 1906. Actually twenty shares were to be held by Brady and Lieb subject to Bowker's right of recall at any time, so that he would not part altogether from the company or permit all the stock to go finally into the hands of the Consolidated Gas Company.

[14] R. R. B. to Gov. C. E. Hughes, in the New York *Evening Post*, April 24, 1907; to G. F. Peabody, August 27, 1912; to T. A. Edison, September 30, 1914; to W. H. Wilmer, February 18, 1916; to J. Lieb, June 10, 1927.

[15] In 1900 the office moved from 59 Duane Street to 298 Broadway; in 1913 to 141 East Twenty-Fifth Street; in 1914 to 241 West Thirty-seventh Street; and finally to 62 West Forty-fifth Street.

[16] *Publishers' Weekly*, December 11, 1909.

[17] Armond C. Frasca, typescript recollections.

ing net profit, and dividing this profit equally with Mrs. Leypoldt and a profit-sharing fund in which the staff participated.[18] Growoll and the others occasionally expressed their opinion that Bowker should take less salary and pay more to the rest, but he was firm in his management policies.[19] Nevertheless, he decided against an enlargement of his publishing program when such a move might have been wise,[20] and he failed to meet the growing competition of the H. W. Wilson Company.

The H. W. Wilson Company was an enterprising Minneapolis firm that showed a progressive, resourceful approach to the bibliographical market which Bowker failed to match, especially in such advances as the extension of the cumulative feature and the introduction of the service basis of price. From 1895 until 1911 the competition grew, Bowker feeling himself unfairly treated by Wilson, Wilson implying that Bowker was incompetent. In 1902, Growoll admitted that "our reputation has already lost lustre. Wilson is covering our field more thoroughly if not better." In 1903, Wilson agreed to give up certain features, but indicated that unless Bowker waked up his bibliographical department, he would lose the field altogether. By 1910, Bowker was obliged to agree that Wilson's *U. S. Catalog* deserved to replace his *American Catalog,* and with the latter's issue for 1908–10, it was discontinued. The agreement was a friendly one, leaving freedom of future action to both houses, and pledging "harmonious co-operation." In 1912 there was actually some talk of merging the two offices into one, but the plan was dropped.[21]

In 1911, Bowker incorporated the R. R. Bowker Company with a capitalization of $25,000 and himself as president, Mrs. Leypoldt as vice-president, and Rider as secretary. The new company now became the owning as well as operating agency for all the Leypoldt publications. It was a move he had contemplated since 1902, but which Mrs. Leypoldt had long resisted. In 1914, Mrs. Leypoldt resigned, and in 1919 she died, the last link with the early days. Meanwhile, Rider had bought a press and started in business for himself, undertaking for a while to do the Bowker publications. In 1918 his place as managing editor of the *Weekly* was taken by Frederic G. Melcher, who also became the company's vice-president. During the twenties the company's activities expanded and prospered: the *Weekly's* gross business grew

18 R. R. B. to Nelson Spencer, March 12, 1906.

19 R. R. B. to A. Growoll, March 4, 1905.

20 *Ibid.,* January 20, 1906.

21 See R. R. B.–H. W. Wilson correspondence, 1906–1907; agreement quoted by H. W. Wilson in letter to R. R. B., January 25, 1927; R. R. B. to Mrs. Leypoldt, October 31, December 12, 1912; to N. Spencer, March 12, 1906; to F. H. Dodd, April 10, 1909.

from $100,000 a year to $400,000, the staff from fourteen to thirty-five.[22] It is especially fitting that the enterprise with which Bowker's name is most widely associated today is one with which he had such a long record of constructive service and which today so admirably carries on the fine tradition of book-trade leadership which he and Leypoldt began.

In 1911 the R. R. Bowker Company owned as well as operated the *Library Journal, Publisher's Weekly, Publishers' Trade List Annual,* and *Book Index;* it published Bowker's *Publications of Societies and State Publications.*[23] It now bought *Book Review* from Rider and issued it as a monthly supplement of the *Weekly* until 1932. In 1913 it published the Daughters of the American Revolution *Monthly Magazine,* but the loss on it proved so considerable that it was discontinued after several months. *Index to Dates,* a monthly with an annual cumulative volume was inaugurated in 1914, its name changed to *Information Annual* from 1915 to 1918, and then sold to Rider, when its name was changed to *Military Digest.* The company also published *Private Book Collectors,* the *American Book Trade Directory,* the *American Library Directory,* the *Bookman's Glossary,* and was agent for such English publications as the *Annual English Catalogue,* Whitaker's *Reference Catalogue of Current Literature,* Whitaker's *Cumulative Book List,* and the *Bookman's Journal.* In 1919 the company purchased and issued *Books of the Month;* it also published the *Bookshelf for Boys and Girls* (later renamed the *Children's Book Parade*), the *Christmas Bookshelf* (later renamed the *Holiday Book Parade*), the *Educational Catalogue,* the *Bookman's Manual, American First Editions, American Book-Prices Current,* and a series of historical maps in the "Booklover's" series.[24]

Bowker's vigorous participation in the copyright campaigns of 1905, 1922, and 1933 has been described. At the same time the editorial pages of the *Weekly* were filled with discussions of various efforts to secure improved postal legislation, and to this end Bowker engaged in both correspondence and personal interviews with Roosevelt, Cortelyou, Champ Clark, the chairman of the House committee on post office, and President Taft. Part of Bowker's campaign of postal education was a popular essay on "The Post Office: Its Facts and Its Possibilities," published in 1905 in the *Review of Reviews.*[25]

[22] See a useful comment, "The American Book Trade Journal," *Publishers' Weekly,* January 1, 1921, pp. 11–12.

[23] *Literary News* discontinued in 1905.

[24] For the company's publishing activities in the nineteen thirties, see Anne J. Richter, "Books from the Office of *Publishers' Weekly,*" *Publishers' Weekly,* January 18, 1947, Section One, pp. 341 ff.

[25] *American Monthly Review of Reviews,* March, 1905. pp. 325–32.

As with the *American Catalogue,* Bowker ran into new competition in the library field. In 1903, a strenuous endeavor to expand the subscriptions of the *Journal* secured very inadequate results, and Bowker wrote in discouragement that "probably the next generation will reap the harvest for which this generation is doing the seed-sowing."[26] It is possible that a growing sense of professional autonomy within the library field justified the American Library Association in the publication of a periodical of its own. Some thought that, for all his fairness, Bowker's close association with publishing interests made it impossible for him to defend the library point of view as vigorously as could be wished. After 1907 the A.L.A. *Bulletin* therefore developed into real competition as the official organ of the association, and as in 1895, when *Public Libraries* was started, Bowker unhappily felt that the move represented a failure of the association to appreciate the sacrifices he had made.[27]

Bowker's relations with the association, however, were not impaired, and he continued to attend its annual conferences. In 1910 he attended the International Congress of Bibliography at the Brussels Exposition. In 1916 he was honored with a handsome loving cup which commemorated "forty years of service to American libraries." During World War I he took an active interest in promoting the war work of the A.L.A., which collected and administered $6,000,000 and 7,000,000 books, and especially in the fortunes of the American Library in Paris which happily survived the war. In 1917 he went on a library tour throughout the midwest, speaking at Cleveland, Toledo, Fort Wayne, Decatur, and St. Louis. In 1920 he made what was probably his finest analysis of the values to democracy of the library movement in a speech given at the dedication of the library building of the University of Michigan, a speech entitled "The Library, Democracy, and Research."[28]

In 1926, at the brilliant semicentennial celebration of the A.L.A., Bowker and Dewey were given special honors as the surviving pioneers of the movement. Bowker's address, "Seed Time and Harvest—The Story of the A.L.A.," was given before twelve hundred of the twenty-five hundred delegates attending, and was an admirable historical review of the fifty years.[29] In 1927 he attended the Edinburgh library gathering, and a few months before his death in 1933 was working to perfect plans for international library representation at the great Library Conference scheduled for that year in Chicago. Meanwhile, he had continued his active interest as a trustee in the Brooklyn Public

26 R. R. B. to W. I. Fletcher, April 11, 1903.

27 See R. R. B. to H. E. Legler, April 30, 1908.

28 *The Library Building with the Addresses* . . . , 25–32; see bibliography.

29 In *Library Journal,* October 15, 1926, pp. 880–86; see references to R. R. B.'s role in W. E. Foster, "Five Men of '76," *ibid.,* 914.

Library and as trustee and president of the Stockbridge Library Association.

Through these years the writing of poetry continued to be a source of relaxation and enjoyment, and Bowker composed verses for his Christmas greeting cards, for his wedding anniversaries, and for his friends' birthdays. His gift of happy expression led him to be asked to compose a score of memorial essays, which included, among those published, the ones to E. M. Shepard, Adolph Werner, Major Delafield, E. P. Wheeler, Frank L. Wing, William M. Murray, Ernst Eurich, J. H. Choate, and several of his Edison associates. For his college he wrote four warmly descriptive essays of reminiscence, printed as "College Days and College Ways," in the *City College Alumnus* for 1926, and a final piece *"Ave Atque Salve"* printed in the same journal in 1928.[30]

True to his crusading ideals to the end, Bowker filled his last three decades with a torrent of communications to the press and to municipal, state, and Congressional leaders pressing for the fulfillment of the liberal program.[31] His basic objectives were embodied in a platform which he advocated on every suitable occasion. It contained such planks as Philippine independence, the direct election of senators, direct primaries, maintenance of the merit system and the short ballot, the initiative, referendum, and recall, absolute home rule for municipalities, economy and business methods in government, a tariff for revenue only, restricted expenditure for the navy and for pensions, and a new tax structure to include both a land tax and a progressive income tax. In 1902 he proposed promoting this platform by organizing "The Friends of Freedom" as a "semipolitical organization somewhat on the lines of the Committees of Correspondence of early days." He pressed the program again in 1905, when he thought the psychological moment had arrived for "a virile forward movement for which the people are ready," either as a movement outside of parties or a revolution within the Democratic party. In 1910 he proposed that his platform be taken up by a "League for Freedom" to be made up of "independent voters in both parties for such concert of action as will enable them to exert effectively the balance of power." Believing that there was need for "a new kind of Mugwump [who] . . . would support Wilson, but on the peace and not war side," in 1916 he again sounded the Mugwump call, writing to the *Evening Post* that "it would be strange indeed if the 'young scratchers' of 1879 should be forced to become the 'old scratchers' of 1916."[32]

[30] See bibliography.
[31] *Ibid.*
[32] R. R. B., "The Mugwump Position," letter dated January 19, 1916, in New York *Evening Post.*

Bowker was especially hopeful, before World War I, of a revival of the Democratic party that would rally radicals, independents, and labor behind real principles. To this end he worked through his friend Peabody, who served as treasurer of the Democratic national committee during the Parker campaign of 1904; Shepard, whose campaigns for governor and United States senator he worked hard for in 1910–11; Champ Clark, in whom he found a rugged champion of the cause and to whom he directed a stream of written counsel; and O. W. Underwood and later Norman Davis. In the national elections Bowker supported Parker in 1904, Taft in 1908, and Wilson in 1912, writing Peabody this year that "all we have been striving for in late years have every opportunity of fulfillment in this campaign." Later, however, he came to be very critical of Wilson's record on civil service and civil liberties.

World War I was a tragedy which a liberal internationalist with a lifetime of European associations felt with particular heartbreak. During these years he vigorously fought war hysteria, excesses of militarism and "Prussianism," censorship and conscription, the suppression of civil liberties, the persecution of conscientious objectors, and a move to give special civil service preference to war veterans.[33] He supported the American League to Limit Armaments and backed Wilson's policy of nonintervention. He described Wilson's great "Peace without Victory" speech as "a new declaration of interdependence . . . a world Magna Charta," and responded whole-heartedly to Wilson's proposal of a League of Nations.

Bowker's support of the League of Nations was insistently coupled with vigorous advocacy of international free trade. This lifelong objective, indeed, as a precondition of genuine peace never seemed more vindicated or more pressing. He pleaded his cause in dozens of essays which have a true prophetic ring. In 1917 he sponsored an "Appeal of American Free Traders to Rt. Hon. A. J. Balfour and M. Rene Viviani," which received a good deal of publicity;[34] in 1923 he published two pamphlets on "Economic Peace" and the League, which were bound together in booklet form.[35] Bowker had worked hard for tariff reform during the debates on the Underwood Bill and continued to be one of the few staunch laborers for the old American Free Trade League. In 1921 he became vice-president of the new Free Trade League, of which Putnam was president and Peabody treasurer, edited a series of bulletins for it, and became its president in 1930 on Putnam's death. In 1930

[33] See especially R. R. B. to T. Williams, January 26, February 3, 14, April 9, 1917; to Newton D. Baker, November 1, 8, 1917.

[34] Reprinted as Leaflet No. 201 of the Cobden Club, London, 1917.

[35] *Economic Peace, Covenant of Sovereign Peoples* (New York, 1923); see bibliography.

he initiated, with Norman Davis, the Council for Tariff Reduction as successor to the league.

Aside from national politics and tariff reform, Bowker dealt blows in season and out of season for liberal causes. He supported the American Civil Liberties Union and the birth-control movement; he protested against child labor, compulsory military training in the colleges,[36] and anti-semitism. In 1903 he contributed capital and counsel to help rehabilitate the *Jewish World*.[37] He wrote in support of Dreyfus in France and of Sacco and Vanzetti in Massachusetts. He contributed enthusiastically to Negro education in the South by giving regularly through thirty years to Hampton and Tuskegee institutes, by supporting the Snow Hill Normal and Industrial Institute, and the W.C.T.U. Settlement School at Hindman, Kentucky; and especially by his special concern for Miss Emma J. Wilson's Mayesville Institute in South Carolina, of which Mrs. Bowker was a trustee.[38] He hoped fervidly for the independence of the Philippines, of Haiti, and of India, and served as a vice-president of the Friends of Russian Freedom to support the liberals in the Russian revolution of 1905.[39] He deeply regretted the Japanese Exclusion Bill, urged Congress to open wider the immigration door to Orientals, and signed a memorial to the President against the occupation of Chinese territory by American troops in 1927. He was lukewarm toward prohibition. He continued his support of the City Improvement Society and of the East Side (Settlement) House, encouraged the City and Suburban Homes Company in Albany to fight an attempt to modify the existing tenement law, and later became enthusiastic about the Sunnyside and Radburn co-operative housing experiments. He was an ardent disciple of Billy Mitchell, and was sure that the airplane made the warship obsolete. "Science," he declared, "has made war suicide."

The twenties were discouraging years for a militant liberal. Bowker looked for younger men who would carry on his old fight. He was especially eager to find some college man who would act as his secretary and serve a sort of apprenticeship in amateur politics. "Is it because I am growing old," he asked Peabody in 1923, "that I fail to find among the young men any to compare with you and Shepard?" To the alumni secretary of his alma mater he wrote in 1930:

[36] See R. R. B. to Board of Trustees, C. C. N. Y., December 15, 1925.

[37] R. R. B. to F. Stein, May 29, July 14, 1903; R. R. B.–Deming letters, May–June, 1903.

[38] Mrs. R. R. Bowker, in the New York *Evening Post*, January, 1916; R. R. B., "Negro Education at the South," letter dated April 6, 1922, in New York *Evening Post*.

[39] R. R. B. to R. Ely, December 16, 1904; to Mrs. A. Ritchie, December 18, 1905; to Miss Picton, February 6, December 21, 1905; May 17, 1906.

We are seeking to find younger men who have—or may develop, such interest in good politics as a number of us had in our youth. . . . It has been most difficult in these latter days to find young men of this type, and some are prone to think that they do not exist. Are there not some who would like to take or make opportunity for themselves to enter "amateur" politics and do public service as private citizens?

This was only one evidence of a low tide of public concern that troubled, though it did not for a minute dishearten, Bowker. His persistent faith in the ultimate triumph of the liberal program shines through a letter which he wrote Peabody in 1923:

I think that we may both feel that our later as well as our earlier years have not been wasted or ill-spent, though it takes strong faith to feel that in this upset world our efforts will ultimately have the results for which we have endeavored. Nevertheless, I do hope that the historians of the future may look back upon these troublous times . . . as the dip in the wave of progress which later will rise again to the crest.

It was typical of the fighting heart of the aging Mugwump. Worthington C. Ford's tribute to Bowker's tireless crusading zeal was well deserved:

The years passed and much that he fought for has been accomplished. There came new conditions, new men, new party alignments, a dropping away of the older workers by death, loss of zeal and conviction, or the temptation of loaves and shes, and finally by a ready willingness to hand the reform activities to a coming and, in some degree, a better equipped generation. Bowker took on new responsibilities—and his increasing affliction narrowed his capacity for work; but he never lost interest in the questions of the day, in the always present and pressing problems due to increasingly complex social relations. . . . To meet him for however brief a talk was to bring a remembrance of comradeship in struggle, of lost and won causes and a refreshing whiff of optimism, of hope for better things to come. His work was unfinished—it never could have been finished; and he held a torch in the procession of reformers to the bitter end.[40]

The last years were full of a happy mellowness. Friends remarked Bowker's power and dignity, his serenity of spirit, his humility of mind.

40 W. C. Ford, in *Library Journal*, December 1, 1933, Part II, p. 1009; see Ford to R. R. B., September 4, 1928.

At Christmas time he continued to send to a long list of friends the laurel wreaths made from the Glendale growth and the cheerful rhymed greetings. He might tend to ramble in committee meetings, but his mind was clear as a bell. One by one the old circle had fallen away, Trask, Shepard, Wheeler, Putnam; but he kept up a warm correspondence with Peabody and enjoyed the company of his old friend Eurich, who more and more became his constant companion as Mrs. Bowker's health gave way to complete invalidism.[41]

Bowker kept remarkably well. He continued to work up to the last minute for free trade, international copyright, the City College, and the library movement; he listened avidly to the latest reports from Washington, analyzed each turn of a complicated business year. "It is better to die in harness," he said when he was eighty-two, "than to be put out to pasture for our few remaining years, or months, or days." His friends made his eightieth birthday a gala celebration. Two hundred letters of greeting and testimony poured in from all over the world; more than one hundred friends dropped in at the Log Cabin to pay their respects; an immense cake, two feet in diameter, was served with eighty candles. It was a community occasion.[42] Five years later the friends again assembled to honor their sturdy old neighbor. Bowker looked well and moved about among his friends chatting and enjoying

[41] Mrs. Bowker had a first serious nervous breakdown in 1920, which left her a semi-invalid, unable to travel with her husband. A second crisis in 1929 and another in 1932 brought serious mental as well as physical deterioration. After several years of complete unconsciousness, she died on January 16, 1941, at the age of 76. Obituaries were carried in the New York *Herald Tribune* and *Times* on January 18, 1941; *Publishers' Weekly*, January 25, 1941; *Library Journal*, February 1, 1941.

[42] See press notices: in the New York *Times* and Springfield *Sunday Union and Republican*, September 2; in Brooklyn *Daily Eagle*, September 3; Boston *Evening Transcript*, September 5; Passaic *Daily News*, September 7; Edison *Weekly*, September 15, 1928.

[43] John Finley wrote an especially fine editorial in honor of the occasion for the September 5, 1933 *Times*, entitled "A Modern Democritus."

[44] Among the obituaries and memorial notices, the following may be noted: New York *Times*, New York *Herald Tribune*, Brooklyn *Daily Eagle*, Springfield *Republican*, November 13, 1933; Passaic (N. Y.) *Herald News*, Providence *Journal*, November 15, 1933; *City College Alumnus*, January, 1934, pp. 5–8; *Publishers' Weekly*, November 18, 1933, pp. 1764–68; *Library Journal*, December 1, 1933, Part II, pp. 1001–1013; Brooklyn Institute of Arts and Sciences, *Bulletin*, December 2, 1933.

[45] *Berkshire Eagle*, October 31, 1934.

[46] The New York Public Library prepared and donated to the Stockbridge Library a memorial scrapbook of clippings, biographical accounts, and selected writings. See Stockbridge Library Association *Bulletin*, August, 1938.

[47] Berkshire *Evening Eagle*, October 26, 1935.

[48] "The Richard Rogers Bowker Memorial Lectures have been established at The New York Public Library as an aid and stimulus to the study of book publishing in the United States, and the problems common to authors, publishers, librarians, readers, all makers and users of books."

their expressions of affection.[43] After the clebration, however, he rapidly weakened, and the end came on November 12, 1933.[44]

Bowker's body was buried in the Stockbridge cemetery beneath a simple gravestone.[45] He would have approved the memorials that were established in his honor: the gift of autographed first editions to the Stockbridge Library,[46] the House Plan group named after him in the City College House Plan Center at 292 Convent Avenue in New York,[47] and the annual R. R. Bowker Memorial Lectures on the book trade at the New York Public Library.[48] His friends, as they thought of his passing, recalled the words he had written in *The Arts of Life:* "What through the years . . . a man has become, what he is in himself, what he is to his fellowmen, this is the test of life." On the memorial stone placed in the Stockbridge cemetery were inscribed the lines from one of his early poems:

Finis Coronat Opus

"The end shall crown the work"—
Ah, who shall tell the end!
It is a woesome way,
And clouds portend.

The work is all we know—
Enough for our faint sight.
The end God knows. Press on!
The crown—is light!

ße

Bibliography

I. R. R. Bowker Manuscript Collections

1. THE NEW YORK PUBLIC LIBRARY

Letters, 1868–1933, 113 boxes.
Edison Collection, 7 boxes.
Copyright Collection, 9 boxes.
Writings, 9 boxes.
Letter Copybooks
    a. Personal and Private Office, 1875–1913, 13 vols.
    b. Brooklyn Free Trade League, 1869–71, 1 vol.
    c. Economic Press, 1888–91, 2 vols.
    d. Society for Political Education, 1889–91, 1 vol.
Accounts, 1870–1932, 7 boxes.
Miscellaneous Papers, 4 boxes.
Scrapbooks, 2 vols.

2. THE LIBRARY OF CONGRESS

MSS speeches by R. R. Bowker and others; original drafts and printed
copies of political documents for 1879, 1880, 1884; letters from
English and American authors; proofs with authors' corrections of
literary MSS; souvenir letters received by Bowker on his seventy-
fifth and seventy-sixth birthdays, etc.

3. STOCKBRIDGE (MASSACHUSETTS) LIBRARY

The Bowker Memorial Collection, a large selection of his printed writings, scrapbooks, and birthday memorials; autographed volumes.

4. IN THE CUSTODY OF THE *Publishers' Weekly*

MS Memoir with fragmentary memoranda, etc.).
MS London Journal, 1880–82, typescript.

MS Letters to his family, 1880–82.
MS Papers relating to the *Publishers' Weekly*.
MS Greetings received by R. R. Bowker on his eighty-fifth birthday, 1933.
MS verse.
Carolyn T. Bowker's MS Journal, 1881.
Carolyn T. Bowker's letters to R. R. B.

II. R. R. Bowker's Printed and Published Writings

1. WRITINGS AND JOURNALS EDITED BY R. R. BOWKER

Songs of the College of the City of New York. New York, 1866. R. R. B., chairman of the Board of Editors.

The Collegian (undergraduate newspaper of the College of the City of New York), November 21, 1866–March 6, 1867 (8 nos.). R. R. B., editor.

The Publishers' Weekly, the American Book Trade Journal, January, 1872–1933. Vols. 1 and 2 have the title, *The Publishers' and Stationers' Weekly Trade Circular*. Publishers: vols. I–XIV, January, 1872–December, 1878, F. Leypoldt (New York, F. Leypoldt, Editor and Publisher); vols. XV–XVII, January, 1879–June, 1880, by R. R. B. (New York, Office of the *Publishers' Weekly*); vols. XVIII–XXIV, July, 1880–December, 1883, by F. Leypoldt; vols. XXV–C, January, 1884–December, 1921, by R. R. B. (New York, Office of the *Publishers' Weekly*); vols. CI–CXXIII, January, 1922–June, 1933, by R. R. B. (New York, R. R. Bowker Company). Editors: January, 1872–January, 1879, F. Leypoldt, assisted by R. R. B.; January, 1879–June, 1880, R. R. B., assisted by F. Leypoldt; July, 1880–March, 1884, F. Leypoldt; April, 1884–November, 1933, R. R. B.

The New Century, Journal of the International Free Trade Alliance for Promoting Industrial and Commercial Freedom and Politico-Economic Freedom. New York, December, 1875–December, 1876. R. R. B., editor.

Library Journal. Publishers: 1876–78, F. Leypoldt; 1879–80, New York, Office of the *Publishers' Weekly;* 1881–March 1884, F. Leypoldt; April, 1884–Decmber, 1910, New York, Office of the *Publishers' Weekly;* 1911–November, 1933, R. R. Bowker Company Editors: 1876–79, Melvil Dewey and R. R. B.; 1879–June, 1880, R. R. B. and Melvil Dewey; July–December, 1880, Leypoldt, Dewey; 1881–March, 1884, C. A. Cutter, Leypoldt; April, 1884–87, C. A. Cutter (and R. R. B.); 1887–89, C. A. Cutter and R. R. B.; 1889–1933, R. R. B. with various assistants.

Harper's New Monthly Magazine, English Edition, December, 1880–October, 1882. R. R. B., editor.

Society for Political Education. *Economic Tracts* (1–31); *Library of Political Education* (six issues).

Economic Fact-Book and Free-Trader's Guide. First edition. New York, The New York Free Trade Club, 1885. R. R. B., editor.

The Occasional Barracoutean, Vol. I, No. 1 (March 14, 1887). Supplement, Vol. I, No. 2 (April 4, 1887). R. R. B., associate editor.

The American Catalogue, July 1, 1876–December 31, 1910. New York, 1880–1911. 18 vols. in 10. Copyright by R. R. Bowker Company. Reprinted in 1941 by P. Smith (New York, by special arrangement with R. R. Bowker Company). Supplemented by the *Annual American Catalogue,* 1886–1900; *Annual American Catalogue Cumulated,* 1900/01–1900/03; *Annual American Catalogue,* 1905–1906, 1908–10.

1876 under the direction of F. Leypoldt. Vol. I. Author and title entries of books in print and for sale (including reprints and importations), July 1876. Compiled by Lynds E. Jones. Vol. II, Subject index, appendix, contributed lists of books published since 1876 with author and title index. *N. Y., A. C. Armstrong and Son,* 1880, 1881. R. R. B. exercises an "advisory" responsibility.

1876–84, compiled under the editorial direction of R. R. B. New York, Office of the *Publishers' Weekly,* 1885, 2 vols. Appendices: U. S. Government Publications. American Literary and Scientific Societies. Books in series. (Each part also issued separately.)

1884–90, compiled under the editorial direction of R. R. B. New York, Office of the *Publishers' Weekly,* 1891, 2 vols. Appendices: U. S. Government Publications. State Publications. Publications of Societies. Books in series. (Each part also issued separately.)

1890–95, compiled under the editorial direction of R. R. B. New York, Offices of the *Publishers' Weekly,* 1896, 2 vols. Appendices: U. S. Government Publications. State Publications. Publications of Societies. Books in series. (Each part also issued separately.)

1895–1900, compiled under the editorial direction of R. R. B. New York, Office of the *Publishers' Weekly,* 1901, 2 vols.

1900–1905, New York, Office of the *Publishers' Weekly,* 1905, 5 vols.

1905–1907, New York, Office of the *Publishers' Weekly,* 1908, 3 vols. in one.

1908–10, New York, Office of the *Publishers' Weekly,* 1911.

Report of the National Executive Committee of Republicans and Independents: Presidential Campaign of 1884. New York, 1885. R. R. B., editor.

The Million. Edited in Des Moines, Iowa, by Henry J. Philpott. R. R. B. an active editorial contributor. Includes R. R. B.'s "Plain Talks on Economics," March 8, 1884–February 28, 1885. *See Economics for the People* in section 2 below.

The Library List, being a list of public libraries in the United States and Canada of over 1,000 volumes, with classification by size and name of librarian. New York, Office of the *Library Journal,* 1887. R. R. B., editor.

The People's Cause. A Journal of tariff reform, ballot reform, civil service reform (successor to *The Million).* New York, January–December, 1889. R. R. B., co-editor with Louis Howland.

The Cleveland Album. A memorial of four years of Democratic administration. New York, 1889. Edited and copyrighted by R. R. B.

The Harrison Album of Republican Leaders. New York, 1889. Edited and copyrighted by R. R. B.

The Reader's Guide to Economic, Social, and Political Science, being a classified bibliography, American, English, French, German, with descriptive notes, author, title, and subject index, courses of reading, college courses, etc. New York, The Society for Political Education, 1891. *(Economic Tract No. XXVII).* R. R. B., co-editor with George Iles.

Campaign Text-Book: National Democratic Party, 1896, 1, 2, 3 editions. Chicago and New York, National Democratic Committee, 1896. R. R. B., editor.

Publications of Societies: A provisional list of the official publications of American scientific, literary, and other societies from their organization. New York, Office of the *Publishers' Weekly,* 1899. Vol. I. R. R. B., editor.

State Publications. A provisional list of the official publications of the several states of the United States from their organization. New York, Office of the *Publishers' Weekly,* 1908. Issued in four parts: I, New England States, 1899; II. North Central States, 1902; III. Western States and territories, 1905; IV. Southern States, 1908.

The Annual Literary Index, 1892–1904. Including periodicals, American and English; essays, book chapters, etc.; with author-index, bibliographies, necrology, and index to dates of principal events. Edited with the co-operation of the American Library Association and of the *Library Journal* staff, by W. I. Fletcher and R. R. B. New York, Office of the *Publishers' Weekly,* 1893–1905. Continued 1905–10 by *Annual Library Index* (New York, Office of the *Publishers' Weekly,* 1906–11, 6 vols.).

American Library Directory . . . a classified list of 1,100 libraries with names of librarians. New York, R. R. Bowker Company, 1923.

Evolved from *Library List,* 1887; *Annual Literary Index,* 1892; *Annual Library Index,* 1906; *American Library Annual,* 1912. *Supplement . . .* comprising subject index to special collections in American libraries, lists of Latin-American libraries and greater libraries overseas, subject index to library literature recorded in 1927, 1928. New York, R. R. Bowker Company, 1928.

2. BOOKS

Of Work and Wealth. A summary of Economics. New York, 1883. Society for Political Education, Economic Tracts 3rd and 4th series, *Tract No. X.* Reprinted by the Society in 1891.

Economics for the People. Being plain talks on economics, especially for use in business, in schools, and in women's reading classes. New York and London, 1886; New York, 1889, in No. 4 of Garnet Seal Series; 3rd ed., revised, New York, 1892; 4th ed., revised, New York, 1893.

Copyright, Its Law and Its Literature. Being a summary of the principles and laws of copyright, with especial reference to books. With a bibliography of literary property by Thorvald Solberg. New York and London, 1886.

The Arts of Life. Boston, 1900; revised ed., 1903. Separate parts: *Of Politics,* Boston 1901; *Of Business,* Boston, 1901; *Of Religion,* Boston, 1903; *Of Education* (with appended addresses on "The Scholar" and "The College of Today"), Boston, 1903.

Copyright, Its History and Its Law. Being a summary of the principles and practice of copyright with special reference to the American code of 1909 and the British act of 1911. New York, 1912.

3. PAMPHLETS, PREFACES, REPORTS, ARTICLES, ADDRESSES

"Hot-House Brains," *Herald of Health,* May, 1870, pp. 216–17.

"Getting at the Masses," *The Christian Union,* June 4, 1870.

"That Boy's Pockets," *At Home and Abroad,* June 18, 1870, p. 14.

"The Small Talk of Journalism," *Aldine Press,* Vol. III, No. 8 (August, 1870), 86–87.

"On Good Resolutions" (signed "The Gentle Optimist"), Lay Sermon I, *Evening Mail,* January 7, 1871.

"On Keeping at It" (signed "The Gentle Optimist"), Lay Sermon II, *Evening Mail,* January 21, 1871. Reprinted in *The Cosmopolitan,* January 28, 1871.

"Bibliomania," *The Cosmopolitan,* January 28, 1871.

"Preaching Up and Preaching Down," *The Christian Union,* August 9, 1871.

"Eternal Death," *Golden Age,* September 16, 1871, p. 2.

"Summering at Lake George," *Appleton's Journal,* October 7, 1871.

"In Re Bridget—The Defence," *Old and New,* October, 1871.

"Literature in America in 1871," Introduction to *The Annual American*

Catalogue for 1871 (New York, 1872), *v–xii;* also in *The Weekly Trade Circular,* Part I, January 18, 1872, pp. 4–7; Part II, February 8, 1872, pp. 97–99; Part III, February 22, 1872, pp. 158–59.

"Science and the Spirits," *Appleton's Journal,* January 20, 1872.

"Our Crimes Against Crime," *Herald of Health,* February, 1872, pp. 67–68.

"On the Tramp," *Herald of Health,* Vol. XXII, No. 3 (September, 1873), 102–104.

"The Shower of Gold," *St. Nicholas,* February, 1876.

"The True Usefulness of the Centennial," *The Christian Union,* April 5, 1876.

"Education and Free Trade," *The World,* April 17, 1876.

"The Centennial and Citizenship," *The Christian Union,* April 26, 1876.

"Address at Eells Memorial Dedication," Utica *Morning Herald,* May 25, 1876.

"The Graduate Associations," Alpha Delta Phi Reunion Dinner, New York, 1875. New York, privately printed, 1876. Pages 35–37.

"Daniel Deronda," *International Review,* January, 1877, pp. 68–76.

Introduction to Graham McAdam's *An Alphabet in Finance* (New York, 1876). Reprinted in the Library of Political Education of the Society for Political Education, New York, 1880.

"Learning to Read in College," *Library Journal,* October, 1877.

"The Harper Brothers," *Publishers' Trade List Annual,* 1877, pp. *v–xvi.*

"Charity—and the Commune," *The Christian Union,* October 9, 1878.

"Books and the Book Trade in America," "Trade Bibliography," "The Library System," in the introduction to *Catalogue of the Collective Exhibit of the American Book Trade* (Paris). Cambridge, 1878.

"On a Co-operative Scheme of Subject Headings," *Library Journal,* November, 1878, pp. 326–29.

"The Brooklyn Bureau of Charities," *The Christian Union,* December 11, 1878.

"A College Camp at Lake George," *Scribner's Monthly,* March, 1879.

"Camping Out," *Appleton's Summer Book* (New York, 1880), 95–99.

"The Star and Crescent," *The Star and Crescent,* May, 1880, pp. 4–5.

"Political Responsibility of the Individual," *Atlantic Monthly,* September, 1880, pp. 320–28.

"The Brooklyn Bridge," *Harper's New Monthly Magazine,* May, 1883, pp. 925–46.

"The Making of the Scholar and the Use of Him," *The Star and Crescent,* June, 1883, pp. 121–31.

"Free Trade, the Best Protection to American Industry." New York, 1883. 2nd and 3rd eds., 1884; 4th ed., 1886; 2nd ed., New York and Lawrence (Kansas); 3rd ed., New York and Lawrence (Kansas).

"The Work of the 19th Century Librarian for the Librarian of the 20th Century," *Library Journal,* September–October, 1883, pp. 247–50.

Bibliography

"A Commemoration Day at Oxford (1882)," *The Star and Crescent,* November, 1883, pp. 3–6.

"The College of Today" (a supposed address before citizens of the city of Hygeia, proposing to found a college), *Princeton Review,* January, 1884, pp. 89–110.

"Frederick Leypoldt," *Publishers' Weekly,* March 29, 1884, p. 379.

"Workingmen's Homes," *Harper's New Monthly Magazine,* April, 1884, pp. 769–84.

Introduction to Jacob Schoenhof's *Wages and Trade in Manufacturing Industries, in America and Europe* (New York, 1884).

"King's College," by John MacMullen (rewritten by R. R. B.), *Harper's New Monthly Magazine,* October, 1884, pp. 715–23.

"Columbia College" (anonymous), *Harper's New Monthly Magazine,* November, 1884, pp. 813–31.

"United States Government Publications," *Library Journal,* September–October, 1885, pp. 236–41.

Political Relations of Tariff Reform. Report and address as honorary secretary of American Free Trade League at National Conference of Free Traders and Revenue Reformers. Chicago, November 11–12, 1885. New York, 1885.

Preface to William E. Foster's *References to the History of Presidential Administrations, 1789–1885* (New York, 1885). Economics Tract *No. XVII* of the Society for Political Education.

The Great American Industries Series, *Harper's New Monthly Magazine:* II. "A Silk Dress," July, 1885, pp. 240–61; V. "A Lump of Sugar," June, 1886, pp. 72–95; VI. "A Sheet of Paper," June, 1887, pp. 113–30; VII. "A Printed Book," July, 1887, pp. 165–88; VIII. "A Piece of Glass," May, 1889, pp. 245–64; IX. "A Suit of Clothes," April, 1890, pp. 685–708; X. "A Bar of Iron," February, 1894, pp. 408–24; XI. "A Steel Tool," March, 1894, pp. 587–602; XII. "Electricity," October, 1896, pp. 710–39.

"The New York Produce Exchange," by Richard Wheatley, reworked by R. R. B., *Harper's New Monthly Magazine,* July, 1886.

"Memories among English Librarians," I, *Library Journal,* October, 1886, pp. 405–409; II, *ibid.,* November, 1886, pp. 437–41.

Civil Service Examinations. Being question papers, with actual answers of successful and unsuccessful candidates. Introduction by R. R. B. New York, 1886. *Economic Tract No. XXII* of the Society for Political Education.

A Primer for Political Education. New York, 1886. *Economic Tract No. XXI* of the Society for Political Education.

"Poore's Catalogue of Government Publications," *Library Journal,* January, 1886, pp. 4–5.

"What a Book Has Done, 'Ten Times One,' and Its Author," *The Literary News,* March, 1887, pp. 65–70.

"The Formation and Organization of Public Libraries," *Library Journal*, March, 1887, pp. 117–19.

"Toynbee Hall, London; an Interesting Social Experiment," *Century Magazine*, May, 1887, pp. 158–59.

The President's Message, 1887, of Grover Cleveland, with Annotations by R. R. B. New York and London, 1888. Reform Club Series II; Questions of the Day No. 48.

"London as a Literary Center," *Harper's New Monthly Magazine*, Part I, May, 1888; Part II, June, 1888.

Electoral Reform. New York, 1889. *Economic Tract No. XXV* of the Society for Political Education.

"Report on Index to Portraits, etc.," *Library Journal*, May–June, 1889, pp. 174–76.

Annual Report as first vice-president of the Edison Electric Illuminating Company of New York to Spencer Trask, president, January 12, 1891; January 5, 1892; January 10, 1893; January 10, 1894; January 10, 1895; January 10, 1896; January 21, 1897; January 20, 1898; January 19, 1899.

"The Nature and Origin of Copyright," in George Haven Putnam's *The Question of Copyright*, pp. 1–7. New York, 1891. Questions of the Day Series No. 68.

"Catalogue of the Publications of the 19th Century," *Library Journal*, December, 1891, pp. C81–C83.

Special Report on Public Documents, *Library Journal*, December, 1891, pp. C118–19.

"The College of the City of New York," *The University Magazine*, I, November, 1892; II, December, 1892; III, January, 1893.

An Index to Newspapers, or Annual Register of Events, *Library Journal*, December, 1893, p. 506.

"Further Ballot Reform," letter to the New York *Times*, November 10, 1893.

"American Library Association and The Library Journal," *Library Journal*, June, 1894, pp. 191–92.

"Some Libraries of the Northwest," *Library Journal*, March, 1895, pp. 77–80.

Address of R. R. Bowker at the Democratic Reform Meeting, Brooklyn Academy of Music, October 22, 1895. Pamphlet, privately printed, New York, 1895.

"Peace Between Kin" (The Speech That Was Not Made, House of Representatives, Wednesday, Dec. 18, 1895). Privately printed, 1895.

"The College of the City of New York, 1847–1895," reprinted from *The University Magazine*, New York, 1896.

"The *Library Journal* and Library Organization; A Twenty Years' Retrospect," *Library Journal*, January, 1896, pp. 5–9. "Postscript," February, 1896, p. 52.

Bibliography

"Libraries and the Library Problem in 'Greater New York,' " *Library Journal,* March, 1896, pp. 99–102; April, 1896, p. 153.

"The American National Library," *Library Journal,* August, 1896, pp. 357–58.

"Recollections of Du Maurier," New York *Times Supplement,* October 25, 1896.

"The City's Traffic" (City Club Lectures, No. 4), February, 1897. New York, 1897.

"Bibliographical Endeavors in America," Second International Library Conference, July, 1897, *Transactions and Proceedings,* pp. 150–53. Printed in *Library Journal,* August, 1897, pp. 384–87.

"Public Control, Ownership, or Operation of Municipal Franchises?" *Municipal Affairs,* December, 1897, pp. 605–30.

Report on Committee on Public Documents, *Library Journal,* August, 1898, pp.117–20. Second report issued July , 1899, *Library Journal,* pp. 100–102.

"Memorandum on Proposed Sale of New York Edison Stock," privately printed, February 23, 1899.

"The Institut International de Bibliographie, Brussels," *Library Journal,* June, 1900, pp. 273–74.

"Libraries and the Century in America: Retrospect and Prospect," *Library Journal,* January, 1901, pp. 5–7.

"On Relationship of Publishers, Booksellers, and Librarians," *Library Journal,* August, 1901, C134–37–40.

"The Piracy of Public Franchises," *Atlantic Monthly,* October, 1901, pp. 463–83; reprinted in *Municipal Affairs,* New York, December, 1901, pp. 886–904.

"Public Control of Corporations," *Municipal Affairs,* Vol. VI, No. 4 (February 27, 1903), 843–46.

"A Theory of Ons: In Reconciliation of the Undulatory Theory of Electricity with Ionization and the Electron Hypothesis," *Electrical World and Engineer,* September 26, 1903, p. 507.

"The Unity of Science," *Transactions* of the American Institute of Electrical Engineers, March, 1903, p. 282.

"On Recent National Bibliography in the United States," *Library Journal,* December, 1904, pp. C121–25, C228.

"The Post Office: Its Facts and Its Possibilities," *American Monthly Review of Reviews,* March, 1905, pp. 325–32.

Annual Reports, Stockbridge Library Association, 1904–28.

The Stockbridge Library. Pittsfield (Mass.), 1905.

"The College of the Past," in Philip J. Mosenthal and Charles F. Horne (eds), *The City College: Memories of Sixty Years,* pp. 3–63. New York, 1907.

"In the Other Half of America," New York *Evening Post Supplement,* November 27, 1909, pp. 2–3.

"In the Continent of Opportunity," New York *Evening Post Supplement*, December 4, 1909, p. 2.

"Associates and Associations in the *Publishers' Weekly* office," *Publishers' Weekly*, December 25, 1909, pp. 1944–45.

"Problems of the Infinitely Little," *City College Quarterly*, Vol VI, No. 2 (June, 1910), 89–100. Also issued as reprint, dated 1911.

"The Literature of Copyright," *Library Journal*, October, 1911, pp. 492–96.

"Edward Morse Shepard," *City College Quarterly*, Vol. VII, No. 4 (December, 1911), 219–38.

"The National Library as the Central Factor of Library Development in the Nation," *Library Journal*, January, 1912, pp. 3–6.

"The Work of Trustees in a Large Library," *Library Journal*, January, 1913, pp. 3–7.

"Address at Memorial Meeting in Honor of John Shaw Billings," *Library Journal*, June, 1913, pp. 335–37.

"Stockbridge History in Brief," *Stockbridge*, I, November 1, 1914 pp. 7–10; II, December 1, 1914, pp. 5–8.

"Making the Most of a Small Library," *Library Journal*, March, 1915, pp. 173–75.

"The After History of the Stockbridge Indians," *Stockbridge*, I, April 1, 1915, pp. 44–46; II, May 1, 1915, pp. 59–62.

"Old Roads of Stockbridge," *Stockbridge*, July 1, 1915, pp. 85–88.

"Music Selections for Public Libraries," *Library Journal*, August, 1915, pp. 579–82.

"Remarks at the 31st Annual Meeting of the Associates of the Edison Electric Illuminating Company, September 16, 1915," printed in the Minutes.

"Of Preparedness," open letter to the Honorable Claude Kitchin. New York, privately printed, December 1, 1915.

"The Library Trustee in the Village Library," *Library Journal*, March 15, 1916, pp. 282–83.

(Address) in a symposium in honor of the memory and in gratitude for the work and influence of Mary Wright Plummer, *Library Journal*, December, 1916, pp. 866–68.

(Address) "For Russia," *Library Journal*, August, 1917, pp. 599–605.

"A Mugwump's Memories of Roosevelt," New York *Evening Post*, February 15, 1919.

"Reminiscences of Lowell," New York *Evening Post* Book Section, March 1, 1919.

"Augusta H. Leypoldt, 1849–1919," *Publishers' Weekly*, June 14, 1919, pp. 1626–28.

"Library Service," *Library Journal*, October, 1919, pp. 627–32.

Co-ordination in Taxation, report of the Committee on Co-ordination in Taxation to the American Economic Association, R. R. B., chairman, New York, 1919; revised edition, New York, 1920.

"The Library, Democracy, and Research," *The Library Building with the Addresses* at the Dedication, Ann Arbor (Michigan), 1920, pp. 25–32. Reprinted in Michigan *Alumnus,* February, 1920, pp. 263–66.

"In Memoriam—Adolph Werner," *City College Quarterly,* Vol. XVI, No. 1 (March, 1920).

"Women in the Library Profession," *Library Journal,* I, June 15, 1920, p. 545–49; II, July 1–15, pp. 587–92; III, August, 1920, pp. 635–40.

"Edward Morse Shepard," *Delta Alpha Quarterly,* July, 1920.

"Major A. D.—Beloved of the Brethren," *Delta Alpha Quarterly,* October, 1920.

"The *Publishers' Weekly,* Through Fifty Years," *Publishers' Weekly,* I, January 1, 1921, pp. 9–11; II, January 8, 1921, pp. 60–61.

"Some Children's Librarians," *Library Journal,* October 1, 1921, pp. 787–90.

"The County Library System of California," *Library Journal,* October 15, 1921, pp. 835–37.

"The Riverside Library Service School and Its Founder," *Library Journal,* November 1, 1921, pp. 893–95.

Economic Peace; Covenant of Sovereign Peoples. New York, 1923. Includes *Economic Peace,* being a brief statement of its basis in economic freedom (Economic Peace Series No. 1, New York, 1923); *Covenant of Sovereign Peoples,* by "Pax Mundi" with an introduction by R. R. B. (Economic Peace Series No. 2, New York, 1923).

Why I Am a Free Trader, Bulletin No. 23 of the American Free Trade League, October, 1924.

"Electrostatic Potential and Human Health," *American Journal of Electrotherapeutics and Radiology,* Vol. XLIII, No. 1 (January, 1925).

"De Mortuis. Everett Pepperrell Wheeler, '56. The Friend and Comrade," *City College Quarterly,* Vol. XXI, No. 1 (April, 1925).

"Frank Luman Wing," *Delta Alpha Quarterly,* April, 1925.

"College Days and College Ways." 4 pts. *City College Alumnus:* March, 1926, pp. 105–17; June, 1926, pp. 251–54; September, 1926, pp. 301–305; December, 1926, pp. 464–68.

Letter to Dr. M. Llewellyn Raney on the Copyright Controversy." *Library Journal* September 15, 1926, pp. 767–69.

(Address) "Seed time and Harvest—the Story of the A. L. A." *Library Journal,* October 15, 1926, pp. 880–86.

"William Maitland Murray, '65" *Delta Alpha Quarterly,* Vol. 8, No. 1, (April 1927), 5–6.

"Why Not the Biggest Navy?" Privately printed leaflet, 1928.

"The Dewey Decimal Classification (12th edition)—An Appreciation," *Library Journal,* February 1, 1928, pp. 129–30.

"Ave Atque Salve," *City College Alumnus,* November 1928, pp. 314–16.

"The Stockbridge Library, 1904–1928," address at the Annual Meeting, September 29, 1929. Pittsfield (Mass.), 1929.

"Remarks on the Preservation of Peace," in *Proceedings* of the Academy of Political Science, January 1929, p. 104.

"The Appointment of Herbert Putnam as Librarian of Congress," in *Essays Offered to Herbert Putnam,* New Haven, 1929, pp. 15–22.

"Ernst F. Eurich," *Delta Alpha Quarterly,* June, 1931.

"Melvil Dewey: Founder and Pioneer," *Bulletin of the American Library Association,* February 1932, pp. 93–94.

4. NEWSPAPER EDITORIALS, FEATURES, LETTERS,
   POLITICAL BROADSIDES
   (All newspapers, unless otherwise specified, are New York papers.)

New York *Evening Mail.* Miscellaneous articles and editorials, 1868–75; "Literary Notes," weekly in *Evening Mail,* 1870–75; "Our Book Table," "The Literary Outlook," "The Magazine Outlook," features in the *Evening Mail* (Weekly Edition) 1872–74.

"New York Letter," Cincinnati *Commercial* (signed Querito), October 23, 1868, and November 11, 1868.

"Bastiat Americanized," *The Free Trader,* November, 1869.

The (New York) *Press.* Occasional editorials in 1869, 1875.

"Wilkie Collins, 'The New Magdalen,' " book review in *The Christian Leader* June 28, 1873.

"The World Priest," book review in *The Christian Leader,* July 26, 1873, p. 464.

"Love in the 19th Century," book review in *The Christian Leader,* August 30, 1873, p. 544.

"Stedman's Poems," book review in *The Christian Leader,* February 14, 1874.

"The Nation's Library," special article for the *Evening Mail,* February 17, 1874.

Boston Daily Globe. Fortnightly and monthly columns of book news, 1874, 1875.

The *Jewelers' Circular.* Occasional editorials in 1869, 1875.

Publishers' Circular, London. Occasional news letters, 1873, 1874, 1875.

Tribune, "Literary Notes," January 15, 1875–June 1878.

"Statesman vs. Politician: Plain Words From a Young Republican" (Signed "A Young Republican"), letter to the *Tribune,* April 15, 1876.

"Scratch and Bolt" (Signed "A Young Republican"), letter to the *Tribune,* April 29, 1876.

"The Party in Power" (signed "A Young Republican"), letter to the *Tribune,* June 10, 1876.

"The People's University," editorial in the *Tribune,* July 9, 1877.

"Librarians in Council," editorial in *Tribune,* September 4, 1877.

"Address of the Council for Tariff Aeform," privately printed, January 1, 1878.

"Justice to the Free College," letter to the *Tribune,* March 9, 1878.

"The British Copyright Report," editorial in the *Tribune,* June 1, 1878.

"International Copyright," special correspondence in the London *Athenaeum,* June 15, 1878, pp. 764–65.

"The Greenback Orator," special article in the *Evening Post,* October 24, 1878.

"The Great Harvest Year," editorial in the *Evening Post,* December 4, 1878.

"The City College," letter to the *Evening Post,* January 8, 1879.

"An Open Letter to Mr. Curtis" (signed "A Young Republican"), *Evening Post,* September 2, 1879.

"No Surrender" (signed "A Young Republican"), letter to the *Evening Post,* September 5, 1879.

"Call for Young Republican Organization," notice in the *Evening Post,* September 6, 1879.

"To the Republicans of New York," memorial by the Independent Republican Executive Committee, September 13, 1879.

"To Independent Republicans," address by the Independent Republican Executive Committee, New York, November 19, 1879; reprinted in the *Independent Republican Campaign of 1879,* (November, 1879).

"The Republican Party for 1880," letter to the *Evening Post,* December 12, 1879. Reprinted as a separate campaign document.

"To Members of the Republican State Convention," circular from the Independent Republican Central Committee, New York, February, 1880.

"Can General Grant Be Elected?" handbill printed by Independent Republican Central Committee, New York, May, 1880.

"Points as to the Selection of The Republican Presidential Candidate," leaflet printed by the Independent Republican Central Committee, New York, May, 1880.

"The Opposition to General Grant and the Opposition to Mr. Blaine," letter to the *Nation,* May 6, 1880.

"Proposed Civil Service Reform Plank," printed sheet used at Republican National Convention, Chicago, June, 1880.

"The Independent Republicans and the Presidential Campaign," letter to the *Nation,* July 1, 1880; quoted in Rochester *Express,* July 3, 1880.

"Letter from 'An American,'" in London *Times,* September 28, 1881.

"The President is Dead," in Editor's Easy Chair, *Harper's New Monthly Magazine* (English edition), October, 1881. p. 875.

"Political Nexts," letter to *Evening Post,* November 10, 1882; reprinted in the *Nation,* November 16, 1882, p. 422; reprinted separately as a campaign document.

"Address to Brooklyn Young Republican Club," October, 1883 (New York, 1883). Printed as a campaign document.

"Political Principles," letter to the *Evening Post,* January 24, 1884.

Free Trade Means High Wages; high tariff means low wages. The ruinous effects of the present tariff upon the wages of labor. Arguments of T. G. Shearman and R. R. B. before the Ways and Means Committee on the subject of tariff. Washington, 1884. Also, *Remarks of R. R. Bowker Before The Ways and Means Committee* (Washington, 1884).

"The Work Before Independents," letter dated March 4, to the New York *Times,* March, 1884.

" 'For President, Grover Cleveland!' Why?" New York *Times,* October 4, 1884.

"To Theodore Roosevelt, the Letter of a Brooklyn Independent Republican," Brooklyn *Eagle* and Brooklyn *Union,* October 29, 1884.

"To The Brooklyn Seventh Ward Republican Association," letter in Brooklyn *Union,* December 10, 1884.

"Letter to Frederick P. Coudert" on the sanitary controversy, a printed handbill, August 14, 1885.

"New Site for the City College," letter to the Honorable Ashbel P. Fitch, controller, in the New York *Times,* March 4, 1894.

"The World's School House," forty-one "lessons" in the *World,* September 21–October 30, 1896.

Letter Addressed to Emplayees, Edison Electric Illuminating Company of New York, December 26, 1899, upon resignation from company.

"A Smashing Letter," R. R. B. to Harrington Putnam, Esq., Brooklyn Democratic Club, *Evening Post,* November 1, 1901.

"Ammunition for Hughes," letter to the Honorable Charles E. Hughes, in the *Evening Post,* April 24, 1907.

"The City College and the Civil Service," letter to Charles S. Fowler, chief examiner of the New York State Civil Service Commission. Privately printed; reprinted in part, *City College Quarterly,* December, 1907, p. 232.

"Danger Points," letter to New York, New Haven and Hartford Railroad, *Berkshire Courier,* July 14, 1910.

"R. R. Bowker for Shepard," statement in *Evening Post,* December 3, 1910.

"The Mugwump Position," *Evening Post,* January 19, 1916.

"Electoral Suggestions," letter dated November 13, 1916 to the *Evening Post.*

"Magna Carta," letter dated January 9, 1917 to the *Evening Post.*

"Appeal of American Free Traders to the Right Honorable A. J. Balfour and M. Rene Viviani" (R. R. B. author and co-signer with twenty-seven others). Reprinted as *Leaflet No. 201* of the Cobden Club, London, 1917.

"Poor Quality of Coal," letter dated December 15, 1917, to the *Evening Post*.

"Proposals for Peace Conference," letter to the *Evening Post,* January 17, 1918.

"Government by Interference," letter to the *Evening Post,* January 26, 1918.

"Mugwump Retrospect and Prospect," letter dated September 4, 1919, to the *Evening Post*.

"The Muzzle Act," letter to the *Evening Post,* November 18, 1919.

"The Treaty and Other Issues," open letter to Senator Lodge, Springfield *Republican,* December 9, 1919.

"Open Letter to Underwood," Springfield *Republican,* January 22, 1920.

"Open Letter to Herbert Hoover," *Evening Post,* October 27, 1920.

"Thanksgiving and Peace Day," letter to the *Evening Post,* November 22, 1921.

"Peace Day," letter dated December 15, 1921, to the New York *Times*.

"Negro Education at the South," letter dated April 6, 1922, to the *Evening Post*.

"Porto Rico's Charms for a Motorist's Eye," signed article in the *Evening Post,* July 7, 1922.

"The New Haven Railroad in the Berkshires," letter to Dr. Arthur T. Hadley, director, in Springfield *Republican,* October 11, 1923. Reprinted as separate leaflet.

"The Stockbridge Indians," *Berkshire Courier,* December 9, 1926.

"At War in Peace Time, A Letter to the President Regarding the Situation in Nicaragua," Springfield *Republican,* February 21, 1928.

"The Havana Conference,—An Open Letter to Mr. Hughes," in the *Evening World,* February 29, 1928.

"Sea Power and Air Power," letter dated October 17, 1928, in Springfield *Republican*.

"Mr. Hoover for 'Stand-pat Conservatism,' and Governor Smith for Progressive Liberalism.' " letter to the Springfield *Republican,* October 29, 1928.

"The Flexible Tariff," open letter to Senator Gillett in the Springfield *Years That Are Past* 1923.

"Walsh and the Tariff," letter to David I. Walsh, dated February 5, 1930, in the Springfield *Republican*.

"For 'Another Kind' of Democratic Platform," planks proposed on tariff, currency, disarmament, prohibition. Letter to the Springfield *Republican,* June 22, 1932.

5. VERSE.

"Toll then no more!" *The Christian Union,* April 9, 1870; reprinted in W. C. Bryant, *Library of Poetry and Song;* being choice selections from the Best Poets. With an introduction by William Cullen

Bryant, New York, 1871. Also reprinted in *From the Pen of RRB* (1916).

"Lake George: A Reminiscence," *Old and New,* September, 1870; reprinted in *From the Pen of RRB* (1916).

"Joy-Song of an American" (translation of *"Jubel-Lied eines Amerikaners,"* by Bayard Taylor), New York *Evening Mail,* September 6, 1870; reprinted in *The Cosmopolitan,* September 10, 1870.

"In Memoriam, L. D." (died February 9, 1871). Privately printed.

"How Old Art Thou?" The *Independent,* February 16, 1871, p. 2.

"Judas and Butler," New York *Evening Mail,* August (?), 1871.

"Runaway Lovelings," The *Independent,* August 10, 1871, p. 3.

"No One to Blame!" The *Independent,* August 17, 1871, p. 5.

"Yawp Hitman Again," Hartford *Courant* (reprinted from the New York *Evening Mail*), September 14, 1871.

"Evening Sadness" (translation from the German of Salis), *Old and New,* October, 1871.

"Darling's Dollies," *The Independent,* November 23, 1871.

"The Abiding Rest," *The Independent,* June 27, 1872.

"Finis Coronat Opus," Scribner's Monthly, December, 1872; also in New York *Evening Mail* (Weekly Edition), November 27, 1872; reprinted in *From the Pen of RRB* (1916).

"Good Friday and Easter Day," *The Independent,* April 10, 1873.

"The Great Tomorrow," *The Independent,* July 24, 1873.

"Quatrains" (1. "Wisdom," 2. "Homeopathy"), *Scribner's Monthly,* December, 1875.

"The Ballad of a Gruesome Butcher," *Scribner's Monthly,* January, 1876.

"My Maidens," *The Independent,* January 20, 1876; reprinted in the New York *Evening Mail,* January 27, 1876, and in (R. R. B.) *From the Years That Are Past,* 1923.

"A Happy Lover," *Scribner's Monthly,* February 1876.

"Through Tears," *The Independent,* April 6, 1876.

"The Master's Work," *The Independent,* May 25, 1876.

"Firelight and Moonlight," *Appleton's Journal,* June 3, 1876; reprinted in *From the Pen of RRB* (1916).

"Autumn," *The Independent,* October 12, 1876.

"Life," *Scribner's Monthly,* July, 1877.

"By the Way," *The Christian Union,* May 1, 1878.

"An Humble Spirit," *Sunday School Times,* July 13, 1878.

"My Lady's Voice," in *A Masque of Poets* (No Name Series), p. 22; Boston, 1878; reprinted in *From the Pen of RRB* (1916).

"Thomas a Kempis," *Scribner's Monthly,* January, 1879; reprinted in E. C. Stedman, *An American Anthology, 1787–1900,* p. 582, New York, 1900; and in *From the Pen of RRB* (1916).

"The Dead President," *Harper's New Monthly Magazine* (English edition), October, 1881; reprinted in the New York *Evening Post,* October 11, 1881; and in *From the Pen of RRB* (1916).

"Mutanter," *Harper's New Monthly Magazine* (English edition), April, 1882.

"A Song of Nests," in *Liber Scriptorum, or Book of the Authors' Club,* 1893; reprinted in *From the Pen of RRB* (1916).

"Peace Out of War, an Ode For the Day of the Dead," New York *Times,* April 27, 1897.

"Ruskin" (sonnet), *Century Illustrated Monthly,* September, 1897, p. 715; reprinted in *From the Pen of RRB* (1916).

"The True America" and "What America Should Say to the Philippines," *The Anti-Imperialist,* Brookline (Mass.), August 20, 1899; also in *From the Pen of RRB* (1916).

"Death Unto Life," *Century Illustrated Monthly,* October, 1899, p. 858.

"Fear and Death (An Arab Legend)." *Century Magazine,* December, 1899, p. 317; reprinted in *From the Pen of RRB* (1916).

"The Semitic Museum," *The American Hebrew,* February 13, 1903, p. 422.

"Lux Benigna; Fama Eterna," in program of annual dinner and celebration of the twenty-fifth anniversary of the development and successful introduction of the incandescent lamp, 1879–1904. American Institute of Electrical Engineers, February 11, 1904, Waldorf-Astoria, New York, Reprinted in *Electrical World and Engineer,* Fbruary 20, 1904, p. 352; also in *From the Pen of RRB* (1916).

From the Pen of RRB. Printed as manuscript, New York, first issue, 1915; second issue with additional poems, 1916.

From Years That Are Past. Printed as manuscript, New York, 1923.

"Menlo Park, 1875–1925." In "Addresses delivered at the Dedication of the Commemorative Tablet near the site of the Edison Laboratories and Workshops at Menlo Park, New Jersey, May 16, 1925."

"To Thomas Alva Edison: Eighty Roses." Printed sheet, February 11, 1927.

III. General Works

1. MANUSCRIPT MATERIALS

Atkinson, Edward A. Letters to David A. Wells, Charles Nordhoff, Worthington C. Ford, 1868–98, in the New York Public Library.

Grover Cleveland Papers, in the Library of Congress.

David A. Wells Papers, in the Library of Congress.

Baldwin, Henry deForrest, MS speech on Reform Club role in 1892. In the possession of the author.

Farnham, Mrs. Edwin P., "My Old Home" and "Memories of the Garden of My Childhood." Unpublished MSS in the possession of the author.

Schlegel, Marvin W. "The Gold Democrats in the Campaign of 1896."

Unpublished MS, 1935. In the possession of the author. "The Silver Issue and the Democratic Party, 1896–1900, with special reference to the State of New York." Unpublished MS, 1935. In the possession of the author.

2. NEWSPAPERS AND PERIODICALS

The Brooklyn *Daily Eagle,* 1879, 1884, 1901.
The New York *Evening Mail,* 1868–75.
The New York *Evening Post,* 1879, 1880,1884, 1892, 1896, 1898–99, 1907.
The New York *Times,* 1880, 1884,1898–99.
The New York *Tribune,* 1876, 1879, 1880, 1884, 1896, 1898–99.
The New York *World,* 1876, 1879, 1880, 1884, 1894, 1896.
Free Trader, 1868–69.
Harper's Weekly, 1879, 1880, 1884.
The Million, 1884-88.
Municipal Affairs, 1879–1903.
The Nation, 1879, 1880, 1882–84, 1896.

3. MISCELLANEOUS ARTICLES, MONOGRAPHS, AND PAMPHLETS

Dickson, Arthur. *History of the Gamma Chapter of New York Phi Beta Kappa, 1867–1931.* New York, 1932.
Edison Electric Illuminating Company of New York. *Annual Reports* of the Board of Directors to the Stockholders, 1887–1900.
———. Memorandum for appraisers, prepared by Mr. Lewis, Supreme Court, New York, June 4, 1902.
"The *Evening Mail,*" *American Newspaper Reporter and Advertiser's Gazette,* June 19, 1871.
Green, S. Dana, *Electrical Review,* November 27, 1895.
Independent Republican Executive Committee (8 Union Square, New York, 1879). "To the Republicans of New York," memorial. September 13.
———. "To the Republican Voters"; "Plain Words from the *Tribune*"; "A Letter to the Union League Club"; "Scratching."
———. "To Disheartened Republicans."
———. "Conscience in Politics."
———. "Independent Republicanism."
———. "To the Independent Republicans of Albany."
———. Address of the Executive Committee, November 19.
———. "Independent Republican Campaign of 1879."
Independent Republican Central Committee (8 Union Square, New York, 1880). "Statement of Principles." January.
———. "Constitution of the Independent Republican Association of the County of New York." January.
———. "Abstract of Constitution and Statement of Principles." February 1.

———. "To Members of the Republican State Convention." February 1.

———. "Can General Grant Be Elected?" May.

———. "Points as to the Selection of the Republican Presidential Candidate." May.

———. "Proposed Civil Service Plank."

Independent Republic Association, 1880. Horace White, *Third Term Politics*. April 5.

———. C. F. Adams, *Individuality in Politics,* No. 2, April 21.

———. Matthew Hale, *Conditions and Limits of Party Fealty,* No. 3, April 26.

———. G. W. Curtis, *Machine Politics and the Remedy,* May 20.

———. Jacob Schoenhof, *The Position of the Independent German Republican in the Presidential Election.*

New York Reform Club. Circulars, 1888–1900.

"Old Ruggles Stable Survives as Home of Litterateurs," *Gramercy Park,* May, 1933.

Osborne, Thomas M. "Address Before the Convention of the National Party." New York, September 5, 1900.

"Richard Rogers Bowker," *Bulletin of Bibliography,* Vol. XII, No. 10 (May–August, 1926).

Shepard, E. M. "To the Honorable David A. Boody," September 11, 1893. Printed sheet.

———. "The First Mayoralty Election in Greater New York," *Atlantic Monthly,* January, 1898.

———. "The Second Mayoralty Election in Greater New York," *Atlantic Monthly,* February, 1902.

Stokes, F. A. *A Publisher's Random Notes, 1880–1935.* New York, 1935.

Supreme Court, New York. Brief on Behalf of Petitioner, W. A. Shortt. 1902.

Warner, John De Witt. "Municipal Betterment in the New York City Elections," *Municipal Affairs,* September, 1901, pp. 625–40. (Issued in mid-November.)

Wetzler, Joseph. "The Edison Electric Illuminating Company of New York," *Electrical Engineer,* January 8, 1896, pp. 25–48.

Whitridge, F. W. "Roscoe Conkling," *International Review,* Vol. II (1881), 375–90.

4. BOOKS

Alexander, D. S. *A Political History of the State of New York.* Vol. III, 1861–82. 3 vols., New York, 1909.

Anderson, Mary. *A Few Memories.* New York, 1896.

Arent, Leonora. *Electric Franchises* in New York City. New York, 1919.

Bancroft, Frederic (ed.). *Speeches, Correspondence, and Political Papers of Carl Schurz.* 6 vols. New York, 1913.

——— and W. A. Dunning. "A Sketch of Carl Schurz's Political Career, 1869–1906," in *The Reminiscences of Carl Schurz*, III, 311–455. 3 vols. New York, 1907–1908.

Beswick, Jay W. *The Work of Frederick Leypoldt, Bibliographer and Publisher*. New York, 1942.

Bigelow, John. *William Cullen Bryant*. New York, 1896.

Bond, F. Fraser. *Mr. Miller of "The Times."* New York, 1931.

Bradley, W. A. *William Cullen Bryant*. New York, 1905.

Brinkerhoff, Roeliff. *Recollections of a Lifetime*. Cincinnati, 1904.

Brooklyn Library. *Annual Reports*, 1887–93.

Brooks, Van Wyck. *New England: Indian Summer*. New York, 1940.

Caldwell, Robert Granville. *James A. Garfield*. New York, 1931.

Camp Manhattan, Lake George, Alpha Delta Phi. Memoranda of Its Beginnings and Doings During Its Continued Existence of Forty Years from 1869–1908.

Cary, Edward. *George William Curtis*. Boston, 1894.

Chidsey, Donald Barr. *The Gentleman from New York*. New Haven, 1935.

Choate, Joseph H. *The Boyhood and Youth of Joseph Hodges Choate*. New York, privately printed, 1917.

Cosenza, Mario Emilio. *The Establishment of the College of the City of New York as the Free Academy in 1847*. New York, 1925.

Davis, Elmer. *History of "The New York Times," 1851–1921*. New York, 1921.

Dawe, Grosvenor. *Melvil Dewey*. Lake Placid (N. Y.), 1932.

Dewey, A. M. *Life of George Dewey . . . and Dewey Family History*. Westfield (Mass.), 1898.

Dunbar, Elizabeth. *Talcott Williams, Gentleman of the Fourth Estate*. Brooklyn, 1936.

[Eaton, Dorman B.] Junius. *The Independent Republican Movement in New York*, as an element in the next elections and as a problem in party government. New York, 1880. Questions of the Day No. 1.

Eckenrode, H. J. *Rutherford B. Hayes, Statesman of Reunion*. New York, 1930.

Edisonia, A Brief History of the Early Edison Electric Lighting System. Prepared by the Association of Edison Illuminating Companies. New York, 1904.

Fish, Carl. *Russell, the Civil Service and the Patronage*. Cambridge, 1920.

Forbes, John Murray. *Letters and Recollections*. Edited by his daughter, Sarah Forbes Hughes. Boston and New York, 1899.

Gosnell, Harold F. *Boss Platt and His New York Machine*. Chicago, 1924.

Growoll, Adolph. *The Booksellers' League*. New York, 1905.

———. *Booktrade Bibliography in the United States in the 19th Century*. New York, 1898.

————. *The Profession of Bookselling.* 3 vols. New York, Office of the *Publishers' Weekly*, 1893–1913.

Hale, Edward E., Jr., *Life and Letters of Edward Everett Hale.* Boston, 1917.

Harper, J. Henry. *The House of Harper: A Century of Publishing in Franklin Square.* New York, 1912.

Hendricks, Burton J. *The Training of an American.* New York, 1928.

Hirsch, Mark D. *William C. Whitney, Modern Warwick.* New York, 1948.

Hoar, G. F. *Autobiography of Seventy Years.* 2 vols. New York, 1903.

Hoke, George Wilson. *George Halford Clark.* Rochester, 1942.

Howe, George F. *Chester A. Arthur, A Quarter-Century of Machine Politics.* New York, 1934.

Hudson, Frederic. *Journalism in the United States from 1690–1872.* New York, 1873.

Johnson, Robert Underwood. *Remembered Yesterdays.* Boston, 1929.

Johnson, W. F., and R. B. Smith. *History of the State of New York, Political and Governmental.* 6 vols. Syracuse, 1922.

Jones, Payson. *A Power History of the Consolidated Edison System, 1878–1900.* New York, 1940.

Joyner, Fred Bunyan. *David Ames Wells: Champion of Free Trade.* Cedar Rapids, 1939.

Lehmann-Haupt, Hellmut. *The Book in America.* New York, 1939.

Lloyd, Caro. *Henry Demarest Lloyd.* 2 vols. New York, 1912.

Lynch, Denis Tilden. *The Wild Seventies.* New York, 1941.

McAdam, Graham. *An Alphabet in Finance.* New York, 1876.

Maltbie, Milo R. *Franchises of Electrical Corporations in Greater New York.* New York, 1911.

Mosenthal, Philip J., and Charles F. Horne, eds. *The City College— Memories of Sixty Years.* New York, 1907.

Mott, Frank Luther. *American Journalism*, a history of newspapers in the United States through 250 years, 1690–1940. New York, 1941.

Murray, William M. *Camp Manhattan, A Retrospect Upon Some of Its Early Years.* New York, 1911.

Muzzey, David Saville. *James G. Blaine.* New York, 1934.

Myers, Gustavus. *A History of Tammany Hall.* New York, 1917.

National Conference of Free Traders and Revenue Reformers, November 11–12, 1885. Chicago, 1885.

National Cyclopedia of American Biography.

Nevins, Allan. *Grover Cleveland, A Study in Courage.* New York, 1932.

————. *The Emergence of Modern America.* New York, 1935.

New York State Historical Association. *History of the State of New York.* Vol. VII (1935). 10 vols., New York, 1933–37.

Official Proceedings of the Anti-Third Term Republican Convention. Chicago, 1880.

Ogden, Rollo. *Life and Letters of Edwin Lawrence Godkin*. 2 vols. New York, 1907.

Osborne, D. *The Authors' Club*. New York, 1913.

Osborne, L. A. *The Electrical Industry*, in H. T. Warshow (ed.), *Representative Industries in the United States*. New York, 1928.

Parrington, Vernon Louis. *Main Currents in American Thought*. 3 vols. New York, 1927–30.

Proceedings of the Republican National Convention, 1880. Chicago, 1881.

Putnam, George Haven. *Memories of a Publisher*. New York, 1916.

Reid, Wemyss. *William Black, Novelist*. New York, 1902.

Ross, Earle Dudley. *The Liberal Republican Movement*. New York, 1919.

Rudy, S. W. *The College of the City of New York: A History*. New York, 1949.

Second International Library Conference. *Transactions and Proceedings*. London, 1898.

Scudder, Horace Elisha. *James Russell Lowell, A Biography*. 2 vols. New York, 1901.

Shelton, Robert. *The Story of Harper's Magazine, 1850–1917*. New York, 1916.

Smith, Ray B. *History of the State of New York*. 4 vols. Syracuse, 1922.

Sonnenschein, William Swan. *The Best Books*. A Reader's Guide to Literary Reference. Both being a contribution towards systematic bibliography. London, 1935.

Starr, Harris E. *William Graham Sumner*. New York, 1925.

Stedman, Laura, and George M. Gould. *Life and Letters of Edmund Clarence Stedman*. New York, 1910.

Tarbell, Ida M. *The Tariff in Our Times*. New York, 1911.

Tassin, Algernon DeV. *The Magazine in America*. New York, 1916.

Taussig, Frank William. *The Tariff History of the United States*. New York, 1914.

Warshow, H. T. (ed.), *Representative Industries in the United States*. New York, 1928.

Wheeler, Everett Pepperrell. *Sixty Years of American Life*. New York, 1917.

Williamson, H. F. *Edward Atkinson: The Biography of an American Liberal*. Boston, 1934.

Wilson, H. W., Company. *A Quarter Century of Cumulative Bibliography*. New York, 1923.

Wingate, Charles F. *Views and Interviews on Journalism*. New York, 1875.

Illustration Credits

From the *National Cyclopedia of American Biography,* through the courtesy of James T. White & Company: Edward Everett Hale and Edmund Clarence Stedman (*facing p. 80*), David A. Wells and George William Curtis (*facing p. 144*), Laurence Hutton, Bret Harte, and James Russell Lowell (*facing p. 176*), Horace E. Deming, Talcott Williams, Thomas G. Shearman, and Edward Atkinson (*facing p. 209*), J. Van Vechten Olcott (*facing p. 240*), Spencer Trask (*facing p. 241*), George Foster Peabody (*facing p. 272*). Brooklyn Academy of Music Building (*facing p. 17*): courtesy Brooklyn Institute of Arts and Sciences. Richard Watson Gilder (*facing p. 80*): courtesy Rodman Gilder. A. D. F. Randolph (*facing p. 81*) photograph by Alfred Stieglitz; J. Henry Harper: courtesy John Harper; W. H. Appleton: courtesy Appleton-Century-Crofts, Inc.; Charles Scribner: courtesy Underwood and Underwood. Through the courtesy of the New York Public Library: Worthington C. Ford (*facing p. 144*) and Mary Anderson (*facing p. 145*). George Haven Putnam (*facing p. 144*): courtesy Mrs. Joseph Lindon Smith. Lady Anne Thackeray Ritchie (*facing p. 145*) from a photograph by Mrs. Cameron at Freshwater, reproduced from *From the Porch* (Charles Scribner's Sons, 1913). Mr. and Mrs. Leypoldt (*facing p. 177*): courtesy Mrs. Frank H. Shafer. Bowker with a group of former presidents of the A.L.A. (*facing p. 208*): courtesy American Library Association. Ernst Eurich (*facing p. 240*) from a portrait by S. J. Woolf, reproduced from *Delta Alpha Quarterly,* April, 1927. Thomas Alva Edison (*facing p. 241*): courtesy Edison's Birthday Committee. Brooklyn Public Library (*facing p. 273*): courtesy of the Library; Stockbridge Library: courtesy Stockbridge Library Association. Camp Manhattan Reunion (*facing p. 336*) and Mr. and Mrs. R. R. Bowker (*facing p. 337*): courtesy Mrs. Herbert Bavington. From *Harper's New Monthly Magazine:* Edwin A. Abbey (*facing p. 145*), June, 1889; William Black (*facing p. 145*), December, 1882; Bronson Howard (*facing p. 176*), November, 1886. From *Harper's Weekly Magazine:* Lord Kelvin (*facing p. 241*), April 26, 1902. From *City College Alumnus:* the Great Tower of City College (*facing p. 17*) from an etching by Walter Pach, June, 1927; Nelson S. Spencer (*facing p. 240*) from a portrait by J. Gordon Stevenson, January, 1927. From *City College Quarterly:* Adolph Werner (*facing p. 240*), March, 1920; Everett Pepperrell Wheeler (*facing p. 272*), April, 1925; Edward Morse Shepard (*facing p. 272*), October, 1912.

Index

UNIVERSITY OF OKLAHOMA PRESS

NORMAN